Healing Our World

In an Age of Aggression

Third Edition

Mary J. Ruwart, Ph.D.

SunStar Press

****

Kalamazoo, Michigan

Published by SunStar Press
P.O. Box 50342
Kalamazoo, Michigan 49005-0342

Library of Congress Cataloging-in-Publication Data

Ruwart, Mary J.
  Healing our world in an age of aggression / Mary J. Ruwart—3rd. ed.
      p. cm.
Rev. ed. of: Healing our world. Rev. ed. c1993.
  Includes bibliographic references and index.
  ISBN 0-9632336-6-1: (trade paperback : alk. paper)
        1. United States—Politics and government—2001–2. United
States—Economic policy—2001–3. United States—Social policy—1993–
4. United States—Moral conditions. I. Ruwart, Mary J. Healing our
world. II. Title.
E902.R89 2003
300′.973—dc21   2002153448

Printed in the United States of America

10 9 8 7 6 5 4 3 2 1

To my sister,
Martie Ruwart.
Without her encouragement, inspiration,
and critiques, this book could never
have been written.
Her story, which appears as this edition's afterword,
was a true healing.

All truth passes through three stages. First, it is ridiculed. Secondly, it is violently opposed. Third, it is accepted as being self-evident.

—Arthur Schopenhauer
German philosopher

Also by Mary J. Ruwart:

Short Answers to the Tough Questions
  (available in part at <http://www.ruwart.com>)

Table of Contents

War and poverty are not caused by "selfish others," but by our own
reactions to them. If we wish to change the world, we must first
change ourselves.

Part One. Give Us This Day Our Daily Bread: Back to Basics

If we assault, cheat, or steal from our neighbors, we create animosity
and strife in our neighborhood. Somehow we believe that these
same actions will create harmony and abundance when undertaken
for the "common good" in our community, state, nation, and world.

Wealth is created when we use existing resources in new ways. Because such creativity is virtually limitless, wealth is too.

Part Two. Forgive Us Our Trespasses: How We Create Poverty in a World of Plenty

When we try to increase the wealth of disadvantaged workers through
aggression, we only succeed in making them poorer.

"Only in America" could the penniless immigrants of the 1800s become
affluent by starting their own businesses. Today, our aggression
keeps the disadvantaged from following in their footsteps.

Licensing laws and regulations give us the illusion of safety. In reality,
our aggression boomerangs back to us, costing us our wealth, our
health, and our very lives.

By using aggression to avoid medications that might harm us, we lose
access to lifesaving drugs.

Part Three. As We Forgive Those Who Trespass Against Us: How We Create Strife in a World of Harmony

Acknowledgments

This edition of *Healing Our World* includes revisions made possible only through the dedicated help of many wonderful co-workers, friends, family, and associates.

I am grateful first and foremost to my husband, Raymond R. Carr, who supported me during this two-year revision both financially and emotionally. Raymond also suggested the concept for the cover design. David Howard, who produced the artwork for the last edition of *Healing*, also provided the original drawing for this one. The cover art was enhanced and converted to digital format by a husband-and-wife team who wish to remain anonymous. Dee Little and Joel Suchecki of Glamour Shots were responsible for the author's makeup and photo. Marvin A. Spehar of Go Graphix provided the final cover layout.

Several individuals provided invaluable critiques along the way. Special thanks go to "J" Milton McGinnis for detailed and painstaking conceptual critiques that inspired my research for the third edition. Jarret Wollstein, Stuart Hayashi, and Ken Schoolland provided the same service for the resulting manuscript. Jarret also made a number of stylistic suggestions, which have made *Healing* much easier to read and understand.

My thanks to Bill and Helen Gaydosh for converting the original manuscript into a more user-friendly digital format. Oil Guillory's wizardry gave me much of my graphic material, layout design, and typesetting. Artist Michael Mason provided a new look for the cartoons, which Brian Betzold had created for the first edition of *Healing*.

My thanks as well to Dan Karlan and Jack Greene for both editorial suggestions and proofreading support. Kay McCarthy, Linda Stringer, and Barbara Hart of Publications Professionals LLC in Fairfax, Virginia, worked tirelessly on the final editorial, stylistic, and proofreading revisions.

Several other individuals deserve special thanks. Zoe Austin created the initial indexes, which Kenya Reed completed. Kenya also worked tirelessly with me on pre-press revisions. Lynn Rohkohl at Malloy Inc. once again walked *Healing* successfully through the printing process.

Last, but by no means least, I want to thank Nancy Tolmacs of SunStar Press for all of her past years of support in making *Healing* and my other book, *Short Answers to the Tough Questions*, successful publications.

The many other readers who gave me support and encouragement along the way also have my heartfelt thanks. My appreciation for my family members has grown over the past couple years for their unwavering support, even when my writing took my time away from them.

Clearly, no one writes a book like this alone. We are all a link in the chain of healing our world.

Foreword

Healing Our World is a rare book that challenges numerous aspects of conventional wisdom that we accept as axiomatically true. For example, a major dimension of this book is linkage between our spiritual perspective and our economic well-being. At first, these two might seem like strange bedfellows, but Dr. Ruwart leads readers with her gentle touch to a world in which the interdependence of the hard sciences, the social sciences, and spirituality becomes clear. Hard facts presented in a sensitive, readable style focus attention on the urgent need for our policymakers to be more careful about the "evidence" upon which many of their policies are made.

Healing Our World gently and provocatively challenges us to recognize the coercive nature of the government intervention that we often consider as inevitable and even desirable. Seldom do we question the morality of government-initiated aggression in prescribing day-to-day regulations and taxes. Dr. Ruwart's book is a refreshing and unusual approach that refocuses public attention on the danger of sanctioning collective action that would be repugnant to us if it were practiced individually. Herein, Dr. Ruwart claims, is the key to a win–win world of abundance and harmony. *Healing Our World* paints a clear picture of a vision within our grasp, thereby empowering and inspiring every person working for a better world.

—Frances Kendall and Leon Louw
Nobel Peace Prize nominees, 1989, 1991, 1992

In the following pages I offer nothing more than simple facts, plain arguments and common sense; and have no other preliminaries to settle with the reader, other than that he will divest himself of prejudice and prepossession, and suffer his reason and his feelings to determine for themselves; that he will put on, rather that he will not put off, the natural character of a man, and generously enlarge his views beyond the present day.

—Thomas Paine
COMMON SENSE

Introduction

The Impossible Dream?

War and poverty are not caused by "selfish others," but by our own reactions to them. If we wish to change the world, we must first change ourselves.

The collapse of the World Trade Center on September 11, 2001, was a gut-wrenching reminder that worldwide harmony and abundance still elude us. War, hatred, starvation, and terrorism are still so prevalent that a peaceful and prosperous world seems like an impossible dream. If we fail to heed this wake-up call or cannot find the path to universal peace and plenty, our civilization, like the Twin Towers, is likely to come tumbling down. We have no place to run; the world has grown too small.

Thankfully, the secret to manifesting our "impossible" dream has been discovered and rediscovered, in part or in whole, by great minds throughout history. The answer is simply an extension of what we already do in our daily interactions with our neighbors. Like many simple things, the answer is overlooked or even ridiculed because we assume that global solutions must be complex. In the end, however, problems appear difficult only because we don't really understand the pattern that creates them.

For example, astronomers struggled for centuries to understand the complex paths by which heavenly bodies crossed our skies. Because they erroneously believed that Earth was the center of the universe, the movement of the stars and planets seemed erratic and complicated. When astronomers realized that Earth and other planets revolved around the sun, predicting their paths became much easier. When we see the cause behind the effect, appropriate action is much easier too. Knowing how the world works makes simple solutions possible.

A simple solution to the world's woes, however, seems almost laughable. For the past century, we've supported widespread social reform. Nevertheless, people are still starving in a world capable of feeding all. Homelessness and poverty still exist, even in the richest of nations. Violence is no longer limited to overseas wars:

our streets, our businesses, even our schools, are no longer safe. The environment that nurtures us is ravaged and raped. We have worked hard to stop such tragedies by passing laws to control the selfishness of other people. Why haven't we had more success?

We have missed our target because our aim was flawed. Rarely are we able to control others, and then only at great expense. We've set ourselves an impossible task. Even a powerful government cannot compel obedience from its citizens against their will. The revolt of the American colonies, the civil disobedience of Gandhi's followers, the widespread use of drugs even in U.S. prisons, and the fall of the Berlin Wall are just a few of the reminders that our ability to control others is largely an illusion.

Does this fact mean that we should simply resign ourselves to a warring world where the rich get richer and the poor get poorer? Of course not! We simply need to stop repeating what doesn't work and find out what does.

The great gift of the twentieth century was an understanding of how our *inner* peace and abundance are created. We discovered that our inner harmony and enrichment depend, not on other people and events, but on how we react to them. Other people do not make us angry; we create our own anger by the way that we choose, consciously or unconsciously, to think about what others do. When we take responsibility for the experience that we create, we are empowered to change our inner world.

The great promise of the twenty-first century is the application of those principles to our outer world to create global harmony and abundance. When we take responsibility for our role in creating the past, we gain control over the future.

When I first recognized this connection, I was full of denial. How could a peaceful, loving person like myself have contributed to starvation, war, and terrorism? Just as I had once resisted responsibility for my inner world, I balked at accepting my role in creating my outer one. Ultimately, however, I persevered, as I trust you will. If we care enough to change the world, we

The essential psychological requirement of a free society is the willingness on the part of the individual to accept responsibility for his life.

—Edith Packer
clinical psychologist

The truth will set you free—but first it will make you damn mad.

—M. Scott Peck
author of THE ROAD LESS
TRAVELED

must swallow our pride and change our own behavior first. Then, and only then, can we heal our troubled world.

Why is the world so troubled? A pervasive belief in our society, our collective consciousness, is in a win–lose world, where one person's gain is another's loss. Starting with this faulty assumption, we blame poverty on those selfish others who "have," believing that they must have plundered, or at least neglected, those who "have not." We try to correct this unenlightened behavior by passing laws to control those selfish others—at gunpoint, if necessary. We try to change the world by changing others, a costly exercise at best.

Selfish others who have been forced, not persuaded, to our way of thinking, ultimately resist the choices we have made for them. Conflicts escalate and voraciously consume resources. A warring world is a poor one.

Attempting to control others, even for their own good, has other undesirable effects. For example, people who are able to create intimacy in their personal relationships know that you can't hurry love. Trying to control or manipulate those close to us creates resentment and anger in them. Attempting to control others in our city, state, nation, and world undermines the universal love we want the world to manifest as well. Forcing people to be less "selfish" creates animosity instead of goodwill. Trying to control selfish others is a cure worse than the disease.

We reap what we sow. In trying to control others, we find ourselves controlled. The laws that we enact to bend others to our will empower the international conglomerates, dictators, politicians, monopolies, and other special interests. Like a stone thrown in a quiet pond, our desire to control our neighbors ripples outward, affecting the political course of our community, state, nation, and world.

We know not what we do. We attempt to bend "selfish" neighbors to our will, sincere in our belief that we are benevolently protecting the world from their folly and shortsightedness. Our desire to control, even for "the common

... collectively held unconscious beliefs shape the world's institutions, and are at the root of institutionalized oppression and inequity. ... By deliberately changing the internal image of reality, people can change the world.
—Willis Harman
PATHS TO PEACE

We are each one of us responsible for every war because of the aggressiveness of our own lives. ... And only when we realize ... that you and I are responsible ... for all the misery throughout the entire world, because we have contributed to it in our daily lives ... only then will we act.
—J. Krishnamurti
FREEDOM FROM THE KNOWN

... whatsoever a man sows, that shall he also reap.
—THE HOLY BIBLE
Galatians 6:7

We are not liberated until we liberate others. So long as we need to control other people, however benign our motives, we are captive to that need. In giving them freedom, we free ourselves.
  —Marilyn Ferguson
  THE AQUARIAN CONSPIRACY

good," is the very means by which poverty and war are propagated. Fighting for our dream without this awareness prevents its creation.

Truly these are tidings of great joy! For if we have been part of the problem, we can be part of the solution! When we stop trying to bend others to our will, the "impossible" dream of widespread peace and plenty unfolds naturally. Others may still act selfishly, but their impact—and their control over us—dwindles to the merest pin prick.

In our seemingly complex world, the secret of universal harmony and abundance is as simple as the basics that we learned as children. Enjoy rediscovering the secret of healing our world!

Part One

Give Us This Day Our Daily Bread:

Back to Basics

Chapter 1

The Good Neighbor Policy

If we assault, cheat, or steal from our neighbors, we create animosity and strife in our neighborhood. Somehow we believe that these same actions will create harmony and abundance when undertaken for the "common good" in our community, state, nation, and world.

How We Create Peace in Our Neighborhood

As children, we learned a great deal about creating a peaceful world. Most of us can remember Mom or Dad prying us apart from a playmate after we came to blows. My parents usually wanted to know "Who started it?" Even at a tender age, we could understand why: *if no one hit first, no fight was possible.*

We contributed to keeping the peace by making sure we did not deliver that first blow. This approach frequently required controlling our reactions to others. No longer did we feed them knuckle sandwiches just because their clothes were "weird." We stopped using our weaker playmates and siblings as personal punching bags. We became tolerant of the peaceful actions and attributes of others.

This tolerance extended to the *property* of our playmates as well. Taking or damaging their toys without their permission was sure to "start it." Lying to or about them also set the stage for physical combat. Consequently, our commitment to keeping the peace required us not only to be tolerant, but also to be honest with others and to respect property that was legitimately theirs. We refrained from threatening "first strike" force, theft, and fraud. This was our first step in bringing peace to our tiny corner of the galaxy.

The second step was just as important. If we struck others, took their toys, or lied about them, we tried to right our wrongs. We replaced the damaged toy out of our meager allowance, perhaps purchasing one just a little better to make up for the distress we had caused. We told those who had heard our lies that we had misinformed them. We carried books for the playmate whose arm we had bruised. By restoring the balance that we had upset, cordial relations might once again be possible. *Therefore, our program for*

Men have the right to use physical force only in retaliation and only against those who initiate its use. The ethical problem is simple and clear-cut: it is the difference between murder and self-defense.
—Ayn Rand
author of ATLAS SHRUGGED

Thou shalt not murder. Thou shalt not steal. Thou shalt not bear false witness against thy neighbor. Thou shalt not covet ... anything that is thy neighbor's.
—THE HOLY BIBLE
Exodus 20:13–17

Most of what I really need to know ... I learned in kindergarten. ... Play fair. Don't hit people. Put things back where you found them. Clean up your own mess. Don't take things that aren't yours. Say you're sorry when you hurt somebody.
—Robert Fulghum
ALL I REALLY NEED TO KNOW I LEARNED IN KINDERGARTEN

He must make full restitution for his wrong, add one-fifth to it, and give it to the person that he has wronged.

—THE HOLY BIBLE
Numbers 5:7

Principles are not legislated or invented, however. They are discovered. A principle was discovered, for example, when rational people first realized that it was not to their ultimate advantage to rob one another. Since mutual plunder led to mutual impoverishment, it was "wrong" (i.e., destructive of life) to steal. This was not "arbitrary social convention," but a fact of life. It was a matter of survival.

—Richard W. Grant
THE INCREDIBLE BREAD
MACHINE

It is not tolerance, it is intolerance, that causes disorder.

—Pierre Bayle
French philosopher

peace had two parts: (1) honesty, tolerance, and respect toward others and their property (i.e., refraining from threatening first-strike force, theft, or fraud); and (2) repairing any damage we caused by violating the first part. We will refer to this dual approach of honoring our neighbor's choice and righting our wrongs as the practice of "nonaggression," or the Good Neighbor Policy.

How We Create Prosperity in Our Neighborhood

As we became adults, our playmates became our neighbors. The degree of tranquillity in our community depended on how many of us practiced the Good Neighbor Policy learned in childhood. Property values tended to parallel the peace. Where theft and assault were rampant, property values plummeted. We learned that *prosperity is possible only when aggression is the exception, not the rule.* Our immediate experience suggests that a peaceful and prosperous world is possible only where the Good Neighbor Policy of nonaggression predominates.

On a one-on-one basis, most of us reject aggression. We would never steal from our next-door neighbor, whom we'll generically refer to as "George." As children, we were taught not to take his toys; as adults, we will not take his car and money. As Good Neighbors, we *respect property* that is legitimately his.

Maybe George likes to wear things we would not be caught dead in, but we wouldn't take a swing at him just because his choices are different from ours. Good Neighbors *use physical force only in self-defense.*

We practice nonaggression by being *tolerant.* If we know that George won't contribute to our favorite charity, we wouldn't lie about where his money is going in order to trick him into giving it. We practice the Good Neighbor Policy when we deal *honestly.*

If we accidentally harmed George or his property, we'd make it right again. We remain Good Neighbors by *repairing the damage that we do.*

We wouldn't join or hire a gang of our neighbors who wanted to steal from George, assault him, or cheat him. If George had an encounter with such a gang, he would probably retaliate, perhaps with a gang of his own. The cycle could repeat itself indefinitely, with aggression begetting more aggression.

"Starting it" is a prescription for neighborhood warfare, with a loss of both peace and prosperity. As Good Neighbors, we just say "no" when we're asked to use aggression against another individual or group. Because we intuitively reject aggression when dealing with our immediate neighbors, war and poverty appear to result from other people's aggression.

How "Good" Neighbors Become "Bad" Ones

Before we absolve ourselves of responsibility for the world's woes, however, let's go deeper. In the 1960s, Stanley Milgram at Yale University conducted a series of studies to determine if gentle, considerate, everyday people could be persuaded, not forced, to hurt their fellow human beings.

In one study, the scientist-experimenter strapped himself in a chair that was supposed to deliver electrical shocks of increasing severity. Whenever the scientist failed to learn a series of word pairs properly, the volunteer, an ordinary person who agreed to participate in this experiment, was supposed to shock him, using a higher voltage each time.

The scientist did not actually receive any shocks; he was only pretending. The volunteer did not know this, because he or she had received a very real, low-voltage test shock as a demonstration. When the shocks reached a third of the maximum level, the scientist pleaded for the experiment to end.

Another experimenter, pretending to be another volunteer, stood by watching the test. He tried to convince the real volunteer that the experiment should continue. However, in each of the 20 tests, the true volunteers refused to keep shocking the scientist. Apparently, a "peer volunteer" could not convince the average person to continue the shocks.[1]

In another study, the results were very different. The two experimenters switched places so that the scientist stood beside the volunteer who then administered shocks to the undercover

... civilization means, above all, an unwillingness to inflict unnecessary pain. ... those of us who heedlessly accept the commands of authority cannot yet claim to be civilized men.

—Harold J. Laski
THE DANGERS OF
OBEDIENCE

experimenter. When the "victim" cried out at one-third the maximum voltage, only 20% of the volunteers withdrew from the experiment. The others, at the insistence of the scientist, continued. At two-thirds maximum voltage, the victim cried out that he had a heart problem and feared for his life. Another 15% of the volunteers refused to continue, even though the scientist claimed that the shocks weren't severe enough to cause permanent damage. A full 65% of the volunteers continued to shock the victim even after he made no other sounds.

Because the victim was hidden in a nearby room, some of the volunteers feared he might be unconscious and were extremely concerned for his safety. Yet, at the insistence of the scientist, they continued to shock him until they had administered the highest voltage three full times![2]

The scientist didn't need to force the volunteers; only verbal commands were required. *Even when the volunteers feared for the life of the victim, they were willing to proceed as long as an authority figure, but not a peer, ordered it.*

When the volunteers were interviewed afterward, the reason for this discrepancy emerged. The 20% who refused to continue when the victim wanted to quit felt that they were personally responsible for shocking him. Administering the shocks was acceptable only if the victim agreed to it. They obviously believed in honoring their neighbor's choice regardless of what anyone else told them to do.

Those who continued shocking the victim were more likely to blame his pain on the scientist or even the victim himself for learning slowly. They felt blameless as long as an authority figure, the scientist (second study), not a peer (first study), gave the orders. Volunteers typically commented, "I was just doing what I was told."[3] Similar statements were made by those who executed Jews in the Nazi concentration camps in World War II or massacred the women and children of My Lai in Vietnam.

We defer to authority figures because we believe that they know more than we do. If a mistake is made, it's easy to lay the blame at

The real evil ... was their acceptance of the principle that the end justifies the means. This is how most human beings ... are introduced to evil. They are not pushed into evil by a strong desire to do wicked things, but by people who persuade them that evil is necessary to achieve some greater good, and that the good justifies the evil.

—Alan Keyes
former U.S. ambassador
to the United Nations

their feet. Ultimately, however, we are responsible for choosing the authority figure to whom we defer. *Our choice to obey someone who urges aggression against others makes us responsible for that aggression.*

Each of us hopes that we would be in the small group that defied the authority figure and refused to shock the victim. When Milgram surveyed people to predict what they would do, none believed that they would continue past two-thirds of maximum shock.[4] *Clearly, what we believe we would do and what we actually would do are quite different.*

We think of ourselves as Good Neighbors who are not responsible for the world's poverty and strife. Milgram's studies show us that we can become aggressors without being aware of it. If we truly wish to help our world, we must first identify ways in which we may be causing its problems. Let us examine an instance of common, everyday aggression to see what we actually practice.

How We Violate the Good Neighbor Policy Daily Without Even Realizing It

If we decided we wanted a new neighborhood park, how would we go about getting one? We could work with other individuals who wanted the same thing. Together we could raise the money to own and operate the park by selling stock in a corporation set up for that purpose or through donations and other voluntary means. If those who did not participate wanted to use the park, we might require them to pay an extra entry fee. The park would be created by relating voluntarily and nonaggressively with our neighbors. If George didn't want to be involved as either a contributor or a park visitor, we would honor his choice.

Usually, however, we vote for a tax to purchase and maintain the park. If a large enough gang of our neighbors voted for the tax, George's hard-earned dollars would be used for a park he didn't want and wouldn't use.

What if George refused to pay our tax? "I haven't committed any wrongs that I need to right," he might argue. "My neighbors just want

In growing up, the normal individual has learned to check the expression of aggressive impulses. But the culture has failed, almost entirely, in inculcating internal controls on actions that have their origin in authority. For this reason, the latter constitutes a far greater danger to human survival.
—Stanley Milgram
OBEDIENCE TO AUTHORITY

In matters of conscience, the law of the majority has no place.
—Mohandas Gandhi
father of modern nonviolent resistance

It is strangely absurd to suppose that a million human beings collected together are not under the same moral laws which bind each of them separately.
      —Thomas Jefferson
      author, Declaration of
      Independence

How does something immoral, when done privately, become moral when it is done collectively? Furthermore, does legality establish morality? Slavery was legal; apartheid is legal; Stalinist, Nazi, and Maoist purges were legal. Clearly, the fact of legality does not justify these crimes. Legality, alone, cannot be the talisman of moral people.
      —Walter Williams
      ALL IT TAKES IS GUTS

A society that robs an individual of the product of his effort ... is not strictly speaking a society, but a mob held together by institutionalized gang rule.
      —Ayn Rand
      THE VIRTUE OF
      SELFISHNESS

me to pay for their park so they can pay less. They aren't honoring my choice."

Such arguments won't sway the tax collector we've hired. If George refuses to pay the tax (let's assume it's a property tax), a lien will be put on his home. George will eventually be evicted if he won't pay. If he refuses to leave, armed officers will remove him. If George resists, he may be shot and killed, even though he has harmed no one.

Wouldn't we be using a gang called "government" to steal from George? Wouldn't we be using first-strike force against a neighbor who hadn't harmed us in any way? Wouldn't we "starting it"?

Of course, George will probably pay the tax rather than risk losing his home. Most likely, George would retaliate by persuading the government to turn its guns on us for projects that he prefers but *we* don't want. We'd alternate as victims and aggressors, as minorities and majorities, while we took turns directing the law enforcement agents at each other.

Through taxation, vegetarians have been *forced at gunpoint* to subsidize grazing land for cattle; nonsmokers have been *forced at gunpoint* to support the production of tobacco, the research to counter its deleterious effect on health, and the lawsuits against the tobacco companies.

Pacifists have been *forced at gunpoint* to subsidize war. People who abhor abortion have been *forced at gunpoint* to pay for it. Those minorities are the victims, not the initiators, of aggression. Their only crime is not agreeing with the priorities of the majority.

Taxation appears to be more than theft; it is intolerance for the preferences, religious, and moral viewpoints of our neighbors. Through taxation, we forcibly impose our will on others in the paternalistic belief that we know better than they. Like Milgram's volunteers, however, we are usually unaware that we've shifted from Good Neighbors to aggressors.

Is There a Better Way?

As individuals, we may not support taxes or other forms of aggression-through-government.

However, the composite of each person's views, as reflected in our laws, indicates that as a nation, as a society, as a collective consciousness, we believe that aggression serves us. For example, we fear that without taxation, the poor will go hungry or that only the rich will be able to enjoy a stroll in the park.

As we'll discover, our own aggression-through-government has created most of the poverty in the world today. Trying to alleviate this poverty with more aggression (e.g., taxation) ends up making the poor poorer. *Aggression creates poverty and strife in our city, state, and nation just as surely as it does in our neighborhood.* Whether aggression is undertaken by individuals or governments, the result is identical. The same means brings us the same ends.

Taxation and other forms of aggression-through-government are so taken for granted that one of our most popular sayings is that "nothing is certain except death and taxes." Taxation is thought to be indispensable to civilization today. Our ancestors had similar thoughts about slavery.

Since most individuals pay assigned taxes before the guns show up, some individuals believe that people have implicitly agreed to taxation as the price of living in society. Most slaves obeyed their master before he got out the whip, yet we would hardly argue that this obedience constituted their agreement to their servitude.

Today, we have an enlightened perspective on slavery, just as we will one day have on taxes and other forms of aggression that we now think of as "the only way."

Just as our ancestors rationalized slavery, we've created the illusion that taxation serves us. Like the volunteers who continued to shock the victim at the insistence of the scientist, we feel that the aggression of taxation is justified, perhaps even noble. We believe that we can create a world of peace and plenty if we are given a free hand to force those selfish others to do things the right way—our way.

We feel taxation is necessary for certain things (e.g., defense, clean air and water, help

... while men usually recognize criminal acts when they are committed by an individual in the name of his own interest, they often fail to recognize the very same acts for what they are when they are committed by some large gang in the name of "social justice" or the "common good."
—Jarret Wollstein
SOCIETY WITHOUT COERCION

Political power grows out of the barrel of a gun.
—Mao Tse-tung
Chinese communist dictator

We are living in a sick society filled with people who would not directly steal from their neighbor but who are willing to demand that the government do it for them.
—William L. Comer
AVOIDING THE HIGH COST OF DYING (AND MANY OTHER FINANCIAL DILEMMAS)

for the poor). Instead, as this book illustrates, aggression backfires every time, destroying what we seek to create. *When we use aggression as our means, our ends are poverty and strife. We reap what we sow.*

In Part II ("Forgive Us Our Trespasses: How We Create Poverty in a World of Plenty!"), we'll see how our well-meaning aggression creates poverty, compromises our health, and destroys our environment, while empowering manipulative monopolies and cartels. Special interests chuckle as they use our fears of "selfish others" to pit us against one another for their benefit. *In trying to control others, we find ourselves controlled.*

We often became aggressors in a futile attempt to prevent aggression by others. Part III ("As We Forgive Those Who Trespass Against Us: How We Create Strife in a World of Harmony") details a better way to deal with those who would harm us. This "other piece of the puzzle" empowers us to create peace and plenty in our community, nation, and world.

We must start, however, by taking responsibility for the acts of aggression that we unwittingly commit. Like the volunteers who refused to shock the victim at the whim of the authority figure, we too must first honor our neighbor's choice. Only when we are innocent of aggression can we deal effectively with those who are guilty of it.

... the moral and the practical are not in conflict, provided one knows what is, in fact, moral.

—Nathaniel Branden
MY YEARS WITH AYN RAND

Aggression hides in our culture under many names. Taxation is only an example, but one of the most widespread, inefficient, and uneconomical ones. If this concept seems incredible to you, consider the shift in awareness that it implies.

Most of us had such a shift when we were children learning to count money. Before we knew how to make change, we could easily be cheated. If someone offered us two small bills, we eagerly traded our single one of a much higher denomination. Because we did not know the rules of counting money, we shortchanged ourselves, all the while believing that we were enriching ourselves. When a concerned adult tried to enlighten us, we at first refused to believe this unsettling truth. Once awareness dawned, however, we could no longer be fooled.

Nor was laborious deliberation necessary. We automatically knew if we benefited from every trade. The complex became simple. Until we had this understanding, however, others could easily cheat us.

Could our social consciousness be like that of a child learning to count money? Do we shortchange ourselves with actions—like taxation—that fuel the flames of war and poverty? To answer those questions, we must first explore the nature of wealth and its creation.

In Summary ...

- As children, we learned that if no one hits first, no fight is possible.
- Therefore, refraining from "first-strike" force, theft, or fraud, is the first step in creating peace.
- The second step is compensating others for any damage that we do.
- These two steps, honoring our neighbor's choice and righting our wrongs, constitute the Good Neighbor Policy or the practice of nonaggression.
- Peace and prosperity are only possible when we are Good Neighbors.
- We can abandon the Good Neighbor Policy without even realizing it when directed to do so by an authority figure.
- When we take from our neighbors what they won't voluntarily give—at gunpoint, if necessary—we call it theft. When majorities take from minorities what they won't voluntarily give—at gunpoint, if necessary—we call it taxation.
- Perhaps we don't have peace in the world because we've abandoned the Good Neighbor Policy without even realizing it.

Chapter 2

Wealth Is Unlimited!

Wealth is created when we use existing resources in new ways. Because such creativity is virtually limitless, wealth is too.

What Is Wealth Anyway?

To determine whether we shortchange ourselves by choosing taxation and other forms of aggression as a means to our ends, we must understand the true nature of wealth. We usually equate money with wealth, but they are really very different things. Imagine a person stranded on a desert island without food, water, shelter, or medicine, but with a billion dollars in gold coin. Is this person wealthy?

Hardly! Food, water, shelter, and medicine—prerequisites for survival—are true wealth. Money can only buy available goods or services. If no wealth is available, money is worthless.

Even the richest of the ancients lived in what we would consider grinding poverty. Two thousand years ago, they had limited knowledge of antibiotics, anesthetics, or surgery. Helplessly, they watched as their children died from commonplace infections and appendicitis. Television, telephones, airplanes, and air conditioning had not yet been invented. News traveled only as fast as horses could carry it. Family members who had migrated to distant lands could not readily visit or send letters. On a sweltering day, even the ruling pharaohs could not enjoy the simple pleasures of an iced drink.

The wealthiest of our ancient ancestors could not imagine many of the things that we take for granted today. Our wealth has increased greatly over the centuries (Figure 2.1).

How Is Wealth Created?

Where did we get all this wealth? The earth certainly did not get more natural resources between ancient times and the present. Instead, we discovered new ways to use the resources the we have. Coal, oil, and natural gas give us an unprecedented amount of power. We send communications via satellite. The Internet allows us to access much of the world's knowledge

... more people who are considered "poor" today have routine access to a quality of food, health care, consumer products, entertainment, communications and transportation that even the Vanderbilts, the Carnegies, the Rockefellers, and 19th century European royalty, with all their combined wealth, could not have afforded.
—Rudiger Dornbusch
GLOBAL FORTUNE

PAST WEALTH

PRESENT WEALTH

FUTURE WEALTH

**Figure 2.1: Pictorial Representation of
the Growth of Wealth Through the Ages**

instantly. Artificial wings fly us all over the world. Assembly lines and robotics mass produce the new products, thereby multiplying the wealth. One advance leads to the next.

For example, fossil fuels create higher temperatures in our furnaces than wood does, allowing us to create new metal alloys. New wealth (e.g., new metal alloys) is created whenever we find new uses for existing resources. When we replicate these ideas (e.g., mass production of metal alloys) we create wealth too.

Natural resources are like seeds that grow into wealth when they are nurtured and developed. For example, oil was once considered a nuisance that contaminated good farmland. Not until we discovered how to pump, refine, and use it did oil turn into "black gold." Even water must be "developed" (drawn from a stream, well, or reservoir) before it can quench our thirst.

When we consider that resources will one day be mined from other planets, that matter and energy are totally interchangeable, and that basic chemical elements can be transmuted, we realize that resources do not limit the creation of wealth. Even if our fossil fuels should be foolishly exhausted, for example, energy is abundantly available in each and every atom when we discover, as we one day will, how to tap it safely. Even land is not a limitation, for a universe of other planets will one day be within our reach. Human resources, our "how to" ideas, and the replication of these ideas determine how much available wealth we have at any one time. *Because human creativity is unbounded, the amount of potential wealth is virtually infinite!*

How Does Wealth Become "Owned"?

The wealth created from using resources in new ways can be mass produced by individuals acting alone or as part of a team. For example, George, our imaginary neighbor, may work in a factory where he makes chairs. The factory owner gets the lumber from a tree farmer. Those three people create new wealth in the form of chairs. They exchange the chairs for money and then trade their money for the wealth (food, clothing, etc.) that others have created.

... most real wealth originates in individual minds in unpredictable and uncontrollable ways.
—George Gilder
WEALTH AND POVERTY

... people have repeatedly overcome crippling shortages by finding new technologies, new materials, and new applications. The creativity of the human mind can overcome the vast majority of obstacles that it comes across, as long as it is not fettered.
—James Bovard
FREEDOM IN CHAINS

All three individuals helped create the chairs. Without their effort, the new wealth would not exist. Thus, the new wealth belongs to its creators, as we instinctively recognize. We wouldn't cheat George out of his wealth with lies and false promises. Nor would we go to George's house with a gun to steal his wealth. If we did, he would retaliate. We'd take turns being victims and aggressors. With continual "warfare," a jungle-like atmosphere would pervade our neighborhood, and property values would plummet. Our time would be spent creating war instead of wealth.

We believe that we can avoid these unwanted consequences if our government enforcement agents call the act of taking George's wealth—at gunpoint, if necessary—a "tax." Sometimes the act of stealing even seems noble if the majority deems it to be for "the common good." As we'll see in the next few chapters, the consequences of aggression are the same, whether performed by an individual or by a group. When *groups* ask their government to steal from other *groups*, we simply take turns as majorities and minorities, aggressors and victims. A jungle-like atmosphere prevails as effort is spent creating war instead of wealth.

Aggression, especially aggression-through-government, has slowed the creation of wealth for most of recorded history. As late as 1820, approximately three-quarters of the world's population lived on the equivalent of $1 per day. For the most part, all countries were equally poor.[1]

In the mid-1800s, however, the countries that we now refer to as "developed" began creating wealth much more rapidly. The Third World nations, however, continued to create wealth slowly (Figure 2.2). Why did some countries grow rich and others stay poor?

What Causes Wealth to Grow?

Although resources contribute to a nation's wealth-creating ability, they are not the primary source of development. Japan, for example, has almost no mineral wealth. Mexico is well endowed, yet the Japanese are certainly more affluent than the Mexicans.[2] North Korea is poorer than South Korea, even though both share a

Amnesty International's listing of human rights abuses shows a definite pattern where those nations with the least respect for human rights are also the poorest. By contrast, those with the greatest respect for human rights tend to be the richest.
—Walter Williams
ALL IT TAKES IS GUTS

common culture and have comparable resources. Similarly, East Germany created much less wealth than West Germany before reunification in 1990. The island of Puerto Rico is wealthier than neighboring Cuba.[3] Obviously, resource endowment is not the primary factor determining a country's wealth.

Rapid population growth and high population density are not major factors in Third World poverty either. In 1996, both Hong Kong and Singapore, with 10 times the population density of China or India, created five-and-a-half times more wealth than either of them.[4] Developing countries that enjoy the highest economic growth rate often have the highest population growth rates as well.[5] Between 1775 and 1975, the United States had the biggest population explosion in history,[6] yet Americans now earn the highest wages in the world. Clearly, rapid population growth and high population density

Figure 2.2: Wealth Creation vs. Time for Developed and Third World Nations

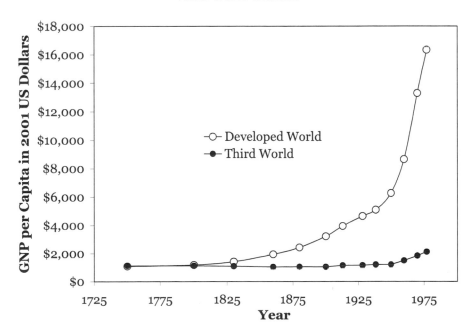

Data from P. Bairoch, "The Main Trends in National Economic Disparities Since the Industrial Revolution," in *Disparities in Economic Development Since the Industrial Revolution*, P. Bairoch and M. Lévy-Leboyer, eds.(New York: St. Martin's Press, 1981), p.7. Inflation-adjusted by the author using CPI-U for first half of 2001.

The GNP of East Germany was an embarrassing $210 billion in 1989 compared to $1.3 trillion for West Germany.
— WALL STREET DIGEST
April 9, 1990

Capitalism is simply what happens in the absence of social planning.
—Richard W. Grant
THE INCREDIBLE BREAD
MACHINE

are no more responsible for poverty than inadequate resource endowment.

In 1996, the country with the highest rate of wealth creation per person[7] was also one of the most densely populated. Over 40% of its population were immigrants and refugees, because of its relatively open immigration policies.[8] Oil, raw materials, and even water had to be imported because this country had so few natural resource "seeds." The government posed virtually no trade restrictions to protect domestic industries. This tiny country with its terrain of eroded hillsides was still a British colony in the year that its wealth creation (gross domestic product per capita [GDP]) was similar to that of the United States. Which country has learned how to create so much wealth under such adverse circumstances? What is its secret?

Hong Kong, the country described above, had the highest level of "economic freedom" of any country in the world for the previous twenty five years.[9] *Freedom, in this context means freedom from aggression, specifically, aggression-through-government.* Freedom is the single most important determinant of a nation's wealth-creating ability today. Because the Good Neighbor Policy sets the stage for harmony and abundance, the people of Hong Kong have prospered, even with so many strikes against them.

Indeed, countries throughout the world create more wealth, as measured by their GDP, when their economic freedom index (EFI) is high.[10] *Cultures with a tradition of rejecting aggression, individually and collectively, enjoy the highest level of prosperity.*

How Can the Poor Gain Wealth?

Does increased wealth creation mean that the rich are getting richer at the expense of the poor? Just the opposite! When developing countries start abandoning aggression, their incidence of poverty goes down as their wealth goes up (Figure 2.3).

As the following chapters show, aggression primarily thwarts wealth creation by the disadvantaged. Thus, the poor gain most from a shift to the Good Neighbor Policy. Nations free from aggression not only have the most prosperity, but also more equality of income and a more even distribution of wealth.[11] In nonaggressive nations, poverty tends to be temporary condition, rather than a life long affliction.[12] As we'll learn in subsequent chapters, the best way to help alleviate world poverty, hunger, and disease is to honor our neighbor's choice.

Until the twentieth century, most Americans, with the notable exception of blacks and Native Americans, faced less aggression-through-government than citizens of other countries. As a result, the United States became the wealthiest nation on earth. Unfortunately, it has been abandoning the Good Neighbor Policy that made it the "land of opportunity" for so long. Consequently, its rate of wealth creation has been adversely affected.

Why would my homeland turn away from a policy that has worked so well? Perhaps we didn't have the other piece of the puzzle. The early Americans knew how to honor their neighbor's

There is no conflict between economic growth and poverty alleviation.
—Dani Rodrik
INCOME DISTRIBUTION AND HIGH-QUALITY GROWTH

GDP growth is correlated with a reduction in poverty, income inequality [and] infant mortality, and an increase in life expectancy.
—The World Bank
THE QUALITY OF GROWTH

Figure 2.3: Economic Freedom Results in More Wealth and Less Poverty

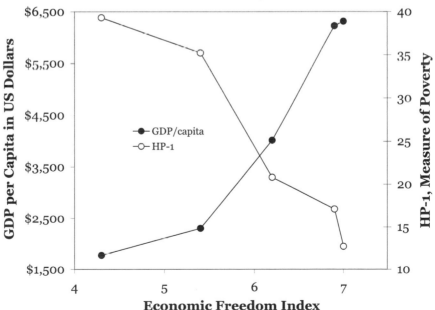

Data courtesy of J. Gwartney and R. Lawson, presented in part in the *Economic Freedom of the World, 2001 Annual Report* (Vancouver: The Fraser Institute, 2002). HP-1 is the United Nations' Human Poverty Index for developing countries. Each point represents one-fifth of the entire sample of developing nations (*n* = 13 for every point except for the middle quintile, where *n* = 14).

choice. *What they did not know was the most effective way to deal with those who aggressed against them.*

Consequently, Americans instructed their government to use aggression in a futile attempt to prevent aggression. Their motto became "do unto others *before* they do unto you." *To fight aggression, they became aggressors themselves, with consequences harsher than those which they sought to prevent.*

By understanding what happened in the United States, other nations can learn a better way. Perhaps, armed with this knowldege, America can regain its proud heritage of freedom and opportunity.

Chapter 2: Wealth Is Unlimited!

In Summary ...

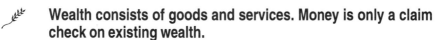

- Wealth consists of goods and services. Money is only a claim check on existing wealth.

- Using resources in new and more productive ways creates wealth.

- Since creativity is unbounded, so is wealth.

- Countries that practice the Good Neighbor Policy create more wealth than those that don't.

- The poverty of ancient times was largely due to violations of the Good Neighbor Policy, especially aggression by governments.

- The poor are harmed most by aggression and prosper most under the Good Neighbor Policy.

- The United States is the wealthiest country on earth because it practiced the Good Neighbor Policy for the longest time.

- By studying U.S. history, we can learn how a country can create great wealth and how it can lose that wealth by abandoning the Good Neighbor Policy.

Part Two

Forgive Us Our Trespasses:

How We Create Poverty in a World of Plenty

Chapter 3

Destroying Jobs

When we try to increase the wealth of disadvantaged workers through aggression, we only succeed in making them poorer.

The previous chapter explained how wealth is created by individuals acting alone or as part of a team. Wealth is virtually infinite, yet we commonly hear that jobs, the means to that end, are limited. As the next two chapters illustrate, we create this limitation by abandoning the Good Neighbor Policy.

The Marketplace Ecosystem: Honoring Our Neighbor's Choice

By the 1800s, when the developed countries started creating large amounts of wealth, people had begun to recognize that the "marketplace" is similar to Nature's ecosystems.[1] People find their "niche" in the marketplace just as different species find their place in the environmental ecosystem.

For example, when workers with special skills are few, employers try to gain their loyalty by paying high wages. When supply is scarce, demand is high and so is employee compensation. Workers who want higher wages train or school to gain skills that are in demand. Eventually, as more people train, the supply of the skilled workers equals the demand, and wages stabilize. The *marketplace ecosystem uses wages and prices to balance supply and demand.* For the most part, the marketplace is self-regulating and creates a natural, harmonious balance quite well without any interference on our part.

In the marketplace ecosystem, interference usually means aggression-through-government. When we don't like the outcomes that we get in the marketplace, we sometimes try to correct its "imperfections" with laws that force our neighbors—at gunpoint, if necessary—to do things differently. As we'll see in the next few chapters, abandoning the Good Neighbor Policy is a cure worse than the disease. Imperfections of the marketplace ecosystem are dwarfed by the havoc created by our well-meaning aggression.

The marketplace is not always neat and orderly and "fair." But it works a whole lot better than the alternatives.

—Richard W. Grant
THE INCREDIBLE BREAD
MACHINE

In the 1800s, most working people correctly perceived that aggression-through-government, a prominent feature of most nations, slowed their ability to create wealth. A flood of immigrants came to the United States hoping for freedom from such aggression.

However, the new immigrants were at a disadvantage in the established marketplace ecosystem. Often, they couldn't speak English. Their customs were different and disquieting. Sometimes, they were unskilled and could produce little wealth. Employers had no incentive to hire them. The immigrants found a way to get employers to reconsider.

A Win–Win Strategy for a New Beginning

The new arrivals created a niche for themselves in the marketplace ecosystem by offering employers a greater-than-usual share of the jointly created wealth. By helping their employers, the immigrants helped themselves. Instead of paying for expensive schooling to learn new skills, they got on-the-job training by initially accepting lower wages than experienced, American-born workers.

Once they learned the language, trade, and customs, immigrants could create much more wealth than before. They were either given a greater share of the jointly created wealth by their employers, or they moved on to better opportunities. Sometimes they opened their own shop; sometimes they went to an employer with a greater appreciation for their recently acquired expertise. Some eventually became quite wealthy. *In offering to serve their first employers well, they ultimately served themselves.*

Young Americans sometimes use the same technique to get that all-important first job. For example, as an undergraduate, I worked in the laboratories of various scientists after class. Sometimes there was a little pay involved, sometimes course credit, sometimes no visible compensation at all. The scientists who hired me really didn't have a job to give. Like the immigrants, I created my niche in the marketplace ecosystem by offering a better deal than any of my classmates would even consider.

By his willingness to accept lousy jobs—to be exploited, if you want to call it that—the immigrant is going to do better in the long run.

—Jose Legaspi
Los Angeles business consultant

Generation after generation, the poor have streamed to America and been lifted out of poverty. This "liberation theology" actually does liberate.

—Michael Novak
WILL IT LIBERATE?

My peers thought I was crazy working for "slave wages." A few years later, they changed their minds. The experience I gained, plus the recommendations of my mentors, turned out to be quite valuable. These intangibles gave me an edge over those with comparable formal education when I applied for more advanced positions. Offering my first employers a good deal resulted in later employers offering *me* a good deal. Letting myself be "exploited" was one of the smartest career moves I ever made.

Bob Burg, author of *Winning Without Intimidation,* once offered to work without pay to prove himself to a prospective employer. My husband hired a young woman who did the same. Both individuals so impressed the decision makers by offering weeks of "free" service that they were enthusiastically hired, with pay well in excess of the minimum wage! By offering to serve others, those eager job applicants served themselves as well.

A Win–Win Strategy for Moving Up

The balance of the marketplace ecosystem evolves naturally. Workers without experience who are willing to start at low (or no) wages can gain the experience and skills to create more wealth. Almost everyone is able to create some wealth, so everyone can find a starting niche. As expertise evolves, job opportunities do too.

An employer will usually reward workers as their capacity to create more wealth increases or will lose them to employers who do. All but the most complacent employees will seek (and find) a better situation if they are underpaid or unappreciated when compared to their peers.

Employers who choose employees on the basis of color or sex or anything other than ability find that their shop creates less wealth than it otherwise would. Less wealth means less profit, providing employers with negative feedback. Discrimination on any basis other than productivity is costly. Employers, for the most part, reap as they sow.

We can observe this "yin-yang," or balance, of the marketplace ecosystem right in our own community when our fictitious neighbor George decides to hire a neighborhood youth, Elaine, to paint his house. Elaine created her job by giving George a better deal than the other teens in the neighborhood. Had Elaine not made such an offer, George would have let the house go unpainted for another few years. The creation of wealth in the form of a well-kept house would have been delayed. By offering to serve George well, Elaine also beautified her neighborhood.

Elaine helped herself too. In the fall, Elaine asked George to put in a good word for her with the corner grocer. As a result of George's glowing recommendation, Elaine was hired instead of other teens who had no one to vouch for them. The following summer, references from the grocer helped Elaine get a temporary job with a nearby factory. When she graduated from high school, Elaine was offered a well-paying job with a local banker because her former employers could vouch for her conscientious performance. Her friends, who had mocked her as she worked for a "pittance," couldn't compete with her experience. By serving her employers well, Elaine also served herself.

Elaine's strategy couldn't guarantee her a well-paying job with an appreciative boss, but it certainly maximized her chances—just as it did mine!

Aggression Disrupts the Marketplace Ecosystem

We'd never dream of putting a gun to George's head and threatening him if he didn't pay Elaine more than what they had jointly agreed on. After all, our neighbors know better than we do what will work for them. Pointing a gun at George would probably end any feeling of camaraderie we might have shared in the past. There's something about looking down the barrel of a gun that isn't consistent with "loving our neighbor." George is likely to call his local sheriff or retaliate with sufficient force so that we won't threaten him again. In trying to control George, we might very well find ourselves controlled. Needless to say, George would no longer consider us Good Neighbors.

Even if we successfully intimidated George, he might decide not to hire Elaine, rather than pay her more. Without the recommendation from George, Elaine might never get the grocery job. Without experience at the grocer's, Elaine might not be picked to work at the factory. Without these part-time jobs, Elaine would not have the experience so valued by the bank. Our attempt to protect Elaine from George's exploitation by using aggression would probably backfire and hurt the person we most wish to help.

The marketplace ecosystem operates in our neighborhood if we let it work its magic. We wisely refrain from threatening our neighbors when they are interacting and contracting with each other without using force or deceit. Those individuals, after all, know their situation better than we do. Honoring their choices is part of being a Good Neighbor.

Exactly the same principles apply in the national work force, but somehow we see it differently. We view low wages as evidence of employer "stinginess" instead of a win–win arrangement providing the employee with on-the-job training, a "foot in the door," job experience, or a chance to get that first work reference. We try to correct the behavior of those selfish others by *forcing* employers to pay a minimum wage. Through our government, we become aggressors, the first party to threaten violence. Our aggression yields the same results on a national scale as it does in our neighborhood.

For example, in the chair factory where George works, employees are paid at different levels ($6 or $7 per hour) depending on their experience. If the minimum wage is raised to $7 per hour, several things could happen.

If the employer pays the least experienced people $7 per hour, he will have to raise the price of the chairs. The people who were earning $7 will probably complain because they are being paid the same wage as the novices. The employer will have to give them a raise too. The price of the chairs goes even higher. Fewer people can now afford to buy the chairs, so the factory will cut back production. Workers will be laid off; the least experienced will be the first to go. Instead of earning $6 per hour, some of the inexperienced workers will be unemployed,

Neumark and Wascher (1998) examined the correlation between state minimum wages and training designed to improve skills on the current job and training to qualify for a job. They found that minimum wages reduced training.

—Mark D. Turner
The Urban Institute and
Institute for
Policy Studies

... low income workers as a group are the major victims of minimum wage legislation.

—Keith B. Leffler
Economics of Legal Minimum Wages

The reduction in employment that results from increases in the minimum wage, which is concentrated among those workers with the fewest skills, is the cruel "dark side" of such legislation. ... The winners will be those who would have fared best in any case.

—Donald Deere et al.
Sense and Nonsense on the Minimum Wage

while the best among them will be making $7 per hour.

George's employer might be able to replace the unskilled workers with machines that end up costing only $6.50 per hour instead of the $7 now mandated for humans. The workers from the factory that makes the new machines are skilled and already make well above the minimum wage. They receive additional orders for machines, so their factory must hire more skilled labor.

Perhaps the employer might simply eliminate part or all of the job that the people earning $6 per hour once did. Maybe their job was to paint the chairs; now finishing is left to the buyer. More unskilled employees are laid off.

Some employers will not be able to use any of these options. There may be no substitute for the unskilled labor and no way to raise prices without losing too many customers. To comply with the law, those employers may cut back on other employee benefits, such as health insurance or vacation time. The unskilled workers make $7 per hour, but lose some benefits that may have been worth more to them than the wage increase.

If none of those options are available, employers may close their factories and retire or switch to a business that needs only skilled workers. In either case, some employees will be laid off. The skilled workers will have an easier time becoming employed again. They are needed in places such as the machine factory that makes labor-saving devices. The unskilled workers will find themselves in less demand and will have more difficulty. The best of the low-paid workers get a raise, but the most disadvantaged are kept from creating any wealth at all!

How Minimum Wage Destroys Jobs for the Poor

In 1938, the Fair Labor Standards Act set the U.S. minimum wage to the average wage in the territory of Puerto Rico. Over the next two years, half of the Puerto Rican work force lost their jobs because employers simply couldn't pay that much and stay in business. To save it from total economic ruin, Puerto Rico was given an exemption from minimum wages.[2]

If making a law "made it so," we could simply legislate $100/hr. minimums for each of us. Like the Puerto Ricans, however, we'd quickly find ourselves without any job at all! Indeed, because of the minimum wage law, an estimated 30,000 to 50,000 workers on the U.S. mainland lost their jobs along with Puerto Ricans, prolonging the country's deep recession.[3]

Subsequent increases in the minimum wage destroyed jobs as well.[4] Consequently, welfare to the unemployed went up each time the minimum wage did.[5] Job loss from minimum wage hikes are so well documented[6] that journalists usually include such estimates when reporting on Congressional minimum wage debates. Aggression backfires, hurting the very people it is intended to help.

Most people paid the minimum wage aren't suffering financially. Eighty-five percent of minimum wage workers don't even come from poor families.[7] Most are part-timers just getting in— or getting back in—to the work force. Those teens and secondary earners averaged just 9 hours of work per week in 1998.[8]

Only about 1% of those paid the minimum wage (less than 60,000 U.S. earners in the early 1990s) were adult heads of households with incomes of less than $10,000.[9] Those individuals, however, are harmed the most if they are laid off because of a minimum wage hike.

How Minimum Wages Discriminate Against the Disadvantaged

Because minimum wages hurt the disadvantaged the most, they are frequently used to legalize discrimination. For example, in South Africa during apartheid, white unions lobbied for minimum wages (called "rate-for-the-job") in order to "reserve" particular jobs for whites.[10] If the unskilled blacks were forbidden by law to negotiate an entry level or training wage, they were effectively barred by law from creating wealth in those occupations.

The same thing happens in the United States. Many disadvantaged workers are black;

A minimum wage requirement mandated by the National Industrial Recovery Act in 1933 halted an increase in employment, lengthening and deepening the Great Depression.
—Richard Vedder and
Lowell Gallaway
National Center for
Policy Analysis

Evidence demonstrates a link between minimum wage increases and the recessions of 1990–91 and 1974–75.
—Richard Vedder and
Lowell Gallaway
National Center for
Policy Analysis

Many studies have been done on the minimum wage over the last 50 years. Virtually all show that increases in the minimum wage reduce employment.
—Bruce R. Bartlett
testifying before
the U.S. House of
Representatives,
May 15, 1996

... changes in the unemployment rate for nonwhites closely parallel changes in the real minimum wage.
—National Center for
Policy Analysis, 1995

A rising minimum wage broadens the income gap between blacks and whites, leaving black families proportionately further behind than ever.
　　　　　—Robert Meyer and
　　　　　　　　David Wise
REPORT OF THE MINIMUM
WAGE STUDY COMMISSION

The minimum wage law is one of the major causes of spiraling unemployment among young blacks.
　　　　　—Walter Williams
THE STATE AGAINST
BLACKS

the most unskilled blacks are the young. Between 1954 (the first year that unemployment data are available by race and age group[11]) and 1980, the number of jobs covered by minimum wage laws rose dramatically. The employment ratio of black to white teens dropped in tandem (Figure 3.1). *What is particularly distressing is that black and white teenage unemployment was almost identical before minimum wage coverage skyrocketed!*

Just as expansion of minimum wage *coverage* significantly contributed to loss of jobs for black male teenagers, *rate increases* in subsequent years shifted jobs from blacks to whites. High minimum wages tempt teens of both races to leave school early and seek full-time employment, hurting their chances for high-paying jobs in the future. Employers choose the most skilled teens from this larger labor pool, which puts the less skilled minorities at a further disadvantage. After minimum wage increased in the early 1990s, teenage minorities were less likely to be

Figure 3.1: Black Youth Unemployment Increases Along with Minimum Wages

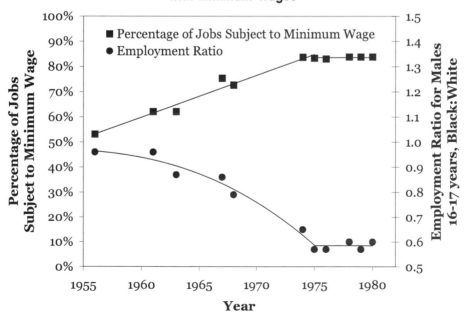

Data from Masanori Hashimoto, *Minimum Wages and On-the-Job Training* (Washington, DC: American Enterprise Institute for Public Policy Research, 1981), p. 2; and Walter Williams, *The State Against Blacks* (New York: New Press, McGraw-Hill, 1982), p. 37.

in school *and* less likely to be employed.[12] The minimum wage disenfranchises minority youths in the United States just as surely as it did in apartheid South Africa.

How Minimum Wage Destroys Jobs for the Disabled

The minorities are not the only victims of the minimum wage laws. The elderly and disabled are hurt as well. This fact was vividly brought home to me in the mid-1980s while renovating low-income housing. A young, unskilled man, who was partially disabled, had been watching our progress and asked if he could do some cleaning and yard work for $2 per hour. He was willing to accept such low wages because he could walk to the work site. He also hoped I might be able to give him a recommendation so others would "give him a chance." I explained to him that minimum wage laws prevented me from hiring him for anything less than $3.35. We both knew that I could hire an able-bodied person at that rate who would do more work. We both would have been satisfied to settle on $2 per hour, but we were forbidden by law from doing so.

Why shouldn't this young man have been able to make his own choices? He viewed working for $2 per hour in the same way I had viewed working in the laboratory—as a stepping stone to something better. Surely he could decide what a particular job was worth to him!

By supporting minimum wage laws, we've condemned many of the disadvantaged to life "on the dole." Destroying entry level jobs for the disadvantaged can keep them from getting the work experience that makes them attractive to employers. When workers end up with no job instead of a low paying job, minimum wage laws create the very poverty that they're supposed to alleviate.

On the average, individuals make better choices for themselves than we can with a "one-size-fits-all" government- enforced choice for everyone. Some employees prefer to accept a lower hourly wage in return for more benefits, better working conditions, more flexible hours, more marketable experience, proximity to work, or

Milton Friedman once called it (the minimum wage law) "the most anti-Negro law on our statute books."
—Richard W. Grant
THE INCREDIBLE BREAD
MACHINE

Past studies by and large confirm the prediction that higher minimum wages reduce employment opportunities and raise unemployment, particularly for teenagers, minorities, and other low-skilled workers.
—Masanori Hashimoto
MINIMUM WAGES AND ON-
THE-JOB TRAINING

... the responsiveness of labor supply to wage changes seems to be greater among the disabled than among the non-disabled. ...
—Andrew Kohen
REPORT OF THE MINIMUM
WAGE STUDY COMMISSION

congenial colleagues. Other individuals may want top wages, even if the work is difficult, the conditions are rough, and the hours are rigid. Without our interference, each person eventually finds the niche with conditions that suits him or her best.

How Low Wage Jobs Provide a Stepping Stone to Success

Few low wage earners stay where they start. Forty percent will receive a raise within four months and almost two-thirds will earn 10—20% more than the minimum within a year. Not surprisingly, part-timers and high school dropouts take longer to advance.[13]

For most people, flipping hamburgers is just the first step up the economic ladder. More than 50% of McDonald's managers started in the kitchen, including Fred Turner, chairman of the board in 1989 and Ed Rensi, former president of McDonald's USA. Because blacks are more likely to start their career flipping hamburgers than whites, it's hardly surprising that blacks accounted for 17% of McDonald's management in the late 1980s.[14] For most workers, entry level jobs are simply humble beginnings rather than dead ends.

Of course, the few who do seem trapped at the minimum wage are the very people those laws are supposed to help. However, employers often respond to the wage hikes by cutting back on hours, demanding more from their remaining workers, or eliminating training programs that improve worker skills and increase their pay. As a result, workers who receive the new minimum wage after a hike are often just as poor afterwards.

Indeed, the total family income of low wage earners may decrease after a minimum wage hike, especially if a spouse or teenage child loses her or his or job as a consequence.[15] Now we see why exhaustive data analysis shows that minimum wages don't alleviate poverty, but often make it worse![16]

Low wages and even poverty itself are generally a temporary condition for most people in the United States. Ninety-five percent of those

Most poor people earn more than the minimum wage when they are working; their problem is not low wages.

—Joseph Stiglitz
Economics

in the bottom fifth of the earning spectrum in 1971 had moved out of that group 20 years later. Indeed, nearly 25% moved out of the bottom category within the first year![17]

Leaving poverty behind is often a matter of obtaining and keeping a full-time job. Most individuals progress if they have steady, full-time employment. Poverty is largely the result of a failure to find full-time work. In 1999, 57% of the poor did not work at all; 31% worked only part-time.[18] When the poor do find work, they usually make more than the minimum wage.[19]

Poverty isn't caused by low wages; it's caused by no wages. Because minimum wages destroy jobs, they actually help to create the poverty that they were designed to cure.

How Davis-Bacon Destroys Minority Jobs

The Davis-Bacon Act of 1931 works much like the minimum wage laws. It was originally designed to protect white union labor from lower paid black construction workers.[20] Private contractors on most federally funded construction projects are forced to pay their workers "prevailing" or union rates, which are higher than average wages. Unskilled workers are paid almost as much as skilled ones; on-the-job training can be provided only through cumbersome apprenticeship programs. Consequently, few inexperienced or unskilled workers can be hired. Minority companies and construction workers are priced out of the market—sometimes right in their own backyards.

For example, when tenants of Kenilworth-Parkside, a public housing project, secured an $18 million grant for improvements, not one of the residents could get a job on the construction team. Contractors who had to pay top dollar for workers because of Davis-Bacon couldn't afford to hire anyone who didn't have either training or on-the-job experience. The community residents, mostly minorities, were not able to help improve their own buildings![21]

Nona Brazier, a minority contractor in Washington state, was approached by her minister, who hoped that Nona would hire some gang members wanting to go straight. Because of

For low income workers earning minimum wage or slightly better, a 10% minimum wage raise has an even greater impact— a 10% job loss.

—Bruce Bartlett National Center for Policy Analysis

The (Davis-Bacon) Act's repeal would also result in the creation of an estimated 31,000 new construction jobs, most of which would go to members of minority groups.
  —Institute for Justice

Davis-Bacon, Nona had no entry level jobs to give. Just as minimum wage coverage of jobs has increased over the years, the reach of Davis-Bacon has extended to 25% of U.S. construction workers. Companies can't afford to hire unskilled minorities or even train them. The paperwork burden that Davis-Bacon requires drives many small companies that sincerely try to comply out of business.[22]

What happens to the disadvantaged who are kept out of the work force by wage laws? Those who can't get jobs often turn to crime, which rises along with unemployment.[23]

A young drug dealer once asked for a job on a public housing project in San Francisco. He approached Chris Albert, president of Willie Electric Company, hoping to get out of drugs and into legitimate work. Unfortunately, because of the high wages dictated by Davis-Bacon, the contractor couldn't afford to take a chance on an unskilled man with no job record. The young man came back two days later and begged to be employed at a lower wage. "I won't tell the law," he promised. "I want to make a better life for me and for my mom and for my little sisters and brothers." Unwilling to risk legal problems, the contractor reluctantly refused. Two days later the young man was shot and killed.[24] Perhaps he'd be alive today if our aggression had not prevented him from getting a job.

In 1993, the Institute for Justice began a legal challenge to the Davis-Bacon Act on behalf of minority construction companies. To counter this challenge, the Clinton administration sought out Norman Hill, president of the A. Phillip Randolph Institute, the "African-American arm of the trade union movement." Although Hill supported the Davis-Bacon Act, he didn't want its wage rates to apply to *his* company. Mr. Hill explained: "We ourselves cannot afford to pay the same level that in most cases a union can."[25] *Even those who lobby for wage control don't want to abide by it!*

When we want others to choose differently, we start by setting an example. If we won't voluntarily change our ways, perhaps we should reconsider forcing others to change theirs.

How Living Wages Destroy Jobs

In recent years, several communities have adopted "living wages," with pay rates greatly in excess of the minimum wage. Initially, the living wage usually applies only to projects funded through taxation.

Most promoters of the living wage erroneously[26] claim that it will not reduce employment. Like the minimum wage and Davis-Bacon restrictions, however, the living wage destroys entry level jobs for the disadvantaged. The Salvation Army, for example, threatened to cancel its contract with the city of Detroit rather than pay an additional $4.2 million per year to its workers. The Salvation Army tries to give the disadvantaged a hand up by giving workers without much to recommend them that all-important first job.[27] The living wage would have left them with no wage at all!

Ironically, the Association of Community Organizations for Reform Now (ACORN), a living wage supporter, sued the state of California in 1995 in order to be exempted from the state's minimum wage laws! In its legal brief, ACORN explained that "... the more that ACORN must pay each individual outreach worker—either because of the minimum wage or overtime requirements—the fewer outreach workers it will be able to hire."[28] *Even those who support the living wage understand its damaging effects!*

The Rich Get Richer with *Our* Help!

Clearly, ACORN has other reasons for supporting the living wage. ACORN believes that "One of the most promising uses of living wage campaigns is to foster union organizing among low wage workers."[29] It hardly seems appropriate to destroy the jobs of some workers so that others will join a union!

Unions frequently lobby for wage controls because they favor their skilled membership by eliminating competition from those working their way up the Ladder of Afflucence.[30] Wage controls limit the number of disadvantaged workers who will rise through the ranks if they are only given a chance. Wage control effectively takes that chance away.

... a 10% increase in the living wage lowers the employment rate by 0.9 percentage point.
> —David Neumark and Scott Adams, Michigan State University

... the law has discouraged some retailers from coming to Oakland. When the retailers found we had a living wage ordinance, they said thanks, but no thanks.
> —Larry Reid vice mayor, Oakland

... if a city passes a living wage that is 50 percent higher than the state's minimum wage, it will raise the average wage of low-income workers by 3.5 percent ... [it will] also reduce employment among low-wage workers by 7 percent.
> —Public Policy Institute of California March 14, 2002

... relatively low-wage union members gain at the expense of the lowest-wage nonunion workers when minimum wages increase.
> —David Neumark et al. INDUSTRIAL LABOR AND RELATIONS REVIEW

... low wage employers may be substituting workers they prefer for more disadvantaged workers. If so, minimum wages are a very undesirable anti-poverty measure.
—Kevin Lang
Employment Policies
Institute

... the minimum wage must reduce total income available to all members of society taken as a whole.
—Sherwin Rosen
REPORT OF THE MINIMUM
WAGE STUDY COMMISSION

... a 20 percent increase (in minimum wage) makes approximately 81 percent of South Carolina workers worse off than before the change.
—James Heckman and
Guilherme Sedlacek
REPORT OF THE MINIMUM
WAGE STUDY COMMISSION

If unions and other advantaged individuals benefit from wage control, should we blame them for its promotion? No—the responsibility belongs to us! Unions are just following our example. The last time we used aggression, unions may have been the victims. Now they are simply taking their turns as aggressors.

Of course, unions and other special interest groups that support wage controls do not actually use aggression themselves. Like the proverbial serpent in the Garden of Eden, they tempt us to disregard the Good Neighbor Policy. We could choose differently. We could say "No!" to those who advocate wage controls, just as Adam and Eve could have said "No!" to the serpent. Without our consent, the unions (and the serpent) are powerless. The choice and responsibility belong to us.

A Lose–Lose Situation

We often agree to minimum wage laws because of our belief in a win-lose world, where wealth and jobs are limited, where gain can be had only at another's expense. When our choice is between winning and losing, aggression appears to be a useful tool. We don't notice that our aggression is limiting wealth and jobs; we take those limitations as a given. Our beliefs become self-fulfilling prophecies.

The gains that skilled workers make when wage control laws put the disadvantaged out of work are largely an illusion. People who lobby for wage control, who enforce these laws, or who lose their jobs because of them will produce no wealth. The world has less wealth and so our money buys less than it otherwise would.

Lost wealth is only the smallest part of the price we pay, however. The laws encourage the disadvantaged to think of their plight as someone else's fault rather than as something that they can change. As they turn the law enforcement agents on us for food, clothing, and shelter, we take turns being victims and aggressors, minorities and majorities. In fighting for control of the guns of government, we consume wealth rather than creating it. Our world is poorer and so is everyone in it.

A Better Way

We have a choice. We can just say "No!" to the aggression of wage control and disempower the special interests (e.g., unions) that promote them. No detailed evaluation of the law or the proponents' motives is necessary. When we find that our enforcement agents will be turned against neighbors who are interacting voluntarily with each other honestly and peacefuly, we know that poverty and strife will follow. The means and ends are intimately related. *Nationwide aggression is every bit as destructive as it is in our neighborhood.*

Without wage control laws, young, inexperienced, or disadvantaged workers could create niches (jobs) for themselves in the marketplace ecosystem by offering employers a greater share of the jointly created wealth in return for training, experience, or a work reference. *Since everyone can create some wealth, everyone could be employed.*

Most job seekers find that the first question a prospective employer wants answered is "How much experience do you have?" Employers know that past performance is the best predictor of future success. In many cases, job experience—any job experience—is more valuable than education of any kind. *Without the aggression of minimum wage laws, this opportunity would be within everyone's reach.*

For the most part, the marketplace ecosystem keeps employers from exploiting workers by simply allowing them to reap what they sow. As a result, *employers already pay 97% of workers 25 years and older more than the minimum wage, even though no laws demand it.*[31]

The marketplace ecosystem regulates the ratio of wealth to wages so precisely that 98% of the change in real U.S. wages can be explained by the change in the amount of capital (wealth) created per worker.[32] *In other words, wages increase at the same pace as wealth creation, indicating that workers, on average, are paid according to how much wealth they produce.* Because both employers and employees have imperfect information when they make choices, a 2% "error" rate is incredibly low. Indeed, in real life, this is as close to perfection as we are likely to get!

How can the marketplace ecosystem work this magic when employers are sometimes prejudiced, when employees aren't always savvy enough to know that they are underpaid, or when employers don't make the connection between what they reap and what they sow? To explore real-life examples, let's consider what happened in the United States to the liberated black slaves after the Civil War.

Many Southern landowners didn't want to have anything to do with the ex-slaves, who would have starved for lack of work. Like the immigrants, blacks found a way to make employers choose between their prejudice and their pocketbook by working for less than whites would. As a result, prejudiced land owners started to hire blacks instead of whites.

The landowners plotted among themselves to pay the blacks "slave wages." Even though such action was perfectly legal, the self-regulating marketplace ecosystem foiled their plans. A few landowners soon found that if they paid their workers a little bit more than everyone else, they had their pick of the skilled blacks. Experienced workers created more wealth than unskilled ones, so profits increased.

Landowners who paid low wages were alarmed to see their best workers leaving to work for more enlightened employers. They either offered higher wages or found themselves without help.[33] Even whites with deep prejudices found themselves persuaded by their pocketbook to treat their black hired hands better than they wanted.

Did blacks receive the same wages as whites? Hardly! However, the marketplace ecosystem convinced landowners to employ blacks rather than leave them without any employment at all. Next, the marketplace ecosystem rewarded employers who were willing to pay the highest wages to their skilled workers. As blacks gained experience, employers paid them more or lost them to those who would. As the cycle repeated itself, wages for blacks began to rise.

One of the most significant things that I saw in the South—and I saw it everywhere—was the way in which white people were torn between their feelings of race prejudice and their downright economic needs.

—Ray Stannard Baker
Pulitzer Prize journalist
and author

Some employers can be slow to recognize the "punishment" that the marketplace uses to discourage prejudice. What can we do to hurry the learning process if aggression doesn't work?

Rather than trying to control selfish others, we can set new standards by our own example. If we feel that workers should be paid more, we can pay our employees higher wages, just as the more enlightened landowners did after the Civil War. Like the plantation owners, who were willing to pay a bit more, we too will have the best employees available. We too will reap what we sow.

We can start the cycle that raises wages and helps the disadvantaged gain experience and training for a better job. *Experience and knowledge are the surest path to higher pay.*

Even former slaves without much education quickly learned how the marketplace worked. If the southern landowners paid them too little, they migrated to Northern factories or offered their skills to the community as blacksmiths or carpenters. The marketplace ecosystem limited black exploitation through the variety of niches (jobs) through which they could create wealth. Slowly but surely, prejudice began to erode as blacks were begrudgingly incorporated into the work place and, against great odds, slowly began to gain respect and affluence.

Had the marketplace ecosystem been allowed to continue its magic, prejudice and prejudicial wage scales might now be a thing of the past. However, the aggression of licensing laws, as described in the next chapter, was used to outlaw the most profitable avenues of wealth creation for the struggling ex-slaves!

The effectiveness of a competitive market is in no way dependent upon the goodwill or honesty of its transactors.
—Thomas Sowell
THE ECONOMICS OF POLITICS AND RACE: AN INTERNATIONAL PERSPECTIVE

The great virtue of a free market system is that it does not care what color people are; it does not care what their religion is; it only cares whether they can produce something you want to buy. It is the most effective system we have discovered to enable people who hate one another to deal with one another and help one another.
—Milton Friedman
Nobel Prize-winning economist

Chapter 3: Destroying Jobs

In Summary ...

- In the marketplace ecosystem (also known as the free market), people with different skills find their job niche, just as different species find their niche in the environment.
- The marketplace is self-regulation and usually functions quite well without our interference.
- Attempts to correct marketplace imperfections with aggression do far more harm than good by destroying the jobs through which wealth is created.
- Immigrants to the United States in the 1800s overcame prejudice by offering employers a greater share of the jointly created wealth. Young Americans sometimes use the same technique to get that all-important first job.
- Almost everyone is able to create some wealth, so everyone can find a starting niche. As expertise improves, so do job opportunities.
- Wage controls intended to help disadvantaged people backfire by destroying their jobs. Instead of low wages, they end up with no wages at all!
- Because poverty is caused by lack of wages, rather than low wages, wage controls increase its incidence, especially for blacks and other disadvantaged groups.
- The marketplace ecosystem slowly but surely dissolves prejudice by rewarding with higher profits those employers who hire workers solely according to their productivity.
- After the Civil War, white landowners tried to pay blacks "slave wages." Because the marketplace penalized such employers, many paid blacks more than they otherwise would. Prejudice was slowly but surely eroded by this natural process.

Chapter 4

Eliminating Small Businesses

"Only in America" could the penniless immigrants of the 1800s become affluent by starting their own businesses. Today, our aggression keeps the disadvantaged from following in their footsteps.

The Marketplace Ecosystem: Honoring Our Neighbor's Choice

In the previous chapter, we learned how the marketplace ecosystem limits the ability of greedy employers to exploit their workers. In the 1800s, when people weren't satisfied with any of their employment options, they often went into business for themselves as farmers, printers, plumbers, carpenters, or stonecutters.[1] Employers had to compete not only with each other for dedicated employees, but also with the benefits that self-employment offered.

The natural balance of the marketplace ecosystem determined whether entrepreneurs succeeded. Startup companies that pleased their customers with better service or lower prices got referrals and repeat business. *Profit (or loss) was a direct reflection of how well they served their customers.*

If businesses charged too much for their products, other entrepreneurs lured their customers (and profit) away with lower prices. Consumers directly regulated the marketplace ecosystem, keeping it in balance without aggression. The customer was the final authority who determined whether a firm would flourish or collapse.

If our fictitious neighbor George decided to go into business for himself, we'd never dream of stopping him because he hadn't gotten our permission. The business that George and his customers voluntarily agree to transact is up to them. We simply honor our neighbor's choice.

In contrast, trying to stop George from serving his customers is likely to destroy any feelings of concern and trust that he may have for us. If we try to force our will on him at gunpoint, George will probably fight back. Perhaps he will call the police or retaliate with sufficient

Take care of your customers and take care of your people and the market will take care of you.
—Tom Peters and Nancy Austin
A PASSION FOR EXCELLENCE

Wealth comes from successful individual efforts to please one's fellow man. ... That's what competition is all about: "out-pleasing" your competitors to win over the consumers.
—Walter Williams
ALL IT TAKES IS GUTS

force to make us unlikely (or unable) to threaten him again. Threatening peaceful people with guns is a prescription for warfare, whether we're adults or children.

If we were successful in preventing George from operating his business, he might have a hard time paying his bills. He would probably feel justified in stealing from us, perpetuating the conflict between us. Our fighting would consume time and effort that would have otherwise created more wealth. As a result, both of us would become poorer.

The same principles apply in our city, state, or nation. We create animosity and poverty when we stop our neighbors from providing service to willing customers. Calling this aggression "licensing" does not change its outcome.

How Licensing Creates Poverty

Licensing laws instruct our government enforcers to stop—at gunpoint, if necessary—businesses without a "permit" from providing service to willing customers. Requirements for a permit or license that are incidental to serving customers, such as requiring high licensing fees, written examinations for manual occupations, and excessive schooling or apprenticeships, create enormous barriers for those who are poor or disadvantaged.

Those barriers enable discrimination to be covertly legalized. For example, licensing laws were instituted to force blacks from several trades in which they had been well represented. The financial progress that ex-slaves had made after the Civil War was effectively thwarted. U.S. citizenship requirements frequently excluded new immigrants from entire professions as well.[2]

Just as minimum wage laws prevent the disadvantaged from getting that first job, licensing laws prevent them from starting their own businesses. Unable to become entrepreneurs or employees, disadvantaged individuals frequently find themselves unable to legally create wealth, leaving them few alternatives to crime or dependence on charity.

In New York City, for example, would-be taxi drivers must purchase a "medallion," or license,

... a favorite method of barring [Negroes] from plumbing and electrical work was to install a system of unfair examinations which were conducted by whites.

—Lorenzo Greene and Carter G. Woodson
THE NEGRO WAGE EARNER

before they can legally carry customers. The number of medallions is limited and has not been increased since 1937. A new driver must purchase a medallion from someone who is retiring. By 1998, those medallions were selling for more than $200,000.[3] Many people who have a car and would be capable of earning a living as a cab driver are forbidden by law to do so because they lack the money for a medallion. Even those who are prosperous enough to purchase one must charge their customers more to make up for the extra expense. Thus, providing safe transportation in New York City became less important than having money or the ability to borrow.

The Poor Get Poorer When We Discriminate Against the Disadvantaged

Most of the licensed taxi drivers in New York City can make a good living servicing only in the better parts of the city. Few venture into the poor areas. Consequently, when those who can't afford a car need to go to the doctor, legal taxi service is usually unavailable. Fortunately, residents able to purchase their own vehicles eventually decided that they would offer such service illegally.

By 1979, these "gypsy" cabs were more numerous than the legal ones. As long as gypsy drivers stayed in the poor areas, police looked the other way. When gypsy cabs came into the business district, however, medallion holders insisted that police stop the gypsy cabs—at gunpoint, if necessary.[4]

We can learn important lessons from the New York experience. First, the gypsy drivers were almost exclusively minorities, mostly black and Puerto Rican,[5] yet they were able to create substantial amounts of wealth, even in their impoverished areas, by providing a desperately needed service.

By 1982, the effect of licensing laws on minority taxicab ownership could be clearly seen. In Washington, D.C., which had few restrictions on taxis, 90% of the cabs were owner-operated;[6] minorities accounted for 70% of those entreprenuers.[7] In Philadelphia, which had restrictions similar to those of New York City, only

Economic regulation is an extremely effective tool for racism, precisely because it does not seem overtly racist.

—Dana Berliner
Institute for Justice

8% of the taxis had black owners.[8] Obviously, licensing requirements keep the disadvantaged from creating wealth.

Is Hair Braiding a Crime?

In 1993, the National Foundation for Teaching Entrepreneurship picked 15-year-old Monique Landers of Kansas for one of its five annual awards. This young black girl had created wealth by starting her own hair-braiding business.

The Kansas state government, however, wanted to put Monique out of business. Monique was even threatened with jail because she did not have a state cosmetology license.[9]

Hair braiders in other states have the same problem. Although few cosmetology schools teach braiding, a cosmetology license is usually required to braid hair legally. In California, the 1,600-hour curriculum costs between $5,000 and $7,000.[10] Only 4% of the curriculum is related to health and safety;[11] trainees focus on manicures, artificial fingernail application, hair coloring, and perms. In New York, 900 hours of training is required for a cosmetology license, compared with 116 hours of instruction for emergency medical technicians.[12] In Ohio, an African-style hair braider needs 1,500 hours of training, compared with 445 for an armed police officer or 600 for a life-saving paramedic.[13] Not surprisingly, such requirements give minorities the impression that they are still living in the days of "Jim Crow."[14]

Should We Harass the Homeless?

When a homeless man, Ronnie Forston, tried to start a shoe shine business in Atlanta, he was arrested seven times in 18 months. His crime? Shining shoes without a license! The license itself was $175, and he needed a vendor's permit and a home address to get it. The city had frozen the issuance of vendors' permits. Ronnie was homeless, so he didn't have an address. Consequently, he couldn't get a permit even if he had been qualified![15] Ronnie's plight clearly illustrates how licensing laws keep the poor from creating any wealth at all!

... a cosmetology school graduate may braid even if she knows nothing about braiding. I've braided for nearly 15 years, but I may not braid because I don't know how to perm. African-American communities nationwide desperately need jobs, but still these stupid rules stand in our way.

—Faith Carey Canton
Ohio braider

Why Make Child Care Unaffordable?

The nationwide shortage of day care provides a perfect opportunity for poor mothers to earn extra money. Unfortunately, these natural child-care providers are often forbidden from providing day care by licensing laws that require extensive remodeling, expensive licensing fees, or expert navigation through a sea of red tape.[16]

We've supported this aggression to protect young children from unsafe conditions and unscrupulous day-care providers. However, most of the licensing restrictions have little to do with safety. Licenses to operate day-care centers have been denied because the yard was deemed to be several feet too short! One center had to replace its four smoke detectors with a five-detector interconnecting system at a cost of $2,000. Another had to remove a wall because the door was 36 inches wide instead of 38.[17] In New York City, day-care employees must meet the same certification requirements as public school teachers. The director must have or be working on a master's degree![18]

The individuals who succeed in upgrading their homes and working their way through the red tape (57 forms in Washington, D.C.)[19] must charge more for their services. In North Carolina, licensing laws increase the cost of day care by 25%.[20] As a result, in most major cities, day care costs more than low wage earners take home. When poor parents must forgo work because they cannot afford day care, their children risk becoming another poverty statistic.

Why Thwart Home Businesses?

In addition to limiting day care, licensing laws often prohibit businesses that start in the home, such as hair braiding.[21] In Chicago, hooking up a home computer to one owned by a business is illegal.[22] In Massachusetts, no goods and services can be produced in the home for a business located elsewhere.[23] Even in areas where home businesses are permitted, they may be prohibited from hiring employees.[24] Where would the computer industry be today if Apple Computer's Steve Jobs has not been able to start his company in the family garage?[25]

They're trying to starve me to death. That's what it seems like to me. I'm just trying to make an honest living. I want to work. I don't believe in soup lines. I can work. I can make it.
—Ronnie Forston
homeless shoe-shiner

To open a group day-care center in one's home, New York City requires that prospective employees meet the same certification requirements as public school teachers.
—William M. Mellor
Institute for Justice

DAY-CARE LAWS LIMIT PRIVATE-HOME CENTERS THAT PARENTS LIKE THE BEST. For about 17 years, Susan Suddath kept other children in her home.... The state of Maryland ... told her she would have to reduce the number of children, or close down ... [because] her basement was too low in one place. Almost 6 feet tall herself, Mrs. Suddath assured the inspector she would be the tallest person in the room. But he couldn't bend the law.
—WALL STREET JOURNAL
October 26, 1982

*Northrup cited an Eagle
Comptronics Company
incident near Syracuse
where a group of women,
who also were single
parents, contracted to
assemble electronic
components in their
homes. The State Labor
Department, he said,
closed them down under
the anti-labor law, so the
work is now contracted
out of the country and the
women, who were
supporting themselves
and their families, now
are on welfare.*

                —ITHACA JOURNAL
                September 11, 1982

*Laws and regulations at
every level of government
stifle competition and entry into myriad jobs and
occupations.... Such rules
are cutting off the bottom
rungs of the economic
ladder, with devastating
consequences for people
with the fewest resources,
particularly minorities
and the poor.*

                —Clint Bolick
                TRANSFORMATION

Throughout my years as a landlady, I've watched how the aggression of licensing laws puts my low-income tenants out of work and on welfare. Those who try to support themselves by taking in sewing, giving piano lessons, or operating day care in their apartments live in fear that one day the government will shut them down or even put them in jail. Eventually, most are indeed caught and forced onto the welfare roles.

We Create Poverty by Limiting Infinite Wealth

Licensing laws, coupled with the minimum wage laws, frequently keep the disadvantaged from ever getting a start. *Infinite wealth through innumerable jobs becomes limited primarily through our aggression-through-government, creating poverty and despair.*

The Ladder of Affluence (Figure 4.1) illustrates this process. If our parents are on the upper rungs of the Ladder of Affluence, they probably have enough wealth to put us through college or professional training so that our first job is on a middle rung of the Ladder. Disadvantaged individuals, however, have to start at the bottom and work their way up. Training jobs at low pay or home businesses often are their first step of the Ladder.

Minimum wage and licensing laws destroy these lower rungs on the Ladder of Affluence, condemning the disadvantaged to a lifetime of poverty. Instead of being *paid* a low wage while getting training and experience, the disadvantaged must *pay* for training or an expensive license. Instead of having the opportunity to work their way up the Ladder of Affluence, they are not allowed to even attempt the climb!

We needn't worry that those who start on the lowest rung of the Ladder will get stuck there. People in the lowest fifth of income earners are just as likely to make it to the top fifth of income earners as to stay where they are in the following 10 years.[26] In the United States, 80% of millionaires acquire their wealth in a single generation.[27] Half of them climb up the Ladder without any inheritance, college tuition from

Figure 4.1: The Ladder of Affluence

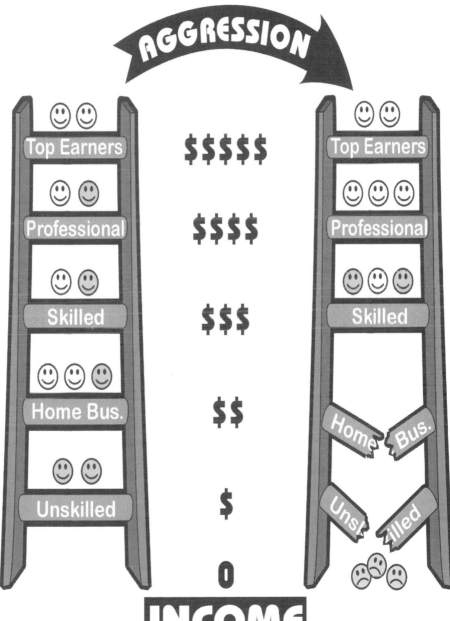

 Advantaged    Disadvantaged    Disadvantaged

Work is the medicine for poverty. Don't put us out of work.

—Lateef Ajala
black van driver fighting
New York City's
licensing laws

their parents, or even substantial financial assistance.[28] Clearly, the Ladder can be climbed by almost anyone able to get a foothold. However, if licensing laws keep the disadvantaged from the lower rungs of the Ladder, they must rely on the charity of others or on a life of crime to sustain themselves.

If licensing laws create poverty, poor countries might be expected to have more of them. Indeed they do. For example, in Peru, it takes an average of 289 days to obtain a business license to open a small garment factory, with fees equal to five months of minimum wage pay. Small industrial firms spend approximately 70% of their profits to pay taxes and conform to regulations. Meeting all legal requirements to build a market mall can take 17 years. A license for a new bus route averages 53 months to arrange and is granted only rarely.[29]

As an experiment, ABC reporter John Stossel tried to open a store selling frisbees that met all regulatory requirements. In Hong Kong, the entire process took hours. In New York City, the multitude of forms took weeks; in India, *years* of paperwork were required and there was no guarantee that a license would even be issued![30] Peruvians and Indians can't create much wealth when they must spend so much time and effort simply getting permission to start a tiny business! Consequently, countries with the most aggression-through-government also have the highest levels of unemployment.[31]

As a consequence, most wealth creation in Third World countries occurs extralegally in the black market. Much of the poverty in those countries is artificially created through the aggression of licensing laws!

The Rich Get Richer with *Our* Help!

When the disadvantaged are legally forbidden to create wealth, the gap between rich and poor widens. Because poverty is usually caused by licensing laws, it is usually accompanied by a huge gap between the "haves" and "have nots." As a consequence, *poor nations generally have a less even distribution of wealth than richer ones.*[32]

Because licensing laws devastate the disadvantaged, increase prices for consumers, and widen the gap between rich and poor, why do our legislatures vote for them?

Usually, unions and professional associations lobby for licensing laws to prevent the disadvantaged from underbidding them.[33] Many locales also outlaw home businesses, which provide another avenue for disadvantaged and part-time workers to create wealth. Because the overhead is low, products are frequently priced lower than similar items manufactured by skilled factory labor. Consumers are usually pleased, but skilled laborers are not. Consequently, in developed nations where unionization is high, unemployment is too, reflecting the tendency for unions to lobby for job-destroying licensing laws.[34]

Does this mean that skilled workers or union members are selfish people who deserve our wrath? Not at all! Those who support licensing laws have seen our willingness in the past to sanction aggression-through-government. Perhaps skilled workers themselves were the victims the last time that we used aggression. We simply take turns being winners or losers when we use aggression as our means. Instead of cooperative win-win scenarios, we perpetrate a win-lose game in which we are constantly at each others' throats.

The skilled workers do not use aggression themselves. Like the proverbial serpent in the Garden of Eden, they only tempt us to do their bidding. We can choose—or we can refuse—to direct our government enforcers to aggress against our neighbors. Without our consent, the skilled workers (and the serpent) are powerless. The choice and the responsibility belong to us.

A Lose–Lose Situation

The gains that skilled workers make through licensing laws are largely an illusion as Figure 4.2 illustrates. When we look closely, we see that aggression is a lose–lose proposition!

Each group lobbies to turn the guns of government away from itself and toward others. In this tug of war, we take turns being victims and aggressors. The only difference between this war

Politics is the conduct of public affairs for private advantage.
—Ambrose Bierce
author of THE DEVIL'S
DICTIONARY

Figure 4.2: The Wealth Pie

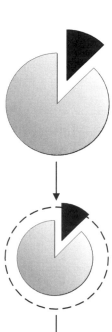

In the absence of aggression, everyone creates goods and services. The Wealth Pie and our Piece of it (black shading) are as large as they can be for our current level of knowledge.

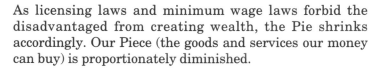

As licensing laws and minimum wage laws forbid the disadvantaged from creating wealth, the Pie shrinks accordingly. Our Piece (the goods and services our money can buy) is proportionately diminished.

Those who lobby for and enforce those laws create no new wealth, so the Pie shrinks once again. As skilled workers, we may see our Piece of the Pie increase *relative* to everyone else's, but the *absolute* size of our Piece is smaller than it otherwise would have been.

The enforcement agents who keep the disadvantaged from producing wealth produce none of their own. Consequently, they must take some of ours in the form of taxes. Our diminished Piece shrinks further.

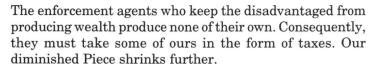

To survive, those who are not legally permitted to create wealth demand that the law enforcement agents take some of ours—at gunpoint, if necessary—to provide for them. Our Piece of the Pie shrinks accordingly.

and conventional ones is that both sides take turns "capturing" the only weapon: the guns of government. Because each side occasionally "wins," both have the illusion of gain. The price of aggression (lobbying, limiting the creation of wealth, supporting those forbidden to create wealth, paying enforcers) is so high that no one comes out ahead.

Hostility is created instead of wealth. Against the background of chronic unemployment, the advantaged come to believe that some "other" people are simply not competent enough to ensure their own survival. The disadvantaged, trapped by aggression and told that only other people can save them, resign themselves to their own impotence. While one segment of society justifies its aggressive actions on the basis of its own alleged superiority, another segment cringes with loss of self-esteem. The stage is set for the lose–lose game known as class warfare.

Licensing laws create division in another manner as well. *As small businesses are thwarted, large companies dominate.* As we'll see in several of the following chapters, licensing laws are the soil in which corporate monopolies and cartels take root.

As entrepreneurial startups are destroyed, employers get the upper hand. As people become poorer, dependence replaces self-sufficiency.

A Better Way

Just as minimum wages keep the disadvantaged from becoming employees, licensing laws keep them from becoming entrepreneurs. Because small businesses hire more people than corporate giants, the laws that thwart startup companies prevent the creation of desperately needed jobs.

For example, between 1991 and 1995, while 3.4 million jobs were *lost* by the largest U.S. companies (5,000+ employees), 3.8 million jobs *were created* by the smallest ones (1–4 employees). Indeed, 90% of all net job creation for those years came from firms with fewer than 100 employees.[35] Small businesses are remarkably stable: 70% of those started in 1985 were still operating nine years later.[36]

Deregulation of the taxi industry helped create a couple hundred new jobs for minorities.

—Tom Rose
assistant to
Indianapolis's
Mayor Stephen
Goldsmith

How many more jobs might have been created in the absence of licensing? Indianapolis decided to answer this question. In 1994, the city ended most of its restrictions on taxicabs. Two years later, the number of cabs doubled, fares dropped, and waiting times fell. Eighty percent of the new cab companies were owned by women or minorities.[37] *The damage done by licensing laws can be reversed!*

Even when companies manage to obtain a license, additional regulations put such a burden on small firms that many, especially the small Mom-and-Pop variety, go out of business. Fortunately, we can undo this damage as well.

For example, between 1980 and 1985, the number of federal regulators in the United States decreased. *More than 150 private sector jobs were created for every regulator who left* (Figure 4.3).

Figure 4.3: Total Federal Regulators vs. Private Sector Job Growth

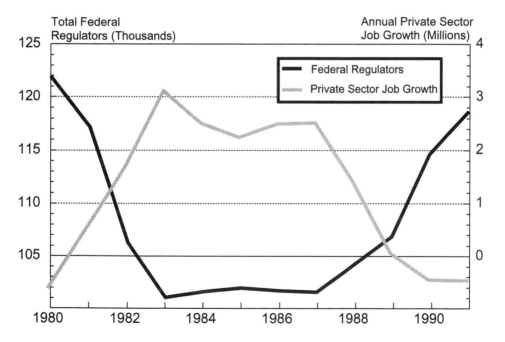

Reprinted with permission from W. G. Laffer III, *How Regulation Is Destroying American Jobs* (Washington, DC: The Heritage Foundation, February 16, 1993). Sources: U.S. Department of Labor, Bureau of Labor Statistics; Center for the Study of American Business, Washington University, St. Louis, MO. Note: Employment data represent a three-year moving average in total nonfarm private employment, according to reports from employers.

During the period of job increases, the number of black-owned businesses nearly doubled.[38] We can create more jobs (and wealth) for the disadvantaged by simply ending the aggression of licensing laws and regulations!

Sadly, we didn't learn from history and are once again repeating it. Between 1988 and 1991, the number of federal regulators in the United States grew once again, destroying more than 150 private sector jobs for every regulator hired.

Because aggression-through-government in the form of minimum wages, licensing laws, and regulations increases unemployment, it increases poverty as well. We can end the poverty we have created by becoming Good Neighbors once again.

When small businesses prosper, employees do too. Many employees would never choose to open their own businesses. However, when employees have this option, employers are more sensitive to their needs. Workers who can leave anytime and open their own shop get more respect than those who can't. When the marketplace ecosystem lets employers reap what they sow, employees benefit—even if starting their own business is the furthest thing from their minds.

In spite of the destruction caused by the aggression of licensing laws, we sometimes hesitate to abandon them. We believe that they protect us in arenas where a mistake by a service provider can be life-threatening, such as electrical or medical work. In the next chapter, we'll see that aggression, as usual, harms the very people it is supposed to help.

Chapter 4: Eliminating Small Businesses

In Summary ...

- Self-employment provides another option for employees who are dissatisfied with their working conditions.
- Businesses that please their customers are rewarded by profit. Those that don't please their customers suffer loss.
- Licensing laws stop entrepreneurs—at gunpoint, if necessary—from providing service to willing customers.
- Many licensing requirements have nothing to do with safety, because they are intended to keep the disadvantaged from competing with established workers.
- The poor have a difficult time climbing the Ladder of Affluence because wage controls keep them from being hired and licensing laws keep them from establishing their own businesses.
- Most people who get a foothold on the Ladder of Affluence are able to climb it. Indeed, someone on the lowest rung is just as likely to advance to the top as to stay at the bottom.
- Licensing laws impoverish all of us because the cost of enforcing them, lobbying for them, and supporting those who are forbidden to create wealth greatly shrinks the Wealth Pie. We get less than we otherwise would, even if our Piece is larger than that of our neighbors.
- Most poverty today is caused by licensing laws that inhibit the creation of wealth. Getting a business license, for example, takes hours in Hong Kong, weeks in New York City, and years in India. The gap between rich and poor is wider in nations with the most regulation.
- The damage done by licensing laws can be reversed. Every time we retire one regulator, we create more than 150 private sector jobs!

Harming Our Health

Licensing laws and regulations give us the illusion of safety. In reality, our aggression boomerangs back to us, costing us our wealth, our health, and our very lives.

How Licensing Laws Can Kill

We've tolerated, even encouraged, the aggression of licensing laws to protect ourselves from shoddy service providers whose mistakes could kill us. However, studies show that the licensing laws themselves are often even more deadly.

For example, licensing laws lower the *number* of electricians in a given area by imposing extra requirements. Fewer electricians mean higher prices. People, especially the disadvantaged, either do without a needed repair or attempt it themselves, resulting in injury or even death. Accidental electrocutions go up when licensing requirements for electricians increase, as people attempt to do their own wiring.[1] *Licensing laws intended to protect us can and do kill.*

By limiting availability, licensing laws lower the overall amount of quality service delivered. The decrease in availability far outweighs any increase in quality that may occur, as the cited studies indicate. For the most part, licensing laws are redundant because few service providers attempt to do work for which they are totally unqualified.

Just as licensing laws created two classes of taxis, the legal ones and the underground gypsy cabs, so too do licensing laws create two classes of electricians and other service providers. For example, in my community, electrical work permits had to be signed by one of the few licensed electricians. Because those electricians were so busy and so expensive, many people actually employed unlicensed workers to do most of their wiring. Referrals from neighbors or even from overworked licensed electricians helped ensure quality service. The licensed electricians finished and "signed off" on the job. *The regulations created a class system of well-paid licensed workers and lower-paid underground ones.*

> *... mainly the research refutes the claim that licensing protects the public.*
> —Stanley J. Gross
> professor of psychology,
> Indiana State University

> *... most of the evidence suggests that licensing has, at best, a neutral effect on quality and may even cause harm to the consumers.... The higher entry standards imposed by licensing laws reduce the supply of professional services. ... The poor are net losers, because the availability of low-cost service has been reduced. In essence, the poor subsidize the information research costs of the rich.*
> —S. David Young
> THE RULE OF EXPERTS

A black person could not obtain an electrician's license. So what they would do is wire an entire house and then pay maybe $100 to a white electrician to connect the wire from the post to the box—about a two-minute job.
—Clarence Thomas
Supreme Court Justice

Because the unlicensed electricians were operating illegally, licensed electricians couldn't work with them directly. Instead, the two groups did their work sequentially, increasing the possibility of error. Thus, even when licensed electricians were involved, the regulations set the stage for dangerous mistakes.

How Licensing Laws Affect Health Care

The observation that licensing laws lower the overall quality of services delivered takes on a very personal meaning when we realize that one of the most highly regulated (licensed) sectors of our economy is the health care network.

For most of us, medical care will be the major factor determining how long and how well we live. Licensing limits the availability of a service, thereby lowering the overall quality delivered. Thus, we would expect our health care to be of substantially lower quality than it could be in the marketplace ecosystem undisturbed by our aggression.

Indeed it is. Dental hygiene is poorer in states with the most restrictive licensing requirements for dentists because fewer people can afford regular checkups. For the same reason, the incidence of blindness increases in areas with the most stringent licensing for optometrists.[2]

Currently, licensing laws for physicians are even more restrictive than those for dental and eye care. Consequently, physician licensing might be expected to cause even greater harm.

The Marketplace Ecosystem: Honoring Our Neighbor's Choice

In the mid-1800s, doctors learned their profession not only in medical schools, but also by apprenticing with another practitioner, or by developing their own therapies.[3] Many individuals limited their practice to specific areas, such as midwifery, preparation of herbal remedies for common ailments, or suture of superficial wounds. Such diversity in the training and type of practice encouraged innovation and allowed individuals to patronize the health care provider who seemed best suited to their immediate needs. Good healers were recommended by their clients, while those unable to help their patients lost business and referrals. Physicians reaped what they sowed. Patients voted with their dollars, thereby regulating the quality of health care. The customer ruled.

Aggression Disrupts the Marketplace Ecosystem

As long as health care providers did not lie about their qualifications and past performance, the marketplace ecosystem evolved a natural balance. Some individuals, however, misrepresented their skills to attract patients. By lying about their expertise, they disrupted the marketplace ecosystem with the aggression of fraud. Patients who entrusted themselves to such individuals sometimes risked their very lives.

Americans were in a quandary. They wished to honor their neighbor's choice but didn't know how to deter aggressors. Had they understood the other piece of the puzzle—the power of having aggressors compensate their victims as described in Chapter 13 ("The Other Piece of the Puzzle"), the balance of the marketplace ecosystem would have been rapidly restored.

Unfortunately, even today the essential role of restitution is not recognized or understood. In Part III ("As We Forgive Those Who Trespass Against Us: How We Create Strife in a World of Harmony"), we'll learn more about this principle and how its application would have defused the practice of medical fraud. For now, however, let's focus on the high price we paid by choosing to fight aggression by becoming aggressors ourselves.

How Licensing Laws Lower Quality

By the early 1900s, every state had agreed to the aggression of physician licensing. Healers who did not meet the requirements it set would be stopped—at gunpoint, if necessary—from treating patients who still wanted their services. *The patient's choice was no longer honored, even if the unlicensed healer was able to cure them![4]* The consumer no longer ruled; the licensing boards did.

The licensing boards soon refused to license health professionals who had not been trained at "approved" medical schools. Only half of the existing medical schools were granted approval, so most of the others closed their doors.[5] By 1932, almost half of the medical school applicants had to be turned away.[6] Those who apprenticed, went to unapproved schools, or developed their own therapies were forced to stop healing, even if their treatments were successful.[7] Specialists, such as midwives, were usually forbidden to practice unless they had a full-fledged medical degree.[8] As a result, the number of medical doctors per100,000 people fell 20%.[9]

As medical knowledge expanded, a smaller number of physicians were available to perform an ever-widening range of services. Although medical treatments got better all the times, the doctor shortage prevented some people, especially the poor, from taking advantage of the latest medical technology.[10]

Only in the 1970s, did the physician-to-population ratio finally return to what it had been in the early 1900s![11] By then, the time that the physician spent with each patient had dramatically increased because more preventative care and diagnostic tests were available. Naturally, with more work and fewer physicians, the price of medical care soared.

One measure of the doctor shortage is the long workweek of the average physician, estimated at 60 hours for practicing physicians and 80 hours for those in training.[12] A transplant surgeon with whom I collaborated once asked why I stayed in research instead of practice medicine. My reply, only half-joking, was that I was unable to function competently after 48 hours without sleep. He admitted in all seriousness that one needed such an ability to get through hospital training and to practice in the more demanding specialties such as transplantation.

Such a long workweek can result in serious mistakes. When my mother was in her late 50s, she went to her doctor because she had discovered a small lump in her breast. The doctor, although aware that five of my mother's relatives had died of cancer, did not even order a mammogram. Embarrassed by the doctor's lack of concern, my mother did not confide in anyone until

Sleep-deprived surgeons make around 20 percent more errors and are 14 percent slower than colleagues who have had rest, a recent study found.

SECOND OPINION
May 1999

the tumor had spread. A few short years later, my mother drew her last breath.

The saddest part of this story is how commonplace it is. My mother's best friend and my mother-in-law had almost identical experiences and met the same premature fate. Another friend survived a rapidly growing oral cancer only because his dentist insisted on its removal in spite of his physician's advice to "wait and see."

Cancer is the second most deadly disease in the United States.[13] Any practicing physician can certainly identify a malignant growth. Were the doctors whom my family and friends visited just too harried to provide that care? Is physician overwork causing major medical mistakes?

Some Californians think so. In 1990, they tried to pass a law prohibiting hospital physicians from working longer than 80 hours a week![14] More aggression is not the answer, however. When doctors are forced to work fewer hours, the physician shortage only gets worse.

How Licensing Inhibits Innovation

Shortages, higher prices, and erratic care are but a few of the many problems caused by licensing laws. Many medical specialties were marginalized by the late 1930s. Students of homeopathic, osteopathic, and chiropractic medical schools could no longer qualify for licensing as medical doctors.[15] Hospitals or medical schools that dared to employ them risked losing licensing board approval, a necessary condition for attracting the students and interns necessary to run the hospital.[16] M.D.s who associated with them, shared facilities, or referred patients to them were branded "unethical," putting their own professional standing at risk.[17] Relying on the advice of licensed M.D.s, insurance companies sometimes denied reimbursements to alternative practitioners, making their service much less affordable.[18] *Those discriminatory practices were so blatant that in 1987 the American Medical Association (AMA) was found guilty of using licensing laws "to destroy the profession of chiropractic in the United States."[19]*

Were we protected from "quacks" by licensing laws that suppressed alternative therapies?

My own experience suggests just the opposite. After I had suffered back pain for several years and had been advised by several M.D.s to take muscle relaxants and live with the discomfort, a coworker recommended an osteopath who had helped him with a similar problem. My spine had been locked in an unnatural position, probably as a result of an accident that had occurred some years before. The osteopath was able to relieve the tension with a gentle adjustment. Although spinal manipulation used to be common practice among osteopaths, chiropractors do most of it today. When my osteopath retired, he turned over his practice to a chiropractor. When I suffered whiplash in an automobile accident years later, I was very grateful to have this alternative therapy. Several studies of workers' compensation records demonstrates that, for certain types of injury, chiropractic was less expensive and more effective than standard medical treatment.[20]

Belatedly, M.D.s have realized the value of chiropratic care. Some physicians are beginning to learn and practice spinal manipulation techniques.[21] By the 1960s, osteopaths were once again permitted to practice in approved hospitals.[22] They assumed the role of general practitioners, since M.D.s had moved into the more lucrative medical specialties.[23] With such tacit admissions that these alternative specialties have a place in medical practice, we can only wonder how many people suffered needlessly over the past 75 years because licensing laws have limited our access to alternatives.

How Licensing Laws Limit Prevention

The suppression of different medical practices by licensing laws can be overt, as with the osteopathic and chiropractic professions. However, the subtle suppression of new therapies may be even more devastating.

The role of nutrition in health and disease is a good illustration. Physicians rarely understand how powerfully nutrition can thwart disease. As a researcher, I quickly learned that most human diseases could be induced in laboratory animals only by taking away their vitamins or

... restricting the practice of what is called medicine and confining it ... to a particular group, who in the main have to conform to the prevailing orthodoxy, is certain to reduce the amount of experimentation that goes on and hence to reduce the rate of growth and knowledge in the area.

—Milton Friedman
Nobel Prize winner in
Economics

minerals. Many of our illnesses, therefore, could probably be prevented by better nutrition.

Many physicians, however, don't recognize symptoms of nutritional deficiency when they see them. For years, alcoholic liver disease was thought to be due to a direct toxic effect of alcohol, rather than a depletion of key nutrients consumed in its breakdown by the liver. Even though baboons fed alcohol gained less weight than control animals, physicians failed to recognize this failure to thrive as a classic symptom of nutritional stress.[24]

Eventually, of course, truth triumphed. When lecithin, a common nutrient, was added to the baboons' diet, much of the alcohol-induced liver damage could be prevented and normal weight gain was restored.[25] Today, nutritional therapy is recognized as an important component in treating alcoholic liver disease.

Failure to recognize classical symptoms of nutritional stress, such as failure to thrive, results from the poor training that doctors receive in this area. As late as 1990, less than one-third of accredited medical schools required even a single course in nutrition.[26] This oversight threatens our health, because major killers such as cardiovascular disease, cancer, and diabetes are intimately related to nutritional status. For example, cardiovascular disease can be cut in half by vitamin E supplementation[27] or by increasing the protein-to-carbohydrate ratio of the average diet.[28] One 10-year study of more than 11,000 adults indicated that vitamin C could lower both cancer and cardiovascular disease, with a resulting increase in longevity.[29] Although medical schools give our doctors little training in nutrition, licensing laws have been used to prosecute health food personnel for "practicing medicine without a license" if they recommend supplements to customers. Licensing laws limit our access to lifesaving information.

How Licensing Laws Limit Innovation

The damage done by licensing laws is compounded when taxes are used to fund medical research. In serving on committees that evaluate such research applications, I've learned that

... by proper orthomolecular measures, mostly nutritional, it is possible for people to extend the length of the period of both life and well-being by about 25 years.
—Linus Pauling
Nobel Prize winner in
Chemistry and Peace

Vitamin C deficiency, as assessed by low plasma ascorbate concentration, is a risk factor for coronary heart disease.
—BRITISH MEDICAL
JOURNAL
1997

... most innovative scientists know that they would never receive funding if they actually said what they were going to do. Scientists therefore have to tell lies in their grant applications. Such views have been explicitly stated by at least two Nobel Laureates.
—WORLD RESEARCH NEWS
1990

innovative ideas rarely get funded. Each evaluator gives the proposal a score; even a single low rating is enough to prevent funding. Research in osteopathy or chiropractic, therefore, receives little money. Research in therapeutic nutrition is also severely limited. Even Linus Pauling, winner of the Nobel Prize for chemistry and for peace, had difficulty obtaining federal funding for his research on the use of vitamin C to treat cancer.[30] As the above citations show, *we now know that people who take vitamin C live longer and have less heart disease and cancer.* How many lives were prematurely lost because our aggression delayed this critical knowledge?

We've agreed to taxation in the belief that profit-motivated industry wouldn't be inclined to fund some important research—such as testing Pauling's theories on vitamin C. However, studies show that only 10% of new technology depends upon such grants.[31] Most of the innovations—a whopping 90%—come from private industry. Over the past 50 years, the spending in both the public and private sector has been similar.[32] Thus, *private funding appears to give us nine times the benefit that forcibly funded research supplies.*

Wasteful use of our taxes is only a portion of our loss, however. If we had kept our money and funded the research of our choice or allowed industry to direct it, we would have gained additional knowledge that could have prolonged or even saved our lives.

Medicine is not as definitive as most people think. Less than 25% of medical procedures have been demonstrated to be useful in controlled clinical trials.[33] Such trials are time-consuming and expensive, and physicians are hesitant to withhold any therapy that might be beneficial just for the study's sake. Consequently, surgery involving coronary bypass, the most frequently performed major surgery in the United States, was shown to be worthwhile only many years after it became the standard of treatment and then only in a select group of heart patients.[34] As a result, many people over the years have undergone needless pain, expense, and risk by having an unnecessary bypass.

To some extent, this situation is unavoidable because rigorous proof of a procedure's efficacy takes time, which some patients do not have. However, through the licensing process, certain types of unproven procedures (e.g., surgery) are permitted, while others are arbitrarily banned as quackery. Such unscientific selection has often led to the ironic situation of yesterday's quackery becoming tomorrow's cure (see adjacent sidebars for an example)!

Medicine is still in its infancy; there is much that we do not know. Like it or not, we are human guinea pigs for medical doctors and alternative practitioners alike. The aggression of licensing laws limits our options without protecting us from unproven cures.

History Repeats Itself As the Rich Get Richer with *Our* Help!

Licensing of doctors was common in the early years of the United States, but was abandoned in the mid-1800s. Licensing excluded competent healers, hindered the development of alternative therapies (e.g., herbal medicine), created a monopoly of established practices (e.g., bleeding), and retarded innovative research.[35] Those problems are familiar because they are caused by the licensing laws of today. If history clearly repeats itself with the aggression of licensing laws, why were they instituted once again in the twentieth century?

Licensing of physicians was largely a result of lobbying by the AMA. This situation is not at all unusual: licensing laws are demanded, not by consumers, but by the professionals themselves! Indeed, professional organizations are frequently founded with the sole purpose of lobbying for licensing.[36]

Service providers want to be regulated because legislators ask the established practitioners to determine the requirements for new entrants. Not surprisingly, practicing physicians gave themselves licenses, set high standards for newcomers, and outlawed entire specialities. Most doctors supported such measures in the belief that the quality of health care would be improved.

Phony "youth cures" ... include products to soften the skin, to "make the person feel young again," to remove brown spots and cellulite. Of course, there is no product that will work in this way any more than there is a product known to medical science that retards baldness or helps grow hair back on a bald scalp.
—CONGRESSIONAL REPORT ON QUACKERY, 1982

Upjohn has introduced Rogaine ... as the "first prescription medication proven effective for male pattern baldness."
—SCRIP, 1986

... state licensing boards, particularly for medicine, but also for other professions, have instead become first and foremost devices for protecting the monopolistic position of the professionals.
—Marie Haus
REGULATING THE PROFESSIONS

Chapter 5

... an oversupply of doctors threatens. ... perhaps there is need for professional birth control.
—JOURNAL OF THE AMERICAN MEDICAL ASSOCIATION, 1932

As you increase the cost of the license to practice medicine, you increase the price at which the medical service must be sold and you correspondingly decrease the number of people who can afford to buy the service.
—William Allen Pusey AMA President, 1927

The proportion and absolute number of women physicians was greater in 1910 than in 1950.
—Stanley J. Gross professor of psychology Indiana State University

AMA leadership appeared to be well aware that fewer physicians would mean higher income for those allowed to practice.[37] Licensing boards even adjust the pass—fail rate of qualifying examinations to keep numbers of service providers (including physicians) low.[38] Choice is diminished, and fees rise accordingly.

Because AMA members control the licensing boards, they can also influence the behavior of practicing physicians by threatening to revoke their licenses. For example, medical doctors giving discounts have been censured by the AMA to keep physicians' incomes high.[39] Similarly, when acupuncture was introduced into the United States, the AMA tried to outlaw its practice by anyone other than licensed medical doctors.[40] Other specialties that are adequately and more economically performed by paraprofessionals have faced similar sanctions.[41]

Should we then blame the negative effects of physician licensing on those selfish others who set AMA policy? Of course not! The AMA leaders simply observed our willingness to use aggression-through-government for a good cause. Perhaps the last time we used aggression, M.D.s were the victims. Like the serpent in the Garden of Eden, the AMA only tempted us to act against our own best interests. We yielded to temptation. The responsibility belongs to us.

The Poor Get Poorer: Discrimination Against the Disadvantaged

As usual, the poor suffer most from the aggression of licensing laws. Indeed, opponents of such laws feared that the poor would be deprived of medical care altogether as costs increased. Rural areas, which could no longer support a full-time physician, had to do without.[42]

Medical licensing radically cut the number of black and female doctors. In 1910, seven medical schools specialized in training black physicians. By 1944, only two had survived.[43] The number of women medical students was cut almost in half as schools reserved the limited medical school placements for men.[44]

The poor were excluded from becoming physicians as well. Students of medical schools that catered to the working class by providing flexible training regimens, such as night school and apprenticeship, were no longer given licenses.[45] Without the ability to work while they trained, only the affluent could become physicians.

A Lose–Lose Situation

The poor are not the only ones harmed by licensing laws. The people who can't afford the high prices caused by physician licensing often ask their government enforcement agents to take wealth from the advantaged (including doctors) to pay for their health care. Those who are harmed by licensing laws are only taking their turn as aggressors.

The government employees who enforce the licensing laws and collect taxes to pay the higher medical costs of the disadvantaged create no new wealth. Their support, therefore, must come from additional taxes. Our piece of the Wealth Pie shrinks further.

Although the plight of the poor is most visible, the aggression of medical licensing hurts everyone. The loss of new, innovative medical therapies (e.g., preventative nutrition) is an invisible one. We all pay the price. When we watch our loved ones die from "incurable" diseases, we suffer deeply because of our refusal to honor our neighbor's choice!

A Better Way

Without licensing laws, how do we find competent electricians or surgeons *before* we put our lives in their hands? One time-honored way to find competent service providers is by referral. However, we might not know someone who can recommend a qualified practitioner. Does this mean that we would have to spend hours of research to find a competent one?

Thankfully, the answer is a resounding "No!" Independent rating services already provide an alternative to licensing. For example, we don't worry that electrical equipment will be faulty, yet our appliances and electrical hardware are not licensed or regulated by government. Instead, a private certifying company, Underwriters Laboratories Inc. (UL) has tested more than six billion individual products and grants its UL Seal

... the study of medical history indicates that quacks flourish whenever physicians are scarce or when their remedies are ineffective. Licensing laws may actually worsen this problem by artificially restricting the supply of practitioners.
—S. David Young
THE RULE OF EXPERTS

Certification provides all the information of licensure while offering a wider choice set.
—Keith B. Leffler
JOURNAL OF LAW AND ECONOMICS

of Approval to those that meet its exacting standards.[46] Manufacturers pay an evaluation fee to fund the testing.

The entire process is voluntary in most countries, including the United States. If you or I wish to purchase an uncertified electrical appliance, our choice will be honored. However, most retailers won't sell an appliance or electrical component without the UL assurance of quality. As a consequence, manufacturers routinely apply for UL certification. The marketplace ecosystem works behind the scenes to protect the consumer, while honoring the choice of those who wish to use an uncertified product.

Why would anyone want to buy an uncertified electrical device? A few consumers might need specialty or custom products that sell in too low a volume to recoup the certification fee. They could still buy such items because the final decision rests with them.

Because the UL mark is prominently displayed on most appliances and electrical hardware, consumers need only look at a product to assure themselves that it is UL certified. No extensive research is necessary.

What keeps UL honest? Why wouldn't it simply give its Seal of Approval to any manufacturer that could pay the testing fee? Because the UL mark is voluntary, product makers will seek it out only as long as it represents quality. If UL certifies defective products, its mark will become worthless; manufacturers will turn to other certifying agencies, which already compete with UL.[47] The dominance that UL now enjoys in the electrical certification market results from its excellent service to the public. UL, like most companies in the marketplace ecosystem, reaps what it sows.

Instead of using the aggression of licensing laws, electricians could be certified by professional organizations, or even by UL itself, in order to ensure quality service. The electricians' Seal of Approval could be prominently displayed on their business cards, advertising, and even their vehicles to let consumers know that they provide quality service. In addition, such certification would test knowledge necessary to do the

We are doing something for manufacturers, buyers, users, and property owners everywhere. We are doing something for humanity.

—UL Inspector William Merrill 1923

job, rather than incidentals, such as citizenship or union membership.

Areas with certification have *more* service providers than areas with licensing laws or without certification. More service providers will mean lower costs and greater availability of quality service for everyone![48]

Similarly, health care providers could be voluntarily certified by their professional organizations rather than licensed through aggression. For example, the AMA might rate practitioners by a variety of criteria, giving "certification" or ratings to those who met its standards. Such ratings would be proudly displayed in advertising and phone listings. Discriminating consumers could simply look for service providers who received high ratings or multiple approvals.

Such a program could be funded through assessment fees just as UL is. Professionals would gladly pay a fee for a certification that meant more business. A professional organization such as the AMA would profit when it *expanded*, rather than *limited*, its membership.

The AMA would have to be careful not to certify carelessly. Otherwise, consumers would no longer trust their Seal, causing practitioners to seek another certifying organization. Specialties that the AMA might not certify (e.g., herbalists and homeopaths) could obtain certification from their own professional organizations.

To protect its Seal of Approval, UL monitors its certified products to make sure that they continue to live up to its standards. Organizations that certify health care providers would need to do the same to protect their seal as well. Licensing boards rarely do a good job of monitoring the quality of service provided by their practitioners.

In 1985, for example, *malpractice insurers sanctioned physicians for poor quality service four times as often than state licensing boards did.*[49] The insurance companies already do a better job of encouraging high-quality service—and of sanctioning poor quality—than the licensing boards. The marketplace ecosystem would give the consumer even more protection with independent certification.

The skyrocketing costs of health care would plummet without the aggression of licensing. Today, health care professionals spend much of their time performing procedures that others could readily do. A Canadian government survey, for example, indicated that 80–90% of dental work could be performed by a high school graduate with only 20 months of additional training. Allowing people to practice at their level of competence could slash dental costs as much as 40% in Ontario.[50]

Similar studies have shown that nurses and other nonphysicians are able to diagnose and treat common conditions as competently as licensed medical doctors.[51] In the United States, however, they were forbidden to do so legally for decades. Today, in most states, nurse practitioners can maintain their own offices and prescribe medication.[52] What a shame that so much wealth creation was sacrificed to establish, enforce, and fight such wasteful regulations!

As an undergraduate, I met a military veteran who had served in Vietnam and who hoped to go to medical school after he graduated from college. Because the U.S. Army never had enough physicians available for the large numbers of wounded, he often found himself performing emergency surgery in an attempt to save soldiers who were otherwise doomed to bleed to death. This man was obviously quite capable of creating wealth by assisting in a hospital operating or emergency room, or by suturing superficial wounds. However, until he completed medical school, he was unable to use the many skills he had. Many veterinary or laboratory personnel are competent surgeons but are currently forbidden by law to perform even the simplest procedures on people.

If these skilled individuals were able to assist surgeons or treat uncomplicated cases, the cost of routine medical care would go down. Lower costs would make health care more accessible, especially to the poor. Quality would be maintained because less-skilled practitioners could—and do—refer difficult cases to those with more training.[53] Instead of being overburdened with routine care, medical doctors could focus on pushing back the frontiers of medicine. They could still enjoy hefty fees for state-of-the-art medical skills, while *routine* medical services would be provided more economically by nonphysician practitioners.

Hospitals and medical centers could hire individuals for their skills, regardless of where, when, and how they received their education. Training for medical practitioners of all kinds would be as diverse as potential job niches. Individuals could once again apprentice, attend part-time medical schools, or develop their own therapies.

Not only would traditional care become more readily available at a lower cost, but also new paradigms of healing would be readily available. People whose conditions warranted treatment by a nontraditional medical practitioner would be able to accept the risks and benefits of doing so. Such individuals would *voluntarily* provide a valuable service to us all as they helped to determine the value of each new treatment.

Such people might be putting themselves at risk as they tried new therapies. However, we all acknowledge that life is not risk free. Between 40,000 to 50,000 people are killed each year in automobile accidents,[54] yet we do not outlaw driving. Everyone decides whether the benefits of driving outweigh the risks. We should honor our neighbor's choice of new medical therapies as well.

By saying "No!" to the aggression of licensing laws, we increase the overall health care quality by increasing availability, decreasing price, encouraging innovation, and allowing full use of each individual's skills. We prosper when we honor our neighbor's choice!

Of course, the benefits of health care deregulation could be sabotaged by the aggression of fraud. Practitioners who attempted to deceive patients by making false claims of certification would perturb the natural balance of the marketplace ecosystem, just as surely as aggression-through-government does. Chapter 13 ("The Other Piece of the Puzzle") explains how to deal effectively with aggressors without becoming aggressors ourselves. We'll see how the second principle of nonaggression, righting our wrongs, restores the balance while rehabilitating and, more important, deterring aggressors. Before examining that concept in detail, however, let's get a better idea of just how much our aggression is costing us by examining the licensing of pharmaceuticals.

Chapter 5: Harming Our Health

In Summary ...

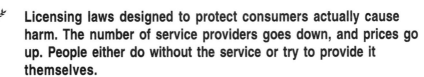

- Licensing laws designed to protect consumers actually cause harm. The number of service providers goes down, and prices go up. People either do without the service or try to provide it themselves.
- Consequently, states with stricter licensing laws for electricians have more accidental electrocutions; states with the most requirements for optometrists have more blindness; states with the most restrictive licensing for dentists have poorer oral hygiene.
- Likewise, licensing for medical doctors creates physician shortage and overwork, as well as higher prices.
- Innovation, especially in nutrition and alternative specialities, is compromised both by licensing and by use of taxes for funding research. Our nation's health suffers as a result.
- The higher income that practitioners gain from licensing laws is more than offset when those unable to afford the higher prices demand tax-supported care.
- Certification provides a better way to insure quality while honoring the choice of each consumer (e.g., electrical equipment certification by Underwriters Laboratories [UL]).

Chapter 6

Protecting Ourselves to Death

By using aggression to avoid medications that might harm us, we lose access to lifesaving drugs.

How "Consumer Protection" Backfires

If a family member had a terminal disease, we'd be furious if our neighbor, George, kept life-saving medicine from our loved one. After all, if George were dying, we'd never rip a potentially lifesaving drug from his hands. As individuals, we honor our neighbor's choice.

If we think our friends are choosing poorly, we might try to convince them to reconsider. We leave the final decision to them, because *their* health is at stake. Within our community, state, and nation, however, we fail to honor our neighbor's choice. Instead, we support laws that keep lifesaving medicine from the terminally ill, all in the name of consumer protection.

We fear that selfish pharmaceutical firms will sell us harmful products just to make money. As a consequence, we feel justified in stopping—at gunpoint, if necessary—any manufacturer who first does not get the permission of our regulatory agencies (licensing boards). Until then, George cannot buy a potentially lifesaving new drug, no matter how desperate his situation may be. We refuse to honor our neighbor's choice. Instead, we let bureaucrats, who have no liability if they choose poorly, decide for George. The results of our aggression are heart-rending.

When four-year-old Thomas Navarro developed medulloblastoma, a deadly brain tumor, his parents were appalled at the frequent side effects (e.g., new cancers, crippling, or even death) of the proposed chemotherapy and radiation treatments. When they expressed their desire to try a gentler experimental treatment called antineoplastons, doctors threatened to take Thomas from his parents and put him in state custody. The Navarros finally relented, but the chemotherapy almost killed Thomas. In spite of the doctors' protests, the Navarros refused further treatments.

It's not good for people to be put in a situation where they're begging for their lives from a central government agency.
—Samuel Broder
National Cancer
Institute director

Cancer patients are willing to risk a new treatment for a chance at life. The FDA is protecting us to death!
—Beverly Zakarian
cancer survivor and
president, Cancer
Patients Action Alliance

When they contacted Dr. Stanislaw Burzynski for antineoplaston therapy, however, they found that the Food and Drug Administration (FDA) regulations wouldn't allow Thomas to try the new treatment unless he finished courses of both chemotherapy and radiation. In frustration, the Navarros went to Congress to plead for their son, as other patients of Dr. Burzynski have for the past 20 years.

After a year and a half of fighting, when Thomas was expected to live for only two more weeks, the FDA finally permitted him to have a "compassionate use" exemption. By that time, Thomas had developed new tumors, called leptomeningial-sarcoma, a recognized side effect from his initial chemotherapy. Nevertheless, the antineoplaston therapy kept Thomas going for several more months.[1] How much longer might Thomas have lived if we had honored his parents' choice?

Of course, the United States isn't the only place where children suffer for our sins of aggression. In South Africa, where more than 20% of expecting mothers are HIV positive, the manufacturer of the drug nevirapine offered to distribute it for free. Nevirapine has been used in other countries to stop transmission of HIV to unborn children and has a 50% success rate. The South African Department of Health, however, claimed that the drug's safety had yet to be proven and would permit only limited distribution. AIDS activists and medical practitioners successfully sued to end the aggression prohibiting widespread distribution of nevirapine. In the interim, an estimated 40,000 South African babies at risk were denied treatment.[2]

In 1994, India was swept by bubonic and pneumonic plague. Health workers called Greer Laboratories in North Carolina to buy plague vaccine, but were turned away. Greer had bought rights to the vaccine in 1992, but the FDA demanded that Greer's product be tested all over again to ensure that the quality hadn't changed along with the new manufacturing site.

Although trials with the U.S. Army had shown that Greer's vaccine was indeed safe and effective, the FDA still hadn't approved it. Greer had the only useful commercial stocks available because demand for such vaccines is low. Even with enough product to protect 280,000 people, Greer had to turn away the World Health Organization, UNICEF, and corporations that wanted to protect their relief workers and employees stationed in India.[3]

With the best of intentions, we have agreed to pharmaceutical regulations (licensing laws) to protect ourselves and our neighbors from harm. By using aggression as our means, however, we've once again compromised our ends.

The Marketplace Ecosystem: Honoring Our Neighbor's Choice

Our aggression is based on the belief that the marketplace ecosystem cannot protect us from unscrupulous drug manufacturers. Is this true? Let's look at what happened in the United States when people were free to choose.

Before the 1938 Federal Food, Drug, and Cosmetic Act, most drug manufacturers did appropriate safety testing before they marketed the drug. A drug that killed people would kill profits as well, since consumers used trusted brand names to guide their purchases. Thus, the manufacturers' quest for profits protected the consumer as well.

Careful manufacturers wooed the public and increased profits by linking their brand name with safety, advertising that "We have never yet had reported a case of sudden death following the use of our Antitoxin." Others pointed out that their products had been tested and approved by various outside laboratories.[4] Brand name loyalty rewarded the drug manufacturer who always gave the customer what was promised. For the most part, manufacturers reaped what they sowed. Producers of questionable products simply had too few customers to stay in business.[5]

Until 1938, Americans decided by themselves, or in consultation with their physician or pharmacist, which medicines were best for them. To help consumers and their physicians evaluate drugs, several groups, notably the

We have a major plague in India, vaccine in the warehouse, people calling for it, and we can't get it to them.
— William White Jr.
president of Greer
Laboratories

When harnessed by competition, self-interest provides business with a strong incentive to serve the interests of the consumers.
— James Gwartney and
Richard Stroup
WHAT EVERYONE SHOULD
KNOW ABOUT ECONOMICS
AND PROSPERITY

American Medical Association and Consumers' Research, began their own testing. Physicians and pharmacists reported their evaluations in trade journals and lay publications.[6] Books[7] and magazines such as *Ladies' Home Journal* and *Collier's*[8] alerted readers to the dangers of specific products.

As early as 1904, the General Federation of Women's Clubs sent out thousands of letters, promoted lectures, and distributed information to educate the public about drug side effects.[9] Even when the modern pharmaceutical industry was in its infancy, the marketplace ecosystem responded naturally to protect and inform the consumer. With the assistance of these independent opinions, consumers made their own choices about which medications to take and honored the choices of their neighbors.

What About Side Effects?

Many of the harmful side effects that occurred in the early days of modern medicine resulted from lack of knowledge.[10] Some toxicity could not be predicted by animal testing and caused devastating side effects in people.[11] Some groups were more sensitive to drugs because of their genetic heritage.[12] "Idiosyncratic" side effects of unknown origin occurred and are still not readily predictable. Most toxicity was attributable to lack of knowledge, not manufacturer neglect.

The exceptions, however, could be tragic. Elixir Sulfanilamide, for example, contained a safe drug which was dissolved in a solvent that proved to be deadly. The new mixture was not tested before its sale in 1937. As a result, 107 people died, and the chemist who made the mixture committed suicide.[13] How might this tragedy have been prevented? What could be done to stop it from happening again?

Third-Party Evaluation Protects the Consumer

The Elixir Sulfanilamide incident demonstrated the importance of third-party evaluation. The AMA had not yet tested Elixir Sulfanilamide or given it a Seal of Approval.[14] Had the marketplace ecosystem been kept free from aggression, the AMA and other independent evaluators would have extended their certification testing in the wake of the Elixir Sulfanilamide tragedy. Manufacturers who were confident of their products would have eagerly paid for such evaluations, knowing that reputable Seals of Approval would boost consumer confidence and sales. The patients, in consultation with their trusted medical professionals, would decide which drugs were right for them.

Aggression Disrupts the Marketplace Ecosystem

Unfortunately, Americans took another tactic. They attempted to deter aggressors by becoming aggressors themselves. In doing so, they created a cure worse than the disease.

In 1938, the Federal Food, Drug, and Cosmetic Act began forcing manufacturers to demonstrate safety to the FDA before selling a drug.[15] Unlike certifying organizations, the FDA does no studies of its own. It simply examines the testing performed by the manufacturer. If individuals wanted to buy the drug before FDA approval, their choice was no longer honored.

The FDA gradually demanded more and more testing, driving small manufacturers of herbal remedies out of business, thereby reducing our choices. As a society, we no longer honored our neighbor's choice; instead, we used aggression to force others to do things our way "for their own good." As the number of tests grew, so did the time taken to perform them. As with all licensing restrictions, the *availability* of new drugs decreased.

The Thalidomide Tragedy Leads Us Astray

By the 1960s, new drugs usually appeared on U.S. pharmacy shelves long after they were available in other countries. Sometimes this drug lag protected Americans from side effects that people in other nations experienced.

Thalidomide, for example, was marketed in Europe for several years as a sedative while its manufacturer sought approval to sell it in the United States. Thalidomide was safer for adults than barbiturates, which killed hundreds of people annually through accidental overdoses.

Over 1,000 people die each year from barbiturate and alcohol interactions who might have been alive if they had used thalidomide instead.
—Sandy Shaw
coauthor of LIFE
EXTENSION: A PRACTICAL
APPROACH

At that time, the drug sensitivity of unborn children to drugs was not widely appreciated, so doctors began prescribing thalidomide to pregnant women. Thalidomide interferes with normal development of arms and legs in unborn humans, monkeys, and a single strain of rabbit.[16] Even if animal testing had been performed in standard test animals (rats and dogs), thalidomide probably would have appeared to be safe. Unfortunately for human babies, it was not. Approximately 12,000 European children were born with deformed limbs.[17] Few American infants were affected, because only a few samples of thalidomide had been distributed in the United States. The FDA physician who had delayed its approval was given the Distinguished Federal Civilian Service Award.[18]

Whereas other countries did not react to the thalidomide tragedy by changing their regulations substantially, Congress gave the FDA a mandate to use more aggression. For the first time, manufacturers had to complete extensive human tests to demonstrate that their drugs were effective as well as safe.[19]

In fact, manufacturers already did such tests, but not in the elaborate way that the FDA demanded. Longer and larger studies had to be undertaken. Foreign testing was rarely considered acceptable, forcing drug makers to repeat research that had been done elsewhere. In the meantime, manufacturers would be stopped from selling drugs to desperately ill people.

Did these additional tests protect Americans from drugs that didn't work? Apparently not! Studies show that consumers bought just as many ineffective drugs in the years following the 1962 changes.[20] Evidently, patients and physicians were usually able to tell if a drug worked and would stop using it if it didn't.

Companies profited only when their drugs acted as promised. The marketplace ecosystem had already done its magic. The new regulations were wasteful and unnecessary. The cumbersome new regulations did not give us better drugs. However, they did keep lifesaving drugs from thousands of desperately ill people.

... the penalties imposed by the marketplace on sellers of ineffective drugs before 1962 ... have left little room for improvement by a regulatory agency.

—Sam Peltzman
REGULATION OF PHARMACEUTICAL INNOVATION: THE 1962 AMENDMENTS

Death by Regulation

While the British continued to enjoy new drugs to treat their illnesses, only half as many drugs were available to Americans after many more years of waiting.[21] One new drug that came late to the American market was propranolol, the first beta-blocker to be used extensively to treat angina and hypertension. In the three years between propranolol's introduction into the United Kingdom and the United States, *approximately 30,000 Americans died prematurely*[22] *because they couldn't get this lifesaving drug.*

Even in 1968, when propranolol became available in the United States, it was approved only for limited uses. Advertising propranolol as a treatment for angina or hypertension was illegal until 1973 and 1976, respectively, so countless other Americans died because their doctors did not prescribe it.

Was the FDA complimented for finally approving propranolol? Not at all! The FDA was criticized by a congressional committee for exposing the American public to a drug with potential side effects![23] Because every drug affects some people adversely, asking the FDA to license only completely safe drugs is asking them to approve no drugs at all!

Consequently, the FDA takes longer and longer to approve even breakthrough drugs. For example, in the early 1980s, FDA team leader Dr. Henry Miller recommended that the agency approve recombinant human insulin only four months after the manufacturer submitted its data for review. At that time, the FDA took an average of two and a half years to grant approvals. Consequently, Dr. Miller's supervisor hesitated to approve this breakthrough for diabetics. He feared that if unpredictable side effects occurred, the short review time would make the FDA appear careless. Fortunately for U.S. diabetics, Dr. Miller convinced upper management to grant approval.[24]

Perhaps we need to heed the adage, "Be careful of what you wish for—you may get it!" We've set the FDA an impossible task by demanding total safety—and we pay for it with our lives.

... rarely, if ever, has Congress held a hearing to look into the failure of FDA to approve a new entity; but it has held hundreds of hearings alleging that the FDA has done something wrong by approving a drug. ... The failure to approve an important new drug can be as detrimental to the public health as the approval of a potentially bad drug.
— Alexander Schmidt
former FDA
commissioner

... there's only one way to play it safe—turn down the application. Or at least stall for time and demand more research.
—FDA regulator
THE FREEMAN

... 82% of all biotech-based drugs came from America, but Europe was the first market for 75% of these products.
—Dr. Robert Goldberg
INSIDER REPORT,
February 1996

The FDA found the [thrombolytic] therapy reduced heart attack fatalities by 18%, but it took two years to approve the new drug application. The result was as many as 22,000 deaths.

—Noel Campbell
Department of
Economics, Gordon
College

After 12 long years of battling the FDA, and after the needless, premature deaths of at least 430,000 Americans, ribavirin was finally approved in June 1998.

—Life Extension
Magazine,
November 1998

We're not prepared to march into people's homes like the Gestapo and take drugs away from desperately ill people.

—Dr. Frank Young
former FDA
commissioner

Although most new medicines are discovered in the United States, Europeans have access to them sooner because of the "drug lag" created by the FDA. *In the mid-1980s, for example, 72% of new drugs approved by the FDA had been available elsewhere for an average of 5.5 years earlier.*[25]

Clearly, as with all licensing laws, regulations governing our pharmaceuticals slash the availability of new drugs. Consequently, 60–80% of U.S. physicians surveyed felt that the FDA, and its slow approval process, had hurt their ability to treat patients.[26] Of course, European countries have their own regulatory bodies that delay drug marketing. Sweden and Norway have long delays too, while development is more rapid in Germany and the United Kingdom.[27]

How the Drug Lag Harms AIDS Victims

AIDS victims are especially aware of the drug lag. They usually can't afford to wait years until testing on new drugs is complete. Those living in the United States often go overseas to bring back effective treatments not yet approved by the FDA (e.g., ribavirin[28] and isoprinosine[29]). Sometimes, on their return, customs agents confiscate their new medications,[30] revealing the true impact of our aggression. Regulations keep effective drugs from desperately ill patients.

As a result of protests by the AIDS community, former FDA Commissioner Frank Young began allowing individuals to import small quantities of medications marketed in other countries.[31] Young's successors did not always share his compassion and sporadically ordered the seizure of imported pharmaceuticals.[32]

Some AIDS and cancer patients were so desperately ill that buyers' clubs contracted with chemists to manufacture new, unapproved drugs.[33] One activist claimed that more bootleg ddC (an anti-AIDS drug then in the early stages of testing) was sold to patients than was given to AIDS sufferers enrolled in the FDA-mandated clinical studies.[34]

When regulations become life-threatening, people turn to underground suppliers for help.

Obviously, black market drugs are more risky than those made by established pharmaceutical firms, but the FDA regulations leave people with little choice.

Had the FDA closed down the illegal buyer's clubs, the hue and cry from the AIDS community would have created a political firestorm and publicized the deadly effects of licensing laws. The FDA wisely looked the other way.

The Drug Lag Kills More People Than It Saves

Obviously, FDA regulation is a two-edged sword. Delaying approval until we see if side effects occur in other countries can save our lives. However, we also get lifesaving medications years later than other countries, causing many Americans to die needlessly. What is the final outcome?

According to a 30-year analysis, for every American saved by the drug lag, another 64–364 Americans were killed by it. Put another way, *between 1950 and 1980, the drug lag saved about 33 American lives per year, while 2,100–12,000 died needlessly.*[35] Since development time has increased since 1980, the annual death toll caused by FDA delays has likely grown. Our aggression, however well-meaning, is deadly. It's a cure that kills!

In today's global economy, U.S. regulations threaten other nations as well. When the world-renowned AIDS researcher, Robert Gallo, developed a blood test for HIV, the FDA took months to approve it. During that time, Dr. Gallo argued that the test should be used to screen the U.S. blood supply. Even an imperfect test, he claimed, would be better than none at all. The FDA disagreed and wouldn't permit the test to be used.

Meanwhile, Japan continued to import U.S. blood supplies for hemophiliacs. *In the three months following the FDA's refusal to allow testing of blood supplies, the HIV infection rate rose from 0% to 13% in Japan.*[36]

The delay in the availability of the HIV test kit increased the U.S. infection rate as well. In addition, the five-year delay in FDA approval for

By what legal or moral right do we abide a system that tells huge numbers of gravely ill Americans that they can't try these therapies until a bunch of people in a federal building in Rockville, Maryland, say so?
—Daniel Henninger
Wall Street Journal

I do not understand how a bureaucrat could sit there in Washington and say what is best for me.
—Terry Sutton
AIDS patient

the AIDS home test kit prevented people from finding out that they were carriers. *About 10,000 Americans were needlessly infected because their partners didn't know of their condition.*[37]

More Regulation Equals Less Safety

As we've seen, the drug lag kills vastly more people than it saves. In addition, the drugs that make it through the labyrinth of regulations are, if anything, less safe than drugs put on the market in earlier years. While only 2% of new drugs were pulled off the market between 1964 and 1983 because of unexpected side effects, Britain, Spain, and the United States withdrew 3–4% of newly-approved pharmaceuticals between 1974 and 1993.[38] Today's drugs may actually be less safe than ever before, possibly because of FDA restrictions on "off-label use."

Drugs that gain FDA approval do so only for a very specific indication. New uses are considered "off-label" because the FDA has not yet reviewed the new claim. Although physicians can legally prescribe drugs for off-label uses, manufacturers cannot tell physicians about them. Instead, long, expensive studies must be performed to obtain another FDA approval.[39] Meanwhile, the patent on the drug may expire, making the added cost difficult to recover. Manufacturers are better off developing new drugs with a longer patent life instead of expanding the approvals for old drugs with established safety records. Because some new compounds will have side effects that won't be discovered until after marketing, we are exposed to additional risk.

Even if manufacturers could afford to apply for approval, off-label uses are so numerous that the FDA wouldn't have time to process the applications![40] Approximately 40% of all prescriptions are for off-label uses,[41] even though drug companies cannot advertise these uses. Consequently, three out of four doctors believe that the FDA's off-label policy makes it harder for them to learn about new uses for older drugs.[42]

An Aspirin Each Day Keeps the Doctor Away

Some of the new uses that physicians might not hear about can mean the difference between

... the U.S. system of approval, in spite of greater restrictiveness and insistence on detail, has not proved markedly superior in the prevention of marketing drugs that are subsequently discontinued in light of safety questions.
—Olav Bakke et al.
Center for the Study of Drug Development,
University of Rochester
New York

... according to George Hitchings, co-winner of the 1988 Nobel prize in medicine, FDA's five-year delay in approving the antibacterial drug Septra cost 80,000 lives.
—Sam Kazman
Competitive Enterprise
Institute

life and death. For example, a study with more than 22,000 physicians demonstrated that an aspirin every other day reduces the risk of heart attack by 44% in men over 50.[43] Although the study was supposed to continue for 10 years, the researchers announced these results in 1989, after only five years. They felt it would be unethical to give a placebo when aspirin might prevent heart attacks and save lives.

The manufacturers of Bayer Aspirin prepared a 28-day "Calendar Pack" to make sure that people received the proper dose of aspirin for heart attack prevention. However, the FDA prohibited aspirin companies from mentioning the new research in their advertising. The FDA would not even allow phrases such as "For patients following a doctor-prescribed daily regimen of aspirin."[44] The FDA was concerned that such statements "may encourage inappropriate self-medication by the lay public with potentially serious adverse health results."[45] Although aspirin, like any drug, has undesirable side effects in some people, many more individuals benefit, because heart disease is the number one killer in the United States. In 1995, one study estimated that a third of the people at high risk for heart attacks were unaware that aspirin might help them.[46]

The poor, who don't see a physician regularly, were especially hurt by the FDA's decision. They were the last to learn how to use economical aspirin to prevent heart disease, because advertising is the main source of information for low-income consumers.[47]

Sadly, we could have learned about aspirin's cardiovascular benefits in the early 1970s. Squibb wanted to study aspirin's benefits back in 1969. The FDA's regulatory demands finally discouraged Squibb from doing so.[48]

Because cardiovascular disease is the number one cause of death in the United States, *10,000[49] to 100,000[50] people have died needlessly each year that the FDA stopped advertisers from promoting aspirin's benefits. For every person killed by the drug lag, another 1–48 Americans died from this single bureaucratic decision![51]*

... the absence of timely information on appropriate—and usually off-label—uses of drugs is implicated in 15% to 30% of drug-related deaths or life-threatening drug reactions in hospitals.
—WALL STREET JOURNAL, April 4, 1996

If I had to use drugs for their approved uses only, half my patients would be dead.
—Dr. Larry Norton oncologist, Sloan-Kettering Cancer Center

The FDA Creates an American Thalidomide

Health claims for unpatentable substances, such as vitamins and minerals, were also prohibited unless manufacturers went through the long, expensive approval process. However, in 1992, the government's Centers for Disease Control and Prevention (CDC) recommended that all women of childbearing age take folic acid supplements, which had been shown to decrease the incidence of birth defects such as spina bifida by 50–75%.[52] The FDA, however, immediately warned folic acid manufacturers that it would prosecute them if they dared to advertise the CDC recommendation![53]

In the United States, approximately 2,500 children per year are born with birth defects that could be prevented by folic acid. Many thousands are aborted when such problems are discovered. Had the FDA not forbidden it, advertisers would have been educating women for 20 years about this inexpensive way to prevent birth defects. *Instead, at least 25,000 U.S. children—over twice the number harmed worldwide by thalidomide—suffered crippling deformities; several times that number may have been unnecessarily aborted.*[54]

Regulation's Most Deadly Side Effect: Inhibition of Innovation

We've seen how the regulations (licensing laws) have delayed the availability of lifesaving drugs and new uses for products already approved. Tens of thousands, perhaps hundreds of thousands of people, die prematurely each year in the United States alone. As large as these numbers are, however, they pale in comparison to the number of needless deaths that result when licensing laws keep innovative, lifesaving drugs from ever reaching the market.

In 1836, Nathan Rothschild was probably the richest man in the world. Yet he died of a simple bacterial infection because antibiotics had not yet been discovered.[55] Infection, the primary cause of death in the early 1900s, can now be vanquished with wonder drugs costing just a few dollars. In the future, heart disease and cancer will likewise be cured at a price that everyone can afford.

Americans are, literally, dying for fundamental reform of drug regulation.
—Henry I. Miller
founding director of the
FDA's Office of
Biotechnology

Innovations in treatment and prevention of disease are largely responsible for the 20- to 30-year increase in longevity experienced during the twentieth century.[56] Anything that discourages such innovation has a devastating impact upon our health. The aggression of licensing laws does just that.

As a researcher in a major pharmaceutical firm, I was intimately involved with the FDA regulations. Some of my work dealt with the natural prostaglandin hormones or their synthetic analogs, which could partially prevent the deleterious effects of alcohol and other toxins on the liver.[57] More than 100,000 Americans die each year from liver disease caused by alcohol, for which bed rest and abstinence are the only, and usually ineffective, treatments.

Even a single alcoholic drink causes changes in the liver. Although most people recover fully, some do not. Adding prostaglandins to alcoholic beverages might have made drinking safer for everyone.

Unfortunately, the regulatory agencies in the United States had already decided that even adding vitamin B-1 to alcoholic beverages was "adulteration."[58] Presumably, the regulators didn't want to promote drinking. Such fears were groundless, however.

For example, when cigarette manufacturers began advertising their "safer" products, consumers recognized the dangers of smoking and consumption slowed. When the Federal Trade Commission used aggression to stop manufacturers from making health claims, cigarette sales rose once again.[59] Had we been able to advertise a "safer" alcoholic product, drinking would probably have decreased as people were reminded of the hazards. People who kept drinking would have done so with less danger to their health.

Nevertheless, regulations prohibited us from adding prostaglandins to alcoholic beverages directly. We decided to try to develop a prostaglandin "pill" instead.

To prove that the prostaglandin prevented or cured liver disease, we would have to study hundreds of people over several years. Because no one had ever done this, we weren't certain

... the pattern of intervention into science from a combination of local, state, and federal sources has moved from reasonable control to something close to chaotic strangulation.

—Donald Kennedy
FDA commissioner,
1976–1979

*If even one new drug of
the stature of penicillin or
digitalis has been un-
justifiably banished to a
company's back shelf
because of excessively
stringent regulatory re-
quirements, that event
will have harmed more
people than all the toxicity
that has occurred in the
history of modern drug
development.*
— William Wardell
professor,
University of Rochester,
New York

*Sir Arthur Fleming, the
discoverer of penicillin,
has said he wouldn't
have gone ahead with the
wonder drug of the centu-
ry if current drug-testing
requirements had been in
effect then. ... penicillin,
which has saved so many
lives, alleviated so much
suffering, and restored so
many people to health,
would have remained un-
known.*
— Edmund Contoski
MAKERS AND TAKERS

how many people we'd need in our tests. If we used too few test subjects, and our product worked with 80% certainty instead of the 95% certainty that the FDA demanded, we'd have to start over with more people. If we didn't guess right the first time, we wouldn't have time to repeat our studies before the patent expired.

Prior to the extensive testing required by the FDA, patents didn't play the pivotal role in drug development that they do today. However, without exclusivity, it's now virtually impossible to recover development costs. Even with a patent, only 3 out of 10 drugs that get to the marketplace ever earn back their manufacturer's investment.[60]

Without a patent, we had no hope of recovering our costs. Even with a patent, the economic risk was great; my employer decided not to proceed. Distressed, the FDA examiner called me, hoping that I could persuade management to go ahead with this important breakthrough. "There's no other treatment," he reminded me. However, even with the support of the FDA examiner, the regulations made development too risky. My employer lost only a potential source of profit; people with liver disease continue to lose their lives.

Drugs that die on the laboratory shelf can't save anyone. No matter how much money we have, we cannot buy cures that no one has developed. *Many more people are probably harmed through the loss of innovative new drugs than through all other regulatory prohibitions and delays put together.* Because these losses are not readily apparent or easily estimated, they are usually overlooked.

Indeed, if FDA regulations had been around earlier, some common medicines could never have made it to our pharmacy shelves. Aspirin, for example, which deforms the unborn young of almost every animal species but humans,[61] could not get FDA approval today. Penicillin, digitalis, and fluroxene would likely have been kept from consumers as well,[62] at the cost of thousands upon thousands of lives.

Paying More for Less

The loss of lifesaving medications is the biggest cost of pharmaceutical regulation. Without medications, we die earlier, suffer needlessly, and pay more for treatment. For example, before antiulcer drugs were developed, almost 100,000 ulcer operations were performed each year at an average cost of $28,000. Less than a decade after the introduction of effective ulcer medication, over 80% of the patients could avoid surgery. The new drugs cost about $900 and occasionally required two or three courses of treatments.[63] However, patients could continue functioning almost normally. Further advances brought the drug price down to $140 per person, saving at least $224 million in health care costs every year.[64] Replacing surgery and hospitalization with medication is an excellent way to lower health costs. When our aggression keeps new drugs off the market, health care costs remain high.

Of course, regulations keep drug prices high too. We can estimate the impact of regulations on drug prices through their increased impact on drug development times, which climbed from 2 years and 7 months before the 1962 amendments[65] to more than 14 years in the 1990s.[66] As we learned earlier, neither safety nor effectiveness was improved by this added aggression, which increased development time by a factor of five!

The five-fold increase in drug development time over the last several decades has increased prices at least five-fold as well. The price increase is probably much larger, since the requirements for more clinical studies, the most expensive part of development, have been responsible for most of the timeline extension. *If we did nothing but stop the aggression put in place by the 1962 amendments, we would slash development costs and the drug prices by at least 80% without compromising safety or effectiveness.*

Some countries have tried to counter the high cost of pharmaceuticals, created by the aggression of licensing laws, with more aggression

... economic studies have been virtually unanimous. ... FDA regulation certainly cannot be proved "safe and effective," thereby flunking its own approval criterion.

—Dale Gieringer
WALL STREET JOURNAL

in the form of price controls. The result: patients in Greece, Portugal, and Spain wait an additional three to four years for new drugs while pharmaceutical companies negotiate with pricing boards.[67] More aggression means that more people die waiting for lifesaving medications.

In 2000, the average drug cost over $800 million to bring to market.[68] With drug development costs so high, pharmaceutical firms don't even try to find cures for rare diseases. The American Medical Association estimates that 10% of the population suffers from such illnesses because they number in the thousands.[69] Clearly, the aggression of licensing laws leaves millions with little hope of a cure.

With costs soaring, small companies can no longer afford to undertake drug development at all. In such a regulatory climate, firms merge into several large companies creating a pharmaceutical cartel. Entry becomes extremely difficult for new competitors.[70] Without hungry small competitors luring away customers, the larger firms become less service-oriented and don't always reap what they sow. The price of drugs skyrocket to reflect not only added regulatory costs, but also the lack of competition.

The Codex Alimentarius Commission, an international group is attempting to "harmonize" the food and drug regulations by making all countries conform to the most stringent regulations.[71] Drug development times and costs will rise. The members of the pharmaceutical cartel will consolidate further, putting new drug development into a handful of mammoth companies.

The real tragedy, however, is that we will have fewer drugs and less innovation. Everyone will suffer, including those in the pharmaceutical cartel and the FDA itself. As an illustration, recall the FDA examiner who encouraged me to develop a prostaglandin for liver disease. He eventually died of cancer. I couldn't help wondering if the drug that might have saved him had also been suppressed by FDA regulations.

When we or our loved ones are dying of "incurable" diseases, we all pay the ultimate price for our aggression. Perhaps we should consider a better way.

A Better Way

If licensing laws do us more harm than good, how do we ensure that our drugs are safe and effective?

Brand Name Loyalty Rewards the Best

In the absence of aggression, drug companies profit long term only when they serve their customers well. When the products perform as advertised, consumers are pleased and buy manufacturer brands again. Consumers "punish" pharmaceutical firms when their drugs harm people by turning to competitive brands.[72]

What would keep unscrupulous manufacturers from making false claims for their products? Perpetrators of fraud would have to compensate their victims as described in Chapter 13 ("The Other Piece of the Puzzle"). Because it is so difficult, *full restitution is the most effective deterrent known*. It not only restores victims, but prevents their victimization in the first place.

Clearing Houses Provide Specialized Information

The AIDS buyers' clubs described earlier spent a great deal of effort to learn about each new compound and instruct their customers on proper dosage and potential side effects. Their two-decade track record was so exemplary that the FDA eventually sanctioned their operation.[73] A great deal of information on nutritional supplements is likewise provided today by nonprofit and for-profit organizations.

Doctors Make Recommendations Too

Most of us want professional guidance when choosing our medications. We don't have the time or expertise to evaluate drugs on our own, examine brand names, or read material supplied by an information clearing house. Consequently, most of us ask our doctors to recommend medications and would most likely continue to do so.

How would our doctors know, in the absence of licensing laws, which drugs to recommend? Besides the sources recommended above, physicians and the pharmacists learn about new drugs from the pharmaceutical firms and would likely continue to do so. Without FDA restrictions, companies could inform doctors of new uses for older drugs.

Because a drug maker may have a biased view of its own product, third-party reviews are crucial. The *Medical Letter on Drugs and Therapeutics*, whose revenue is derived from subscriptions, is a modern-day example of how the marketplace ecosystem can meet the demand for an unbiased review of pharmaceutical data.[74]

Reliable Certifications by Third Parties

Today, the FDA simply reviews studies performed by the pharmaceutical firms; it does no research itself. Third-party evaluation, popular early in the 20th century would likely make a comeback in the absence of FDA regulations. Certifying firms would work closely with manufacturers to ensure pharmaceutical safety and efficacy. Manufacturers would gladly pay for such service because certification would reassure consumers and make physicians more likely to recommend their products.[75]

Indeed, Europe uses such certifying bodies in its approval process. Medical device manufacturers pay a private device certifying body (DCB), to oversee their studies and recommend them to the regulators for rapid approval. As a result, in the early 1990s, medical device approval in Europe took an average of 250 days compared with 820 days in the United States.[76]

If DCBs can safely certify medical devices in Europe, surely similar organizations could evaluate pharmaceuticals as well. Like UL, which has certified electrical products longer than the FDA has been in existence, DCBs would profit only as long as consumers regarded their Seal of Approval highly. Thus, they would have little incentive to certify unsafe or ineffective products.

Certification is already evolving in the nutritional supplement industry because some brands don't always contain the amount of active ingredient indicated by the label. Organizations such as Good Housekeeping, Consumer Reports, and ConsumerLab.com all perform independent testing on nutritional products to help guide buyers.[77] The supplement manufacturer

USANA Health Services, Inc., voluntarily and proudly adheres to the Good Manufacturing Practice guidelines followed by pharmaceutical firms to ensure uniform potency.[78] The Life Extension Foundation uses independent laboratory evaluation for its own products and that of other firms. In addition, the foundation reviews the vast scientific literature to educate its customers of both benefits and potential side effects of nutritional supplements.[79]

Certification puts the customer back in control. Each person, in consultation with trusted medical professionals, decides which products to use. When we are Good Neighbors, each of us is free to choose!

Less Aggression Means Longer Life

The rewards of honoring our neighbor's choice are many. Certification would allow life-saving therapies to reach us more quickly than under the current regulatory system. Cost would plummet at least 80% without needless regulation. Since drugs could make up their development costs more rapidly, prices would likely drop even further.

As new uses for marketed drugs were discovered, manufacturers could freely educate physicians and the public. Safety would improve because older compounds with well-defined side effects would be used in preference to new drugs. Pharmaceuticals that were sold for more than one indication would pay for themselves more quickly, driving prices down even further.

The biggest benefit from deregulation, however, would be increased innovation. When development costs go down, more drugs and nutritional supplements become potential profit makers. Treatments for diseases that affect only small segments of the population become commercially feasible. Innovation flourishes, giving us cures for diseases that we now consider terminal or hopeless. Longer, more healthful lives reward us when we honor our neighbor's choice!

Will some people choose poorly? Of course! However, most of the time, people choose poorly because they have few good alternatives. A dying person, for example, makes desperate choices when there's no proven cure available. Today, the terminally ill find many "healers" ready to take their money, even with medical and pharmaceutical licensing.

If we end the regulations that inhibit innovation and keep effective drugs off the market, fewer people will find themselves in such desperate straits. The only way to end quackery and exploitation of the terminally ill is to provide them with effective treatment. Nothing does this better than the marketplace ecosystem free from aggression.

Chapter 6: Protecting Ourselves to Death

In Summary ...

- If a loved one were dying, we'd never snatch lifesaving drugs from their grasp. Yet, we unwittingly do just that with FDA "consumer protection" regulation.
- The FDA's mandate to approve only drugs that are completely safe and effective can be fulfilled only by approving no drugs at all. Because the FDA is unfairly blamed when drugs affect some people adversely, it drags out the approval process.
- Consequently, drug development time and cost has increased five-fold since the early 1960s without any improvement in either efficacy or safety. We pay five times as much for drugs as we should!
- The true cost, however, is measured in lives, as tens of thousands of people die waiting for the FDA to approve breakthrough drugs.
- The FDA limits the information that drug companies can share with doctors and consumers. Consequently, 10,000–100,000 Americans died needlessly from heart disease each year because aspirin makers couldn't advertise aspirin's role in prevention; 25,000 children were born with preventable deformities because vitmain sellers weren't permitted to advertise folic acid's protective effects.
- The biggest cost of regulation, however, is the stifling of innovation that could transform life-threatening diseases (e.g., infection) into a mild inconvenience.
- Innovation lowers the cost of health care dramatically. In the 10 years after its introduction, ulcer medicine slashed the cost of treatment from a $28,000 surgery to $140, a savings of 99.5%!
- When certification replaces aggressive regulations, prices drop, safety improves, and innovation thrives. More treatments become available, lessening the chances that quackery will prevail.

Chapter 7

Creating Monopolies That Control Us

Most monopolies are created, not by selfish business-people, but by our own aggression.

In the last few chapters, we've seen how the aggression of licensing laws keeps the disadvantaged from creating wealth, makes all of us pay higher prices, and decreases our safety.

Small businesses can't always survive the increased cost of regulations. Larger firms become dominant. The aggression that we use to protect us from businesses that might exploit us actually delivers us into their hands. In trying to control others, we find ourselves controlled.

The Pyramid of Power

This concept is graphically illustrated by the Pyramid of Power (Figure.7.1). In the absence of aggression, the base of the Pyramid is as broad and wide as our choice of goods and services. Our cost is low when aggression is absent. Service providers compete for the privilege of serving us. We are in control.

Additional layers of aggression in the form of licensing laws or regulations outlaw some goods and services. As a result, first-layer goods and services are not as numerous. Prices go up as availability goes down, as described in Chapters 4–6. Consumers must buy a licensed product or service, do without, or provide their own.

Licensing is *exclusive* when only a single monopoly provider is legally permitted to serve consumers. All other businesses will be stopped—at gunpoint, if necessary—from supplying willing customers. When this second layer of aggression is added to the first, costs go up further as the choice of goods and services is narrowed to one. Consumers must buy the monopoly service, do without, or provide their own.

Utilities are usually the most common example of second-layer aggression. With every layer of aggression, companies empowered by the licensing laws grow larger and gain more control over our lives. In turn, our choices become more limited and our costs higher.

A third layer of aggression is added when people who don't use the second-layer monopoly service are forced to subsidize those who do. Usually, such services are provided by a government department rather than by a private firm. The U.S. Postal Service, for example, usually needs tax subsidies because it operates at a loss even though it charges for its services.

Public services typically cost *twice* as much as those provided by a private firm, for reasons we'll explore shortly. With third-layer aggression, even if consumers choose to do without or provide their own service, they must still subsidize the monopoly!

A fourth layer of aggression is added to the Pyramid when consumers are forced to *use* the subsidized monopoly service. Doing without or

Bureaucratic Rule of Two: Removal of an activity from the private to the public sector will double its unit cost of production.
—Thomas Borcherding
BUDGETS AND
BUREAUCRATS: THE
SOURCES OF GOVERNMENT
GROWTH

Figure 7.1: Pyramid of Power

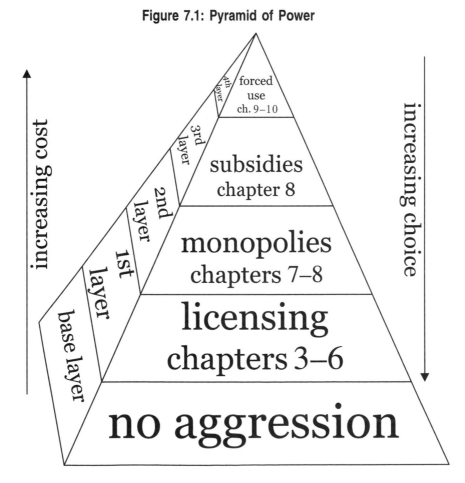

providing their own is no longer an option. With every layer of aggression, consumers have fewer choices until finally they have no choice at all. Chapters 9 ("Banking on Aggression") and 10 ("Learning Lessons Our Schools Can't Teach") explore the money and education monopolies that we are forced to use.

Aggression-through-government is the tool through which each successive layer of the Pyramid of Power is added. That's why the U.S. government is sometimes referred to as "Uncle Sam, the Monopoly Man."[1] Let's take a look at history and see how this happens.

John D. Rockefeller and Standard Oil

Occasionally, consumers vote with their dollars to give their business almost exclusively to one exceptional service provider. John D. Rockefeller, for example, through efficiency and innovation, helped lower the price of kerosene from 58 cents to 8 cents per gallon between 1865 and 1885.[2] He was able to accomplish this remarkable feat because his employees were the best that money could buy. Rockefeller was an enlightened employer who paid his managers well. He was one of the first employers to initiate a retirement plan.[3]

Because Rockefeller shared more of the jointly created wealth with his workers than other employers did, his team was highly motivated. Standard Oil scientists developed better refining methods (e.g., "cracking");[4] found a way to use culm, a by-product of coal mining, for fuel;[5] and learned how to purify oil contaminated with sulfur.[6] Before this research, only the well-to-do could afford the expensive candles or whale oil for nighttime lighting.

With these innovations, kerosene, for pennies per hour, transformed evening activities for Americans of more limited means.[7] Americans voted with their dollars to make Rockefeller's Standard Oil their kerosene provider; by 1879, it had 90% of the world's refining business.[8]

Working-class Americans were not the only ones to benefit from lower kerosene prices. As the cost of kerosene lighting decreased, the demand for whale oil did too. Whaling became less

We must ever remember we are refining oil for the poor man and he must have it cheap and good.
—John D. Rockefeller
founder, Standard Oil

... the richest people in the world are those who have done best at pleasing others, especially the common man. ... Henry Ford became richer than Bentley; Ford made cars for the common man. ... The pursuit of profits is the activity most consistent with human needs.
—Walter Williams
ALL IT TAKES IS GUTS

Had the whaling industry matched the 300 percent population growth from 1850 to 1900, many species of whale would have been extinct long ago.
—James S. Robbins
The Foundation for
Economic Education

profitable. The 735-ship whaling fleet of 1846 was reduced to 39 vessels by 1876.[9] Without the creation of new wealth in the form of inexpensive kerosene lighting, whales might have faced an early extinction. Instead, Rockefeller substituted the more abundant resource (kerosene) for the scarce one (whale oil). Our present dependence on fossil fuels will eventually be eliminated by substituting an even more abundant resource, such as solar or nuclear power.

How the Marketplace Ecosystem Protects Consumers

Standard Oil reaped what it sowed and gained industry dominance. However, it was unable to raise prices without inspiring fledgling competitors to lure customers away by selling for less. The marketplace ecosystem, free from the aggression of licensing laws, protected the consumer from being overcharged.

Rockefeller tried to organize independent oil refiners to keep prices high.[10] However, profits from underselling the monopoly were so tempting that at least one refiner always attempted it. Prices couldn't be fixed. Rockefeller found that the marketplace ecosystem, when free from aggression, regulated his attempts to exploit his customers. He was not the last to learn this lesson. In 1907, members of the steel industry tried to fix prices with exactly the same result.[11]

Encouraged by Rockefeller's story of rags to riches, young hopefuls tried to lure customers away from Standard Oil. Naturally, some consumers were willing to take a chance on a new refiner that offered them better prices than Standard Oil would.

In frustration, Rockefeller tried to buy out those who tried to undersell him. However, Rockefeller still could not secure a monopoly. Some people went into the refining business hoping that Rockefeller would make them an offer!

While the marketplace ecosystem thwarted Rockefeller's quest for monopoly, aggression-through-government worked in his favor. Most railroads were government subsidized. Had the marketplace ecosystem developed transportation alternatives naturally, oil transport would likely have been more decentralized, to the benefit of Standard's competition.

The railroads helped Rockefeller maintain market dominance with large volume discounts.[12] In addition, the railroads engaged in some unsavory collusions with Standard Oil. In return for Rockefeller's exclusive business, some railroads secretly agreed to pay Rockefeller a "drawback" for every barrel of oil they shipped for Standard's competitors.

When news of this scheme leaked out, oil drillers stopped selling to Standard Oil. Thousands of people demonstrated against Standard and refused to buy from it.[13] Suppliers and consumers punished Rockefeller for behavior that they felt was unbecoming. Rockefeller stopped putting Standard's banner on new acquisitions to avoid losing business.[14]

The only way that Rockefeller could thwart the marketplace ecosystem was with aggression-through-government. Rockefeller asked state legislators to put his competitors out of business for him. When Tidewater Pipe Line Company threatened Rockefeller's dominance, he successfully lobbied to get Standard Oil a monopoly on pipeline building in states where Tidewater was operating.[15]

In spite of Rockefeller's maneuvering, however, the marketplace ecosystem protected consumer from monopoly exploitation. Rockefeller had to keep his prices low or lose customers to his competition. Consumers benefited. Nevertheless, barely four years after attaining 90% of the market, Standard Oil's competitors had doubled their volume.[16] In 1884, almost 100 refineries were processing crude oil.[17] By 1911, Standard refined only 64% of the domestic petroleum. The competition included Gulf, Texaco, Union, Pure Oil, and Shell.[18] The antitrust conviction against Standard Oil that same year, paid for with our tax dollars, was obviously redundant. The natural balance of the marketplace ecosystem had already controlled Standard Oil.

Indeed, Rockefeller's empire had dwindled even more than the above numbers show. In 1882, Standard refined 85% of the world's oil; by

... economists have long known that business (that is, non-governmental) monopolies are short-lived.

—Peter Drucker
INNOVATION AND
ENTREPRENEURSHIP

The entire structure of antitrust statutes in this country is a jumble of economic irrationality and ignorance.

—Alan Greenspan
Federal Reserve
chairman

1888, Russian oil had cut Standard's world market share to 53%.[19]

In addition, kerosene, which had replaced whale oil for lamp lighting, was itself displaced by natural gas and electricity in the early 1900s.[20] Innovative new products ultimately keep the most determined monopolist in check in the marketplace ecosystem!

Bill Gates and Microsoft

The marketplace ecosystem also prevented Microsoft's dominance from turning into an exploitive monopoly long before the antitrust case was heard. In 1997, Microsoft was charged as a monopolist largely because the International Data Corporation had predicted that Microsoft Windows would soon control 95% of the operating system market. By 1998, Apple, which utilizes the MacOS system, had gained 10% of the computer market.[21] By mid-2000, Microsoft made only two-thirds of the retail operating system sales; Linux and MacOS accounted for most of the remainder. Microsoft's performance in the business sector was dismal: less than a third of commercial networks used Windows.[22]

Clearly, Microsoft did not have an operating system monopoly and was fast losing ground. The ongoing development of Web-based platforms might even make Windows obsolete within a few more years.[23] The marketplace ecosystem protects the consumer from a Microsoft monopoly through competitive innovation.

Microsoft's products were rarely overpriced. The cost for Windows, adjusted for inflation, dropped 53% from 1990 to 1998.[24] Microsoft's success was based on low prices and high volume. As a result, when Microsoft created application software such as word processing, prices fell four times as fast as they did in areas where Microsoft didn't compete.[25] Microsoft gained customers much as Rockefeller had done—with high quality, low-priced products.

Indeed, Microsoft gave away Internet Explorer with its Windows operating system. The Justice Department considered this "predatory pricing" because other producers of browsers, like Netscape, presumably could not compete.

You're gouging on your prices
If you charge more than the rest.
But it's unfair competition
If you think you can charge less!
A second point that we would make,
To help avoid confusion:
Don't try to charge the same amount,
For that would be collusion!

—R.W. Grant
THE INCREDIBLE BREAD MACHINE

Of course, Netscape, which had market dominance before Internet Explorer did, gained it precisely the same way—by giving its browser away for free.[26] Nevertheless, Netscape and other Microsoft rivals complained about this "predatory pricing" to the Justice Department.[27] Netscape wanted to keep charging for its browser, but many people wouldn't pay Netscape if they could get Microsoft's product for free!

Netscape and other Microsoft competitors could have put their time, money, and effort into winning back consumers. They turned instead to aggression-through-government in order to stop Microsoft from giving better service.

Such tactics are not uncommon. Indeed, most antitrust cases are based on the complaints of competitors, not consumers.[28] Both antitrust and licensing laws are backed by special interest groups who want to thwart competitors without having to win customer loyalty.

Naturally, the politicians who wield the guns of government favor those who contribute generously to their campaign chests. As late as 1995, Bill Gates gave his attention to Microsoft products rather than politics. Microsoft had only one full-time lobbyist in Washington, D.C., and a political action committee with a scant $16,000.[29] However, by 1996, Microsoft spent almost $250,000 on political contributions.[30]

Naturally, this political tug-of-war between Microsoft and its competitors consumes resources. No new wealth is created, and our world is poorer because of it. Wealth is transferred from consumers and taxpayers to politicians and attorneys.

We don't need to turn to aggression to prevent monopolies; the marketplace ecosystem is self-regulating. The only way a company can maintain market dominance is to serve its customers better than anyone else. Few companies can manage this feat for extended periods of time.

Alcoa Aluminum

One such company, the Aluminum Company of America (Alcoa) maintained its 90% market share for nearly 50 years. (The other 10% came from imports.) During that time, Alcoa brought

... even the government's chief expert, economist Franklin Fisher, admitted Microsoft had harmed competitors, but had done nothing to harm consumers "up to this point."
—David Kopel
INTELLECTUAL AMMUNITION

Microsoft would not likely now be in the legal straits it is in if it had not been so competitive and if it had curried more favors with politicians in Washington—made more payouts—over the years.
—Richard McKenzie
University of California, Irvine

down the price of aluminum from $8 to 22 cents per pound, much as Rockefeller had done with oil and Bill Gates has done with software. Unlike Standard Oil and Microsoft, however, Alcoa was not accused of unsavory business tactics.

Nevertheless, the Justice Department prosecuted Alcoa for unfair monopolist practices which included being "... a great organization, having the advantage of experience, trade connections, and the elite of personnel."[31] In other words, Alcoa served customers so well for so long that other businesses couldn't do better.

Alcoa was simply reaping what it had sown. The antitrust suit brought by the U.S. government served no useful purpose. Indeed, consumers were harmed since Alcoa eventually had to pass its legal costs on as increased prices. The taxpayers' money was wasted as well.

Patents Create the Bell Monopoly

In the marketplace ecosystem free from aggression, monopolies are rare. They exist only when a company serves its customers better than any other competitor. However, monopolies created by aggression-through-government are actually quite common.

Indeed, the term "monopoly" originally referred to a privilege granted by government. Rulers would grant a monopoly to a single service provider and outlaw all of their competitors.[32] In return for the privilege of monopoly, the favored company would share its profits with its benefactor.

Monopoly: A right granted by a government giving exclusive control over a specified commercial activity to a single party.
—AMERICAN HERITAGE DICTIONARY, 2000

In many nations, patents give inventors an exclusive monopoly, enforced by government, on their product. In the United States, the standard patent life is 17 years. In theory, patent protection encourages innovation by rewarding inventors with exclusivity.

Patents only became essential in the pharmaceutical industry after the FDA's imposition of artificially long development times. Indeed, in a survey of 12 major industries, drug manufacturers were by far the most highly regulated and the most dependent upon patents. Over 60% of medicinal products would not have been developed in their absence.[33] Because development time has increased substantially since the early 1980s when this study was performed, the pharmaceutical industry today is even more dependent upon patents.

Discovering new ways to use old resources creates wealth, as it did with the invention of the telephone. However, since one idea builds on another, several people often create similar versions of a new product almost simultaneously. At least three individuals, Alexander Graham Bell, Elisha Gray, and Antonio Meucci, developed different versions of the telephone. However, the U.S. Patent Office awarded the monopoly to Bell, because he had reached their office three hours earlier than Gray.[34] Meucci had filed years before either Bell or Gray, and sued when Bell's patents were issued. Court battles ultimately favored Bell.[35]

Why shouldn't all the inventors be able to replicate and sell the new wealth that they created? Bell's monopoly prohibited Meucci and Gray from using their own ideas!

Bell Telephone's patents, thought by some to be the most lucrative patents in history, made it a legal monopoly until 1894. Bell catered primarily to the business sector and to the wealthy. When the patents expired, other companies began providing affordable telephone service in middle class and rural areas.[36] The independents charged less because customers could call only those serviced by the same company. Consumers were evidently pleased to make such a trade-off; by 1907, some 20,000 independents controlled half of all the new telephone installations. Between 1895 and 1910, when Bell no longer had a monopoly the rate of phone installations soared (Figure 7.2).

Competition from the independents slashed Bell's annual profits 80%[37] as consumers chose the independents who served them best. The marketplace ecosystem protected consumers from monopoly profits.

As telephones went from a curiosity to a standard household utility, the independents began developing a plan for sharing each other's lines.[38] The marketplace ecosystem promoted cooperation. The independents, by avoiding duplication,

The Patent Office granted Bell the telephone patent on March 3, No. 174,465, which has earned more money than any other piece of paper ever issued by this office.

—Joseph C. Goulden
Monopoly

could give customers better, less expensive service and profit as a result.

The Big Get Bigger

Theodore Vail, Bell's new chairman, was determined to regain Bell's monopoly. Instead of giving customers better service than the independents, he wanted an exclusive licence, enforced by aggression-through-government. He wanted consumers to have no choice but to come to Bell or do without telephones.

To convince Americans to use the guns of government to destroy Bell's competition, he claimed that competition caused duplication and penalized the customer (i.e., telephone service was a "natural" monopoly). Had this been true, the independents would never have been able to lure customers from the established Bell monopoly in the first place!

It has been in periods of untidy, tumultuous competition that products have been democratized and have gone through their most rapid rate of growth and innovation.
—Peter Samuel
UNNATURAL MONOPOLIES

Figure 7.2: How Bell's Monopoly Slowed Phone Installations

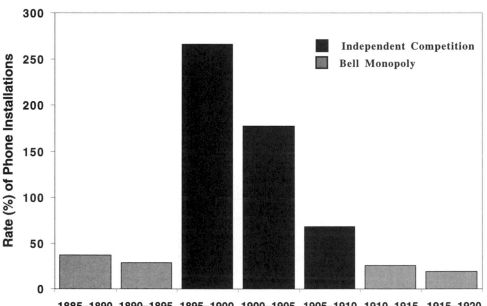

Rate of phone installations expressed as the percentage increase in telephones per 1,000 people from the prior period. Data from L.S. Hyman, R.C. Toole, and R.M. Avellis, *The New Telecommunications Industry: Evolution and Organization*, Vol. 1. (Vienna, VA: Public Utility Reports, Inc., 1987) as reported in A.D. Thierer, "Un-natural Monopoly: Critical Moments in the Development of the Bell System Monopoly," *Cato Journal* 14: 267–285, 1994.

If our neighbor George asked us to stop everyone other than himself who tried to provide services to willing customers, we'd probably be very suspicious of his motives. Nevertheless, by 1910, local governments would allow only one telephone company to operate in that region.[39] Other companies would be stopped from providing service to willing customers. Because Bell was the largest single company, it was in the best position to lobby the state utility commissions effectively and was almost always chosen over the independents.

Although Vail had claimed that Bell's monopoly would result in universal service, installations began to fall as Bell put the independents out of business. Indeed, phone installation rates after 1910 were comparable to what they had been during Bell's earlier monopoly period (Figure 7.2). Since there was only one phone per 10 people, the lower growth rate probably reflected dissatisfaction with Bell's monopoly rates, rather than market saturation.[40]

Consumer Exploitation

How were consumers to be protected from predatory pricing by the new AT&T monopoly? The new licensing law allowed the company to charge enough to cover all costs and to generate a fixed profit. With costs and profits guaranteed, AT&T paid top dollar for its research staff, who then developed patented products in radio, television, movies, and electronics. AT&T had little incentive to innovate in the telephone market, because technology that would lower costs to customers generated no new profit for the company. Consumers paid for research that gave AT&T an edge in other industries.[41]

During the depression of the 1930s, AT&T stock continued to pay handsome dividends.[42] If subscribers didn't like subsidizing AT&T's new ventures and its investors' portfolios, they had to do without telephone service.

Our aggression cost us more than high-priced phone service, however. As the wealth of AT&T increased and its research began to affect other industries, the U.S. Justice Department began antitrust suits to keep AT&T out of radio,

The dominant fact of American political life at the beginning of this century was that big business led the struggle for the federal regulation of the economy.

—Gabriel Kolko
THE TRIUMPH OF
CONSERVATISM

*Monopoly favors the rich
(on the whole) just as
competition (on the whole)
favors the poor.*
                —George Watson
        JOURNAL OF ECONOMIC
                      AFFAIRS

television, and cinema.[43] In addition to paying higher prices, Americans paid $1.1 billion in taxes each year to regulate the monopoly.[44] In the marketplace ecosystem free from aggression, those expenses would have been unnecessary.

In 1984, an antitrust suit eliminated AT&T's 75-year monopoly in long-distance service. Rates plummeted 30% over the next five years, as new long-distance companies competed to serve consumers better for less.[45] When aggression was outlawed, the marketplace ecosystem protected consumers well. However, the cost of local service, still monopolized by exclusive licensing, went up 50% during the same period![46]

Seven of the "Baby Bells," created by the antitrust ruling, earned 25% more than the top 1,000 U.S. firms in 1987. Local phone companies were allowed to charge extra fees as compensation for loss of AT&T's long-distance monopoly![47] Is this consumer protection?

During the time when other U.S. companies could not sell local phone service, they were allowed to bypass AT&T's network by using their own phone lines, microwave routing, or satellite systems. By the late 1980s, more business phones were serviced through private exchanges than by conventional phone lines.[48] Businesses found these systems more economical, confirming that AT&T had been overcharging the consumer. Even the Federal Communications Commission, the U.S. government agency in charge of regulating the telephone companies, bypassed the local phone network![49]

As cellular phones became less expensive, people began using them as a replacement for the standard home phone. The innovation of the marketplace ecosystem protected consumers, even from monopolies created by aggression! Bowing to the inevitable, competition in local phone service has recently been permitted.

The telephone industry is just one example of a natural monopoly that is not so natural after all. Cable television is another one. We create these exploitive monopolies through our own aggression-through-government.

Even when we lower the guns of government enough to permit just one additional service provider, we empower ourselves as consumers.

For example, in the few cities that license two power companies instead of one, prices are lower than in regions where only one company is permitted to provide service.[50] Unfortunately, higher costs are only a small part of the price we pay for our aggression.

How Licensing Laws Harm the Environment

Monopolies created by aggression have contributed greatly to our dependence on fossil fuels. In the early 1900s, for example, several paper companies produced cheap electricity from steam. They were stopped from selling their electricity because the exclusive monopoly belonged to the public utilities.[51] Small plants using alternative energy sources were also banned. Centralized energy production with its dependence on fossil fuels became the norm. As with AT&T, utilities had no incentive to conserve fuel or develop alternative energy methods. Their profit was determined by politicians, not by consumers. Politics ruled, not people.

A Lose–Lose Situation

No one wins when second-layer aggression creates exclusive monopolies. Small firms, like the independent phone companies, are put out of business leaving consumers at the mercy of the monopolies. Consequently, consumers pay more for less.

However, even monopoly firms lose. When innovations, such as cell phones, make the regulated monopoly obsolete, it is ill prepared to compete. Eventually, the monopoly itself may be subjected to antitrust action, as AT&T discovered. In 2000, AOL, which supported government action against Microsoft, became a target of the U.S. Federal Trade Commission because of its dominance in the instant messaging market.[52] Such suits also mean bigger tax bills and higher prices for the average American.

The marketplace ecosystem is so efficient in weeding out monopolies that antitrust laws are redundant and wasteful. Because antitrust action consumes resources without creating new wealth, our world is poorer. When companies have to defend against antitrust action or lobby to prevent it, they have less money to invest in production. Consequently, they hire fewer workers. As a result, unemployment rises when antitrust action does.[53]

However, the greatest loss is the innovation that never happens under a regulated monopoly. For example, AT&T did little research to improve phone service, because it reaped the same guaranteed profit with or without innovation.

If our aggression had given IBM a monopoly on computers, the desktop and laptop might never have been developed. In 1943, IBM chairman Thomas Watson Sr. believed that "there is a world market for about five computers." As late as the mid-1970s, a Xerox executive asked Steve Jobs, founder of Apple Computer, "Why would anyone ever need a computer in their home?"[54] A great deal of innovation comes from small start-ups, such as the one that Jobs began in a garage. When regulations outlaw hungry new competitors, we all lose. Our wealth cannot buy what has not yet been invented.

A Better Way

Monopolies are rare in the marketplace ecosystem. Only firms that can serve customers best for long periods of time can maintain market dominance. If firms raise prices, competition quickly sets in. Only aggression can maintain exploitive monopolies for any length of time.

Fortunately, the financial and ecological costs of monopolies maintained by aggression are becoming so obvious that they are starting to be dismantled. In 1978, U.S. Congress ended the utilities' monopoly in generation of electricity. Public utilities now buy electricity at favorable rates from power plants that rely on renewable sources such as wind, water, or cogeneration from steam. Small local power plants are springing up that run on fuel as diverse as cow dung and old tires![55] Before 1978, if you had wanted to put up a windmill and sell your extra electricity to George and other neighbors, the federal government would have stopped you to protect the not-so-natural utility monopoly.

Deregulation of electrical utilities is becoming more common. Consumers in Australia and the United Kingdom saved an average of 24% and 26% respectively after deregulation.[56]

In the United States, many states still have an electrical utility monopoly even though Congress no longer requires it. In 1996, Pennsylvania began deregulating its electrical generation monopoly. Consumers paid 30% less and could choose environmentally friendly "green power."[57]

Lower prices mean that wealth is being created more efficiently. The less time and energy spent creating "old" wealth, the more resources we have to create "new" wealth. Because wealth is created through jobs, employment rises. Pennsylvania's secretary of revenue estimated that deregulation of electric generation would result in 36,000 new jobs by 2004.[58] The Good Neighbor Policy works for the common good.

Deregulation means less aggression-through-government. Instead of trying to control our neighbors, we honor their choices. In 1996, however, California attempted to "deregulate" by increasing aggressive control of its electrical utilities. Private utilities were forced to sell their generating plants and buy their power through a Power Exchange utility monopoly. The monopoly no longer sold its power through long term contracts that enabled the utilities to anticipate and fix their costs.[59]

Although many companies have applied for permission to build generating plants in California, the state government stops them from doing so. Like the FDA, California's regulators are so slow to give licenses (approval) that no major plants have been built in the past decade, even though the demand for electricity in the state has risen over 25%.[60]

Not surprisingly, California reaped as it sowed. Prices skyrocketed and electricity had to be rationed. True deregulation means less aggression, not more.

Adding that second-layer of aggression carries some hefty costs in terms of selection, cost, and environmental quality. As we'll see in the next chapter, however, adding third-layer aggression makes second-layer environmental insults look like tender loving care!

Within the first two years of deregulation, prices had fallen by 4–15 percent, and sometimes more for certain groups of customers. Within 10 years, prices were at least 25 percent lower, and sometimes close to 50 percent lower.

—Robert Crandall and Jerry Ellig
ECONOMIC DEREGULATION AND CUSTOMER CHOICE: LESSONS FOR THE ELECTRIC INDUSTRY

Chapter 7: Creating Monopolies That Control Us

In Summary ...

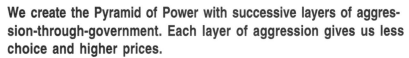

- We create the Pyramid of Power with successive layers of aggression-through-government. Each layer of aggression gives us less choice and higher prices.

- The first layer outlaws some goods and services; the second layer outlaws all but a single service provider to create a monopoly. The third layer of aggression forces us to subsidize the monopoly and the fourth layer forces us to use it.

- Rockefeller gained 90% of the oil refining market with innovations and low prices. The marketplace ecosystem made it impossible for him to raise prices and exploit consumers. However, the aggression of exclusive licensing allowed him to stop some of his strongest competitors.

- Bill Gates, like Rockefeller, gave consumers quality products at low prices. His competitors complained to the U.S. Justice Department instead of wooing their customers back with better service.

- Bell Telephone enjoyed a monopoly for many years because its patents gave it an exclusive monopoly. When the patents expired, Bell's competitors brought phone service to the masses. When Bell regained its monopoly through exclusive licensing, the rate of phone installations plummeted.

- Deregulation returns control to the consumer. Service providers compete with each other to provide the highest quality, lowest cost service. Everyone wins!

Chapter 8

Destroying the Environment

We are more likely to protect the environment when we own a piece of it and profit by nurturing it.

In this chapter, we'll learn how third-layer aggression harms the environment and increases costs of many important services. With third-layer aggression, we are forced—at gunpoint, if necessary—to *subsidize* the exclusive monopolies created by second layer aggression, even if we don't use them!

Of course, we can be forced to subsidize service providers who do not have an exclusive monopoly. In real life, the layers of aggression that create the Pyramid of Power may change order from time to time. What doesn't change is that each additional layer of aggression decreases our choices and increases our costs.

Increasing Costs

Many subsidized exclusive monopolies are public services. On average, we pay *twice* as much through our taxes for these services as we would if they were provided by the private sector.[1]

Bureaucrats have little incentive for efficiency when consumers must pay for the service whether they use it or not. The proof of this inefficiency is the enormous savings enjoyed when public services are contracted out to private firms instead of being performed by government employees. California cities save between 37% and 96% by contracting out their street cleaning, janitorial services, trash collection, traffic signal repairs, grass cutting, street maintenance, and road construction.[2] Private municipal transit service saves taxpayers 30–50%.[3] Savings have also been realized in various locales by contracting out fire protection,[4] emergency ambulance service,[5] building or operation of water and sewage treatment plants,[6] and solid waste recycling.[7] The monopoly services are still subsidized, but they cost less.

Encouraging Waste

Whenever people do not pay the full cost of something they use, they have less incentive to

If we can prevent the Government from wasting the labors of the people under the pretense of caring for them, they will be happy.

—Thomas Jefferson
author of the
Declaration of
Independence

Forces which impede innovation in a public service institution are inherent in it, integral to it, and inseparable from it.
　　　　—Peter Drucker
　　　　INNOVATION AND
　　　　ENTREPRENEURSHIP

conserve. For example, when people pay the same amount of taxes for solid waste disposal whether they recycle or not, fewer people are inclined to recycle. As a consequence, we have more waste and disposal problems.

Conversely, when subsidies decrease, conservation automatically follows. In Seattle, during the first year that customers were charged by the volume of trash they generated, 67% chose to become involved in the local recycling program.[8] Because about 18% of our yearly trash consists of leaves, grass, and other yard products,[9] composting coupled with recycling can dramatically lower a person's disposal bill. As less waste is generated, fewer resources are needed to dispose of it. What could be more natural?

Discouraging Conservation

Water utilities are usually public monopolies subsidized by our tax dollars. In California's San Joaquin Valley, 4.5 million acres of once-desert farmland is irrigated by subsidized water. Taxes are used to construct dams for irrigators, pay many of their delivery costs, and support zero-interest loans to farmers who pay only a tenth of what residential customers do![10] These subsidies encourage wasteful over irrigation, resulting in soil erosion, salt buildup, and toxic levels of selenium in the runoff. Kesterson Wildlife Reservoir has been virtually destroyed by irrigation-induced selenium buildup, which now threatens San Francisco Bay as well.[11]

As long as our tax dollars subsidize the irrigators, however, they have little financial incentive to install drip sprinkler systems or other conservation devices. As a result, less water is available for other uses, so prices increase for everyone else. Without subsidies, irrigators would be motivated to conserve, making more water available for domestic use.

Destroying the Environment

The above examples of third-layer aggression deal solely with exclusive monopolies, where service is provided by a public works department, subsidized in whole or in part by taxes. Subsidies also go to maintain the federal and state lands which encompass over 40% of the U.S. landmass,[12] including nearly all of Alaska and Nevada.[13] Land ownership is not an exclusive government monopoly, but the sheer size of the government's holdings and the subsidies necessary for maintaining them, allow us to treat them as a product of third-layer aggression.

Rather than exclusive licensing, aggression-through-government takes the form of forcible prevention of homesteading. Lands in the United States were originally settled by homesteading, a time-honored way of creating wealth.

Individual or groups find unused land and clear it for agriculture, fence it for grazing, make paths for hiking, build a home, and so on. To own the new wealth (farm land, ranch land, etc.) that they have made, creators lay claim to the property on which it resides. When others settle nearby, they choose different property on which to stake their claim.

Government holds land by forcibly preventing homesteading. Sometimes we condone this aggression to protect rangeland, forests, and parks from abuse and destruction. By using aggression as our means, however, we endanger the ends that we seek.

Overgrazing the Range

The incentives of the congressional representatives who oversee the U.S. Bureau of Land Management, are very different from individual land owners. The following imaginary conversation between a congressman and some of his constituents illustrates the dilemma that our sincere lawmakers have.

"Mr. Congressman, we represent the ranchers in your district. Things are pretty tough for us right now, but you can help us. Let us graze cattle on all that vacant rangeland the government has in this area. We'll be properly grateful when it comes time to contribute to your campaign. As a token of our goodwill, we'll make a substantial donation just as soon as we come to an agreement."

The congressman has twinges of conscience. He knows that the ranchers will overstock the government ranges, even though they carefully

The most entrepreneurial, the most innovative people behave like the worst time serving bureaucrats or power hungry politicians 6 months after they have taken over the management of a public service institution, particularly if it is a government agency.

—Peter Drucker
INNOVATION AND
ENTREPRENEURSHIP

control the number of cattle on their own land. Since they can't be sure of having the same public range every year, however, they cannot profit by taking care of it. They cannot pass it on to their children. They profit most by letting their cattle eat every last blade of grass. When the congressman shares his concern with the ranchers, they respond with:

"Mr. Congressman, we will pay a small fee for 'renting' the land. Renters don't take as good care of property as owners do, it's true, but the land is just sitting there helping no one. People who want to save the land for their children and grandchildren must not have the problems we do just keeping our next generation fed. If you don't help us, sir, you'll have trouble putting food on your table too. We'll find someone to run against you who knows how to take care of the people he or she represents. We'll make sure that you're defeated."

The congressman sighs and gives in. After all, the ranchers gain immensely if allowed to graze cattle on the land he controls. They have every incentive to make good their threats and their promises. The person they help elect might not even try to protect the environment. The congressman reasons that he should give a little on this issue so that he, not some "yes man," can remain in office.

The congressman finds that his colleagues have constituents who want the government to build a dam on public land or harvest the national forests. He agrees to vote for these programs in return for their help in directing the Bureau of Land Management to rent the grazing land to his ranchers. Naturally, these changes set precedents for many of the resources controlled by the government, not just the ones in this congressman's district.

Because of these skewed incentives, almost half of our public rangelands are rented out to ranchers for grazing cattle at one-fifth to one-tenth the rate of private land.[14] By 1964, three million additional acres had been cleared with environmentally destructive practices, such as "chaining,"[15] to create more rentable rangeland. Because the ranchers and their representatives cannot profit by protecting the land, they have little incentive to do so. As early as 1925, studies demonstrated the inevitable result: on overgrazed public ranges, cattle were twice as likely to die and had half as many calves as animals raised on private lands.[16]

Are the ranchers and their representatives selfish others whom we should condemn for overgrazing the range? Not at all! Had ranchers been permitted to homestead these lands in the first place, the rangeland would now be receiving the better care characteristic of private grazing. Our willingness to use aggression to prevent homesteading has taken the profit out of caring for the environment. When this aggression is even partially removed, the environment greatly improves.

For example, in 1934, Congress passed the Taylor Grazing Act to encourage ranchers to care for the public grazing land. By allowing ten-year transferable leases, ranchers had control of the land for a decade. Ranchers who improved the land were given the positive feedback of good grazing or a good price when selling their lease. In essence, the lease gave them partial ownership. As a result, almost half of the rangeland classified as poor was upgraded.[17]

However, in 1966, leases were reduced to only one year, giving ranchers little incentive to make improvements. After all, they could not be sure that they would be able to renew their lease. As a result, private investment in wells and fences in the early 1970s dropped to less than a third of their 1960s level.[18]

When vast tracts of public property are misused, the environment can suffer great damage. Overgrazing of public rangeland was permanently destructive in many cases, contributing to the formation of a "dust bowl" in the Midwestern states.[19]

Logging the Forests

As subsidies increase, so does environmental destruction. Most of the trees in our national forests wouldn't be logged without subsidies, because the cost of building the roads necessary to transport the timber exceeds the value of the

What is common to many is least taken care of, for all men have greater regard for what is their own than what they possess in common with others.

—Aristotle

lumber. Once again, however, the special interests found a way to use the aggression of taxes to their own advantage. Let's listen to an imaginary conversation between the timber companies and their congresswoman.

"Ms. Congresswoman, the Forest Service has money in its budget for hiking trails. Now we're all for hiking; we just think we should get our fair share of the forest and our fair share of the subsidy. Some of that money for trails should be used to build logging roads. Consumers will benefit by increases in the supply of timber. We'd profit too and see that you got your 'fair share' for your campaign chest. We'd pay some money for replanting too, so the environmentalists will be happy."

The congresswoman considers their offer. She knows that the loggers, like the ranchers, have little incentive to log sustainably on public lands. She also knows that if the hikers complain, she can ask Congress for a larger subsidy so that the Forest Service can build more trails. Some of that subsidy can be siphoned off to build more logging roads. More logging roads mean more campaign contributions. Since hikers don't make money off of the forests, they won't help her out the way that loggers will.

The congresswoman won't protect the forests by fighting the loggers. Special interests reap high profits with subsidies, so they'll spend large amounts of money to protect them. If the congresswoman doesn't agree to the timber companies' demands, they'll put their considerable money and influence behind her opponent. The timber companies will be able to log the forests. The only question is which congressional representative will reap a share of the profits. The congresswoman sighs and agrees to fight for more logging subsidies.

As a result of subsidies' adverse influence, the Forest Service uses taxpayer dollars to log the national forests. By 1985, almost 350,000 miles of logging roads had been constructed in the national forests—eight times more than the total mileage of the U.S. interstate highway system![20] Construction of roads requires stripping mountainous terrain of its vegetation, causing massive erosion. In the northern Rockies, trout and salmon streams are threatened by the resulting silt. Fragile ecosystems are disturbed.[21]

The Forest Service typically receives 20 cents for every dollar spent on roads, logging, and timber management.[22] Even though the timber companies are charged for the cost of reforestation, 50% of these funds go for "overhead."[23] Between 1991 and 1994, $1 billion more in taxes were spent to log the national forests than the loggers paid.[24]

Although logging is encouraged, hiking is discouraged. The number of backpackers increased by a factor of 10 between the 1940s and the 1980s, but trails in the national forests dropped from 144,000 miles to under 100,000.[25]

Should we blame the timber companies and their congressional representatives for this travesty? Hardly! After all, if we sanction aggression to prevent homesteading, we take the profit out of protecting the forest.

While national forests are being depleted through special interest subsidies, trees on private property are flourishing. In the United States, 85% of new tree plantings are made on private lands; in Western Europe, private plantings increased forest cover by 30% between 1971 and 1990.[26]

The largest private U.S. landowner, International Paper, carefully balances public recreation (e.g., backpacking) with logging. In the Southeast, 25% of its profit is from recreation.[27] Industry grows 13% more timber than it cuts in order to prepare for future needs and increase future profits.[28] When we honor the choices of others, the desire for profit works hand-in-hand with sustainable environmental activities.

Slaughtering Wildlife

Governments often prevent individuals from claiming wildlife just as they prevent homesteading on land. In essence, wildlife management has become a public monopoly.

Tax subsidies to "manage" wildlife give it the characteristics of third-layer aggression. Subsidies have often paid for the killing of wildlife, sometimes to the point of near extinction.

By the 1990s, International Paper alone planted more than 48 million trees a year—five times more than it harvested—and donated or sold the rest for [the purpose of] additional reforestation.
—Larry Schweikart
THE ENTREPRENEURIAL ADVENTURE

At the peak of the 1,885 bounty period, Dr. C. Hart Merriman, chief of the U.S. Biological Survey, noted that Pennsylvania paid $90,000 in bounties for hawks that may have killed $1,875 worth of chickens. ... his calculations estimated that farmers lost nearly $4 million in grain crops because of increased rodent populations resulting from the decreased number of hawks. Merriman concluded, "In other words, the state has thrown away $2,105 for every dollar saved!"

—Robert J. Smith
Center for Private
Conservation

State governments encouraged the shooting of hawks. Some, like Pennsylvania paid hunters a tax-subsidized bounty. Aghast at this slaughter, Mrs. Rosalie Edge bought one of the hunters' favorite spot with voluntary contributions from like-minded people and turned it into a sanctuary. Hawk Mountain, in the Pennsylvania Appalachians, has been protecting hawks since 1934.[29]

In 1927, the owner of Sea Lion Caves, the only known mainland breeding and wintering area of the Stellar sea lion,[30] opened it to visitors as a naturalist attraction. Meanwhile, Oregon's tax dollars went to bounty hunters who were paid to shoot sea lions. The owners of Sea Lion Caves spent much of their time chasing hunters off their property. Although the owners of Sea Lion Caves and Hawk Mountain Sanctuary were protecting the wildlife on their land, they were also forced to pay the taxes that rewarded hunters who endangered it!

Not everyone in a group wants resources treated in the same way. When all people use their property as they think best, one owner's careless decision is unlikely to threaten the entire ecosystem. When bureaucrats control vast areas, however, one mistake can mean ecological disaster.

In addition, special interest groups struggle for control. For example, Yellowstone National Park, the crown jewel of the national park system, has been torn apart by conflicts of interest. In 1915, the Park Service decided to eradicate the Yellowstone wolves, which were deemed to be a menace to the elk, deer, antelope, and mountain sheep that visitors liked to see.[31] Park officials induced employees to trap wolves by allowing them to keep or sell the hides. Eventually, the fox, lynx, marten, and fisher were added to the list.[32] Without predators, the hoofed mammals flourished and began to compete with each other for food. The larger elk eventually drove out the white-tailed deer, the mule deer, the bighorn sheep, and the pronghorn. As their numbers increased, the elk ate the willow and aspen around the river banks and trampled the area so that seedlings could not regenerate.

Without the willow and aspen, the beaver population dwindled. Without the beavers and the ponds they created, water fowl, mink, and otter were threatened. The clear water needed by the trout disappeared along with the beaver dams. Without the ponds, the water table was lowered, decreasing the vegetation growth required to sustain many other species. When park officials realized their mistake, they began removing the elk (58,000 between 1935 and 1961).[33]

Meanwhile, the elk overgrazed, greatly reducing the shrubs and berries that fed the bear population. In addition, the destruction of willow and aspen destroyed the grizzly habitat, while road construction and beaver loss reduced the trout population on which the grizzlies fed. When the garbage dumps were closed in the 1960s to encourage the bears to feed naturally, little was left for them to eat. They began seeking out park visitors who brought food with them. Yellowstone management began a program to remove the problem bears as well. In the early 1970s, more than 100 bears were removed. Almost twice as many grizzlies were killed.[34]

Subsidies create tension between special interests with different views. Yellowstone visitors wanted to see deer and elk. Some naturalists would have preferred not to disturb the ecosystem, even if it meant limiting visitors and disappointing some of them. Since everyone is forced to subsidize the park, each person tries to impose his or her view as to how it should be run. The resulting compromise pleases no one.

Contributors to private conservation organizations, in contrast, choose to donate to a group that shares their common purpose. For example, at Pine Butte Preserve, the Nature Conservancy replanted overgrazed areas with chokecherry shrubs for the grizzlies and fenced off sensitive areas from cattle, deer, and elk—animals that thrive in the absence of predators.[35] The Nature Conservancy has preserved more than 2.4 million acres of land since 1951.[36]

The Audubon Society also uses ownership to protect the environment. The Rainey Wildlife Sanctuary in Louisiana is home to marshland deer, armadillo, muskrat, otter, mink, and

... government ownership has another kind of impact on society: it necessarily substitutes conflict for the harmony of the free market.
—Murray Rothbard
POWER AND MARKET

Ninety-eight percent of the ducks on this conti- nent are raised not on ref- uges, public wetlands, or waterfowl production projects but on privately owned land.

—Jim Kimball
former Minnesota
conservation
commissioner

snow geese. Carefully managed natural gas wells and cattle herds create wealth without interfering with the native species.[37] Other private organi- zations investing in wilderness areas for their voluntary membership include Ducks Unlimited, the National Wild Turkey Federation, the Na- tional Wildlife Federation, Trout Unlimited, and Wings Over Wisconsin.

The story of Ravena Park, Seattle, illustrates how aggression compromises the care given to the environment. In 1887, a couple bought up the land on which some giant Douglas firs grew, added a pavilion for nature lectures, and made walking paths with benches and totems depict- ing Indian culture. Visitors were charged admis- sion to support Ravena Park; up to 10,000 people came on the busiest days.

Some Seattle citizens weren't satisfied with this nonaggressive arrangement. They lobbied for the city to buy and operate the park with tax dollars—taken at gunpoint, if necessary. In 1911, the city took over the park, and one by one the giant fir trees began to disappear. Concerned citizens complained when they found that the trees were being cut into cordwood and sold. The superintendent, later charged with abuse of pub- lic funds, equipment, and personnel, told the citi- zens that the large "Roosevelt Tree" had posed a "threat to public safety." By 1925, all the giant fir trees were gone.[38] The superintendent could personally profit from the beautiful trees only by selling them, not by protecting them.

Power Corrupts

The above example succinctly illustrates the dangers of third-layer aggression. Subsidies give few bureaucrats the *power* to trade public assets for personal gain. Unlike the personal power that comes from wisdom, inner growth, and hard work, this power comes from the point of a gun. This power of aggression corrupts those who use it, impoverishes those who have little, and de- stroys the earth that supports us.

A Better Way

In earlier chapters, we saw how the aggres- sion of exclusive licensing inhibited innovation, increased costs, and lowered quality of service.

Adding another layer of aggression in the form of tax-funded subsidies encourages inefficiency and waste as well.

Ironically, we often sanction the aggression of exclusive, government-run monopolies because of the erroneous belief that they promote improved efficiency and prudent use of resources. Subsidies are sometimes tolerated in the equally mistaken belief that they allow the poor access to services they otherwise couldn't afford. The cost of aggression, however, is so great that the poor are harmed instead of helped.

Helping the Poor Pay Less

The poor do pay for these inefficient services, they simply don't do so directly. For example, those too poor to own their own home pay no property taxes, but their rent reflects the taxes that their landlords must pay. The poor pay higher rents to subsidize inefficiency and waste.

Privatizing Government Monopolies

Many countries with exclusive, subsidized government-run monopolies are realizing that aggression doesn't pay. They are privatizing these monopolies, including railways and highways, by selling them to investors or giving them to employees and citizens.[39]

In the early 1980s, for example, Britain privatized its oil, gas, coal, telecom, water, electrical power, and steel holdings, as well as its ports, railways, and airports. By 1992, two-thirds of state-owned businesses had been moved to the private sector. Although the newly privatized companies often laid off workers, by the late 1990s, Britain's unemployment rate was lower than Europe's.[40] More efficient wealth creation raised purchasing power, fueling the demand for more goods and services, thereby expanding employment opportunities.

Comprehensive studies in both developing and industrialized nations have confirmed the British experience. Privatization turns subsidized utilities and industries into profit-makers. Employment, on average, increases.[41]

Costs to consumers go down. For example, New Zealand, as well as Sweden and the Netherlands, has privatized its post office. Without

Today, in response to the high costs of control and the disillusionment with its effectiveness, governments are privatizing. It is the greatest sale in the history of the world.

—Daniel Yergin and
Joseph Stanislaw
THE COMMANDING
HEIGHTS

increasing rates, the private postal service was still able to maintain service to all addresses, increase on-time delivery of first-class mail from 84% to 99%, and transform an annual loss of $37 million to a profit of $76 million![42] Because losses before privatization were usually made up by the taxpayer, *real* postal rates actually went down as quality went up!

How can privatizing decrease costs so quickly? When provision of services is not restricted to a subsidized government monopoly, the profit motive spurs businesses to adopt the latest, most efficient technology possible. For example, instead of dumping refuse into landfills, waste disposal companies find ways of turning trash into cash. Recomp (St. Cloud, Minnesota) and Agripost (Miami, Florida) use composting whenever possible and sell the resulting loam to landscapers, Christmas tree farms, and reclamation projects. Other uses for the nutrient-rich compost include topsoil replacement for the farms, rangelands, and forests[43] that have been devastated by third-layer aggression.

Better quality at lower cost is only the beginning of the natural beauty of the marketplace ecosystem, however. Private companies can offer ownership to employees through stock options. Surly employees are transformed into dedicated service providers when they profit from their company's growth. Consequently, privatization increases employee output.[44]

Letting Everyone Win

Increased efficiency means more wealth creation, resulting in higher GDP and more employment.[45] Everyone wins: owners, employees, and consumers!

As noted in Chapter 2, higher GDP results in less poverty as well. Less inefficiency and waste mean more wealth for everyone! We can readily see why 40% of state-owned businesses throughout the world were privatized between 1979 and 2001.[46]

An Added Bonus: Retiring the National Debt

The equivalent of privatizing state-owned monopoly would be to sell state-owned land. If the money were used to retire the national debt, the taxes now used to service it would no longer be necessary. The decrease in wealth creation caused by taxation[47] would be reversed, and tremendous economic growth would result.

Some people don't worry much about the national debt because they believe we simply "owe it to ourselves." In a way, that is true. The government I.O.U.s are held by individuals, corporations, and pension plans (including Social Security and other government-sponsored retirement programs). For our pensions to pay us, taxes will have to increase to pay off these I.O.U.s. The net result is that we may have no pension at all!

To understand how we came to such an impasse, we should look at the apex of the Pyramid of Power—the money monopoly.

Chapter 8: Destroying the Environment

In Summary ...

- Third-layer aggression forces us to pay subsidies, usually to exclusive monopolies created by second-layer aggression.
- Subsidizing these monopolies, usually government services, increases costs, encourages waste, discourages conservation, and destroys the environment.
- Federal and state lands, which cover over 40% of the United States, are maintained through subsidies. The natural process of homesteading is stopped—at gunpoint, if necessary.
- Because the bureaucrats who supervise government lands do not profit by caring for them, special interest groups, such as loggers and ranchers are allowed to abuse them.
- When loggers and ranchers are allowed to own the forests and ranges, however, they take better care of the land.
- Similarly, when bureaucrats control our parks, they upset the ecological balance as they did in Yellowstone. Some states even subsidized bounties to kill hawks and other predators.
- Private parks, like Sea Lion Caves and Hawk Mountain Sanctuary, do a better job of protecting wildlife.
- When Ravenna Park was under private ownership, the giant Douglas firs were protected. A few years after the city took over the park, the beautiful trees were all cut down for cordwood.
- Since people protect the environment when they own a piece of it, privatizing our parks would ensure better care. When we end the subsidies that make parks and government monopolies possible, we get better service for lower cost.
- Privatizing government-owned services gives us more for less. Privatizing government-owned lands might even retire the national debt, while protecting our ecological heritage.

Chapter 9

Banking on Aggression

We established the "money monopoly" in the hope of creating economic stability. By using aggression as our means, we created boom-and-bust cycles instead.

Fourth-layer aggression—forced use of subsidized, exclusive monopolies—creates the controlling apex of the Pyramid of Power. One example of fourth-layer aggression is the money monopoly, a central bank with an exclusive license to issue currency. By empowering the money monopoly, we have created inflationary boom-and-bust cycles, which redistribute wealth from the poor to the rich. Let's learn how the apex of the Pyramid of Power controls us with this sleight of hand.

How the Marketplace Ecosystem Sets Prices

Earlier we learned that wealth consists of goods and services. Money is a claim check on the goods and services that constitute wealth. The more money people have, the more goods and services they are able to claim (buy).

The price is the amount of money that we pay to buy a particular item. Prices tell us how abundant and desirable a particular item is. For example, when farmers have a bad year, the harvest is poor and prices rise to reflect scarcity. When farmers have a good year, and food is abundant, prices decline. Grocery prices fluctuate when supplies do.

If a valuable resource, such as oil, became scarce, oil producers would raise their prices as demand began to outstrip supply. To avoid high fuel bills, consumers would cut back on their usage, insulate their homes, car pool, and take other steps to conserve. If a new supply of oil was suddenly discovered, producers would lower prices accordingly.

New ways of creating wealth also lower prices. When Rockefeller's staff developed new refining technologies, oil could be processed more efficiently and inexpensively. Wealth creation lowers prices.

As Rockefeller discovered (Chapter 7), prices can't be kept artificially high. The marketplace ecosystem sets them naturally with supply and demand.

How Money Was Born

Historically, gold and silver were used as money because they could easily and accurately be coined or weighed. Moreover, in societies where precious metals were made into jewelry or used industrially, gold and silver were goods as well. They served both as wealth and money.

As people prospered, carrying gold and silver around became burdensome. People began to deposit their gold and silver with bankers. Some bankers simply charged a fee for this service. Others found that if they loaned part of the gold to someone else, interest could be collected and shared between the bank and the depositor.

Bankers gave depositors a promissory note, which was a pledge to return the gold "on demand." A bank with many customers could usually keep this promise, because everyone would not want to withdraw money at the same time.

In the interim, the depositor could exchange the promissory note for goods and services as if it were gold. Thus, promissory notes began to function as money or claim checks for the available goods and services. The currencies of most western nations were once notes of this type, redeemable with stored gold and silver.

How Banks Create Money

Because everyone did not want their gold and silver at the same time, banks kept a portion of the precious metal on reserve and loaned out the rest. In doing so, they "created" money. Today's banks still create money this way, although they use additional methods as well.

For example, assume that your bank needs to put 20% of its funds on reserve to operate optimally. You deposit $1,000 in your favorite bank; the bank puts $200 into reserve and loans out the other $800. The person who borrowed the $800 deposits it in a bank account. That person's bankbook says he or she has $800. Yours says you have $1,000. Together, the two of you have $1,800 in the bank. But wait: only $1,000 is there to begin with! The bank has "created" the $800 it lends out!

Next, the bank puts 20% of the newly deposited $800 (i.e., $160) in reserve and lends out the remaining $640, which is then redeposited and goes through the same process. When the reserve is 20%, the $1,000 eventually becomes $5,000. The lower the reserve requirement, the more money is created. For example, when the required reserve is 10%, every deposit is multiplied by 10 instead of 5. How amazed I was when my father, a bank manager and economics teacher, first explained this process, called "fractional reserve banking," to me!

How Banks Cause Inflation and Deflation

Creating this extra money can cause price inflation when there is no compensating increase in goods and services. To appreciate how this happens, imagine yourself at an auction where you and your neighbors bid for food, clothes, and other necessities. Such an auction is essentially a smaller version of the marketplace.

After you've attended the auction several times, you can anticipate how much your favorite items will be. However, if George's wealthy cousin leaves him a big inheritance, George has more money and can bid higher. The prices you must pay at auction go up.

The increase in the money available at the auction drives up prices by increasing demand. Initially, supply is not affected. We use the word "inflation" to describe price increases triggered by an increase in the money supply.

Deflation is the opposite process. If George and several of your neighbors go on vacation, you'll have fewer people to bid against. You'll probably be able to buy what you want for less. The decrease in the money available at the auction drives down prices by decreasing demand.

How Inflation and Deflation Work

Banks can cause price inflation and deflation by changing the amount of money that they create. When banks expand the money supply, prices rise just as they do when George brings his inheritance to the auction. When banks contract the money supply, prices fall just as they do in the auction when your neighbors go on vacation. In real life, however, the inflation and

Whoever controls the volume of money in any country is absolute master of all industry and commerce.

—James A. Garfield
U.S. president,
assassinated in 1882

deflation caused by changes in the money supply don't affect everyone equally.

For example, immediately after you deposit your $1,000 in the bank, the bank could send a representative to the auction. The bank knows from past auctions that you usually spend less than $200. Consequently, the bank can bid up to $800 with your money and not be caught short when you make your withdrawal. Your $1,000 deposit has already created an extra $800 that works against you and other bidders to the bank's advantage.

If the bank puts 10% of your deposit on reserve and lends out the rest, your $1,000 will turn into $10,000. The people who borrow this money can come to the auction and bid against you too. Prices become *inflated,* so you are able to buy less with your original $1,000.

By allowing extra money to be created from your savings, you unwittingly decrease its buying power. On the other hand, the buying power of the bankers and the borrowers grows.

Of course, you can become a borrower too. You buy a house because continuous inflation means a continuous increase in housing prices. However, the interest that you pay on the mortgage probably negates much of the anticipated appreciation that comes from inflation.

Because real property appreciates with inflation and money loses its value, more families will use their money to buy homes. The extra demand drives up prices. The higher housing prices mean some people will no longer be able to afford them.

If banks raise the reserve rate, interest rates go up and fewer people borrow money to buy homes. Now the price of houses stagnates or even declines.

Realtors, builders, and other people who depend upon house sales for a living are now making less money. Consequently, they buy less too. Businesses that sell to them must cut back on production. People are laid off and can't make their house payments. With the decline in home prices, some people can't even sell their home for enough to cover their mortgage, so the bank forecloses. Depending upon its severity, the "bust" that follows the "boom" is called either a recession or a depression.

Clearly, anyone who can't anticipate these cycles can be financially devastated. However, since interest rates can be changed overnight for totally political reasons, these cycles can't be anticipated by the public. Consequently, we are constantly at risk.

In most developed nations, the banking system alternates high inflation with moderate deflation. Without alternating the cycles, inflation would run rampant, as it has in several Third World countries. In nations with rapid inflation, prices rise hourly! Workers in such countries rush to buy necessities as soon as they receive their paycheck. Hyperinflation can be so bad that a wheelbarrow of currency is required to make a purchase![1]

The Myth of "Stimulating" the Economy

We often hear that inflation "stimulates" the economy to grow, but the "fix" is temporary and accompanied by the backlash of recession or even depression.

Inflation expands the money supply, and prices rise. Suppliers increase supply to meet the new demand. They hire more employees to make the new product, causing wages to rise as well.

Workers are excited by their higher wages, but their raises are offset by the increase in product prices. Indeed, workers have already started paying higher prices by the time the demand for their labor increases. Product prices drive the demand for labor, so wages are always one step behind prices. Inflation hurts workers, while appearing to benefit them.

Eventually, the banks slow the creation of money to prevent hyperinflation. The "hangover" from "stimulating" the economy is invariably a recession, or even a depression. Consequently, *inflation slows wealth creation.*[2]

Marketplace Ecosystem Protects the Consumer

Luckily, the marketplace ecosystem regulates banks in the absence of aggression so that the destructive boom–bust cycles are minimized.

It isn't unusual for South American shoppers to see the price of bread increase between the time they enter a grocery store and the time they leave it.
    —Gerald Swanson
    associate professor,
    University of Arizona

... an increase by 10 percentage points in the inflation rate is associated on impact with a decline by 0.3 percentage point in the annual growth rate of GDP.
    —Robert Barro
    economics professor,
    Harvard University

The banking system in Scotland between 1793 and 1845, for example, was almost entirely free from aggression.[3] Each bank issued its own money, promising to return depositors' gold on demand or with interest if the customer had to wait.[4]

This situation could have been very confusing. However, banks accepted the money of other banks as if it were their own. In Scotland, banks were Good Neighbors and had to make good on their promises. If a bank ran out of reserves, its owners (stockholders) had to pay the depositors out of their own pockets. Bank owners, therefore, were highly motivated to control the creation of new money. When both new wealth and new money were created at the same rate, prices remained stable.

Occasionally, however, a bank would foolishly print so many notes that it could not meet depositors' demands. If the stockholders of a failing bank were unlikely to be able to pay off their debts, sound banks sometimes did so to retain the confidence of the Scottish people and gain grateful new customers.[5] Scottish prosperity was attributed in part to the efficient banking system that evolved in the absence of aggression-through-government.[6]

Between 1793 and 1933, Canada, Sweden, Australia, China, and South Africa had periods when their banking systems also operated relatively free from government regulation. In contrast, U.S., English, French, German, and Italian banks were subjected to more aggressive licensing laws.

In the United States, for example, banks often had to keep government securities as part of their reserve, limiting their available cash and making them vulnerable when depositors needed large amounts of currency. Because banks were often prohibited from having multiple sites or branches, high depositor demands in one locale could not be offset by low demands elsewhere.[7] In some countries, one central bank was given an exclusive monopoly. Because of this interference with the marketplace, banks hindered by aggression had *eight times as many crises* as those which operated with more freedom from

It was the combination of bond deposit provision and the fiscal instability of some states that was the root cause of most of the "free bank" failures. The failures were a case of government rather than market failure.

—Kevin Dowd
professor, Sheffield
Hallam University

it (Figure 9.1)![8] When crises did occur in the relatively free banking systems, they were usually less severe as well.[9]

Banking Regulations Bankrupt Americans

Unfortunately, the U.S. banking system was never free from aggression. In 1914, however, even more aggression was instituted. The Federal Reserve (Fed) was given an exclusive monopoly to issue U.S. currency. Like AT&T, the Fed is a private corporation, owned by its member banks. The Fed is a powerful institution; some believe it is the most powerful in the world. Let's find out why.

Before the creation of the Fed, banks needed reserves of approximately 21% to have enough money to cover customer withdrawals. When the Fed took over the reserves of the national banks, it slashed the reserve requirement in half.[10] The Fed itself kept only 35% of the money entrusted

When the President signs this bill, the invisible government of the Monetary Power will be legalized.
—Congressman Charles A. Lindbergh, 1913 referring to the Federal Reserve Act

Figure 9.1: Countries with Less Aggressive Banking Systems Have Fewer Crises

Countries with More Aggression	Period	Number of Crises	Crises/100 Years
United States	1793–1933	18	12.9
United Kingdom	1793–1933	8	5.7
France	1847–1933	6	7.0
Germany	1857–1933	5	6.6
Italy	1893–1933	4	10.4
			Average 8.4

Countries with Less Aggression	Period	Number of Crises	Crises/100 Years
Canada	1819–1933	3	2.6
Scotland	1793–1933	1	0.7
Sweden	1833–1933	1	1.0
China	1891–1933	1	0.0
South Africa	1833–1933	1	1.0
Australia	1819–1933	0	0.9
			Average 1.0

Data from G. Selgin, *Bank Deregulation and Monetary Order* (New York: Routledge, 1996), pp. 195–200.

If the American people ever allow banks to control the issuance of their currency, first by inflation, then by deflation, the corporation that will grow up around them will deprive the people of all of their property until their children will wake up homeless on the continent their forefathers conquered.

—Thomas Jefferson
author of the
Declaration of
Independence

This great government, strong in gold, is breaking its promises to pay gold to widows and orphans. ... It's dishonor, sir.

—Senator Carter Glass,
1933
principal author of the
Federal Reserve Act

Governmental intervention in monetary matters, far from providing the stable monetary framework for a free market that is its ultimate justification, has proved a potent source of instability.

—Milton Friedman
Nobel Prize laureate,
Economics

to it on reserve.[11] The balance was loaned out, mostly to the government, with the wealth of the American people as collateral.

Lowering reserves created more money. As a result, the money supply doubled between 1914 and 1920[12] and once again from 1921 to 1929.[13] In contrast, gold in the reserve vault increased only 3% in the 1920s.[14] The bankers would obviously be unable to return gold to depositors if a large number of people were to withdraw their money at the same time.

Businesses could not use all the newly created money, so banks encouraged stock speculators to borrow.[15] Many people got heavily into debt, thinking that the boom would continue.

In 1929, the Fed started deflation by slowing the creation of new money.[16] People who had counted on renewing their loans to cover stock speculations or other investments found that they could no longer borrow. They were forced to sell their securities, and a stock market plunge ensued.

People who lost money spent less on goods and services; business began to slow. With banks unwilling to renew loans,[17] businesses began to reduce their work force. People nervously began withdrawing their gold deposits as banks in other countries quit honoring their promise to return depositors' gold. Rumors circulated that the Federal Reserve would soon be bankrupt as well,[18] and that President Franklin D. Roosevelt might devalue the dollar.[19] If that happened, customers would receive only a fraction of the gold that they had deposited.

Eager to get their gold before the paper currency lost value, people began withdrawing their funds. A run on the banks began wiping out reserves. Naturally, banks couldn't exchange all of the inflated dollars for gold.

Had this situation happened in Scotland between 1793 and 1845, bank owners (stockholders) would have had to pay depositors, even if it meant digging into their own pockets. In the United States, however, the government made the American citizenry pay instead!

In 1933, Congress made gold ownership a crime.[20] Americans were forced to exchange their valuable coins and bullion for Federal Reserve notes, which had no intrinsic value. Foreigners could still exchange their dollars for gold, but Americans could not!

The Federal Reserve's manipulation of the currency supply was a major contributor to the Great Depression. Other forms of aggression, notably tariffs (see Chapter 18), played a role as well. Nevertheless, *one study estimated that the Federal Reserve's money monopoly aggravated the crisis ten-fold!*[21]

Even before the Fed started contracting the money supply, U.S. banks were already in trouble. A number of regulations, most notably the restrictions on branch banking, created a wave of failures from 1921 to 1929. During that same time, however, no Canadian banks failed. American depositors lost an estimated $565 million, while Canadian losses were less than 3% of that.[22]

Canada enjoyed a banking system similar to the one described earlier for Scotland—few licensing laws, negligible restrictions on branch banking, and no central bank with an exclusive monopoly on currency issue.[23] Each bank issued its own notes, thereby protecting itself and its depositors from rampant money creation. Just as in Scotland, the stockholders of Canadian banks were obligated to make good the inflated currency. Unfortunately for Canada, aggressive regulations were instituted in 1935.[24]

The Rich Get Richer

Why did the Canadians abandon the system that protected them from bankruptcy? Why did England eventually impose its inferior system of aggressive regulations on Scotland? Why was the Fed introduced in the United States and relieved of its promise to return gold that was deposited by our great-great-grandparents and their contemporaries? Why did the Fed slow money creation in 1929, precipitating the stock market crash? Why does the Fed alternate inflation and deflation at the expense of the American public today?

Several authors have proposed that the evolution of central banks represents a collusion

Depressions and mass unemployment are not caused by the free market but by government interference in the economy.
—Ludwig von Mises
THE THEORY OF MONEY
AND CREDIT

Every effort has been made by the Fed to conceal its power but the truth is—the Fed has usurped the government. It controls everything here and it controls all our foreign relations. It makes and breaks governments at will.
—Congressman Louis T. McFadden
chairman, Banking and Currency Committee, 1933

The entire banking reform movement, at all crucial stages, was centralized in the hands of a few men who for years were linked, ideologically and personally, with one another.
—Gabriel Kolko
THE TRIUMPH OF CONSERVATISM

The bold effort the present bank had made to control government, the distress it had wantonly produced ... are but premonitions of the fate that awaits the American people should they be deluded into a perpetuation of this institution or establishment of another like it.
—President Andrew Jackson

between politicians and a small elite who control the major banking institutions.[25] Bank owners want to create as much money as possible, without having to dig into their own pockets when depositors want their money. Politicians long to fulfill their grandiose campaign promises without visibly taxing their constituency. Central banking can give both groups what they want.

Through the aggression of exclusive licensing, politicians give the central bank a monopoly on issuing currency. As long as banks must make good on their promises to depositors, however, they are still subject to the regulation of the marketplace ecosystem. The politicians grant corporations limited liability (see Chapter 13, "The Other Piece of the Puzzle" for further details) so that owners and managers who make risky loans can simply walk away from their mistakes, as President George W. Bush's brother Neil did.[26] Depositors either lose their life savings or are reimbursed with taxes taken from their neighbors.

The bankers, of course, must give the politicians something in return for their currency monopoly and limited liability. Bankers lend the government a great deal of the Fed's newly created money. When special interest groups want more subsidies, our representatives pacify them with borrowed money rather than an unpopular tax increase. The special interest groups thank the politicians by funding their reelection.

Like any special interest group, the Fed helps politicians who protect it. By manipulating the money supply to cause boom or bust, the Fed controls the illusion of prosperity—an illusion which can determine which politicians people will vote for or against.

For example, the exclusive monopoly of the Second Bank of the United States, an earlier but temporary central bank, was scheduled to end in 1836. Andrew Jackson swore not to renew its charter if he were reelected president in 1832. Soon after his victory, he removed the government's deposits from the Second Bank.

The bank's president, Nicholas Biddle, tried to create a depression by cutting back on the creation of money, just as the Federal Reserve would do almost 100 years later. Biddle hoped to blackmail Congress into renewing the banks' monopoly by making voters miserable. Fortunately, the American people were not fooled, and the bank charter was not renewed.[27] Unfortunately, this lesson was forgotten, and central banking was reestablished with the Federal Reserve.

A Lose–Lose Situation

The price we pay for the money monopoly is staggering. In the 50 years prior to the creation of the Federal Reserve, we experienced a small, gradual deflation as banks created money at a pace somewhat slower than wealth creation (Figure 9.2). After the Fed was given a currency monopoly, the money supply inflated rapidly and the dollar's purchasing power decreased. During the Great Depression, the collapse of the stock market and bank failures deflated the money supply.

After 1933, when the Fed no longer had to give depositors gold, it could inflate the currency without limit. Consequently, the Federal Reserve created money faster than new wealth was produced. As a result, prices rose and money lost over 90% of its value between 1933 and 2000.

In other words, 90% of the new wealth created in this time period has been taken from the American public, primarily for the benefit of bankers and borrowers. *The largest borrower is the U.S. government, so inflation acts like a hidden tax.*

If we lose so much of our wealth to the money monopoly, how has our country's standard of living risen so much since 1933? The answer: wealth creation is so rapid that we come out ahead even when most of it is taken from us. Instead of living well, we could instead be living like royalty without the inflation tax!

The Poor Get Poorer

Inflation hurts those on fixed incomes the most. For example, if inflation continues at the rate shown in Figure 9.2, if George retired in 2000 on $2,000 per month, he would be able to

History shows that the money changers have used every form of abuse, intrigue, deceit, and violent means possible to maintain control over governments by controlling the money and the issuance of it.

—James A. Madison
fourth U.S. president

By a continuous process of inflation, governments can confiscate, secretly and unobserved, an important part of the wealth of their citizens. ... The process engages all the hidden forces of economic law on the side of destruction, and does it in a manner which not one man in a million is able to diagnose.

—John Maynard Keynes
English economist and board member of the Bank of England

buy only half as much with his money in 2020. The lost value of $1,000 per month is a devastating inflation tax for George. An income that was adequate, even comfortable, could easily become too little to pay for food and rent!

Most of George's lost buying power ends up with the banks. Those who borrow may reap some of George's loss as well. Because governments are the biggest borrowers, they, along with the banks, capture most of the losses suffered by people who live on a fixed income.

People with property have partial protection from inflation, since the value of the goods they own rises along with prices. Naturally, the poor own little of this "inflation insurance."

Without the money monopoly, politicians would be unable to borrow the large sums of money that create deficits. Without these deficits, the enforcement of licensing laws and the provision of special interest subsidies could be financed only by more taxes. Taxpayers would

Figure 9.2: The Inflation Tax

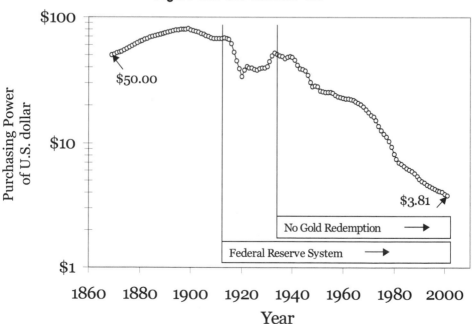

Purchasing power of the dollar in the period 1869–1912 is based on the Implicit Price Index of Kuznets as reported in Table B-2 of *Capital in the American Economy* by Kuznets. For purchasing power in the period 1913–2001, the urban consumer price index (CPI-U) of the U. S. Bureau of Labor Statistics is used.

be unlikely to support subsidies and waste if their true cost was reflected in their tax bills.

By redistributing wealth from those who have little to those who have much, the money monopoly increases the gap between rich and poor. When everyone is forced to use the money monopoly to pay taxes and settle debts," central banks like the Fed become so powerful that they control the economic fate of the entire nation. Virtually overnight, they can send us reeling into a depression or hyperinflation simply by manipulating the money supply.

We can hardly blame selfish bankers for this state of affairs, however, if we elect politicians who promise to fund our favorite programs. However, we usually expect that other taxpayers will be forced to shoulder part of the burden so that we don't have to. Politicians who tell us that we can't have something for nothing are rarely elected, so they obligingly use the money monopoly to hide the truth from us.

How can we blame the owners of the Federal Reserve for wanting the same exclusive monopoly with which we favored AT&T? How can we blame them for seeking the same subsidies that we are willing to give the ranchers and timber companies? Like our biblical ancestors in the Garden of Eden, we want to blame the serpent because we ate the apple. As always, the choice and responsibility belong to us.

The fragility and instability of real-world banking systems is not a free market phenomenon but a consequence of legal restrictions.

—George Selgin
BANK DEREGULATION AND
MONETARY ORDER

A Better Way

Clearly, if we wish to minimize boom-and-bust cycles, our banking system needs to be free from aggression. Bank failures may still occasionally happen, but they won't be as frequent or as devastating as they are today. The demise of the Second Bank of the United States demonstrates that central banking charters can be revoked when we choose to say "No!" to the money monopoly.

A modern banking system free from aggression might be similar to the Scottish system described earlier.[28] Because owners/managers could be liable if the bank lost its depositors' money, they would probably buy liability insurance to protect themselves and their depositors.

A successful self-regulating system of bank liability insurance is much more than a pipedream; it is the mechanism that characterizes the only successful liability insurance systems in the historical record.
    —Charles W. Calomiris
    ECONOMIC PERSPECTIVES

Unlike the Federal Deposit Insurance Corporation (FDIC) or the Federal Saving and Loan Insurance Corporation (FSLIC) of today, premiums would differ for each institution, depending on how well each bank invested its depositors' money. Poor managers would be saddled with high premiums, just as poor automobile drivers are today. As premiums went up and profits went down, poor managers would be fired.

Today, each bank, by law, pays the same premium regardless of the way it does business. Managers can make risky loans that generate high closing fees, letting the taxpayer pick up the tab if the loan isn't repaid. Consequently, *states that have such mandatory deposit insurance have more bank failures than states with voluntary or no deposit insurance.*[29]

When the taxpayers shoulder the bill, it can wipe out a family's entire savings. Every man, woman, and child in the United States will pay an average of $6,000 to cover savings and loan defaults of the 1990s.[30] With a banking system free from aggression, the working class would no longer subsidize the failures of investors and money managers.

The marketplace ecosystem is already creating alternatives to the money monopoly. For example, e-gold converts currency into precious metals (gold, silver, palladium, or platinum) and stores it for depositiors.[31] The company facilitates buying and selling among its depositors. Popularization of such programs would effectively reduce the inflation tax.

Several programs for buying services with time rather than money are also evolving. With Time Dollars,[32] for example, George might mow our lawn and "bank" the hour he spent doing so. Later, if he needs someone to mend his clothes, a neighbor might trade him an hour of sewing for his banked "Time Dollar" in exchange. When she needs a baby-sitter, she trades her Time Dollar for an hour of baby-sitting.

Several time trading programs have begun in various communities that allow for negotiation. For example, a physician might want to trade a 15 minute office visit for a full hour of baby-sitting, a reasonable exchange since years of training go into doctoring.[33]

Because people "bank" their hours, a baby-sitter in Seattle could trade her time for a resume written by a wordsmith in New York. Although most hours are traded locally, a national network could become popular as well.

Bankers can't inflate our time and precious metals as they inflate our currencies. In spite of all the aggression stacked against it, the marketplace ecosystem may yet save us from the Pyramid of Power that we have created!

Chapter 9: Banking on Aggression

In Summary ...

- One example of fourth-layer aggression is the Federal Reserve, an exclusive, subsized monopoly on currency issue. We are forced to use the Fed's currency "for all debts, public and private."
- When banks lend, they expand the money supply, causing inflation. When banks slow lending, the creation of money slows too, causing deflation. By manipulating the money supply, banks can control a nation's economy.
- For example, the Second Bank of the United States, a precursor of the Fed, tried to create a depression when President Andrew Jackson refused to renew its charter.
- The Federal Reserve is subsidized invisibly by devaluing the currency through expansion of the money supply. Between 1933 and 2000, this "inflation tax" was more than 90% of all newly created wealth.
- People without property, such as the poor and those on fixed incomes, pay most of the inflation tax. At current rates, the inflation tax on retirees will cost them half of their purchasing power over the next 20 years.
- In essence, the inflation tax redistributes wealth from the poor to the rich.
- The Federal Reserve is supposed to protect us from booms and busts. However, highly regulated banking systems, like the Fed, have *eight times* as many crises as banking systems free from aggression.
- In the past, "free" banks expanded the money supply carefully since they, not the taxpayers, were obligated to make up any shortfalls. Consequently, prices were more stable as money and wealth creation proceeded at approximately the same rate.
- The marketplace is reacting to the inflation tax by creating alternative currencies based on precious metals or work hours.

Chapter 10

Learning Lessons Our Schools Can't Teach

**How can our children learn to be Good Neighbors when
we teach them in a school system built on aggression?**

The Bitter Fruits of Aggression

In the past 100 years, technological progress has been amazing. At the turn of the twentieth century, horses were still the mainstay of the transportation industry. Today, automobiles and planes take us all over the world. Letters used to take weeks to cross a continent; today, e-mail is delivered within minutes to any place on earth. Just a few generations ago, people died from simple infections. Today, with modern nutrition, antibiotics, and sanitation, infection is rarely fatal. In most arenas, radical progress has been made over the past century. Unfortunately, our educational system is one of the few exceptions.

In the early 1900s, our great-grandparents trudged off to the neighborhood school. For the better part of the day, the teacher stood in front of the class, chalk in hand, to expound on lessons contained in the schoolbooks. Today, our children take cars or buses to school, but once there, students listen as the teacher stands in front of the class to expound on the lessons contained in the schoolbooks. The facilities are newer, the chalk has become a whiteboard marker, and the curriculum includes some additional subjects, but otherwise our schools are still stuck in the horse-and-buggy days.

The cost of doing things the same old way, however, has skyrocketed. The United States, for example, spent 14 times as much per pupil in 1996 as in 1920, even after adjusting for inflation,[1] yet educational surveys find the United States to be "A Nation at Risk."[2] Almost 25% of our high school students do not graduate, and another 25% know too little to get a job or go to college.[3] By 1997, 20% of companies had to teach their new employees reading, writing, and arithmetic even though most of the new people hired had high school diplomas![4]

Literacy in the United States is on a steep decline. Before the end of World War II in 1945, 18 million men were tested to see if they could

In no other industry in U.S. history has there been so little technological change as in the field of public school education.
—National Center for Policy Analysis
THE FAILURE OF OUR PUBLIC SCHOOLS: THE CAUSES AND A SOLUTION

... it isn't just cheap labor that's attracting companies to India, Ireland, or the Philippines—it's their "educated, trainable workers."
—SCHOOL REFORM NEWS
April 1998

read well enough to be soldiers. Only 4% failed. By 1952, during the Korean War, 19% of the men tested were turned away as illiterate. The U.S. Army hired psychologists to find out how high school graduates were faking illiteracy, only to discover that they really couldn't read![5] By the end of the Vietnam War in 1973, 27% of potential inductees read too poorly to be accepted.[6]

Reading isn't the only arena in which our students are doing poorly. During international competition, U.S. eighth graders were asked, "Here are the ages of five children: 13, 8, 6, 4, 4. What is the average age of these children?" The correct answer, 7, was one of the multiple choice answers, yet an embarrassing 60% of the U.S. students missed it.[7]

Perhaps students have difficulty with tests because their teachers do too. Some states now require instructors to pass literacy tests themselves. In 1998, 59% of would-be teachers in Massachusetts failed the test, even though they were college graduates and the test's difficulty was at the junior high level.[8]

Fourth-Layer Aggression: Monopoly Education

We shouldn't be too surprised that both our students and teachers are floundering academically. After all, our schools are examples of fourth-layer aggression, exclusive, subsidized monopolies that we are forced to use. All schools, even the more flexible private and home schools, must meet requirements of the state's licensing boards, which usually dictate the core curriculum, the hours and years of attendance, the list of acceptable textbooks, and the educational standards for teachers.[9] The result is predictable. The aggressive education monopoly gives us high prices, low quality, and little innovation.

Government education is heavily subsidized by taxes. Subsidies encourage waste. As a result, public schools consume twice as many dollars in operating costs as do private ones,[10] even though private school students consistently do better academically. Increasing the public school budgets does not improve learning and may even have a negative effect.[11]

Decreasing literacy means that our children have fewer skills with which to create wealth. If learning hadn't declined after World War II, the United States would have been 39% richer by 1989.[12]

School-age children are forced—at gunpoint, if necessary—to attend a licensed school. Because we want all children to get a good education, we view tuition-free public schools and mandatory attendance as a way to ensure that neglectful parents don't deny their children this valuable asset.

As always, aggression gives us results we'd rather not have. Specifically, fourth-layer aggression, which forces our children to use the subsidized, exclusive monopoly service, gives others control of what the children are taught. Literacy is no longer a priority.

The Most Literate Nation in the World

In the 1800s, Americans were considered to be among the most literate people in the world. A visiting French aristocrat, Alexis de Tocqueville, claimed that the new nation had the best educated people in history.[13] The complex novel *Last of the Mohicans*, published in 1818, sold five million copies[14] at a time when the U.S. population was less than 20 million.[15] By 1840, literacy in the North and South, exclusive of the slave population, was over 90% and 80%, respectively.[16] In other words, literacy was more prevalent than it is today!

Schooling was neither compulsory nor free, although private "charity" schools provided education to those too poor to afford formal instruction.[17] Many of those schools taught hundreds of children at a time, using a monitoring method pioneered by the British Quaker schoolmaster Joseph Lancaster. The teacher would instruct several older children, and they, in turn, would instruct others under the teacher's supervision. Lancaster perfected his method so that he was able to teach a thousand pupils at one time—for free![18]

Schools could try new and better methods of teaching because the licensing requirements for instructors and schools were few. Students left if they didn't learn, so the marketplace ecosystem regulated schools without aggression, which allowed for innovative improvements.

In no country in the world is the taste for reading so diffuse as among the common people of America.
—Per Siljestromm
Swedish visitor, 1853

When I perceive that many boys in our school have been taught to read and write in two months who did not before know the alphabet ... and when I perceive on great assembly of a thousand children under the eye of a single teacher ... I confess that I recognize in Lancaster the benefactor of the human race.
—DeWitt Clinton
founder of the New York Free School Society and governor of New York

In 1812, Pierre Du Pont de Nemours published "Education in the United States." ... Du Pont said that fewer than four of every thousand people in the new nation could not read or do numbers well.
—John T. Gatto
1991 New York State Teacher of the Year

Before 1850, when Massachusetts became the first state in the United States to force children to go to school, literacy was at 98 percent.
—Sheldon Richman
SEPARATING SCHOOL AND STATE

Our purpose it to teach our students to be responsible adults who will be of benefit to society.
—posted in every classroom, Mililani High School, Mililani, Hawaii

In the early 1800s, Boston had schools that were partially tax-supported, but twice as many children attended the private ones. Admission to public schools required that students *already* know how to read and write. They were usually taught these basic skills either by their family, a tutor, or a private school.[19]

An 1817 survey revealed that over 90% of Boston's children attended some type of local school.[20] Education in America was so readily available that school attendance didn't change in New York City when it began offering tax-subsidized, tuition-free public education.[21]

Parents had a variety of schools to chose from, especially among institutions not subject to the conditions attached to state support. Some schools prepared students for the university, and some taught trades. Some schools provided a broad-based education, while others focused on a particular area of expertise. Private tutoring was available for those unable to attend ordinary day school, and some children were taught by their parents or older siblings. The marketplace ecosystem, free from aggression, provided education to fit every budget and schedule. Parents voted with their dollars to support the educators who served them best. In this way, parents determined both the content and process by which their children would be educated.

Aggression Disrupts the Marketplace Ecosystem

Clearly, private education and the literacy it produced were virtually universal by the mid-1800s in the United States. How then did tax-supported compulsory education evolve?

Supporters of a uniform system of "American" education hoped to mold immigrant children into their idea of proper citizens. If public schools were tax-supported and didn't need to charge much tuition, immigrants might send their children to the "free" schools instead of the private ones that they generally favored.

Of course, tax support meant that parents would be forced to turn over their hard-earned dollars over to the public schools. Only the wealthy could then afford to send their children to private institutions. Like the serpent in the

Garden of Eden, the so-called reformers tempted the American citizenry to use aggression against the new immigrants, presumably to create harmony throughout the land.

Many immigrants had come to the United States to escape this holier-than-thou attitude. In spite of the additional financial burden, struggling immigrants made great sacrifices to educate their children as they saw fit rather than send them to inexpensive or even free public schools. Catholics saw the public schools as vehicles for Protestant propaganda and established parochial schools; German immigrants sent their children to private institutions when the public ones refused to teach them in German as well as in English. Immigrants who wanted their children to learn their native tongue and their Old World history opted for private or parochial schools that catered to their preferences.[22]

Schools Built on Aggression Teach It

The willingness of poor parents to send their children to private instead of public school tells us how highly they valued education, specifically education that reflected their beliefs and culture. Many people had come to the United States for a chance to pull themselves away from the poverty trap spun by Europe's guild-style licensing laws and other forms of aggression. Perhaps they didn't want their children in schools that were created by the aggression from which they had recently fled. Perhaps they feared that schools built on aggression would teach aggression. If that seems farfetched, consider your own education. As you've read through the past few chapters, have you been saying to yourself, "That's not the way my teachers told me the world worked"?

Can you imagine a school system funded by taxation hiring a teacher who equated taxation with theft? Hardly! Consequently, our children are instructed by teachers who believe that first-strike force, fraud, or theft is acceptable as long as it's for a good cause. An obvious underlying assumption of this philosophy is that the ends are not influenced by the means used to obtain them. To parents with an enlightened view of

A general State education is a mere contrivance for molding people to be exactly alike one another; and as the mold in which it casts them is that which pleases the predominant power in government, whether this be a monarch, a priesthood, an aristocracy, or a majority of the existing generation; in proportion as it is efficient and successful, it establishes a despotism over the mind, leading by a natural tendency to one over the body.

—John Stuart Mill
English philosopher

By this mode of education, we prepare our youth for the subordination of laws and thereby qualify them for becoming good citizens of the republic. ... Let our pupil be taught that he does not belong to himself, but that he is public property.

—Benjamin Rush, 1786
signer, Declaration of Independence and public school advocate

how the world works, this idea is analogous to teaching their child that $2 + 2 = 5$!

We interpret facts according to our world view. If our interpretation is correct, we can predict which actions will take us to our goal. We will be able to create peace and plenty in our hearts, our families, our communities, and our world. If our interpretation is faulty, we will create problems instead of solving them. No wonder parents who wanted the best for their children were willing to make great sacrifices to send them to a school that would complement their home instruction.

... public schooling often ends up to be little more than majoritarian domination of minority viewpoints.

—Robert B. Everhart
professor of Education,
University of California,
Santa Barbara

One-Size-Fits-All Education

If the law demanded that all children must receive an education, it also needed to define exactly what constituted one. School boards, not parents, decided what children would learn. Because school boards were drawn from the upper class and professional groups, the curriculum was often geared toward a liberal arts education in preparation for college.[23] For students who didn't want to attend college, the curriculum seemed irrelevant. Boredom and frustration led them to loud, boisterous behavior that hurt other children's chances of learning.

One desperate public school teacher, Steve Mariotti, asked his inner-city students why they were so disruptive. "You're boring!" they replied. In frustration, Steve asked the class if anything he had taught interested them. One young man told Steve that his stories about his former import-export business had been wonderful. Indeed, the young man was able to recall that class in great detail.

... during the high point of the whole language era of popularity, I and my department neglected to promote phonics. The results, as shown by the NAEP reading results in California in 1992 and 1994 were catastrophic ... the theory is dead wrong.

—William Honig
California Schools
superintendent

For youngsters enmeshed in the poverty trap, making money in business is a ticket to a better future.[24] However, public schools rarely have the autonomy to introduce classes in entrepreneurial skills.

When the monopoly school boards make a mistake, a great number of children are adversely affected. Sometimes the error lies in failure to promote courses that interest students and help them succeed in the real world. Sometimes the error is a substitution of experimental methods for the tried and true, as when phonics instruction was replaced by "whole word." Regrettably, school boards seem unaware that comprehensive studies have determined which methods are most effective in teaching basic skills. Direct Instruction ("Distar") not only ranked first in reading, spelling, arithmetic, and language, but it also gave children the highest sense of self-esteem. In spite of these exciting results, Distar was discontinued in public schools.[25]

Schools Built on Aggression Beget Violence

When schools don't provide relevant and interesting classes, and yet force attendance, some youngsters do more than create distractions for other children. As attendance has risen, so have theft, drugs, and violence perpetrated by students unmotivated by the curriculum.[26]

By 1992, 24% of teenage students reported fearing for their physical safety while at school.[27] In Detroit, 63% of parents cited violence as their child's biggest problem at school.[28] One Arizona mother had only one wish for her boy's schooling: that he be alive at the end of his high school years.[29]

Children who have difficulty focusing in such an environment, run the risk of being "diagnosed" with ADD (attention deficit disorder) by a school administrator and put on powerful drugs like Ritalin or Prozac. Approximately 5 million children are on psychotropic drugs. Parents who refuse to medicate their children on demand are threatened with medical neglect and child abuse suits.

However, these powerful drugs have side effects in children that are truly frightening. One 12-year-old boy, Michael Mozer, pleaded with his mother to stop the drugs because "there's a person inside my head telling me to do bad things."

Indeed, both 18-year-old Eric Harris and his 17-year-old friend Dylan Klebold were on Luvox when they massacred their classmates and teacher at Columbine High School in Littleton, Colorado on April 20, 1999. Just a month later, T.J. Solomon, a 15-year-old who had been on Ritalin, shot six of his fellow students at Heritage High in Conyers, Georgia. In Oregon, Kip

... when it [the State] controls the education, it turns it into a routine, a mechanical system in which individual initiative, individual growth and true development as opposed to a routine instruction becomes impossible.
—Sri Aurobindo
SOCIAL AND POLITICAL
THOUGHT

One reason Johnny can't read may be that he is simply too busy surviving.
—William Plummer and
Luchina Fisher
PEOPLE MAGAZINE

... a Metropolitan Life study released in late 1993 reported that over 10 percent of teachers and about 25 percent of their students had been victims of violence in or near their public schools ... This seems to be a problem exclusive to public schools.
—Sheldon Richman
SEPARATING SCHOOL AND
STATE

What is most disturbing, however, is the growing awareness that the increased violence among school children may have more to do with the drugs than with the guns they use to carry out their violence.
—Samuel Blumenfeld
WORLDNETDAILY

I have no doubt that Prozac can contribute to violence and suicide. I've seen many cases. In a recent clinical trial, 6% of the children became psychotic on Prozac. And manic psychosis can lead to violence.
> —Peter R. Breggin
> author of TALKING BACK
> TO PROZAC and TALKING
> BACK TO RITALIN

It is difficult to find a group of people that has been dealt a worse hand by modern government schooling than African Americans.
> —Andrew Coulson
> MARKET EDUCATION

I will find a way to have my children attend private school even if it means less food on the table. A quality education for my children is that important.
> —Pilar Gonzalez
> Milwaukee parent

Kinkel, 15, killed his parents and two classmates, as well as wounded 22 others in his school cafeteria. Kip was on both Ritalin and Prozac.[30]

We tell our children not to use drugs, yet we give them powerful psychoactive medication when they are more boisterous than we want them to be. Rather than doping our children, perhaps we should find out why they are restless. Perhaps they are having a natural reaction to an education based on aggression.

The Poor Get Poorer: Discrimination Against the Disadvantaged

Learning problems are most pronounced in the inner-city schools populated by minorities. Only 12% of black high school seniors were proficient in reading in 1995, compared with 40% of whites. In 1997, 76% of white fourth graders had acquired basic math skills, whereas only 41% of Hispanic and 32% of black children had done so.[31]

Inner-city parents usually pay hefty school taxes through their rent, which reflects the high cost of this poor education. Even though private school tuition is an immense hardship for them, many enroll their children in the local parish or independent neighborhood schools—even if they have to pay tuition with their welfare checks![32] As a result, the proportion of poor and minority children in private schools has been increasing.[33] By the late 1970s, more private school students came from families in which the parents earned between $5,000 and $10,000 a year than from families with incomes of $25,000 or higher.[34] Vandalism, crime, drug abuse, student apathy, and disrespect for teachers are much lower in private schools, even after adjusting for socioeconomic and demographic differences.[35]

The Marketplace Ecosystem Offers Hope

Most parents cite superior academic quality as the reason for sending their children to private schools. The Catholic school system is the largest single private educational network.

Even after adjusting for race, family background, and social class, the average Catholic high school student gained over three years of learning above that of the average public school student.[36] Whereas minorities in public high schools lose ground each year compared with their white counterparts, that gap narrows each year for minority students in Catholic and private high schools.[37] The "Catholic school advantage" was evident to me when, as a high school student, I watched Catholic students take a disproportionate share of awards at the Detroit Metropolitan Science Fair.

Not only do private schools promote academic excellence, they do so in a setting that is more integrated, both racially and economically, than in public schools.[38] Twice as many private school students (36.6%) are in well-integrated classrooms compared with public school students (18.3%).[39] Even voluntary lunchroom seating patterns are more integrated in private schools.[40]

Public schools draw their students from the surrounding neighborhood more often than the regional private institutions do. Zoning restrictions, another form of aggression-through-government, increase the price of housing in the suburbs, effectively eliminating lower-income, minority buyers.[41] The segregation promoted by zoning laws becomes reflected in our neighborhood public schools as well.

Private school students are more socially conscious in other ways. They, more than public school attendees, are likely to report that they've volunteered recently and that such community action is important to them.[42]

For the most part, private schools do not obtain their superior results in academic and social arenas by admitting only the very best students. More than a quarter of inner-city parochial schools have no admission criteria at all; the typical Catholic school takes 88% of all who apply. In urban schools, like those in Cleveland, three-quarters of the students are not even Catholic.[43] Twenty percent of Catholic schools report accepting students expelled from the public system![44]

Indeed, public schools send almost 100,000 problem students to private schools specializing in helping such youngsters.[45] Students include delinquents, troublemakers, and the emotionally disturbed.

... Chicago's Catholic schools are able to offer a good education at a cost of $1,500 per elementary student and $3,200 for secondary students; the Chicago public schools spend $5,500 per pupil ... [and] 46% of entering freshmen fail to graduate, while in the parochial schools only 22% drop out.
—William Tucker
FORBES
November 25, 1991

... a 1995 challenge to New York City officials from Cardinal John J. O'Conner: send us the lowest-performing 5 percent of public school students and we guarantee they will succeed.
—Clint Bolick
TRANSFORMATION: THE PROMISE AND POLITICS OF EMPOWERMENT

The expected graduation rate for minorities in Catholic schools is 94 percent; the rate in public school is 64 percent.
—George A. Clowes
SCHOOL REFORM NEWS

The existence of thousands of private schools that focus on nothing but difficult-to-educate children lays bare the myth that private schools just skim the cream and leave the toughest kids to the public schools.
　　　　—Joseph Lehman
　　Mackinac Center for
　　　　　　Public Policy

One such private school, specializing in dropouts, boasts an 85% graduation rate. By utilizing self-paced computer learning and high teacher-to-pupil ratios, Jim Boyle's Ombudsman Educational Services helps students advance one grade level in basic skills for each 20 hours in his program. Ombudsman achieves these remarkable results while spending half as much money per pupil as the public schools do![46]

A quarter of the students at Marva Collins Preparatory School in Chicago have learning disabilities, yet almost all of the students read at least one level above their grade.[47] The school's tuition is less than a third of what the neighboring public schools receive per pupil.[48] Sylvan Learning Centers, a tutoring service for students who want more progress, *guarantees* a one-grade-level leap with 36 hours of instruction![49]

While private schools offer to guarantee results, courts in Colorado have ruled that public schools have no "contractual duty" to provide a good education. Parents are obligated to pay for public schools in their tax bill, yet schools have no reciprocal obligation to teach children even basic skills![50]

Even Public Employees Go Private!

If you're becoming eager to send your children to a private school, you're not alone. On a nationwide basis, approximately 14% of students are enrolled in private schools.[51] Almost half of the Milwaukee public school teachers send their children to private institutions. When Wisconsin state legislator Polly Williams wanted to force employees of Milwaukee's public school system to enroll their children in it, she was harassed with death threats![52] Presumably, at least some school employees would rather kill than have their children attend Milwaukee public schools!

Members of Congress send their children to private schools more frequently than the average parent. At least 34% of U.S. representatives and 50% of the senators chose private education for at least one of their children. During their terms of office, former president Bill Clinton and vice president Al Gore sent their children to private schools as well.[53]

Private schools raise achievement, promote voluntary community service, lower violence, and heal race relations—at half of the per pupil cost of the public schools.[54] Lower administrative costs are a significant factor in the savings. For example, Chicago public schools have 37 times as many administrators per pupil as the Catholic ones; in New York City, the ratio jumps to 60![55]

Teachers' salaries average 50% more in the public sector,[56] which may account for their unions' violent antagonism toward the private sector. In 1995, Pepsi announced that it would give scholarships to low-income children living in Jersey City so that they could attend private schools. The public school teachers' union began discussing a statewide boycott of Pepsi products. The company's vending machines were vandalized. Faced with such hostility, Pepsi withdrew its offer.[57] Sadly, teachers who deny poor children a chance for a better education and destroy property in the process will ultimately teach students to be aggressors too.

Public school teachers needn't fear that a fully privatized school system would mean a cut in pay. Indeed, as explained in "The Better Way," teachers would probably earn more when money wasn't wasted on excess administration and other inefficiencies of public education. By harming students to maintain the status quo, teachers only hurt the very people they are trying to help.

Aggression vs. Choice

Our schools have failed low-income children, but the marketplace ecosystem stands ready to serve them—at half the cost. Simply by sending our children to private schools, we could slash the price of education and increase its quality, especially for the disadvantaged.

With this vision in mind, minority parents are supporting reforms that enable them to take their tax dollars to the school of their choice. Vermont[58] and Maine[59] have had such programs since the 1870s. Milwaukee gives each child about half of the $9,500 per pupil cost of public school education.[60] Because private schools cost so much less than public ones, "vouchers" allow

Giving every school-aged child ... vouchers for the full average tuition charged by private schools would save over one hundred billion dollars a year nationwide.
—Andrew Coulson
MARKET EDUCATION

*... the absence of political
control over the schools
is a determining factor
of private school
effectiveness.*
          —Eugena F. Toma
University of Kentucky

*... education, like reli-
gion, is too important to
be left in the hands of the
state.*
          —Jacob Hornberger
Future of Freedom
Foundation

students to pay tuition and have money left over. As a result, a total of $1.2 million of taxpayer funds was returned to the state in 2000.[61]

If private schools don't live up to parents' expectations, they lose their students and their money. This natural regulation by the marketplace ecosystem keeps educational quality high. As a result, most voucher programs boast academic gains and increased parental satisfaction.[62]

School choice programs end the aggression of forcing children to attend a particular neighborhood school, but maintain the aggression of tax funding. Tax-supported private schools in Belgium, France, New Zealand, Ontario, and the United States still outperform the public ones, because overall aggression is less. However, when public school regulations are imposed on choice programs, the private schools lose their effectiveness.[63] Ultimately, only complete separation of school and state will protect our children's education.

Investigators recently constructed an Education Freedom Index, measuring the level of aggression-through-government that each state experienced in the educational realm. As might be expected, students from states with less aggressive school regulations scored higher in an eighth grade standardized math test.[64]

Perhaps the best evidence that public schools have failed our children is the incredible increase in after school education. Sylvan Learning Centers, with affiliates in Canada, Germany, France, England, and Spain, guarantee students a one-grade-level leap with 36 hours of after-school instruction.[65] In other words, Sylvan guarantees to do in 2 months of daily instruction what the public schools often fail to do in 10 months.

In Japan, 70–90% of students regularly attend *juku,* an "after-school school" by the ninth grade. Top juku instructors can make as much money as professional Japanese baseball players. As with Sylvan, the juku curriculum is adapted to each child's learning style and goals.[66]

More and more parents are choosing to keep their children out of schools and teach them at home. In some states, home schooling is permitted only with a state-licensed teacher, even though such training does not improve student learning.[67] Parents without this qualification have been fined or jailed for home schooling, even when the education has been progressing well.[68]

Home schooling has now been legalized in every state, but only 1–3% of the U.S. school-age population learns at home.[69] *In spite of home schoolers' small numbers, the top three finalists at the 2000 National Spelling Bee were home schoolers, as were 4 of the 10 National Geography Bee finalists.*[70] Home schoolers score higher on standardized tests than 75–85% of conventionally schooled children. Parents typically pay between $200 and $2,000 dollars for materials, with a median cost of $400.[71] Home schooling is more economical than even private schools, but usually one parent stays out of the work force to provide the learning environment.

Do home-schooled children lag behind their peers in social development? Just the opposite! Trained counselors saw no difference between the two groups with regard to self-concept or assertiveness. However, children schooled by their parents were better behaved and exhibited higher self-esteem.[72] An entire network of support groups now provides sports and social activities to home schoolers, giving them the best of academic excellence and social interaction.[73]

A Better Way

As we've learned from the above examples, less aggression results in better education, especially for the disadvantaged. If we were to honor our neighbor's choice, to what educational heights could we aspire? Let's try to imagine what a successful school might look like if education were totally deregulated (i.e., completely free from aggression). Although this school, which we'll call Quest, doesn't actually exist, many of its components do. These factors are referenced to allow comparisons with what we have today.

Quest would probably start out small, expanding each year as its reputation for excellence grew. New students would take tests to discover their aptitudes and their optimal learning modes, much as Sylvan Learning Centers

Young home school students test one grade level ahead of their counterparts in public and private schools. As they progress, the study shows that home schoolers pull further away from the pack, typically testing four grade levels above the national average by eighth grade.

—Lawrence Rudner
University of Maryland

do today. Some children are visual learners who remember best what they see; auditory-oriented youngsters learn fastest when they hear their lessons; kinesthetic children understand best what they are able to feel and manipulate.[74]

Subjects taught at Quest would come in each of these three learning modes. A kinesthetic child, for example, could be introduced to math by adding and subtracting with blocks before working with numbers on paper.[75] The curriculum would make effective use of computers and audiovisual equipment, which have long been known to double a student's learning.[76]

Tuition for the standard Quest program would probably be comparable to the private school tuition of today, roughly half of what public schools currently cost. A student's classes might begin with an "edutainment" video or Internet program. Since the producers of these lessons would receive royalties based on usage, exceptional broadcast teachers could make as much money as professional athletes, just as *juku* instructors do today.[77] Because student achievement increases along with teacher expertise,[78] broadcast educators might include Nobel Prize winners, who would likely donate their time and expertise to promote quality education. Unlike the public school system, which turned away such offers,[79] a results-oriented school like Quest would gladly accept such generosity.

After the edutainment, students might go into one of several "query" classrooms where the resident teacher could answer their questions. Students would naturally gravitate to teachers who relate best to their learning style. Not all Quest teachers would have advanced degrees, but those who didn't attract students to their query sessions wouldn't be at Quest long. Employment at Quest would be performance-based, rather than dependent on seniority, as it is in public schools today.

Teacher excellence would be rewarded with bonuses.[80] Most teachers would be partially paid in Quest stock, which would give them incentive to share successful teaching techniques with other Quest faculty. Teachers would thus reap what they sow.

The instructors would enjoy working at Quest because they could do what they were hired to do—teach. Extensive high-tech learning programs would take the repetition out of their job, so that they could devote most of their time to answering students' questions, guiding their choice of curriculum, or teaching writing and other skills that require personal instruction. Some teachers would supplement their income by creating edutainment in their field of specialty. The combination of royalties, Quest stock, and regular paychecks would give most teachers better compensation than public school teachers make today.

Quest's teachers would be highly regarded in their community because of their dedication to helping students meet their goals. Teachers could track student progress through the interactive computer programs that students use for learning and testing. For example, students who did poorly on the computerized test following each lesson would review their material again. After successful retesting, students might attempt more sophisticated problems or simply move on to the next lesson.

Because student computer time is monitored by the staff, slow learners would quickly be identified and given special attention so that they can meet their predefined goals. Motivation would be kept high by reward systems. For example, Sylvan has found that giving out milestone tokens gives students a sense of completion and accomplishment that motivates them to complete the next learning segment.[81] For major achievements, such as graduation from their pre-defined programs, both students and their teachers might receive a monetary bonus.[82]

The curriculum at Quest would be designed taking into account a student's strengths and weaknesses. For example, one student might excel in history and the social sciences but do poorly in math and the physical sciences. When the student keys in her password on the teaching computer, she might be able to access her math problems formulated in terms of historical events.

Depending upon their goals, students might stay at school all or part of the day. Quest teachers would likely work in shifts, so that families would have maximum flexibility to design the best schedule to mix school, work, and play.

Quest would probably help students relate their academic lessons to real-life situations, unlike most schools of today. For example, Quest could cultivate relationships with community professionals so that students could be exposed to various career opportunities and work environments (e.g., hospitals, laboratories, computer firms, manufacturing plants, auto repair shops). Students could visit these organizations, or even work part-time for pay or class credit. Such exposure to different careers would help students discover what their aptitudes are and inspire them to study subjects appropriate to possible careers. For some Quest students, such contact might eventually evolve into an apprenticeship or even full-time employment.

Early exposure to a wide range of career possibilities is essential for wise curriculum choices. As a research scientist, I supervised several pre-med students who found out, in their last year of college, that they couldn't stand the sight of blood during surgical procedures. Had they recognized this earlier, they might have chosen another program. By the time they discovered that they really didn't want to go into medicine, it was too late to change their major.

With exposure to a variety of experiences, students would discover their strengths and weaknesses. For example, a student who has an exceptional grasp of math or science and a weaker understanding of literature and the arts might choose to spend more time on liberal arts courses to match his proficiency in other areas. Alternatively, he could focus only on the basics in his weak areas and accelerate his strong ones, perhaps even earning college credit in his specialties. Some students might want to explore specialized curriculum, such as the courses in offered by Steve Mariotti's National Foundation for Teaching Entrepreneurship. Quest counselors would keep abreast of new offerings to help students and parents choose wisely.

Most colleges rely heavily on standardized test scores when evaluating prospective students. Quest would almost certainly post student scores to show new applicants the effectiveness of the school's program. Schools that are hesitant to display such records would likely be viewed with suspicion by parents considering enrollment for their children. Because high school diplomas don't always mean that graduates can read and write, test scores are evolving into the standard by which employers and colleges select among applicants.

At Quest, studies would continue until test scores indicate that the proficiency target has been met. A state-of-the-art school like Quest would probably guarantee that students have 12th grade proficiency by the time they are 12 years old.[83] Indeed, such progress by properly taught youngsters is probably conservative, given the progress that Sylvan and other learning programs are already able to achieve. For example, Hope Academy in Lansing, Michigan, gives parents a money-back guarantee that their kindergartners, by year end, will read as well as second-graders.[84] What a refreshing change from the public school system, which has no obligation to ensure that students learn anything!

Social skills development would be well integrated into the Quest curriculum. Children would learn how to tutor and mentor younger classmates, how to engage in constructive teamwork with peers, and how to assume leadership roles in various types of projects.

Although Quest would be less expensive than the old-style public school system, the yearly tuition might still be beyond the means of many who would like to attend. Fortunately, Quest would most likely have a number of programs enabling parents to pay all or part of their children's tuition by contributing their labor. Some parents might help maintain the buildings or grounds; others might staff the office; still others might work in the cafeteria. Much of the nonteaching function of Quest would likely be provided this way.[85]

As they progress, students could help pay their tuition by supervising younger children,

Children born into poverty have special gifts that prepare them for business formation and wealth creation. They are mentally strong, resilient. ... They are long-suffering in the face of adversity. They are comfortable with risk and uncertainty. They know how to deal with stress and conflict. ... In short, poor kids are "street smart" or what we call "business smart."

—Steve Mariotti
National Foundation for Teaching Entrepreneurship

working with the cafeteria staff, and tutoring less-advanced students. Not only would such students get a first-rate Quest education, but they would leave with a work reference as well!

Problems with drugs or violence would probably be minimal, since students could be expelled for disruptive behavior. However, rather than abandoning such children, Quest might provide a specialized home-study program for such youngsters.

A Quest home-study program might also be popular with those who prefer to keep their children at home. If the family had a home computer, it could tap into the Quest system via the Internet so that student progress could be monitored by Quest instructors as if they were on-site. Quest instructors might also be available by video phone, so that students won't get stuck if their caregiver isn't able to answer their questions. By providing space for several children of working parents, stay-at-home parents could earn enough to pay for an at-home Quest education for their children.

For families without Internet access, Quest might have a comparable video program and home workbook. Instructors could be contacted by telephone for questions and consultations. Every couple of weeks, students could visit Quest for evaluation and program alterations. For example, a child who has trouble with math might receive a special series of videos and workbooks to resolve his or her problems. Quest is likely to guarantee results in its home-study program, just as it would in its classrooms.

Of course, Quest's excellence might also make it more expensive and structured than many parents would prefer. Such parents might choose instead to subscribe to educational cable television. For a monthly fee similar to that of the entertainment channels, a family would probably be able to order a "school" station that specializes in K–12 education. Such channels are not yet available, since today's children are mostly in a classroom. However, such an alternative would almost certainly develop if parents had full choice in educational options.

Indeed, alternatives are already beginning to appear. A number of correspondence courses are now available in subjects for which a professional's evaluation is desirable (e.g., essay writing).[86] Indeed, Internet schools, like Class.com[87] and VirtualHighSchool.com,[88] provide standard and elective courses in a more interactive environment.

In addition to "school" cable stations, educational television would continue to be supported by advertising, just as other sponsored shows are. *Sesame Street*, which taught preschoolers their letters and numbers, would have many K–12 imitators. Virtually every child in the country would have access to this "free" classroom!

Churches and other support groups would most likely provide inexpensive day care and schooling through such advertiser-sponsored educational television. A volunteer staff would probably run the center, providing low-income parents with affordable schooling and day care while they work. Like *Sesame Street*, educational television is likely to be highly participatory. Children would probably sing their alphabet to catchy jingles and march around the room chanting historical dates, names, and happenings. Madison Avenue techniques could be used to produce stimulating programs to entice advertisers to pay top dollar to sponsor them, as they do for high school programs today.[89]

With so many options available at costs ranging from substantial to trivial, few parents would be unable to provide their children with a good education. Those parents who need assistance, however, would probably have access to a number of scholarship programs. Children First CEO America, which began in 1991, has already provided over $500 million to low-income students for private school tuition. Funds come primarily from the business community,[90] although other charitable organizations also contribute. Most likely, such efforts would continue in an educational system free of aggression.

Would parents take advantage of these widespread educational opportunities? All of the available evidence suggests that they would. Over

90% of Boston's children enrolled in some sort of learning program in the early 1800s. Today, although high school is optional in Japan, over 90% of Japanese 17-year-old youths *voluntarily* attend. In contrast, the United States was only able to *force* 72% of its teens to enroll.[91]

The few children who would be without a formal educational program most likely have parents who don't value learning or their children's future. Because family background is a significant factor in a child's scholastic achievement, few of those children would benefit from being forced into a learning program. Instead, they would only disrupt the learning of others with drugs and violence, while learning little themselves. Such children cannot be helped by forcing their parents to send them to school.

However, such children can be helped. By taking aggression out of education, learning aids would become widely integrated into our culture (e.g., advertiser-supported educational TV programs). Children might find it difficult *not* to learn the basics. After all, when education becomes as easy as pressing buttons on the TV remote, even a child can do it!

Nonaggression is the education of choice!

Chapter 10: Learning Lessons Our Schools Can't Teach

In Summary ...

- The education monopoly is an example of fourth-layer aggression: a subsidized, exclusive monopoly that we are forced to use. Even private and home schools must abide by rules set by the school licensing boards.
- In the early days of the United States, when most education was private and voluntary, Americans were among the most literate nations in the world.
- Modern public schooling, however, has failed our children. Costs are twice that of private schools and test scores are lower. Drugs and violence are more prevalent In public schools as well.
  It schoolchildren rebel when forced into the one-size-fits all educational mold, they are given potent psychotropic drugs to quiet them. These drugs often have severe side effects, including violent behavior, in children.
- Black and minority children suffer the most in public schools. Consequently, parents will often go to great extremes, such as cutting back on groceries, to give them a private education.
- Private schools are better integrated than public ones, both in the classroom and in the lunch room.
- Public school teachers and members of the U.S. Congress send their children to private schools more frequently than the rest of the American public.
- Public schools are not legally obligated to teach our children.
- Private institutions, like Sylvan Learning Centers and Hope Academy, however, *guarantee* to teach students up to five times faster than public schools!
- A fully privatized educational system would teach our children better for less than half the cost in an environment that was safer and more integrated. Indeed, with Internet, educational cable TV, and advertiser-sponsored programs, even children who didn't study could hardly help learning the basics!

Chapter 11

Springing the Poverty Trap

When we use aggression to help the poor, we end up hurting them instead!

Aggression Disrupts the Marketplace Ecosystem

As we've seen in earlier chapters, most poverty in today's world is a result of aggression-through-government. Minimum wage laws, for example, make unskilled workers unemployable. As a result, welfare payments to the newly unemployed go up when the minimum wage does.[1]

Licensing laws drive small companies, which provide 80% of all new minority hires,[2] out of business. When unemployment rises, so does poverty.[3]

Poverty today is largely created by the aggression of minimum wages and licensing laws through increases in unemployment. As licensing laws become more exclusive, they create legal monopolies, and the price of services skyrockets, further penalizing the poor. If, in spite of all these setbacks, disadvantaged individuals manage to acquire something, they are the first to flounder in the alternating waves of inflation and deflation produced by the money monopoly. Moving to the poor side of town has grave consequences, however. Unless parents are willing and able to make heroic sacrifices, their children will go to inner-city public schools, from which they will be lucky to leave with some basic literacy skills, a diploma, or even their lives.

As we look at the plight of the poor, we are usually unaware of the role we have played in creating their poverty. Without such awareness, we repeat our mistake. In the United States, for example, the aggression of taxation was used to support a massive war on poverty created by earlier aggression.

Two wrongs don't make a right. Welfare supported by taxation uses aggressive means in an attempt to achieve benevolent ends. Instead of helping the poor, welfare backfires by ensnaring them in a never-ending cycle known as the poverty trap.

Economic control is not merely control of a sector of human life that can be separated from the rest; it is the control of the means for all our ends.

—Ludwig von Mises
HUMAN ACTION

The first thing a welfare state does is take money away from people against their will—an obviously harmful, destructive activity. Only after it has inflicted this certain harm is it in a position to do some possible good by giving it away.

—James L. Payne
OVERCOMING WELFARE

No matter how worthy the cause, it is robbery, theft, and injustice to confiscate the property of one person and give it to another to whom it does not belong.

—Walter Williams
professor of economics,
George Mason
University

The fundamental fact in the lives of the poor in most parts of America today is that the wages of common labor are far below the benefits of AFDC, Medicaid, food stamps, public housing, public defenders, leisure time and all the other goods and services of the welfare state.

—George Gilder
WEALTH AND POVERTY

... the welfare system is responsible for at least 15 to 20 percent of the family disintegration in America.
—William Galston
President Clinton's
deputy assistant for
domestic affairs, 1993

How the Poverty Trap Works

As a landlady renting to low-income tenants, I found out just how the poverty trap works. In the United States, many different programs of aid, such as cash, food stamps, housing, and medical care are available. Taken together, these programs can combine to give a person on the dole a substantial tax-free income.

By 1979, welfare benefits were as much as $1,500 higher than the median family income.[4] By 1995, every state had tax-supported aid programs that, in combination, exceeded the take home pay of a minimum wage earner. In Hawaii, a welfare recipient would have had to make $17.50/hour to exceed total available welfare benefits![5] On average, the United States spent three times as much per low-income person in 1993 than it did during the peak of the Great Depression![6]

Consequently, to a young person just beginning a career, starting out at minimum wage may seem less attractive than going on the dole. Indeed, for girls raised on welfare, getting pregnant has become a way to receive aid and establish their own households. They can't marry, because aid is usually denied if the child's father lives in the same household.[7]

Once young mothers started receiving welfare, they realized that more children meant more welfare benefits. They had one child after another until they reached the maximum number that the state would support.

Because of such incentives, most unwed teen mothers have their babies deliberately.[8] A number of studies in the United States and Canada show that illegitimate births rise and fall in parallel with the baby's welfare entitlements.[9] Even after researchers accounted for variables such as income, education, and neighborhood, a 50% increase in welfare benefits was accompanied by a 43% increase in out-of-wedlock births![10] No wonder one out of eight U.S. children was on welfare by 1993![11]

One of my tenants took me aside one day and chided me for working at my day job and at the apartments at night. "You need to quit your job, have some kids, and get on welfare," she counseled me. "Then you can have a life!"

Of course, opting out of the work force at a young age has grave consequences later. Although a working person might start out with less than someone on welfare, the working person's experience will eventually bring raises and a higher standard of living.

For the person on welfare, however, living standards don't change. Because most welfare benefits are in the form of food, medical care, and shelter, putting away cash for a rainy day is almost impossible. When their working counterparts are ready to buy their first house, those on welfare can't even afford their first car.

Once a woman realizes that she won't progress on the dole, however, she's already had several children in order to increase the size of her welfare check. Because she has little or no work experience, she usually must start at an entry-level job. Until she gains experience and the pay raise that goes with it, she's can't afford day care costs for her expanded family. Once she begins working, her state-supported medical coverage ends. This loss can be devastating since entry-level jobs rarely include such benefits.

If a young mother can somehow persist, however, and keep working for two years, her income will usually surpass what she received in aid.[12] However, few welfare recipients persevere under such conditions. Instead, they usually quit their job and get back on the dole. Unable to work their way up the Ladder of Affluence, they're caught in the poverty trap.

Welfare makes breaking out of poverty so difficult that only 18% of state aid recipients were able to do so in 1987, compared with 45% of equally poor individuals who never received aid.[13] Because welfare keeps people poor, poverty increases in states with high welfare benefits.[14]

In the United States, people seldom end up in poverty if they obtain a high school diploma, marry, and wait until their twenties before having children.[15] By "helping" unwed teenage mothers, our welfare programs discourage them from ever achieving self-sufficiency.

Continued dependence upon relief induces a spiritual and moral disintegration fundamentally destructive to the national fiber. To dole out relief in this way is to administer a narcotic, a subtle destroyer of the human spirit.
—Franklin D. Roosevelt
U.S. president

How Welfare Entraps Minorities

The disadvantaged, at the bottom rung of the Ladder of Affluence, are most likely to be lured into the welfare trap. Most of the disadvantaged are minorities. Between 1940 and 1960, black poverty rates fell from 87% to 47%.[16] By 1982, however, after the "War on Poverty" had been in effect for almost 20 years, the number of black children living in poverty had tripled.[17]

Welfare enticed blacks into the poverty trap by subsidizing unwed teen pregnancies. In the 1940s, less than 10% of all black babies were born out of wedlock;[18] by 1994, 70% of all black children were illegitimate, compared with 25% of white children.[19] In trying to help the poor with aggression, we've hurt them instead!

An economic split developed between working class minorities and those on the dole. Between 1975 and 1992, income for the wealthiest fifth of the black community rose by 23%, while income for the poorest fifth decreased by 33%.[20] Blacks who escaped the poverty trap could look forward to unprecedented gains. Unfortunately, our aggression made that escape more difficult.

Welfare enticed the disadvantaged to choose dependence over self-sufficiency, poverty over getting ahead, and illegitimacy over marriage. Like overprotective parents, we've stifled the development of self-reliance and self-esteem in our poor by trying to give them the wrong kind of help. Dependency may hinder cognitive ability as well. The IQ of welfare children is only 80% as high as children of similar race, income, and parental IQ who are not aid recipients.[21]

History Repeats Itself

Even in the 1970s, studies with over 9,000 people predicted these ruinous results. One group of people, who served as controls, received no aid. An experimental group received a guaranteed income, created by supplementing whatever was earned by whatever was necessary to reach the predetermined target. Those in the experimental group who worked would receive less money than those who didn't, so everyone in that group received the same income for three consecutive years.

It is welfare dependence and single parenthood, not skin color, that determine the likelihood a child will live in poverty.
—Robert E. Rector and David Muhlhausen
Heritage Foundation

... we could end up in an absurd situation where a third of the population produces goods and services, another third are social workers and the last third are welfare cases and pensioners.
—Jens Aage Bjoerkeoe
Danish social worker

When the control and experimental groups were compared, the results were unequivocal. Young unmarried men with a guaranteed income worked 43% less than their peers in the control group. Men who worked the least also gained less experience, thereby jeopardizing their future earnings.

Wives in the experimental group cut their work hours by 20%, and their husbands reduced their work week by 9%. If a female head of household lost her job, it took over a year for her to find a new one if she was receiving a guaranteed income. Her counterpart in the control group found new employment in less than half the time.[22] Clearly, welfare decreased the incentive to work, especially for individuals with no family responsibilities.

Divorce rates went up by 36–84% in the experimental group. The economic benefits of a family unit evidently help to bind people together. Guaranteed incomes made it easier to say good-bye. In one group, couples thought that their guaranteed income would be stopped if they separated. Divorce rates in that group were comparable to those of the controls.[23] Clearly, income guarantees significantly influenced life-changing decisions.

We shouldn't be surprised that welfare leads to dependency. We discourage people from feeding porpoises and other wildlife so that the animals won't forget how to fend for themselves.[24] Perhaps we should have the same concern for our neighbors!

Ending Welfare Leads to Self-Sufficiency

How many people choose welfare over work? Almost 90% of my tenants who were receiving tax-supported aid were able-bodied. Oregon estimated that 70% of its welfare recipients would be able to work; the state even paid employers to hire them. Within a year, all but 4% had found themselves employment on their own.[25]

Earlier estimations that one-sixth of aid recipients are able to work[26] have proven low. A third of welfare recipients stopped taking aid within a year when states began requiring them to clean parks or perform other chores.[27] The

The combination of welfare and other social services enhance the mother's role and obviate the man's. As a result, men tend to leave their children, whether before or after marriage. Crises that would be resolved in a normal family way break up a ghetto family. Perhaps not the first time or the fifth, but sooner or later the pressure of the subsidy state dissolves the roles of fatherhood, the disciplines of work, and the rules of marriage.

—George Gilder
WEALTH AND POVERTY

The more that is given, the less the people will work for themselves, and the less they work, the more their poverty will increase.

—Leo Tolstoy
author of WAR AND PEACE

My kids see a difference in me. They see their mother making it. ... I feel so good about myself.
   —Michelle Crawford
      Wisconsin mother
      formerly on welfare

The Children's Defense Fund claimed that welfare reform would cast millions of children into poverty and hunger. The Urban Institute predicted that the welfare law would cause the incomes of one out of 10 American families to fall and throw 1.1 million children into poverty. Obviously, these predictions were inaccurate. The exact opposite occurred. In 1995, prior to reform 14.7 million children lived in poverty; by 2001, the number of poor children had fallen to 11.7 million. ...Opponents ... argued that ...when a recession hit, children would be thrown into poverty in unusually large numbers. Again, the exact opposite has occurred. Far from rising at above average rates, child poverty, for the first time, has remained flat during the recession.
   —Robert E. Rector
      Heritage Foundation

exodus off the welfare rolls was similar regardless of the state's unemployment rate.[28]

Wisconsin, the first state to implement a work program in the late 1980s, cut its welfare rolls in half by 1996, even though the national caseload increased by 25%. During the two decades before these changes, child poverty rates had soared; seven years after the work program started, Wisconsin's child poverty rate was down by 13% and child abuse decreased by 15%.[29] Clearly, getting parents off the dole improved life for the children as well.

Indeed, the 1996 nationwide welfare reform dramatically reduced child poverty, especially in groups historically linked to welfare: children of single mothers, blacks, and Hispanics. *Black child poverty, for example, which had been 40–47% since 1970, plummeted after welfare reform. Although still decreasing in 2000, black child poverty had already reached a historic low of 30%.*[30]

How Aggression Backfires

We pay handsomely to keep people poor. In 1992, enough taxes were budgeted for aid to give every poor family of four $35,756, or $4,700 more than the average family income![31] The poor get very little of this windfall, however. Instead, *as much as 74 cents of every dollar goes to program administrators!*[32]

With so much of intended charity going to the welfare bureaucracy and able-bodied recipients, the hard-core needy and their children are literally left out in the cold. Those truly incapable of producing significant wealth, especially the mentally disabled, may end up homeless. In San Francisco, where I lived for a year, many of those unfortunates roamed the parks and cities scrounging for food and shelter. No social workers sought them out. The paperwork burden barely leaves them enough time to assist those who walk in the door.[33]

The most destitute and helpless of our society rely almost entirely on the private sector for aid.[34] People donate their spare change; church-run soup kitchens provide an occasional hot meal, compassionate health care workers give free medical attention.

Unfortunately, many freelance humanitarians are thwarted by government regulations. For example, Carol Porter was feeding needy children up to 20,000 hot meals a week—until Houston regulators made her stop. Carol was told she couldn't *give away* hot meals unless her kitchen underwent expensive remodeling to meet standards imposed on restaurant owners. In frustration, Carol stopped cooking and started giving the children cold sandwiches instead.[35]

Most homelessness is caused by the aggression of rent control, zoning restrictions, building codes, and construction moratoriums, which drastically limit the availability of inexpensive housing.[36] During my years as a landlady to low-income tenants, building inspectors told me to install new kitchen counters a couple of inches longer or to rebuild staircases to increase width by an inch. When I pointed out that these expensive and unnecessary changes would increase rents for the poor who lived there, one inspector replied, "Good. We'll get these people out of our city." Other Michigan landlords told me similar stories. Frustrated with the attitudes of the building inspectors, I eventually stopped attempting to provide safe and affordable housing to the poor.

Even Mother Teresa's helpers were no match for aggressive regulators. In 1988, the Sisters of Mother Teresa's order, the Missionaries of Charity, bought two abandoned buildings from New York City at $1 apiece and raised $500,000 for repairs.

The city approved their plans for a homeless shelter, but after construction had begun, inspectors demanded installation of a $100,000 elevator. The nuns didn't want to spend that much money on something that wouldn't really help the poor. In frustration, they abandoned the project. The street people of New York City, who would have been thrilled to live in these buildings even without an elevator, remained homeless.[37]

When construction and renovation are limited by aggression, rents go up. When rent controls are also imposed, a severe housing shortage results. Landlords then rent only to the most

Cities with rent controls had, on average, two and a half times as many homeless people as cities without them.

—William Tucker
THE EXCLUDED
AMERICANS:
HOMELESSNESS AND
HOUSING POLICIES

... during the whole two years of my residence in America, I saw but one beggar.

—D. Griffiths Jr.
English visitor to the
United States, 1830s

During the 19th century, before the federal government ever got involved, a war on poverty, much more successful than our own, was waged by tens of thousands of local, private charitable agencies and religious groups around the country. These 19th-century warriors did not abolish poverty, but they did help millions of families to move out of it.

—Marvin Olasky
University of Texas,
Austin

affluent tenants who are less likely to be late in their payments. The poor are literally forced out into the cold.

A Better Way

A Hand Up, Not a Handout

With the best of intentions, we've used aggression in an attempt to help those less fortunate than ourselves. Because our means were flawed, we hurt those we wished to help. As a result, the most destitute are literally left without a roof over their heads. How can the Good Neighbor Policy do a better job?

History provides the answer. In the 1800s, some of the poor made the rounds of various help groups on a regular basis. These "rounders,"[38] who made up as much as 70% of the applicants, stopped coming by if they were required to chop wood for their supper.[39] *Charities used the work test for the able-bodied to distinguish between the needy and the freeloaders.*

An extensive network of charitable organizations actively assisted the poor,[40] as evidenced by the large number of rounders who tried to take advantage of them.

Charity workers recognized that giving a handout instead of a hand-up created dependency. Consequently, most money or food was given only in exchange for work, some of which might assist others in need.

In addition, volunteers developed relationships with their clients as "befriending leaders." Their friendships became a springboard to teach the poor thrift, better habits of sanitation, and marketable skills.[41]

Even today, our disadvantaged are sorely in need of such personal mentoring. After all, it's much easier to climb the Ladder of Affluence if someone who has already done it can point the way!

Charity That Really Works

For the homeless. A caring person who works directly with the poor is more likely to help them become productive. Guy Polhemus, a soup kitchen volunteer, realized that New York City's homeless could help themselves and the city by collecting discarded beer and soda cans. He established a nonprofit organization, We Can, to redeem the cans gathered by the homeless. Industrious collectors earned $25 to $30 a day cleaning up the city's litter while recycling cans that might otherwise end up in landfills. Indeed, since 1987, We Can has recycled 16,000 tons of trash, while paying collectors about $30 million in refunds.

Critics felt that scavenging cans was too degrading for the poor. Obviously, the homeless, who participate voluntarily, disagree. We Can's expansion allowed Polhemus to give some of his collectors jobs in the nonprofit organization. His employees even have the opportunity to work their way up into management positions—all on account of their "can-do" attitude![42]

Attitude is why job-training programs like East Harlem's Strive work so well today. Strive is one of six organizations that received a commendation from the General Accounting Office, even though Strive refuses to take government funds and the strings that go with them.

For the outcast. Twenty-five percent of Strive's clients are ex-offenders, half are on welfare, many are on drugs, and some are even homeless. Strive helps their clients can the self-defeating attitudes that give potential employers pause. Strive instructors, who come from the same difficult backgrounds, help their clients shed their ghetto outlook and become cooperative, motivated workers. The program is tough; only 60% graduate.

In five years, Strive put 14,000 people to work in New York, Boston, Pittsburgh, and Chicago for a mere $1,500 a piece. After two years, 80% were still working.[43] In comparison, the $53 billion tax-funded job-readiness program CETA (Comprehensive Employment and Training Act) placed only 15% of its recruits in unsubsidized jobs. Two separate studies concluded that the program actually created "negative effects" and "earning losses" for men, while having no effect on female enrollees.[44] Aggression backfires every time!

For the disabled. Pride Industries of Roseville, California, became frustrated with

It's me using my own mind to do something for me. It gives me pride. It's not like we are living off welfare or stealing.
—Jack Miller
a We Can customer

For most people who are deemed needy, the main barrier to economic and social success is not a lack of dollar bills; it is a lack of healthy values and motives.
—James L. Payne
OVERCOMING WELFARE

"warehousing" their disabled clients. Instead, they began a rehabilitation program designed to get the disabled full-time, well-paying jobs.

Before this shift in emphasis, Pride served 50 individuals with disabilities; 90% of its funding came from taxes. By 1996, 1,200 disabled workers were on Pride's factory payroll and 95% of Pride's revenue came from electronics assembly, packaging, snowshoe manufacture, property maintenance, woodworking, and fees from its excellent rehabilitation program.

How do Pride's clients like the shift from dependency to self-sufficiency? "Most of them will tell you it's the best thing that ever happened to them," the president of Pride, Michael Ziegler, states. "They smile just like you and I do on payday." Rather than feeling disenfranchised from a normal working life by their physical condition, the newly enabled are on the job like everyone else. That's what Pride is all about!

Pride blurs the line between helper and employer, because it plays both roles. It makes a profit, although its mission is to create opportunities for people with disabilities. "When you're struggling financially, you really can't offer much," board member Bob Selvester explains. "It takes a lot of skilled people to take folks from zero to where they can actually go to work for somebody else, live by themselves, and get off Social Security."[45] Profit allows Pride to hire the best professionals to rehabilitate its clients. Perhaps the best way to teach individuals with disabilities how to become self-sufficient is for their supporting organization to set the example!

For those in need of ongoing support. Some people need more than a training program to achieve self-sufficiency. Delancey Street Foundation provides a two-to-four year program in a family-like shelter for repeat offenders, addicts, and illiterates. Residents have to earn their keep by working in the foundation's award-winning restaurant, print shop, moving company, or auto-detailing center.

Senior residents become befriending leaders, helping newcomers gain reading skills, discipline, manners, and work standards that will help them become self-sufficient. Delancey now operates shelters in five cities and is 80% self-sufficient; only about 20% of its major project funding comes from charitable donations.[46]

Teaching Self-Sufficiency by Example

Organizations similar to Delancey can be found throughout the United States. Union Gospel Mission in Portland, Oregon and Step 13 in Denver cater to the homeless who want a better life. Not all do. Like the rounders of yesteryear, they quickly fade into the shadows when the handout they're seeking turns into a hand-up.[47]

Like many other organizations teaching self-sufficiency, Delancey, Union Gospel Mission, and Step 13 do not take government money. The strings that are attached to such grants can conflict with their missions.

For example, recipient organizations are often required to tone down their no-nonsense message. Faith-based institutions are especially hampered by such restrictions. St. Martin de Porres House of Hope in Chicago, which provides shelter to homeless women (especially addicts) and their children, is one of these. Although the founder, Sister Connie Driscoll doesn't evangelize, she does want her clients to see her faith at work. Only 5% of graduates from Sister Driscoll's program return to shelters, one of the best success rates ever recorded.[48]

Another faith-based drug rehabilitation program, Teen Challenge, takes no tax money and has more than 100 chapters across the country. Its long-term cure rates are 67–85%, earning it praise from the National Institute on Drug Abuse. The Texas Commission on Alcohol and Drug Abuse (TCADA), however, threatened to shut down the San Antonio branch because it violated trivial regulations (e.g., frayed carpeting) and employing unlicensed drug counselors. TCADA wanted Teen Challenge to follow state guidelines imposed on other drug rehabilitation centers which had a success rates of a mere 10%. Only when a nonprofit group, the Institute for Justice, threatened a lawsuit did the TCADA officials back off.[49]

Kimi Gray, a 29-year-old coordinator for her public housing project, was approached by three

When I mention redistribution, people think I'm talking about taking all the money from the rich and giving it to the poor. That wouldn't help a bit! ... Our redistribution must involve us—our time, our energy, our gifts, and our skills.

—John Perkins
WITH JUSTICE FOR ALL

teens who wanted to escape the poverty trap by going to college. Because they knew no college graduates, they weren't sure how to prepare. Kimi started a prep group, College Here We Come, which met regularly to study, drill, and practice taking exams. The dream of college seemed like an impossible one.

The enthusiasm of the determined students was catching, however, and soon the parents started a booster club to raise money through raffles, bake sales, and sundry other projects. Slowly but surely, the dream materialized. In August 1975, 17 youngsters left for out-of-town colleges amid the cheers and best wishes of the entire housing project.

College Here We Come continues and boasts more than 600 success stories. Kimi Gray and other residents eventually convinced the City of Washington, D.C., to let them manage the public housing project where they live. Rent receipts went up by 60%, and management costs went down by the same amount. Welfare and teenage pregnancy were cut in half, and crime fell by an incredible 75%.[50]

The Best Gifts That We Can Give

These success stories demonstrate that our poor, disabled, addicted, and homeless are quite capable of becoming self-sufficient when assisted by befriending leaders. Good role models, high expectations, and tough love are needed most: hand-ups, not handouts. Our time is the gift that's truly required; monetary donations are secondary and sometimes not even necessary. Charity-through-aggression only gives us the illusion, but not the reality, that we are helping the less fortunate.

For many of the impoverished, our aggression was a major contributing factor. Not understanding our own role in their plight, we compound our error by using more aggression in the hopes of helping. When our aggression backfires once again, we're too busy congratulating ourselves on our "compassion" to notice!

The best way to help the poor is to do away with the aggression that entraps them. For those who truly cannot support themselves and their families, voluntary contributions of time or money would be more than adequate.

The Generosity of the Human Spirit

In spite of rising taxes for aid programs, Americans donated twice as many inflation-adjusted dollars to charity in 1996 as they did in 1970. Half of the adult population does some type of volunteer work. *Their contributions in time and money exceed the poverty budgets of federal, state, and local governments combined.*[51]

The people of other developed nations are just as generous. Because they care about their neighbor, they support the redistribution programs of their governments in the belief that those in need will be helped.

Generosity will only increase when government programs end. In the past, private contributions made up the difference when government backed away. In the 1980s, President Ronald Reagan's spending and welfare cuts gave Americans the money and the incentive to increase their charitable contributions, which had declined after the War on Poverty had begun.[52] When they were no longer forced to support failing welfare programs, they voluntarily increased their giving.

When disaster strikes, Americans contribute readily to help those in need. In 1871, when one-third of the City of Chicago burned to the ground, the Chicago Relief and Aid Society coordinated private donations that poured in from all over the country.

Able-bodied victims of the fire were put to work clearing away rubble and salvaging what remained in return for aid. Only the infirm, elderly, widows and children were exempted from the work requirement. Because the Society used the donations carefully, it was able to help resupply businesses, build new housing, and even open a garment factory to replace jobs lost in the fire.[53]

When the Twin Towers were devastated on September 11, 2001, Americans responded immediately. When the Red Cross put out a call for blood, people waited in line for hours to give blood. *Over $2.7 billion in donations flooded the*

Americans make really great sacrifices for the common good, and I have noticed a hundred cases in which, when help was needed, they hardly ever failed to give each other support.
—Alexis de Tocqueville
DEMOCRACY IN AMERICA

American Red Cross and other relief agencies, dwarfing collections for any previous disaster. Indeed, most of the agencies were so overwhelmed by the outpouring of funds that they were still distributing it a year later![54]

Because New York City lost its fire truck in the disaster, White Knoll Middle School of Columbia, South Carolina, raised almost $450,000 to buy the city a new one. Back in 1867, New York fire fighters had donated a fire wagon to Columbia, which was still using bucket brigades. The truck was lost en route, so New York fire fighters had supplied a second one. Former Confederate Colonel Samuel Melton was so touched that he promised Columbia would come to New York's aid should it ever be needed. In 2001, the promise was remembered and fulfilled.[55]

The return gift of the fire truck is reminiscent of how the marketplace safety net worked in early America. The poor helped each other. One social worker reminded his colleagues that their assistance paled in comparison to what neighbors offered to other neighbors in trouble. He wrote: "If there were no resources in times of exceptional distress except the provision which people would voluntarily make on their own account and the informal neighborly help which people would give to one another ... most of the misfortunes would still be provided for."[56]

The Tried and True Safety Net: Mutual Aid

Spontaneous, mutual aid among neighbors created a safety net against misfortune long before social work became a profession. When society was much poorer than today, a family could easily become destitute if the breadwinner became ill, was incapacitated, or died. Consequently, neighbors spontaneously supported each other in times of crises, knowing that they might one day be grateful recipients of such aid.

Eventually, some of these informal networks became models for mutual aid societies. Almost half of the working class belonged to one or more of these groups, which collected small annual dues used to help members in the event of misfortune. Many of the organizations were staffed by volunteers, who made sure that claimants received help tailored to their needs.

Mutual aid societies covered virtually every eventuality that insurance companies and social safety nets do today, including death, disability, sickness, accident, and retirement benefits. As mutual aid societies grew, they built hospitals, old age homes, sanitariums, and orphanages for their members.[57] Society members considered themselves part of an extended family where emotional support could also be found in times of need.[58] Because they generally prohibited formal distinctions on the basis of class or income, such societies promoted a sense of equality among members.[59]

Mutual aid societies pioneered affordable health care for low- and middle-income families. The society would hire a physician, usually a new one without an established practice. Women doctors were particularly favored by fraternal societies at a time when social and professional barriers made it difficult for women to practice. The lodge paid doctors an annual fee for the care of all local members as needed. The annual cost to the average worker was a single day's pay.[60] Because medical access was through his mutual aid society rather than his employer, a worker took his insurance with him from job to job.[61]

This win–win practice for the doctor and the workers ended with the aggression of medical licensing laws. Physicians who contracted with a mutual aid society, and sometimes even their patients, were denied access to the local hospital, which feared loss of its teaching accreditation if it didn't exclude them as the physician licensing boards demanded. Doctors were threatened with the revocation of their licenses for contracting with lodges.[62]

Some societies reacted by establishing their own hospitals, but the aggression of licensing laws eventually forced them to close their doors. Hospitals for treating blacks were informally exempted from such scrutiny so that their black patients wouldn't need to use resources at "white" hospitals.

In the 1960s, however, regulators started citing black hospitals for inadequate storage and bed space, doors that didn't swing open in two directions, unlicensed practitioners, and so on.

... practically every provision embodied in the Social Security Act has been carried successfully by the fraternal societies of America for years, and all without cost to the taxpayer.

—James J. Davis
Mooseheart Board of
Governors

Regulatory pressures eventually caused the demise of the remaining society hospitals.[63]

Aggression Kills Mutual Aid

Mutual aid societies continued their work through the Great Depression. To remain solvent, many merged with other organizations, but *few failed to deliver the promised benefits.*[64]

Regulations and licensing laws eventually destroyed the societies. Regulations limited the benefits societies could offer and required an prohibitively high reserve requirement, in spite of their excellent performance record.[65] In addition, government programs, like Social Security and welfare, lulled people into assuming that mutual aid societies were no longer necessary.

Clearly, the marketplace ecosystem pioneered an effective and affordable safety net that survived both World War I and the Great Depression. Mutual aid, however, was destroyed through our well-meaning aggression-through-government. Forced charity and licensing laws extinguished mutual aid, taking us from self-sufficiency to dependency.

The freedom from aggression that makes it possible to create great wealth also inspires generosity of spirit. However, the belief that our taxes are taking care of the poor discourages us from giving them the time and attention that would be even more valuable.

As a befriending leader, we can help others learn to climb the Ladder of Affluence. Ultimately, showing someone how to be independent of our charity is the best gift that we can give!

Each man should give what he has decided in his heart to give, not reluctantly or under compulsion, for God loves a cheerful giver.
　　—THE HOLY BIBLE
　　2 Corinthians 9:7

Chapter 11: Springing the Poverty Trap

In Summary ...

- Poverty is caused by unemployment, which usually results from minimum wage and licensing laws.
- By trying to alleviate poverty with tax-supported welfare, we tempt the disadvantaged to accept an aid check instead of a pay check.
- Welfare breaks up the family by encouraging multiple illegitimate births and discouraging marriage.
- By the time young mothers realize that welfare is a dead-end, they are caught in the poverty trap. Entry level jobs don't pay enough to support her many children, but while she is on welfare, no progress is possible.
- When welfare recipients are required to do community work, more than half get a job and get off the dole.
- Welfare reform in 1996 slashed black child poverty to the lowest levels ever seen by 2000.
- While tax-supported charity doesn't help the poor, private charitable groups have been incredibly effective in helping the homeless, the addicted, the criminal, and the illiterate.
- The most successful private programs accept little or no tax support. Indeed, their existence is often threatened by regulations imposed by bureaucrats. Even Mother Teresa's helpers were put out of business in New York!
- An entire mutual aid network that once provided a social safety net for low- and middle-income Americans, survived both World War I and the Great Depression. Regulations, however, destroyed mutual aid.
- The human spirit is so generous that the time and money contributed by Americans exceeds the entire poverty budgets of federal, state, and local governments. Without the aggression-through-government that makes people poor, befriending leadership and charitable donations would be more than sufficient to care for the truly needy.

Chapter 12

By Their Fruits You Shall Know Them

It's just as well that aggression creates poverty instead of wealth. Otherwise, we'd be eternally at war with each other!

What Have We Learned So Far?

We began our journey through the topics in this book searching for a way to create a world of universal harmony and abundance. In the first half of this book, we discovered that *freedom from aggression, especially aggression-through-government, is the single most important factor in modern-day wealth creation.*

Put another way, freedom from aggression means that others, including government officials, do not confront us with first-strike force, fraud, or theft. If they do harm us, they make it right again. We treat them with similar respect, honoring their choices and righting any wrongs that we do. We act as Good Neighbors.

We learned these basics principles as children. The Good Neighbor Policy kept our little part of the world a safe haven where we could prosper and grow (Chapter 1).

The Good Neighbor Policy or parts of it are widely embodied in our culture (e.g., the Golden Rule, the Ten Commandments). Individuals are usually expected to be Good Neighbors, but governments are not. Consequently, in the modern world, governments are the greatest aggressors.

In the 1800s, both Britain and the United States had less aggression-through-government than other nations. Consequently, these countries began to create wealth at a rate much faster than other nations (Figure 2.2).

Prior to this time, the only way to be free from aggression-through-government was to bribe or lobby government officials. Clearly, the poor were at a disadvantage in such a system. When they became free from this aggression, the numerous poor created great wealth. The prosperity of the English-speaking countries, therefore, was accompanied by a decrease in poverty, just as it is today (Figure 2.3).

In the 1800s, most people recognized that aggression-through-government was the single

The moral lesson we learn as children becomes simple realism in adult life: ultimately the methods used to reach a goal do end up determining the outcome.

—Frances Moore
Lappe et al.
BETRAYING THE
NATIONAL INTEREST

... more financial wealth has been generated in the United States over the past 50 years than was created in all the rest of the world in all the centuries before 1950.

—Stephan Moore and
Julian Simon
GLOBAL FORTUNE

greatest hindrance to wealth creation. Freedom from this aggression meant prosperity and an end to widespread starvation, disease, and premature death. Other factors (e.g., education, percentage of working adults, investment), even combined, have much less impact.[1] Consequently, people valued this freedom above all else.

Freedom from aggression-through-government allowed people freedom to choose their profession. They no longer had to get the permission of bureaucrats to create wealth. Freedom to choose was an outgrowth of freedom from aggression-through-government. Freedom to choose allowed people to create wealth, giving them freedom to live their dreams. Freedom, in its political context, has many shades of meaning, but all stem from freedom from government aggression.

Confusion about what "freedom" means has muddied our intellectual waters. We want everyone to be free to live their dreams and see lack of wealth as the greatest obstacle for most people. Rather than asking why some people aren't able to create wealth, we assume that wealth itself is limited and must therefore be "redistributed." We see poverty as a failure of the rich to "share." We blame selfish others for the world's plight, instead of taking responsibility for the manifestations of our own ignorance.

This mentality of separation (us/them, win/lose, sharing/selfish) ripples outward to create the illusion of winners and losers. For example, if we believe that poverty results from the low wages paid by stingy employers, we enact minimum wage laws (first-layer aggression) to bend these selfish others to our will (Chapter 3). We teach workers to blame employers for low wages, rather than to acknowledge their own lack of skills. *Resentment flares between employers and employees.* The foundation for strife has been laid.

Just as the aggression of minimum wage laws encourages animosity between employers and employees, the aggression of licensing laws creates *suspicion between businesses and consumers.* As licensing laws become stricter, the number of service providers diminish, and the remaining few providers can charge more for less. Consumers then feel that they are being exploited. They are indeed being cheated; not by service providers, but by first-layer aggression that eliminates their choices (Chapters 4–6).

Eventually, licensing laws become so restrictive that they exclude all but a single service provider, creating monopolies that give us high prices and poor quality (Chapter 7). *Second-layer aggression favors the big at the expense of the small.* When competition is eliminated, we experience the dominance of large, exploitive corporate monopolies.

Coercive monopolies, especially those run by bureaucrats (e.g., the U.S. Postal Service), often require tax subsidies for their survival. Third-layer aggression enables special interest groups to exploit forests, rangelands, and other sensitive environments (Chapter 8). Not only does wealth creation suffer, but our earth is harmed as well. Subsidies set the stage for *conflicts between industrialists and environmentalists.*

Fourth-layer aggression, which forces us to use subsidized monopolies, are even more harmful. Forced use allows the people who control the money monopoly to manipulate the value of our savings at their whim (Chapter 9). *In trying to control others with layer upon layer of aggression, we ultimately find ourselves controlled.*

We don't notice how our fear of selfish others creates the very world that we want to avoid. Our minds are trained by the education monopoly (Chapter 10), itself a creature of fourth-layer aggression. We can hardly expect to learn the follies of aggression from an institution built on it. Instead, our instructors, paid by taxation, teach us that such aggression is necessary and beneficial. Like the volunteers who shocked the victim at an authority figure's request (Chapter 1), *we allow ourselves to be persuaded that our violence will do no harm and may even do good.*

When we adopt aggression as our means, we impoverish ourselves. Many functions of modern government are actually acts of aggression perpetrated against one group at the request of another. Even defense against the aggression of

Government is not reason; it is not eloquence. It is force. And force like fire is a dangerous servant and a fearful master.
—George Washington
first president of the
United States

The state spends much time and effort persuading the public that it is not really what it is and that the consequences of its actions are positive rather than negative.
—Hans-Hermann
Hoppe
A THEORY OF SOCIALISM
AND CAPITALISM

Low-growth cities spend, on the average, $1.71 per person for every $1.00 spent in high-growth cities.

—EXECUTIVE ALERT
July/August 1993

... a 10 percentage point increase in government expenditures as a share of GDP leads to approximately a 1 percentage point reduction in economic growth.

—James Gwartney,
Randall Holcombe, and
Robert Lawson
THE SCOPE OF
GOVERNMENT AND THE
WEALTH OF NATIONS

individuals or other nations is paid for through the aggression of either taxation or inflation. (We'll discover a better way to pay for these services in Part III.) Consequently, government spending of today only increases through aggression. The more that government spends, the more limited wealth creation becomes (Figure 12.1). The negative impact of total government spending on wealth creation holds true at the state[2] and city[3] level too.

Even when government spends "for a good cause," society becomes poorer. For example, between 1960 and 1996, Swedish government spending went from 31% to 66% of GDP. Wealth creation fell from 4.9% (1960–1965) to a mere 0.6% (1990–1996).[4] Sweden, which prides itself on its social safety nets, is destroying its ability to create the very wealth it wishes to redistribute! If wealth creation continues to fall, Swedish citizens will become poorer every year instead of richer. Sweden's poor will not be helped by policies that put the entire nation at risk.

Rich nations like Sweden can lose their ability to create wealth simply by increasing government spending.[5] Freedom from aggression is not something that countries can "afford" only after they become wealthy. Freedom from aggression is a necessary precondition for wealth.

Aggression, however well intentioned, creates poverty. Using aggression to help the poor only creates more poverty (Chapter 11).

How the World Really Works!

The discovery that aggression harms, rather than helps, the poor often surprises us. In government schools, we have been taught that aggression-through-government is the salvation of the poor. Clearly, the high cost of counteracting aggression leads to its use as a tool of the rich. Only the well-to-do can afford to lobby, bribe, or threaten our elected representatives effectively. Unlike the well-to-do, the poor cannot afford to pay licensing fees or meet exhaustive requirements. Inflation may force a wealthy person to cut back on luxuries, but it forces the poor to go hungry. Poor nutrition can limit energy and cut back further on wealth creation by the poor, which only perpetuates their downward spiral. Aggression creates poverty and sustains it. Aggression is the poor's greatest enemy.

Conversely, freedom from aggression is the poor's greatest benefactor. As we'll find in subsequent chapters, *most poverty in the world today is caused by aggression-through-government.* The illusion that this aggression benefits the poor at the expense of the rich is just that—an illusion. It is the wolf in sheep's clothing, the temptation in the Garden of Eden, the spark from which the flames of war and poverty spring. We should not be surprised that aggression, however well meaning, creates poverty and strife in our city, state, and nation just as it does in one-on-one interactions in our neighborhoods. *The same means always create the same ends.*

All government intervention is "not merely ineffectual, but also pernicious and counterproductive." And that means all.
—FORBES, March 6, 1989

Figure 12.1: Wealth Creation vs. Government Spending

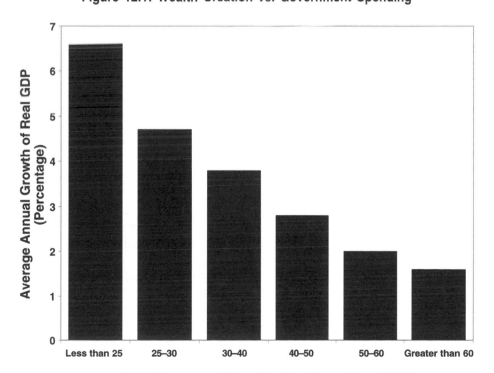

Total Government Spending As a Percentage of GDP

Reprinted with permission from J. Gwartney, R. Holcombe, and R. Lawson, "The Scope of Government and the Wealth of Nations," *Cato Journal* 18: 171, 1998.

Don't be tricked into believing the choice is between sacrificing yourself to others or others to yourself. ... You wouldn't accept it if someone told you your only choice was between sadism and masochism, would you? The same principle applies here.

—Ayn Rand
author of THE VIRTUE OF
SELFISHNESS

Aggression, undertaken individually or undertaken collectively through government, can never create its opposite—harmony and abundance. Our desire to use aggression (first-strike force, theft, or fraud) to create a peaceful and prosperous world is like asking for a circular triangle. Something cannot have three sides while, at the same time, have no sides at all! We cannot create harmony by taking up arms against peaceful neighbors when we disagree with their choices. Unprovoked, armed attack is a declaration of war.

Those who wish to control us encourage our belief in a win-lose world where we must do unto others before they do unto us. Once we accept this premise, we willingly defer to the authority figures who attack those selfish others on our behalf. When we recognize that we live in a win-win world, *we no longer need to choose between the welfare of ourselves and that of others.* Instead, we recognize that both conditions rise and fall together. Consequently, it is in our own best interest to offer our neighbor love instead of war. *Honoring our neighbor's choice is the political manifestation of universal love.*

How wonderful it is that our world works this way! If striking first brought us a plentiful world, we would have to choose between either war and wealth *or* peace and starvation. A peaceful, prosperous world would be impossible. Instead, we can enjoy both harmony and abundance by honoring our neighbor's choice. Truly, we live in a win-win world!

Now we can see why aggression-through-government is generally more destructive to a nation's wealth creation than individual aggression. Government aggression (e.g., taxes and regulations) affects the whole country. Rarely, if ever, do all the individual aggressors (thieves, murderers, *etc.*) destroy as much total wealth as aggression-through-government does.

The good news is that this process can be reversed! The only three developed countries that substantially decreased their government expenditures between 1960 and 1996 also increased their wealth creation significantly (Figure 12.2).[6] Less aggression results in more wealth.

How Much Wealth Could We Create If We Didn't Use Aggression?

Of course, wealthy nations are not entirely free from aggression. What could they hope for if they were?

A conservative estimate based on the economic freedom index (EFI), suggests that the United States would experience 2.7 times as much wealth creation as it did in 1995.[7] Another model predicts that wealth creation in the United States would increase to 18.5 times the 1995 rate if federal taxation were abandoned.[8] This figure is 18.5 times the 1995 wealth creation rate. In theory, it may be an *upper estimate* should the United States become free from aggression.[9]

Most likely, adopting the Good Neighbor Policy in the United States at our current level of knowledge would increase wealth creation by somewhere between 3 and 18 times! Part of the

... raising one dollar through the tax system carries a waste of 33.2 cents in lost production.
    —James L. Payne
    Overcoming Welfare

When taxes are too high, people go hungry.
    —Lao-tsu
    Tao Te Ching

Figure 12.2: Wealth Creation vs. Government Spending

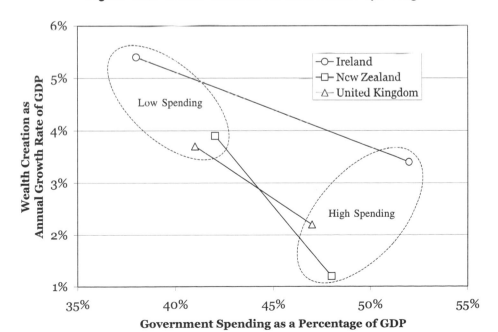

Data from J. Gwartney, R. Holcombe, and R. Lawson, "The Scope of Government and the Wealth of Nations" in *Cato Journal* 18: 185, 1998. Low spending periods were 1987–1996 for Ireland, 1993–1996 for New Zealand, and 1983–1989 for the United Kingdom. High spending periods were 1960–1986 for Ireland, 1974–1992 for New Zealand, and 1960–1982 for the United Kingdom.

wealth consists of new discoveries that help us create even more wealth. As our knowledge increases, the amount of wealth we can create grows as well!

What would you do if your paycheck tripled, quadrupled, or soared even higher? Would you send you children to better schools, take more vacations, work less, donate time and money to your favorite charity? Would you be able to pay off your credit card debt and mortgage, start your own business, or retire early? The increase in wealth would be so dramatic, it's difficult to even imagine it!

The most dramatic change of all would be new goods and services that are the true wealth of a nation. Most likely, we'd have cures for our deadliest diseases: cancer, heart disease, AIDS, and the deterioration of old age! Perhaps we'd visit other planets of even colonize them as new technologies gave us travel speeds that we can only dream of today.

I let go of all desire for the common good, and the good becomes as common as the grass.

—Lao-tsu
Tao Te Ching

We'd be able to take better care of our earth as well, since we'd be able to learn more about Nature's ecosystems and how best to maintain them. Poverty, as we know it today, would become a historical curiosity. We'd be able to create more wealth in less time, increasing leisure for study, play, friends, or family.

The loss that we experience because of our aggression is staggering: the damage done to our forests and prairie lands; the boom-and-bust cycles that cripple the poor; the hopeless future of millions of illiterate children; the absence of lifesaving drugs and antiaging therapies; the space explorations that never launch; starvation; poverty. *The lost wealth means that the suffering we could have stopped must continue.*

Why, then, did the developed countries stop honoring their neighbor's choice when it served them so well? While many people understood the dangers of aggression-through-government, they did not know how to cope with *individuals* who aggressed against others. They didn't have the other piece of the puzzle. As a result, they tried to prevent aggression by becoming aggressors themselves, with consequences more terrible than those they sought to prevent. In the following chapters, we'll explore a better way to deal with those individuals who would aggress against us while still remaining Good Neighbors!

The Fruits of Honoring Our Neighbor's Choice

Chapter 12: By Their Fruits You Shall Know Them

In Summary ...

- Freedom from aggression-through-government is the most important determinant of a country's rate of wealth creation.
- Since modern government can only collect the money it spends through taxation or inflation, government programs start with aggression.
- Consequently, as government spending increases, wealth creation increases.
- When Sweden increased government spending from 31% to 66% for its social safely net, wealth creation plummeted from 4.9% annually to a mere 0.6%.
- Slowing wealth creation hurts the poor the most. Consequently, aggression-through-government is the poor's greatest enemy.
- Most poverty in the world today is caused by aggression-through-government. When nations cut back on government spending, they automatically cut back on this aggression.
- The three countries that have slashed government spending in recent years (Ireland, New Zealand, and the United Kingdom) increased their wealth creation dramatically.
- Without aggression, we'd create wealth 3 to 18 times faster!
- When we recognize that we live in a win–win world, we no longer need to choose between our welfare and that of others, between what's good for the individual and what's good for society. Instead, we recognize that our mutual welfare rises and falls together.

Part Three

As We Forgive Those Who Trespass Against Us:

How We Create Strife in a World of Harmony

Chapter 13

The Other Piece of the Puzzle

Justice does not consist of punishing the aggressor, but of making the victim whole.

Righting Our Wrongs

So far, we've seen how our aggression, meant to protect us from selfish others, is a cure worse than the disease. Can we deter those who would harm us without becoming aggressors ourselves?

We know what we'd do if we accidentally put a baseball through our neighbor George's window. We'd go to him and offer to fix it. If George had been cut by flying glass, we'd pay his doctor bills. We might even offer George something to make up for his discomfort. George would be unlikely to hold a grudge against us if we "made things right" again.

If we didn't volunteer to pay for the window, George would probably be angry. If he had us arrested, we might go to jail. George would still have a broken window to fix and perhaps doctor bills as well. In today's system, he'd also pay taxes to cover the cost of apprehending, convicting, and imprisoning us. It's doubtful that George would feel very positive about dealing with us in the future.

The situation would become even more unbalanced if we were to actually gain from our "crime." Had we stolen George's valuable coin collection instead of breaking his window, we might come out ahead, even if we spent a few days in jail. We might decide that crime pays and continue our aggressive behavior.

Apparently, many criminals have come to the same conclusion. Of those imprisoned, 70% will be arrested again.[1] Crime today is often committed by "career criminals," who average more than 100 offenses per year.[2]

Perhaps we should not be surprised that aggression permeates our culture. As we saw in earlier chapters, we've condoned aggression of the majority against the minority. We've taught others that a "good cause" can justify stealing George's wealth—at gunpoint, if necessary. Burglars, rapists, and murderers may rationalize that looking out for Number One is the best cause of all!

Nonaggression Wins the Game

The first step in putting an end to aggression is to stop teaching it by example. We cannot cast stones when we ourselves are guilty. Next, we must respond to aggression in a way that will *deter* aggression in the future rather than perpetuate it.

The second principle of the Good Neighbor Policy, righting our wrongs, discouraged us from aggression as children. Breaking other children's toys didn't make much sense if we were going to have to replace them out of our allowance. When what we gave out was reflected back to us, we learned quickly how to be Good Neighbors.

A well-known psychological game, the Prisoner's Dilemma, which mimics how honesty is learned, actually predicts this outcome. In the Prisoner's Dilemma, two prisoners must decide, when held apart from each other, whether to keep their pact to remain silent. If they are both true to their promise, they will each gain freedom (3 points apiece). If both break their promise and incriminate the other, they both end up in prison (1 point apiece). In both cases, they reap what they sow.

However, if they each choose differently, the promise breaker goes free (5 points), but the incriminated prisoner goes to jail (0 points). When both prisoners choose differently, one ends up feeling like a "sucker" and the promise breaker feels that dishonesty is the best policy. In addition to the physical outcome (prison or freedom), there is a psychological payoff as well, reflected by more points for the promise breaker and less for the sucker. Now each prisoner is not reaping as they have sown. The aggressor (promise breaker) comes out ahead.

The point system reflects the cynical view of human nature that is prevalent in our culture today. If selfish others betray our trust, we can lose only by being honest. If they are honest, we still gain more by cheating! Doing unto others before they do unto us seems to be the best alternative. This viewpoint is reflected in our aggressive laws, as described previously in Part II.

How did honesty, cooperation, and the Good Neighbor Policy ever evolve in a system that seems to favor aggressors and penalize those who keep their promises or contracts? If the Prisoner's Dilemma has any relation to reality, some other factor must be involved.

Indeed, it is! When players have to deal with each other repetitively, they adapt to each other's response.

This discovery was make when computers were programmed to play the Prisoner's Dilemma repetitively with prisoners using different strategies. One strategy always cheated. Another strategy always was honest. One strategy cheated twice for every time the other broke a promise. Another was honest until the other prisoner broke his promise, and so on.

Some of the strategies were quite complex. Computers were used to play each strategy a specified number of times and keep score. The tournaments were replicated many times, varying strategies and the number of repetitive interactions. One strategy, however, almost always came out ahead.

This winning strategy was called TIT FOR TAT. In its first interaction with another strategy, it dealt honestly. After that, TIT FOR TAT reflected back what the "other" had done last. If the other program had been honest, TIT FOR TAT was too. If the other program had defrauded, TIT FOR TAT cheated in the next interaction. Other computer strategies quickly learned how TIT FOR TAT worked and began to deal honestly to create a win–win scenario.[3]

TIT FOR TAT practiced the first principle of nonaggression, and so did every program that scored in the top half of the games. TIT FOR TAT never was the *first* to defraud. When TIT FOR TAT encountered an aggressor (a program that defrauded *first*), it reflected exactly what the other gave it—nothing more, nothing less.

TIT FOR TAT won the game by converting aggressors to nonaggressors. It first set a good example and then allowed aggressors to experience the fruits of their actions. In essence, TIT FOR TAT modeled the Good Neighbor Policy.

Of course, computer games and real life often bear no relation to each other. However, the TIT FOR TAT strategy is commonly used throughout the animal kingdom to teach cooperation. Stickleback fish, divorcing couples, and even enemy combatants in trench warfare instinctively use TIT FOR TAT to create cooperation in the midst of strife. Such findings have made the Prisoner's Dilemma and the TIT FOR TAT strategy a starting point for studies in many diverse fields ranging from evolutionary biology to networked computer systems.[4] Because TIT FOR TAT so strongly resembles the Good Neighbor Policy, it may give us insight for creating a world of peace and plenty.

As seen in the preceding chapters, we often try, unsuccessfully, to deter aggression with aggression. *Similarly, the tournaments with the Prisoner's Dilemma suggest that aggression elicits retaliation, not cooperation.* Perhaps that's why we found in Part II that aggression was a cure worse than the disease!

TIT FOR TAT's success also implies that we deter and rehabilitate aggressors best when we allow them to experience the fruits of their actions. If we break George's window, we repair it and thereby learn to be more careful in the future. Righting our wrongs "rehabilitates" us and dissipates any hostility that we have caused. We re-create the peace and wealth that we have destroyed.

Unfortunately, in our society aggressors rarely experience the fruits of their actions by making their victims whole again. Most are never caught. We'll learn a better way to deal with this problem in Chapter 16.

Even when they are caught, however, less than one-third of convicted burglars are even imprisoned.[5] Because only one prison term is served for every 164 felonies committed,[6] aggressors often look at imprisonment as simply the cost of doing business as a career criminal.

Usually, aggressors are not required to repair the damage they've done. Imprisonment as punishment does not help them experience what their actions have cost others or defuse the hostility that they have caused. Thus, aggressors rarely take responsibility for their crimes and may actually feel victimized by "the system." As a result, they continue their aggression and prey on others.

A Better Way: Restitution

How could we implement TIT FOR TAT's strategy to deter aggression? To a large extent, Japan already has. *Its system of apology and restitution to domestic crime victims has made Japan the only industrialized country where crime rates have fallen every year since World War II.*[7]

In Japan, once a wrongdoer has been caught, he or she is expected to negotiate a settlement with the victim. Usually, a mediator, often a relative of the offender, visits with the victim. First, through the intermediary, the aggressor apologizes to the victim and offers restitution. After a period of negotiation, the victim may accept both the apology and the settlement. He or she will then write a letter to the judge, expressing satisfaction with the offer. The offender receives a light fine or sentence, because the judge is satisfied that the wronged party has been made whole again.

If the victim and aggressor cannot agree on a settlement, the judge must decide if the victim is simply being unreasonable or if the aggressor is not sorry enough to make a good-faith bargaining effort. If the judge finds fault with the criminal's offers, a harsh sentence is imposed. Thus, offenders have a great deal of incentive to make things right for their victims.[8]

When aggressors experience the harm that was done, they are, in essence, receiving the "punishment" that TIT FOR TAT gives cheaters. They learn honesty, as evidenced by Japan's lower crime rates[9] and fewer repeat offenses.[10]

Most career criminals start with small offenses. In Japan, they are twice as likely to get caught as in the United States,[11] partially because victims have something to gain by turning to the authorities. Only if the victim reports the crime can the aggressor be apprehended and

The principles of restorative justice are consistent with those of many indigenous traditions, including Native American, Hawaiian, Canadian First Nation people, Aborigines in Australia, and the Maori in New Zealand. These principles are also consistent with values emphasized in nearly all of the world's religions.
—Mark Umbreit
WESTERN CRIMINOLOGY
REVIEW

offer restitution. When criminals reap what they sow, they are more likely to turn away from crime before it becomes a career.

Western nations are starting to reintroduce restitution into their victim–offender mediation programs. In face-to-face dialogues, both victims and aggressors can express their feelings. Ninety-five percent of such meetings result in a consensus on appropriate restitution, much as similar negotiations in Japan might do. Restitution is usually financial, although personal service to the victim and community service are sometimes included as well.[12] Mediation programs report contract fulfillment of 79–98%.[13]

Reconciliation meetings between victims and aggressors can be healing to both parties. Ms. Brugger of Elkhart, Indiana, plagued with insomnia after two burglars raided her home, was finally able to rest soundly after speaking her piece and receiving promises of restitution.[14] Although the possibility of restitution motivates many victims to enter mediation, they often find that telling the offender how they feel is even more satisfying.[15]

Aggressors also feel differently after mediation, making comments such as "I realized that the victim really got hurt and that made me feel really bad" and "I had a chance of doing something to correct what I did without having to pay bad consequences."[16] As one might expect from such comments, offenders involved in mediation are less likely to commit additional crimes.[17]

Although most mediation in Western countries has been with juvenile offenders for theft and minor assaults, recent reconciliations have involved murder and sexual assault as well.[18] Both victims and offenders find that a great deal of healing occurs in these supervised meetings. When aggressors express sorrow at the suffering they cause, victims find a measure of peace.[19]

An Even Better Way: Full Restitution

Requiring aggressors to *fully* right their wrongs might deter criminals even further. Victim restoration is only part of the true cost of aggression. Catching offenders, holding them until the case is resolved, and even the mediation

A thief must certainly make restitution, but if he has nothing, he must be sold to pay for his theft.
—THE HOLY BIBLE
Exodus 22:3

process itself are costly. Taxing other members of society, including the victim, to pay those costs creates additional victims. Indeed, those expenses are likely to dwarf the value of goods stolen in most burglaries. Full restoration requires that aggressors cover these costs as well.

How might such a justice system work? Because most aggression involves theft or burglary,[20] let's first examine how such violators might fully right their wrongs.

Thieves would be expected to negotiate a settlement to compensate the victim and pay for the costs of apprehension, mediation, and any other losses resulting from their crime. If the victim carried insurance, the company could pay the victim immediately and collect from the thief. Uninsured victims might receive payments, with interest, from the offender. Depending on the crime, some victims might accept personal services (e.g., painting, grass cutting) from the wrongdoers as part of the compensation.

Thieves who refused to make payments might be put in a prison factory. They could earn money to pay their debts along with the added costs of their imprisonment. The harder the inmates worked, the sooner they would be released. Prisoners could choose the prison that helped them make the most money in the least amount of time, given their particular skills or experience. The ability to choose a prison and transfer at will would help minimize inmate exploitation and maximize prisoner pay.

Private prisons keep costs down[21] and quality up. In addition to outperforming public facilities, private prisons have lower escape rates and fewer inmate disturbances.[22] If inmates had transfer privileges, an abusive facility would lose prisoners. Business and profits would suffer. Each prison would reap what it sowed.

Contrast this self-regulation of the marketplace ecosystem with our current situation. Although 150 county governments and 39 states were charged with violating prison regulations in 1984, prisoners are unlikely to receive any compensation for their mistreatment.[23] Transferring to a more humane institution is not an option.

... inmates rate the private facilities as "substantially better" in staff treatment, safety, medical care, recreation, education, visitation, and substance abuse programs and that the inmates' mood was substantially better in the private facilities as well.
—Bruce Benson
TO SERVE AND PROTECT

During the nineteenth century many state prisons actually were able to finance their own operations and turn over surplus funds to state treasuries.
—Bruce Benson
TO SERVE AND PROTECT

Obviously, imprisonment greatly increases the debt a thief would be required to pay. Most thieves would make regular payments to the victim or the victim's insurance company to avoid prison and its added costs.

Taxpayers would no longer need to support those who did not agree to right their wrongs. Because food and other commodities would have to be purchased from the prison store, criminals who refused to work would have to rely on charity for sustenance. Inmates would be motivated to take responsibility for their lives.

Prisoners who refused to work would be unlikely to starve to death, however. Most prisons would probably provide a simple, but not necessarily appetizing diet for such individuals. Charitable individuals or groups could help support prisoners if they felt circumstances warranted such compassion. Repentant young offenders facing a lifetime of payments for a single mistake might find charitable sponsors to shoulder part of their debt.

Nevertheless, some uninsured victims might never be fully compensated. Partial payment, however, would be better than nothing, which is what they usually receive today.

Are prisoners capable of creating wealth even when imprisoned? In the early 1900s, my great-grandfather's factory gave inmates of the Missouri State Penitentiary jobs making saddle parts. Not only was the prison self-supporting, it also made a small profit![24] The inmates grew their own food and manufactured brooms and men's clothing. The prison prided itself on the health of the prisoners, noting that epidemics were rare and the death rate was "less than that of the average village." Self-financing prisons were common in the nineteenth century.[25]

In recent years, more than 70 companies have employed inmates in 16 states.[26] Best Western International uses prisoners to operate its telephone reservation system. Trans World Airlines hires young offenders in California to handle its telephone reservations. A private corporation, Prison Re- habilitative Industries & Diversified Enterprises (PRIDE) of Clearwater, Florida, manages 53 prison work programs.

Wages are used to pay taxes, costs of imprisonment, restitution, and family support.[27] Some individuals on probation contribute to the cost of their supervision while working at regular jobs.[28]

Before 1980, inmates of the Maine State Prison manufactured arts and crafts, which were sold through the prison store. Individuals made as much as $30,000 per year, the equivalent of about $64,500 in 2001. Some of their businesses were so successful that the prisoners no longer wanted to commit crimes.[29]

In such an environment, inmates could gain work experience. Unskilled prisoners could participate in training programs to raise their hourly earnings. Instead of learning better ways to steal, they would learn alternatives to stealing. *Restitution through productive work is the most successful rehabilitation known.*[30]

Of course, aggressors sometimes harm others in ways that cannot be totally undone. Monetary compensation to a person who has been raped or maimed, or to families whose loved ones have been killed, does not make things right again. In some cases, the victims, their family, or their insurance company might accept a monetary settlement as the best compensation available. A repeat offender might be imprisoned permanently so he or she could not harm others. In a self-supporting prison system, victims would not have to clothe and feed those who had harmed them, as they do now.

Less Aggression Equals Less Crime

Today, it's difficult for young people to learn how to create wealth. When we destroy jobs by implementing minimum wages and licensing laws, unemployment and criminal activity rise.[31] Increasing welfare payments by 50% doubles the crime rate among young black men,[32] probably by encouraging breakup of the family as described in Chapter 11. When our aggression keeps the disadvantaged from creating wealth, stealing becomes an attractive option. When we destroy jobs with aggression, our chances of becoming crime victims increase. We reap what we sow.

Making sure that aggressors repay their victims could require the use of *retaliatory* force. Retaliatory force, by definition, is not *first-strike* force, but a *response* to first-strike force. Retaliatory force stops aggressors or compels them to compensate their victims. Using more force than is necessary to accomplish these ends can make us aggressors too. In the computer games, strategies that defrauded twice for every time that the other cheated did not do as well as TIT FOR TAT.

Turning the other cheek can discourage aggressors when they are not aware of what they are doing. India's Mohandas Gandhi understood this principle well. He and his followers engaged in nonviolent civil disobedience, allowing themselves to be imprisoned, beaten, or even killed to demonstrate the true nature of the British colonial government. The more violence the British employed, the worse they looked. The British, who did not wish to consider themselves aggressors, eventually changed their ways.

Gandhi's experience suggests that we do better when we err on the side of forgiveness, especially in situations where people "know not what they do."

Indeed, when the computer tournaments described earlier were changed so that a cooperative move was occasionally mistaken for fraud, a "generous" TIT FOR TAT scored more points than the original version. Forgiving aggression 10% of the time ensured that a misinterpreted move didn't create an endless echo between two TIT FOR TAT players. Because mistakes in the real world are frequent, erring on the side of forgiveness is a practical strategy.

In the real world, we may be the ones who make a mistake or have an accident. In the tournaments, a "contrite" version of TIT FOR TAT continued to be honest 10% of the time when a player that it had cheated tried to strike back. The contrite version scored more points than the original TIT FOR TAT. When we hurt others and we are attacked because of it, retaliation may not be the best policy.[33]

In summary, TIT FOR TAT teaches cooperation better than any other strategy. However, when we mistake how the other person is reacting to us, or if we occasionally send the wrong signal, erring on the side of forgiveness and contrition is appropriate.

Computer games have their limitations, but they do give us valuable insights. The successful TIT FOR TAT strategies all suggest that we should err on the side of less force not more. Good Neighbors win the game!

A Win–Win Scenario

When aggressors right their wrongs, everyone benefits. Victims are made whole again. Aggressors have the satisfaction of knowing that they have truly paid their debt. Taxpayers get relief when aggressors pay the costs of their capture and imprisonment. Prisoners don't lose years of earning power and work experience or suffer as much abuse. Prisons profit. Everyone wins!

What Might Have Been

In Part II, we examined how we've used aggression-through-government to control those who would harm us. In many Western nations, punishment was more common than restitution. Victims understandably felt cheated and wanted more prevention. Rather than deterring crime by moving from punishment to restoration, we tried to fight aggression by becoming aggressors ourselves. We could have made a better choice.

Instead of enacting licensing laws, for example, we could have required fraudulent service providers to compensate those they had harmed. Physicians who lied about their training and experience or pharmaceutical firms that made false claims about their drugs would have faced a powerful deterrent. Restitution, especially when it includes the costs of apprehension, mediation, and imprisonment, could absorb a lifetime of earning power. Although such offenders would be able to keep some of what they earned for survival and motivation, they would be unlikely to enjoy much luxury.

Bankruptcy would not be the easy option that it is today, because only victims or their surviving family could forgive the debt. Any service providers who lied about their credentials would be more visible and easier to catch than a hit-and-run driver or a thief in a dark alley. The high probability of being caught would serve as a powerful deterrent against fraud.[34] *Restitution would deter dishonest service providers without the negative consequences that accompany the aggression of licensing laws.*

Of course, individuals and businesses would not be held liable for risks that the consumer had agreed to take. People who chose to take a drug, even though the manufacturer advised against it, might have little recourse in case of injury. A person who hired a surgeon who freely admitted that he had no training would have difficulty mounting a successful lawsuit.

Restitution would also influence corporate liability. A corporation is a business that is held responsible for the damage it does only to the extent of its holdings. Owners (stockholders) and most corporate officers cannot be held personally liable except in unusual circumstances. Aggression-through-government prevents victims from obtaining justice either from the decision makers or the owners who hired them.

A better way of protecting businesses and investors from unforeseen liabilities while permitting victims to seek compensation is through insurance. Careful businesses would enjoy low premiums, while insurers would charge careless firms more. As a result, businesses would reap what they sow.

Victims with too few resources to prosecute their aggressors could hire a lawyer on contingency, just as many do today. Frivolous lawsuits would be less usual, because those who brought them could end up paying the legal costs of the person they unjustly accused. Today, a wealthy person or business can bankrupt a poor opponent simply by instigating a suit that requires an expensive defense. Rarely are the victims awarded costs as they would be in a system based on restitution.

Crime just doesn't pay when aggressors right their wrongs. As a result, restitution is the perfect "pollution solution," as described in the next chapter.

Chapter 13: The Other Piece of the Puzzle

In Summary ...

- Righting our wrongs is the second part of the Good Neighbor Policy.
- TIT FOR TAT is a well-known social strategy that acts very much like the Good Neighbor Policy. In both computer tournaments and diverse situations of strife, it has proven effective in convincing aggressors to become peaceful and cooperative.
- In addition to our own experience as children when we re-created the peace by righting our wrongs, TIT FOR TAT's record suggests that letting aggressors experience the harm that they have done is the best way to teach them to be Good Neighbors.
- When aggressors make their victims whole again, they experience the harm they have done to others. Restitution through productive work is the most successful rehabilitation known.
- Restitution also deters crime better than imprisonment. Japan has an extensive program of restitution and is the only industrialized nation in the world that has seen a consistent decrease in crime since World War II.
- Full restitution, which would include all the costs of trial and apprehension, would end the aggression of taxation that currently subsidizes these functions.
- When in doubt, erring on the side of forgiveness and contrition is less likely to provoke further aggression.
- When we used licensing laws and regulations in an attempt to stop individual aggressors, we slashed our wealth creation. When we substitute restitution for these laws, we will deter individual aggressors more effectively and increase wealth creation once again.
- Corporate irresponsibility would lessen if aggressors were required to right their wrongs. Forgiveness could only come from victims, not from an arbitrary limitation of liability by government.

Chapter 14

The Pollution Solution

When we can only make things right by cleaning up our garbage, we're less likely to dump it in the first place.

Righting our wrongs is the perfect solution to pollution. When dealing one-on-one with others, we practice this second principle of nonaggression naturally. If we accidentally dump trash on George's lawn, we clean it up. George is unlikely to hold a grudge if we make things right again.

If we refuse to clean up our mess, however, George will probably make us pay in other ways. He may arrange to have the trash picked up and take us to court if we don't pay the bill. Perhaps he will dump trash on *our* lawn. Unless we right our wrongs, we will destroy the harmony between ourselves and our neighbors.

We gain nothing by dumping trash on George's lawn if we have to clean it up. Therefore, we have no reason to pollute in the first place. Righting our wrongs is the best deterrent of all! Taking responsibility for the damage we cause is the "pollution solution."

How Restitution Saves the Environment

Unfortunately, this common-sense pollution solution is seldom used. If we listen to a conversation between our mayor and an industrial polluter, we see why.

"Mr. Mayor, it's true we dump chemicals in the river, but that's a small price to pay for the many jobs we provide in your district. If we have to take these 'toxic wastes' and dispose of them 'properly,' we'd have to lay off workers. You'd be mighty unpopular. Your opponent won't be, though. She wants to see her constituents employed. That's more important to everyone than a few dead fish."

The mayor sighs in defeat. A few fish are dying, but without further investigation, he can't be sure that the chemicals are responsible. A few residents have complained, but workers who lost their jobs would be much more vocal. The company has a lot to lose if it can't use the river for dumping, so it will help elect whichever candidate will look the other way.

"You're right," the mayor concedes. "People's jobs *are* more important than a few fish." *Including my job*, he adds silently. He hopes he has done the right thing. He can't help thinking that there must be a better way.

The mayor is right. There *is* a better way. The British have been using it for decades. Their government allows people to "homestead" rivers. Consequently, individuals, rather than government, own the fishing rights in many British waterways. When a polluter, kills *their* fish, the owners have every incentive to stop the polluter, and they do! The owners of Britain's rivers have successfully sued hundreds of polluters, individually and collectively, for the past century.[1] The aggressors stop polluting and pay restitution.

When we encourage homesteading, we put the environment in the hands of those who profit by caring for it. When private ownership is forbidden, our government officials are bought out by special interests—or lose their jobs. It's a no-win situation for the environment!

Sovereign Immunity Poisons the Playground

The Love Canal incident illustrates the contrast between private ownership and public management. Prior to 1953, Hooker Electrochemical Company and several federal agencies dumped toxic wastes into a lined trench[2] near Niagara Falls, New York, and sealed them there to prevent leaching.[3] As the population increased, the local school board tried to persuade Hooker to sell this cheap, undeveloped land to the city for a new school. The company felt that it was unwise to build on such a site and refused to sell. The school board simply threatened to seize the land through "eminent domain." Eminent domain allows a government agency to force a person to give up his or her land for the so-called "common good."

Hooker finally stopped trying to fight city hall and sold the land to the school board for $1. Hooker took the board members to the canal and showed them the dangerous chemicals[4] so they would not build any underground facilities.

Indeed, a provision against building was put in the deed of sale.[5]

The city ignored these clear warnings and its contractual obligations. In 1957, it began constructing sanitary and storm sewers. By 1958, children playing in the area came into contact with the exposed chemicals and developed skin irritation. Hooker again warned the school board to stop excavation and to cover the exposed area. The school board again refused to listen.

By 1978, reports of chemical toxicity came to light. The Environmental Protection Agency (EPA) filed suit, not against the school board, but against Hooker Electrochemical! Taxpayers had to pay $30 million to relocate Love Canal residents;[6] Hooker paid over $200 million in settlements.[7] Thankfully, extensive testing of the residents found no significant long-term differences between their health and the health of the general population.[8]

The Love Canal incident is a classic case of the role of aggression in polluting our environment. The officers of Hooker Electrochemical took responsibility for their toxic waste by disposing of it carefully. Hooker did not want to turn the property over to the school board because they feared that it wouldn't be as careful. Hooker relented only when the school board threatened to use the guns of government (eminent domain) to force the company to its will.

The company's fears were well founded. The school board was protected by sovereign immunity, which holds government officials and agencies blameless for damage they cause.

Public officials are no different from you or me; they respond to incentives. Anyone who is not held responsible for mistakes has little incentive to avoid them. For example, the school board members knew they would not be personally liable for a bad decision. However, they *were* under pressure to find cheap land for the school. If they excavated Love Canal and nothing went wrong, they'd be heroes. If the chemicals caused problems, Hooker would take the heat. The board had everything to gain and nothing to lose by acting irresponsibly. How different things would have been if school board members had been personally liable for the damage that *they* had caused!

Our Greatest Polluter Has Sovereign Immunity

Government's sovereign immunity is probably responsible for more pollution than any other single cause. For example, in 1984, a Utah court ruled that negligence in nuclear testing was responsible for health problems in 10 out of 24 cases brought before the court. The court of appeals, however, said that the government had sovereign immunity; therefore, the victims received nothing.[9]

This ruling was particularly distressing because, as documented in Congressional testimony, the Atomic Energy commission knew that the fallout would harm area residents but did nothing to warn them of the dangers.[10] Officials probably feared that compensating the victims would put a damper on nuclear test programs.

However, the required restitution would have given us a better measure of the true price of this "defense." Such information could have helped us decide the worth of this approach and whether it was worth continuing. Instead, sovereign immunity forced a few to bear the entire fallout of nuclear testing, both medically and financially. The true cost of nuclear testing was hidden from the American public.

Hundreds of people in the St. George, Utah, area were seriously injured by the nuclear fallout, including area residents, uranium prospectors, miners, military personnel, and workers at the testing site. In high fallout areas, childhood cancers increased almost two-and-a-half times.[11] Thyroid cancers increased fourfold.[12] In total, more than 1,100 people developed cancers probably caused by the fallout.[13]

Local ranches were devastated too. More than 4,000 sheep died from eating the radioactive sage.[14] The sheep farmers lost their case in court, primarily because of misrepresentation by government employees. In 1983, the cover-up was made public. However, the U.S. Court of Appeals refused the sheep herders, request for a new trial.[15] By 1997, more than 250,000 Americans had been exposed to dangerous levels of

There is no question the government has covered up the health aspects from radiation fallout during the atmospheric nuclear testing. ... The record will show that for over twenty years, the federal government placed the citizens of Utah at risk without their knowledge and without taking proper precautions.
—Senator Edward Kennedy, 1979

nuclear fallout, and up to 75,000 may face thyroid cancer as a result.[16]

If we want polluters to right their wrongs, we must first require the enforcement agencies who act in our name to do so! However, we often look the other way when the project that harms others is one we favor. We don't want government to right its wrongs, because the resulting tax increase might jeopardize our favored project. Ultimately, however, what we do unto others is done unto us.

Because we don't require our government to right its wrongs, the U.S. military has become the greatest toxic threat to all of us. Thousands of sites at home and abroad are now highly contaminated by the heavy metals used in bombs and bullets, jet fuel, toxic chemicals, and radioactive waste.[17] Cleanup costs from government pollution are estimated at $350 billion, approximately five times the Superfund[18] liability of the private sector.[19] The Departments of Energy and Defense simply refused to comply with EPA cleanup orders.[20] When we ask our government to aggress against others, we ultimately see that aggression turned back on us.

Perhaps the clearest example of how our aggression backfires is the contamination of the groundwater at military bases and surrounding metropolitan areas (e.g., Minneapolis, Cincinnati, Denver, Sacramento). Toxins were dumped on the ground or even into sewers by base personnel over years, perhaps decades![21] Sovereign immunity protected government polluters, who would have been more careful if they were required to right their wrongs.

Sovereign immunity violates the second principle of nonggression. It allows some people (government officials) to harm others without having to make things right again. We could not expect to enjoy a prosperous and peaceful neighborhood if we dumped garbage on George's lawn and then refused to clean it up. Nor can we expect our country to be bountiful and harmonious when government can poison our property or bodies without liability. When we don't hold all polluters accountable, we set the stage for the degradation of our land and water.

... the Pentagon's vast enterprise produces well over a ton of toxic wastes every minute, a yearly output that some contend is greater than that of the top five U.S. chemical companies combined.
—Seth Shulman
THE THREAT AT HOME

With 15,000 known contaminated sites, the military is the nation's greatest polluter.
—Heather Booth
UTNE READER

The military is the single largest generator of hazardous wastes in the United States.
—Michael G. Renner
WORLD WATCH

As usual, our aggression ripples out beyond our own boundaries. The U.S. military has many hundreds of overseas bases. The contamination at these sites has caused popular resistance to U.S. troops. The aquifer in Germany supplying Frankfurt's water has been contaminated by 300,000 gallons of toxic jet fuel leakage.[22] Poisoning the wells of our allies won't win us many friends.

Our lawmakers have extended the concept of sovereign immunity to include favored private monopolies. For example, in 1957, a study by the Atomic Energy Commission predicted that a major accident at a nuclear power plant could cause up to $7 billion in property damage and several thousand deaths. The marketplace ecosystem protected the consumer from such events naturally: no company would insure the nuclear installations, so power companies were hesitant to build new plants. Congress passed the Price-Anderson Act to limit the liability of power plants to $560 million. In the event of an accident, the insurance companies would have to pay only $60 million. The other $500 million would be paid through taxation![23] If the damages were more extensive, the victims would just have to suffer.

Sovereign immunity is a way of hiding the true cost of aggression-through-government. If our taxes reflected the cost of cleaning up pollution caused by the defense industry, we might not be so eager to let it pollute. If we had to compensate those harmed by nuclear testing, we might demand that such testing, if it were truly necessary, be conducted more carefully. If the price tag for insuring nuclear power plants were reflected in our electric bills, we might prefer alternative fuel. If we shouldered the full cost of our aggression, we'd do things differently.

Death by Regulation

We all want an environment free from cancer-causing chemicals. Unfortunately, half of all chemicals, both natural and synthetic, were carcinogenic when tested at high doses in animals. Plants make natural, carcinogenic insecticides that protect them from attack. Americans eat approximately 1,500 mg per day of these natural pesticides. In contrast, the FDA estimates we eat 0.15 mg per day of synthetic pesticides.[24]

Fortunately, these levels are well below established acceptable daily intakes.[25] When healthy, our liver is easily able to destroy small amounts of cancer-causing agents. When researchers give rats large quantities of potential carcinogens, however, the liver is overwhelmed. Many compounds that are actually quite safe may appear to be carcinogenic in such skewed tests.

One such chemical, ethylene dibromide (EDB), was banned by the EPA in 1984. EDB can cause cancer when given to animals in huge amounts. However, in the 50 years of its manufacture, workers exposed to many thousand times more EDB than consumers receive haven't developed more cancers than the rest of the population.

EDB was used as a grain pesticide, preventing the growth of molds that produce aflatoxin, the most carcinogenic substance known. Naturally, farmers didn't want their grain contaminated with a potent cancer-causing substance, so, after the EDB ban, they turned to the only other effective substitute: a mixture of methyl bromide, phosphine, and carbon tetrachloride/carbon disulfide.

Carbon tetrachloride and methyl bromide are both potent carcinogens in animals; phosphine and methyl bromide must be handled by specially skilled workers because they are so dangerous.[26] By using the aggression of prohibitive licensing, the EPA left us to choose between moldy grain with highly toxic natural carcinogens or dangerous mold-controlling pesticides!

DDT Ban Kills Millions

One of these bans killed millions of our overseas neighbors. By 1946, the insecticide DDT (dicholordiphenyl tricholororethane) had been recognized as one of the most important disease-preventing agents known to humans. Used extensively in the tropics, DDT eradicated the insects that carried malaria, yellow fever, sleeping sickness, typhus, and encephalitis. Crop yields increased as the larva that devoured them

You can't eat a meal that doesn't have carcinogens. ... Human blood wouldn't pass the Toxic Substances Initiative if it got into a stream.

—Dr. Bruce Ames inventor of the Ames test for carcinogenicity

While approximately 9,000 people die from bacteria-caused food poisoning each year, there is no scientific evidence showing that residues from the lawful application of pesticides to food have ever caused illness or death.

—C. Everett Koop former U.S. surgeon general

DDT has had a tremendous impact on the health of the world. ... Few drugs can claim to have done so much for mankind in so short a period of time as DDT did.

George Claus and
Karen Bolander
ECOLOGICAL SANITY

The DDT-malaria issue is a stark illustration of the conflict between the developed and the developing world. For the sake of a possible environmental threat to birds of prey in the "civilized" world, millions of people in developing countries are dying. This must stop.

—Lorraine Mooney
THE WALL STREET JOURNAL

Compared with its agricultural use, public health uses of DDT are too trivial to merit banning with any urgency.

—NATURE MEDICINE
July 2000

were destroyed. Without seasonal malaria to keep farmers from the fields, an additional crop could be planted.[27]

In Sri Lanka (then Ceylon), with 2.8 million malaria sufferers and over 7,000 malaria deaths per year, 15 years of DDT spraying reduced these numbers to 17 cases a year and no malaria deaths at all![28] Fatalities in India dropped from 750,000 per year to 1,500, thanks to DDT.[29]

Because malaria takes such a great toll, even on survivors, countries with a high incidence of this disease create less wealth than similar countries without this problem.[30] DDT contributed greatly to wealth creation in Third World nations. As malaria was eradicated, wealth creation in Sri Lanka rose by almost 10%.[31]

Human side effects from DDT were rare even though thousands had their skin and clothing dusted with DDT powder or lived in dwellings that were sprayed repeatedly. DDT replaced the more dangerous and less effective pesticides, some of which contained the poison arsenic.[32]

Massive quantities of DDT were applied to land and water. Fears that the bird population was being harmed, that DDT remained too long in the environment, and that it might cause cancer led the EPA to ban DDT in 1972, even though its own hearings concluded that "The uses of DDT under the regulations involved here do not have a deleterious effect on freshwater fish, estuarine organisms, wild birds, or other wildlife."[33] This single bureaucratic decree sentenced millions of people to death.

Any country receiving U.S. foreign aid had to obey the DDT ban.[34] As a result, malaria cases once again skyrocketed in the poor countries of the tropics.[35] Within six years, 800 million cases were reported each year and over 8 million died in the affected countries.[36] Frustrated by expensive and ineffective alternatives, developing nations started sprayed homes with DDT once again. Even this limited use resulted in dramatic drops in malaria deaths.[37] Even widespread use of DDT in this manner would be just a fraction of its former agricultural use,[38] while it would save millions of lives. Nevertheless, worldwide bans of DDT are still under discussion.

EPA Bans Cause Cancer Too

Banning additives to prevent cancer might actually increase our risk of dying from it. Pesticides improve our health by making fresh fruits and vegetables more affordable. Increasing consumption of produce is one of the best ways to fight cancer, according to the National Research Council.[39] The tiny risk of cancer from pesticides is vastly offset by the larger consumption of fruits and vegetables that pesticides make possible. Perhaps higher produce consumption is the reason that less breast cancer is seen in women with higher tissue levels of DDT![40]

Even the EPA acknowledges that dying from pesticides is less likely than dying in an automobile accident.[41] Tobacco smoking is a much greater threat; it is thought to be responsible for 30% of all cancer deaths.[42] Convincing people not to smoke would seem to be the best way to lower the incidence of cancer in the United States.

Instead of attacking the big problems, the EPA focused on minor risks, such as cancer caused by asbestos. Although asbestos can promote lung cancer during manufacturing, it appears to be quite safe when placed in buildings and left undisturbed. When it is removed, however, the fibers break, releasing the asbestos. As a result, workers removing the asbestos at the orders of the EPA were placed at risk. Because of fiber breakage during removal, asbestos levels in schools and other public buildings were *higher for two years after asbestos was removed*.[43] Money that could have gone to educate people about the dangers of smoking was instead used to endanger our schoolchildren— and our astronauts!

Because of the 1977 ban on retail asbestos products, the removal of asbestos from public buildings, and the impending ban on all use, the maker of an asbestos-containing putty used in the space program stopped production. Another asbestos-containing putty not as well suited to high temperatures was substituted. In January of 1986, its failure brought down the space shuttle Challenger, killing the astronauts and teacher Christa McAuliffe.[44]

We should rename the EPA the Tobacco Protection Agency, because it focuses public attention away from the biggest risk of all to some of the very smallest.

—Rosalyn Yalow
Nobel Prize winner,
Medicine

... the $6 to $10 billion spent on removal of asbestos from schools and public buildings was wasted.

—Tom Harris
THE ASBESTOS MESS

The EPA was not sanctioned for endangering our children by removing asbestos in schools, killing our astronauts, or destroying our space shuttle—it enjoys sovereign immunity!

A Better Way

Accidents do happen. If we were to accidentally spill a harmful chemical on George's arm, we'd probably offer to pay his hospital bills. We'd also make sure that whatever caused the accident didn't happen again. If a company puts a toxin in the air, water, or soil that makes people ill, it needs to restore, as much as possible, those it has harmed. The extra cost is passed on to consumers, encouraging them to use less of the company's product. The more pollution the product caused, the more restitution would be required. As the price of the product skyrocketed, its use would be restricted to necessary and important uses (like saving lives). In this way, the self-regulating marketplace ecosystem would ensure that benefits were maximized and risks were minimized without the aggression of bans.

Today, some polluters simply go bankrupt. Victims are left to suffer, while the polluters just start over. We could do things differently. Those responsible for the decision to pollute could compensate a victim through time payments or could be sent to a work prison if they did not voluntarily make amends. Victims who were insured against such injury would get immediate payment from their insurance companies, which would, in turn, collect from polluters.

Naturally, many companies would want to insure themselves against poor decisions by their corporate officers. The premium for such insurance would probably depend on the company's record for environmental pollution as well as the reputation of the individual manager.

To protect its interests, the insurance company would examine its clients' policies concerning pollution and suggest changes that would lower the clients' risk and premiums. Companies with the potential to pollute would effectively be regulated by the marketplace ecosystem, free from aggression. The high cost of paying for cleanup simply would be so great that few would dare to pollute. No tax dollars would be required to fund this effective program.

The Good Neighbor Policy deters polluters naturally! If a particular food additive or pesticide had adverse effects that didn't show up in animal testing, publicity would enable consumers to quickly boycott the product. In 1990, a news program questioning the safety of Alar caused a dramatic drop in apple sales virtually overnight.[45]

Pesticide manufacturers, like pharmaceutical firms, know that poisoning the customer is bad for business. However, independent testing to prevent honest mistakes is always highly desirable. Consumers might wish to avoid foods grown with new pesticides until those chemicals were given a seal of approval from a trusted evaluation center. Such testing agencies would be similar to those described for pharmaceuticals in Chapter 6 (*Protecting Ourselves to Death*).

Of course, *all* polluters should right their wrongs, including government officials. Rule of law, under which everyone is treated equally, increases a country's wealth creation. When sovereign immunity exempts some individuals or organizations from the law, victims of aggression are not restored. Their wounds still fester, setting the stage for future strife.

The pollution solution requires *all* who damage the property or the body of another to make them whole again. Making aggressors right their wrongs teaches them that pollution doesn't pay. In the next few chapters, we'll learn why such common-sense justice is so rare in the world today.

Chapter 14: The Pollution Solution

In Summary ...

- Righting our wrongs is the ideal pollution solution. Restoring the person or property of another is so costly that it acts as an effective deterrent.
- Government officials are actually penalized if they try to protect the environment. In contrast, if they cause great harm, sovereign immunity protects them from personal liability.
- The Love Canal disaster happened because the Niagara Falls school board disturbed buried chemicals after repeated pleas by Hooker Chemical not to do so. When the chemicals caused skin irritation, Hooker was blamed, but the school board was not. Taxpayers had to pick up the bill for relocating residents. Hooker had to clean up the mess that the school board had made.
- When nuclear testing damaged rangeland and more than doubled childhood thyroid cancer in Utah, courts denied compensation to the victims because the U.S. government has sovereign immunity.
- The U.S. military is the greatest polluter in the world, but it rarely cleans up its mess. Sovereign immunity protects it from legal action.
- DDT saved millions of lives by nearly eradicating malaria in the Third World. The DDT ban killed millions of people in developing countries when malaria returned.
- Asbestos removal in schools, as ordered by the EPA, endangered our children by increasing airborne concentrations of this carcinogen for years afterward.
- All polluters, public or private, should compensate their victims. Restitution, by deterring pollution, will contribute greatly to environmental protection.

Chapter 15

Dealing in Death

Using aggression to stop drug abuse kills more people than the drugs themselves!

In the last two chapters, we discovered that when aggressors right their wrongs, they are less likely to commit another crime. However, this deterrent works only if criminals expect to get caught.[1]

Today, an aggressor's chance of apprehension are low. Police in the United States don't spend much time going after rapists, murderers, and thieves. Instead, they focus on catching drug users. In 1998, the total number of marijuana arrests, 88% of them for possession, exceeded arrests for homicide, rape, robbery, and aggravated assault combined.[2] *Our police spent more time chasing pot smokers than violent criminals.*

People who rape, steal, and attack are clearly aggressors violating the Good Neighbor Policy. Marijuana smokers, drug users, alcohol drinkers, and tobacco smokers relaxing in their own homes clearly are not. However, we fear that those who use certain mind-altering substances will become aggressors in the future. We try to prevent the anticipated aggression by becoming aggressors ourselves. We stop people—at gunpoint, if necessary—from selling or using these drugs.

As we've seen in Part II, trying to deter aggression with aggression is a cure worse than the disease. Our experience with alcohol prohibition illustrates how our aggression boomerangs back to us, hurting the very people we are trying to help.

Prohibition Didn't Work Earlier

In the early 1900s, Americans used aggression-through-government to stop the consumption of alcohol. As we all know, Prohibition just didn't work. People still drank, but they had to settle for homebrews, which poisoned over 4,000 people per year.[3] Aggression killed the very people it was supposed to protect.

About 80 percent of all felony criminal cases in Los Angeles County and Orange County are drug-related. ... These people are clogging the court dockets, the prisons, the entire system.
—Judge James Gray
Superior Court

Vices are simply the errors which a man makes in search after his own happiness. In vices, the very essence of crime—that is, the design to injure the person or property of another—is wanting.
—Lysander Spooner
NO TREASON

The more prohibitions you have, the less virtuous people will be. ... Try to make people moral, and you lay the groundwork for vice.

—Lao-tsu
TAO TE CHING

Prohibition ended in 1933 because the nation's most influential people, as well as the general public, acknowledged that it had failed. It had increased lawlessness and drinking and aggravated alcohol abuse.

—Thomas M. Coffey
author of THE LONG THIRST: PROHIBITION IN AMERICA: 1920–1933

Because businesses could no longer sell alcohol, organized crime did. Innocent bystanders were caught in the crossfire of turf battles. In the early 1900s, the homicide rate, less than 4 per 100,000, began climbing as more and more states went "dry."

Nationwide Prohibition took effect in 1920, causing crime to skyrocket throughout the country. By the time Prohibition ended in 1933, the homicide rate was 10 per 100,000 people and still rising.[4] Aggression was ineffective and expensive, both in terms of dollars and lives.

Police found that they could make more money taking bribes than jailing bootleggers. Corruption spread, turning law enforcers into law breakers.

People who had supported Prohibition soon realized that it was a cure that was worse than the disease. Pauline Sabin, the first woman to serve on the Republican National Committee, was one of them. She had thought that Prohibition would "remove temptation from the path of my boys," but later realized that the crime, lawlessness, and corruption endangered her family more than alcohol did.[5] She started fighting for Prohibition's repeal.

After Prohibition ended, professional producers brought quality control back into brewing and distilling. As a result, people stopped dying from bathtub gin. The turf fighting ended, because there was no turf to fight about. The murder and assault rate that had skyrocketed during Prohibition fell steadily after its repeal[6] and did not rise again until drug prohibition began in the 1960s.

Did the United States turn into a nation of alcoholics once drinking was legal again? Just the opposite! Over the past several decades, Americans switched from hard liquor to beer and wine.[7] Educating people about the harmful effects of alcohol has proven more effective than force. People who abuse alcohol are now more likely to get help and community support (e.g., Alcoholics Anonymous) than a jail term. Good Neighbors have succeeded where our aggressive laws have failed.

Prohibition Isn't Working Now

Unfortunately, we've forgotten the lessons of Prohibition. As a result, its terrible consequences have been re-created in the War on Drugs.

In spite of drug prohibition, an estimated 20% of Americans age 20 to 40 years use illegal recreational substances regularly.[8] Approximately 80% are marijuana smokers.[9] Drugs are freely available, even in our prisons![10]

How many lives are lost each year from drugs? In the mid-1980s, heroin and cocaine killed about 3,000 people per year,[11] fewer than the 7,000 annual deaths from aspirin and other perfectly legal anti-inflammatory drugs.[12] By 2000, overdose deaths commonly involved multiple drugs, including alcohol and a wide range of prescription narcotics. Nevertheless, accidental drug-induced deaths from both legal and illegal drugs combined were less than 13,000 nationwide.[13] No deaths have been reported from marijuana overdose.[14]

In contrast to the death toll from illegal drugs, alcohol kills over one million Americans each year,[15] while as many as 400,000 people die each year from tobacco,[16] considered by many to be the most addictive drug of all.[17] Tobacco's popularity has made it the most serious drug-related threat to worldwide health. The biggest killer in the Western world is overeating, believed to be responsible for close to one million cardiovascular deaths each year.[18]

Clearly, the expense of drug prohibition is directed at a relatively minor problem. Indeed, drug prohibition actually kills more people than the drugs themselves! Approximately 80% of the overdose deaths are caused by black-market side-effects.[19] For example, legal drugs are tested for safety; street drugs are sold even when they are highly toxic. They are frequently cut with other substances, such as quinine, caffeine, and amphetamines, which makes them even more dangerous. Users seldom know how much drug they are taking, making overdose and death much more likely. Prohibition, a form of prohibitive licensing, puts more people at risk.

If the government cannot stop people from using drugs in the prisons over which it has total control, why should Americans forfeit any of their traditional civil rights in the hope of reducing the drug problem?

—inmate, Federal Correctional Institution, El Reno, Oklahoma
TIME MAGAZINE, October 16, 1989

Street drugs are 100 times more expensive than they would be without prohibition.[20] If drugs were cheaper, some would be swallowed rather than taken intravenously. However, the safer oral route requires more drug, because absorption is slow and inefficient. Because prohibition makes drugs expensive, many users choose the more dangerous intravenous route, thereby increasing their chances of dying through overdose or hepatitis.

In addition to making drugs more deadly, laws prohibiting the sale of drug paraphernalia contribute greatly to the spread of AIDS. Almost 16,000 new U.S. AIDS cases or 35% of the total number reported in 1991 resulted from intravenous drug use with shared needles.[21] In Spain and Italy, over 60% of new AIDS patients are IV drug users. In the Netherlands, where addicts get free needles, only 7% of new AIDS cases are drug-related.[22] In Hong Kong, where needles can be bought without a prescription, AIDS is not spread by contaminated needles.[23]

When users get in trouble, they delay seeking medical help for fear of arrest. The basketball player Len Bias had three seizures before his friends finally called the medics. By then, it was too late.[24]

Drug prohibition encourages a great deal of gang warfare just as Prohibition did. In 1988, over 50% of New York homicides were drug related. Turf fighting, rather than drug-induced psychosis, was mostly to blame.[25] The murder rate would plummet if we ended the War on Drugs, just as it did when alcohol Prohibition ended. *Indeed, homicide rates across countries, cities, and counties rise and fall in parallel with drug-related arrests and seizures.*[26]

Property crime goes up as well when our police stop chasing thieves and go after drug users instead.[27] Contrary to popular opinion, most drug users do not *become* thieves to support their habit. Criminal activity is likely to precede drug use by a couple of years. A life of crime evidently predisposes a person to start using drugs.[28] Consequently, if we deter crime through restitution, we would most likely lower drug use as well.

Studies estimate that a 1 percent increase in drug law enforcement in Florida relative to Index 1 enforcement, as measured by arrests, leads to approximately 0.2 percent to 0.34 percent decrease in the probability of arrest for property crime.

—Bruce Benson and
David Rasmussen
ILLICIT DRUGS AND CRIME

We pay dearly to make ourselves better targets for thieves and murderers. By 1999, the federal government was spending nearly $18 billion on drug prohibition; state governments typically spend twice as much.[29] Nevertheless, between 1992 and 1995, drug consumption *doubled* among U.S. teens.[30] Drug prohibition hasn't worked any better than alcohol Prohibition did.

The Bottom Line

We pay a high price for the failure of drug prohibition. *Since 1989, the War on Drugs has killed 10–14 times as many people each year as the drugs themselves.* These deaths include AIDS spread by contaminated needles, overdose deaths caused by black-market side effects, and homicides resulting from turf fighting and other drug-related murders.[31]

Like alcohol Prohibition, drug prohibition is a cure much worse than the disease. *Even if everyone in the country took drugs regularly, instead of the one in ten who do so now,[32] the death toll from overdose would still be lower than the deaths caused by today's drug prohibition.*

Entrapping the Young and the Innocent

The War on Drugs can ruin a teenager's life just as surely as drug addiction can. Joey Settembrino made the kind of mistake that gives parents nightmares.

Joey picked up some acid for a friend and delivered it to a "buyer" for him. Joey had never sold drugs before, but like most teen "dealers," he was enticed by the money that his friend offered him.[33] When Joey made the delivery, the "buyer" turned out to be a Drug Enforcement Administration agent. Joey had been set up on his first "sale." The 18-year-old received a 10 year mandatory sentence because he wasn't able to turn over another "pusher" to the prosecution.[34]

Joey's case is not unique. *Nonviolent, first-time drug offenders make up almost 30% of the federal prison population.*[35] Unless they are willing and able to testify against another "dealer," they face years in prison. Not surprisingly, many people choose to accuse an innocent person rather than face the horrors of incarceration.

Orlando Magrunder, 15, stunned "experts" at a Washington, D.C., conference on kids and violence with his simple statement that kids sell drugs for money.

—Beth Frerking
Kalamazoo Gazette, July 25, 1993

Suzan Penkwitz, for example, was coming back from Tijuana, Mexico, with her friend, Jenny, when border agents found drugs in Jenny's car. Jenny confessed to drug smuggling, but told authorities that Suzan knew nothing. A few hours later, however, Jenny implicated Suzan in return for a six-month sentence at a minimum security prison. Since Suzan didn't know about the drugs, she couldn't turn anyone else in. Even though she didn't have a criminal record, she was sentenced to 6.5 years in federal prison—10 times what the actual drug smuggler received.[36] By offering a reduced sentence to each offender, prosecutors double their conviction rate. Defendants must choose between serving a long sentence and testifying against someone else. The temptation to lie is great.

Lonnie Lundy fared much worse than Suzan. One of his employees (we'll call him Richard) was caught smuggling drugs. Richard was promised a reduced sentence if he would testify that Lonnie dealt in large quantities of drugs. The prosecutor could then get credit for convicting a big-time drug dealer. Richard agreed to lie and Lonnie got *life without parole*, even though no drugs were found in his possession.

Later, Richard confessed that he had been lying, but the judge wouldn't listen.[37] Perhaps the judge was afraid that if Lonnie were released, the public would be outraged to learn that he had sentenced an innocent man to such a harsh sentence.

Merchants can be imprisoned just for selling innocuous indoor gardening equipment if marijuana growers buy it. Gary Tucker, for example, owned a small hydroponics store in Norcross, Georgia. The DEA wanted to put cameras in his store to film his customers, who *might* be growing marijuana with his perfectly legal indoor gardening equipment.

Gary refused. As a result, Gary, his wife Joanne, and his brother Steven were all convicted of conspiracy to manufacture marijuana, even though searchers found no marijuana or illegal drug paraphernalia.[38]

Real estate agent Loren Pogue was sentenced to 22 years in prison after he helped a part-time employee close a land sale in Costa Rica. The employee was paid to entrap Loren. The investors buying the land were undercover agents supposedly intending to build an airstrip for drug smuggling. The airstrip was never built.

Sixty-four-year-old Loren was a missionary, a former serviceman, and father to 15 adopted children.[39] Although he had no previous drug history, Loren was imprisoned for what someone else said they *intended* to do!

Jacquie Fogel quit her job when she sensed that something about it wasn't quite right. Two years later, she was charged with conspiracy to distribute marijuana because she hadn't gone to the police with her suspicions. She's now serving 10 years.[40]

Jacquie, Loren, Gary, Lonnie, and Joey weren't sent to prison because they assaulted, defrauded, or stole from anyone. Except for Joey, they didn't sell or possess drugs. Nevertheless, their lives were ripped apart by the aggression of drug prohibition.

Putting nonaggressors in prison harms other innocents. When nonviolent drug offenders serve long, mandatory sentences, thieves, rapists, and murderers are paroled earlier than they otherwise would be. For example, Florida tripled the number of drug-related prisoners in its system between the fiscal years of 1983/84 and 1989/90. As a result, Frank Potts was released in 1988. Potts had only served 6 years of his 15-year sentence for molesting an 11-year-old girl. Before 1984, most Florida prisoners served half of their sentences; by 1989, they served only one-third.

Potts's parole officer warned that Potts would strike again—and he did. A few years later, Frank Potts was arrested for molesting another 11-year-old girl. He is believed to be guilty of at least 13 murders since his release.[41] Our aggression boomerangs back to us, killing the very children that the War on Drugs is supposed to protect.

Taking Medicine Away from the Dying

People suffering from painful, even terminal, diseases are becoming Drug War casualties as well. They are often prohibited from using

There were no drugs involved. The government agents said they were going to fly 1,000 kilos of drugs into the U.S. and that is what I was sentenced on.

—Loren Pogue
casualty of the War on Drugs

I have watched murderers and child molesters go home and come back, bank robbers leave and make the next heist and come back like it was nothing out of the ordinary. But let a first-time nonviolent drug-related offender be given a mandatory minimum sentence, and they will stay here for 10 years or more. If I had used a gun and killed someone, I would be home right now with my children.

—Jacquie Fogel
casualty of the War on Drugs

... more than twice as many pot smokers have been imprisoned under California's "three strike" law as murderers, rapists, and kidnappers combined.

—Justice Policy Institute, 1996

The advanced stages of many illnesses and their treatments are often accompanied by intractable nausea, vomiting, or pain. Thousands of patients with cancer, AIDS, and other diseases report they have obtained striking relief from these devastating symptoms by smoking marijuana. The alleviation of distress can be so striking that some patients and their families have been willing to risk a jail term to obtain or grow the marijuana. ... It is also hypocritical to forbid physicians to prescribe marijuana while permitting them to use morphine. ... there is no risk of death from smoking marijuana.
—Dr. Jerome P. Kassirer
NEW ENGLAND JOURNAL OF
MEDICINE, 1997

drugs that could make the difference between life and death.

Marijuana, for example, was listed in the *U.S. Pharmacopeia* for its many medical uses until it was outlawed. Marijuana can slow the progress of glaucoma, keep cancer patients from being nauseated by chemotherapy, alleviate certain types of pain, and help treat multiple sclerosis.[42] However, even in states that have passed laws permitting medical use of marijuana, patients and their doctors have been prosecuted by the federal DEA.

In the 1970s, Robert Randall successfully won court battles, enabling him and a few other glaucoma patients to use medical marijuana.[43] However, in recent years, glaucoma patients have been treated as criminals.

For example, James Burton, a Vietnam War veteran, grew marijuana to treat his hereditary glaucoma rather than go blind like so many of his male relatives. Kentucky police raided his farm. Dr. John Merritt, the only physician at the time legally allowed to treat glaucoma patients with marijuana, testified that it was the only medication that could save James's sight. Nevertheless, James was sentenced to a year in prison. After his release, the Burtons went to the Netherlands, where he can legally purchase marijuana.[44] What message does this lack of compassion send to our children?

Other medical marijuana users have fared even worse than James. After Proposition 215 passed in California in 1996, patients with a doctor's prescription were legally able to use marijuana. Nevertheless, renowned California author Peter McWilliams was arrested, even though his doctor had prescribed marijuana to control the violent nausea caused by his chemotherapy. Peter was forbidden to use marijuana while awaiting trial.[45] He finally plea-bargained when the court would not allow him to use his medical condition (AIDS and cancer) or Proposition 215 in his defense.[46]

While awaiting sentencing, Peter was forbidden to use marijuana and was subjected to drug tests. If he had tested positive, his mother's and brother's homes would have been seized.

Without marijuana, Peter McWilliams could not control his violent nausea. On June 14, 2001, he died choking on his own vomit.[47] How many other patients fighting for their lives will needlessly suffer the same fate?

Californian Todd McCormick, an associate of Peter McWilliams, has had recurring bouts with cancer since the age of 10. The radiation treatments left him with crippling pain, which was relieved only by marijuana. As with Peter McWilliams, the federal court did not permit Todd to use his condition or Proposition 215 in his defense. In March 2000, he was sentenced to five years in prison—without marijuana.[48] How many people needlessly suffer from devastating pain because of our prohibitive licensing?

Steve Kubby, 1998 Libertarian Party candidate for governor of California, used marijuana to treat his adrenal cancer and high blood pressure. He, too, was arrested. Unlike Peter and Todd, Steve was actually allowed to use his medical condition and Proposition 215 in his defense. He was eventually given a 120-day jail sentence (without marijuana). Rather than die in prison from lack of medication, Kubby appealed his conviction and moved to Canada with the permission of the court. Placer County, California, then notified the Canadian government that Steve was a "fugitive."

Because of Placer County's charge, Steve was imprisoned for three days in British Columbia before posting bail. He became so ill without medical marijuana that he lost 20 pounds. Steve's blood pressure soared, and he suffered severe diarrhea and vomiting.[49] His doctor claimed that four days without marijuana would have killed him. Steve has now applied for refugee status in Canada.[50]

Seven other states now allow the sick to use marijuana for medical purposes.[51] However, the federal government claims that its use is still illegal and continues to prosecute. Our enforcement agents still take medicine from the sick. When our loved ones suffer intractable pain or lose their battle with cancer because they literally can't stomach their medication, we reap the bitter fruit of our aggression.

... marijuana has been accepted as capable of relieving the distress of great numbers of very ill people. ... It would be unreasonable, arbitrary, and capricious for the DEA to continue to stand between those sufferers and the benefits of this substance in light of the evidence.
—Judge Francis Young
chief administrative law
judge, DEA

Why Do We Do It?

Clearly, drug prohibition hasn't worked any better than alcohol Prohibition did. Why, then, do we continue this failed program?

Perhaps Rep. Randy Cunningham, (R-Calif.) knows the answer. Rep. Cunningham is a typical drug warrior, advocating mandatory prison sentences and even the death penalty for big-time drug dealers. In January 1997, his son was caught with *400 pounds* of marijuana. The representative urged the judge to go lightly with *his* son because "He has a good heart. He works hard."

The prosecution, moved by the drug warrior's plea, agreed to a scant 14–18 months in a halfway house. However, while out on bail, the young Cunningham *tested positive for cocaine three times*. Even so, he was given two years, half the mandatory minimum.[52]

Why didn't "tough on drugs" Cunningham want his son to follow in the footsteps of Joey Settembrino? Most likely, Rep. Cunningham sees his own son not as a bad person, but simply a fallible one, much like an alcoholic. Other people's children, he probably feels, are responsible for tempting his son with drugs and should be imprisoned or killed.

Had the judge not been sympathetic, Rep. Cunningham would have suffered the anguish that his policies have forced other parents to endure. To the extent that we support drug prohibition, we weave the net that could one day ensnare our own children.

Jailing other people's children to protect our own backfires, hurting the very people we wish to help. The temptation to make poor choices is everywhere. The best protection we can give our children is to spend time teaching them how to make the best choices for themselves. Had the representative chosen to spend more time with his son, rather than crusading for tougher drug laws, perhaps his son would have made better choices.

The Rich Get Richer With Our Help!

Drug prohibition has become such an emotional issue that it's sometimes difficult to look

... virtually every contender in the 2000 presidential primaries acknowledged that he had used drugs in his younger days. But not one of them claimed that he should have been sent to prison for his "youthful indiscretions."

—Harry Browne
2000 presidential
nominee, Libertarian
Party

beyond the hype-induced haze. We are addicted to the War on Drugs, and it impairs our decision making just as surely as alcohol and other mind-altering substances can.

How did we acquire our habit? As we've learned in previous chapters, special interest groups often tempt us to use aggression against our neighbors for their benefit. The Marijuana Tax Act of 1937, which effectively outlawed both marijuana and industrial hemp, was backed by such groups.

Industrial hemp is a variety of the same plant species (cannabis) that produces marijuana. Hemp contains such a small amount of the mind-altering chemical, THC, that it is useless as a recreational drug, just as poppy seeds, which contain trace amounts of opiates, are.

Industrial hemp, however, makes excellent paper. Its fiber has literally thousands of uses. Until the 20th century, the canvas (cannabis) sails that captured wind power for oceangoing ships were made of hemp.[53] Ben Franklin used hemp paper to establish a free press in America.[54] Unlike trees, hemp grows to maturity in 100 days and doesn't require environmentally damaging bleaching agents for its paper processing. Hemp could literally save our forests, 40% of which we now harvest for paper production.[55]

Hemp fiber is stronger than cotton, which uses one-quarter of the world's pesticide production for its cultivation. Hemp requires only a small fraction of the chemical fertilizers and pesticides that cotton needs.[56] The U.S. government begged farmers to grow hemp during World War II for the strong ropes needed on naval ships, and then outlawed its cultivation once the war ended.[57] Indeed, hemp parachute lines kept George H.W. Bush alive when he bailed out over the Pacific![58]

Shortly before the Marijuana Tax Act was passed, a new machine was developed that would have made hemp processing more economical and efficient. Needless to say, the wood-pulp paper producers, cotton farmers, and synthetic fiber manufacturers feared that industrial hemp would take over their markets. By exaggerating the mind-altering properties of marijuana, the

The so-called "WAR ON DRUGS" is itself an addiction. It's an addiction more harmful to the fabric of American society than drug use ever could be.
—Sheriff Bill Masters
Telluride, Colorado

True, the Founding Fathers had provided for a specific right to bear arms, but the only reason they'd nothing to say about the right to plant seeds [was] ... because it never would have occurred to them that any state might care to abridge that right. After all, they were writing on hemp paper.
—Will Fulton
HARPER'S MAGAZINE
1997

"killer weed from Mexico," they encouraged Americans to use aggression to destroy hemp farming in the United States.[59]

Most other industrial countries, even if they have outlawed marijuana, still permit industrial hemp farming. Until recently, Americans could import all hemp products. However, in 2001, the DEA banned edible hemp foods, even though they are not psychoactive.[60] Suppression of industrial hemp may very well be the hidden agenda behind the War on Drugs.[61]

When we automatically reject aggression as our means, we need not worry about being manipulated into destroying what is good for us (e.g., industrial hemp) for the benefit of special interest groups (e.g., wood pulp producers, synthetic fiber manufacturers, and cotton farmers). When tempted by catchy slogans to use aggression against our neighbors, we can "Just say, 'No!' "

A Better Way

If we end drug prohibition, how can we protect our children from the destructive potential of drugs? Wouldn't ending the War on Drugs create a nation of addicts?

Apparently not! When small amounts of marijuana were decriminalized in 11 states, consumption did not increase significantly.[62]

In Amsterdam, marijuana coffeehouses openly sell different varieties of the plant. With marijuana, a so-called gateway drug, freely available we might expect the Netherlands to be a nation of addicts. However, heroin addiction is half that of the U.S. rate, and crack is not widely available.[63]

Addiction rates for native Hollanders is probably quite low, because almost 40% of Dutch addicts are refugees of the War on Drugs like James Burton.[64] The Dutch treat addicts as patients in needing treatment rather than criminals deserving prison.

Pushers have virtually abandoned the Dutch schools. Teenage consumption of alcohol and tobacco is similar in the Netherlands and the United States, but use of marijuana and cocaine in the Netherlands is only 10–40% of U.S. rates, depending upon the age group compared.[65] The

The real question is why are millions of people so unhappy, so bored, so unfulfilled, that they are willing to drink, snort, inject or inhale any substance that might blot out reality and give them a bit of temporary relief.
—Ann Landers
syndicated columnist

Drug addiction is a health problem; it should be treated medically, not criminally.
—Jesse Ventura
Minnesota governor

age of the average Dutch addict is rising, as fewer youngsters become involved with drugs.[66] Clearly, the Dutch are protecting their children from drugs by using less aggression and more compassion. *The best way to get the pushers out of schools is to take the profit out of drugs by ending prohibition!*

Many people find it difficult to believe that re-legalizing drugs will actually decrease consumption. However, in the early 1900s, when children could buy alcohol or medicinal heroin in any drugstore,[67] addiction was less of a problem than it is today. Even in our prisons, drugs are readily available, which should alert us to the impossibility of *forcing* people to stop taking them.

Like alcoholism, dependence on drugs is a medical problem. People who are willing to sacrifice their health, wealth, families, and friends for chemical highs require our help, not our condemnation.

Ending drug prohibition might even make our roads safer if people substitute marijuana for alcohol. Although alcohol drinkers are often hazardous drivers, pot smokers rarely are. *Pot smokers have fewer accidents because, unlike drinkers, they drive less aggressively when under the influence of marijuana.*[68] Today, with the mandatory minimums for drug-related crimes, we could end up putting dangerous drunk drivers back on the road in order to keep pot smokers behind bars!

No matter how much we wish it, we cannot protect people from themselves. When we reach out to them with compassion, rather than aggression, however, we have the best chance of helping them. Ironic as it may seem, honoring our neighbor's choice gives us the best chance of changing it.

Just as bootleggers were forced out of business in 1933 when Prohibition was repealed, making the sale of liquor legal (thus eliminating racketeering), the legalization of drugs would put drug dealers out of business.
—Abigail Van Buren
"Dear Abby"

If even a small fraction of the money we now spend on trying to enforce drug prohibition were devoted to treatment and drug rehabilitation, in an atmosphere of compassion not punishment, the reduction in drug usage and in the harm done to users could be dramatic.
—Milton Friedman
Nobel Prize winner,
Economics

Chapter 15: Dealing in Death

In Summary ...

- Although people who rape, steal, and murder are clearly ag-gressors, people who use alcohol, tobacco, or other drugs peacefully in their own homes are not.

- Alcohol Prohibition failed to stop people from drinking. Orga-nized crime thrived and the murder rate increased two and one-half times.

- The War on Drugs kills more than 10 times as many people as the drugs themselves by increasing homicides from turf wars, AIDS from shared needles, and accidental overdose caused by contaminated drug supplies.

- Because our police spend more time arresting pot smokers than thieves, murderers, rapists, and child molesters, crimes of violence increase when drug enforcement does.

- Mandatory minimum sentences for drug-related crimes have forced overcrowded prisons to release violent felons to prey on the innocent.

- The desperately ill are condemned to unnecessary pain and premature death because some drugs with documented medici-nal uses are prohibited.

- Marijuana's cousin, industrial hemp, may be the real target in the War on Drugs.

- In Amsterdam, where marijuana can be legally purchased, heroin addiction is dropping and pushers have left the schools. Cocaine and marijuana use by Dutch teenagers is only 10–40% of U.S. rates, depending upon age group.

- Even if everyone in the United States took drugs once they were re-legalized, the death toll would still be less than we have today from the War on Drugs.

Chapter 16

Policing Aggression

We can protect ourselves from aggression only by refusing to be aggressors ourselves.

The High Cost of Aggression

Throughout the world, law enforcement has many characteristics of fourth-layer aggression. Police, courts, and prosecutors are often part of tax-subsidized government monopolies that we are forced to use. As with all such aggression, we end up with high-cost, low-quality service and little innovation. We pay too much for too little.

Conversely, a little less aggression goes a long way. For example, Reminderville, Ohio, and the surrounding township were aghast when the Summit County Sheriff's Department wanted to charge the community $180,000 per year for a 45-minute emergency response time and an occasional patrol. Corporate Security, a private police organization, offered to provide a six-minute emergency response time and twice as many patrols for one-half of the cost.[1]

The private company saved its customers money by using used cars and equipment.[2] The private police officers enforced the law, while clerical personnel took care of the "social-worker, caretaker, baby-sitter, errand-boy" activities that can consume 80% of public police work.[3]

The police force remained a tax-subsidized monopoly. However, aggression no longer dictated which police force (public or private) could provide security to the community. Reminderville could choose to get more service for less money by hiring Corporate Security.

Oro Valley, Arizona, enjoyed similar savings when the town hired the private firm, Rural/Metro in 1975. The Arizona Law Enforcement Officers' Advisory Council, however, objected, arguing that Oro Valley residents should be forced—at gunpoint, if necessary—to hire public police. Ironically, the public police wanted to use aggression against the very people they were supposed to protect from it.

The court expenses were too much for Rural/Metro, which stopped serving Oro Valley. In 1975, the city had paid $35,000 to Rural/Metro;

by 1982, it needed $241,000 to subsidize the public police. *In just seven years, the cost of paying public police rose by a factor of seven!*

The Oro Valley community lost more than money, however. Rural/Metro saw profit in *preventing* crime instead of *fighting* it after the fact. Consequently, Rural/Metro did things the public police didn't do, such as checking homes twice a day when residents went out of town. These measures cut burglary rates by 95%![4]

Rural/Metro kept Oro Valley's support by providing better service than the community could get anywhere else. The public police, however, would not honor the choice of Oro Valley residents.

By asking our police to bend others to our will, we have taught them to use aggression. We should hardly be surprised when they use their knowledge to sabotage our choices. By threatening lawsuits, public police have limited private policing in the United States.[5]

In Switzerland, the private firm Securitas provides police services for several dozen cantons, villages, and townships. Private police keep crime rates lower on Paradise Island in the Bahamas than on the main island of New Providence, which still relies on public police.[6]

Discriminating Against the Disadvantaged

As usual, poor people are hurt the most when critical services are provided by aggression-through-government. Their rent reflects the high property taxes required to pay for the public police. As a percentage of their income, the poor pay more for police protection than their middle-income neighbors do. Most crime occurs in poor neighborhoods; nevertheless, the residents are largely ignored by those sworn to serve and protect them.

For example, my mother and sister left a drugstore one day to find that a couple of young men had stolen their bicycles. They silently followed the thieves to a low-income apartment complex, where my mother and sister could see their bikes just inside the open door. They called the police, who told them that it was far too dangerous for officers to go into that area. Instead,

Blacks have suffered more from being left unprotected or underprotected by law enforcement authorities than from being mistreated as suspects or defendants.

—Randall Kennedy
RACE, CRIME, AND THE
LAW

the police advised my mother and sister to get whatever money they could from their insurance company.

If my mother and sister couldn't get the police to rescue bikes that were in plain sight, what chance would a resident have of police support? If the poor could use their tax dollars for hiring less expensive private security, they would at least have some leverage. Without the option to vote with their dollars, poor people are largely ignored.

When frustrated victims have sued unresponsive police, the courts have ruled that "the police do not exist to provide personal protection to individual citizens."[7] If we hired private security, and they didn't come when we called, we'd sue them for breach of contract. With the aggression of taxation, we must continue to pay police even when they won't come when we call—and they don't come 30% of the time in some metropolitan areas![8]

As usual, we have only ourselves to blame. In our addiction to the War on Drugs, we want our police to make chasing peaceful "outlaws" (e.g., pot smokers) their top priority. Because pot smokers outnumber violent criminals, police have little time to chase down aggressors or come when we call.

More Guns, Less Crime

We call the police when someone is breaking into our house or threatening our families because the police have the training and the weaponry to deal with robbers. However, even when our police do respond, they usually can't arrive soon enough to stop a crime in progress. To protect ourselves against aggressors, therefore, we must be able to defend ourselves, with deadly force if necessary.

Naturally, most of us would find the act of killing another person repugnant. However, banning or regulating weapons will not prevent all situations in which we must kill or be killed. Gun bans themselves are acts of aggression. They stop people—at gunpoint, if necessary—from having or using firearms. Gun control is the ultimate contradiction.

In Massachusetts, a man was sentenced to a year in prison for shooting a co-worker who was busy knifing him—for the second time—even though the Massachusetts Supreme Court admitted that "it is possible that the defendant is only alive today because he carried the gun that day for protection."

—James Bovard
Lost Rights

Our futile hope is that gun bans, waiting periods, and registration will stop criminals from arming themselves. However, over 85% of gun-toting criminals purchase their weapons illegally. Consequently, these laws do little to stop aggressors, while they prevent innocent victims from adequately defending themselves.[9]

Guns themselves are neutral, just like a man's reproductive equipment. Even though a man can use his sexual equipment to cherish or to ravage, castrating all men as a preventive measure is clearly a cure that is worse than the disease!

Similarly, guns can be used to save lives or to take them. For example, studies show that in 98% of the confrontations, armed citizens needed only to brandish their weapons and aggressors fled unharmed.[10] Simply by showing that they were armed, 30% of intended victims "almost certainly" or "probably" saved their lives or that of a bystander.[11]

Felons go out of their way to avoid victims who might be armed.[12] Intuitively, we know this even if we personally find guns abhorrent. Posting a sign in our front yard declaring "This home is a gun-free zone" is an open invitation to aggressors. Such signs are never seen, even in the yards of staunch gun control advocates.

Why are criminals more cautious when citizens are armed? By the late 1970s, armed citizens were killing more criminals in self-defense than the police were.[13] Yet armed citizens kill only a tenth as many innocent people by mistake as police do.[14]

Defending oneself with a handgun makes sense: a victim who submits to an attacker is twice as likely to be injured as a victim who resists with a gun. Defending oneself without a gun, however, is more dangerous than simply giving attackers what they want.[15]

To take advantage of the fear that criminals have of armed victims, the Orlando police began in 1966 a highly publicized program to train women in the use of firearms. The rape rate, which had been rising, dropped from 34 incidents for every 100,000 inhabitants in 1966 to 4 incidents per 100,000 in 1967, almost a 90% drop!

Surrounding areas still suffered from high rape rates.

Burglary in Orlando also fell by 25% because more criminals were deterred by the fear of encountering an armed victim. These remarkable results were achieved without injury; no woman ever had to use her gun. By 1971, Orlando's rape rate was still below its 1966 level, although rape had increased in the surrounding area by 308%.[16]

In Albuquerque, New Mexico;[17] Highland Park, Michigan; New Orleans, Louisiana; and Detroit, Michigan,[18] crime rates, especially burglaries, plummeted when shopkeepers publicized their acquisition of handguns. When the city council of Kennesaw, Georgia, passed an ordinance requiring each household to keep a firearm, crime dropped by 74% the following year.[19]

Recently, an exhaustive study of all U.S. states and counties found that the locales with the fewest restrictions on carrying concealed firearms were also the safest. Indeed, violent crime (assault, rape, robbery, and murder) plummeted in states and counties that adopted "nondiscretionary" concealed carry (right-to-carry) laws, where permits *must* be granted if a person meets some basic qualifications (Figure 16.1). Ten states have enacted right-to-carry laws since 1987; over 30 states now have them.[20] When we stop *our* aggression of gun control laws, we stop those who would aggress against us.

How Guns Make the Meek Mighty

Although everyone benefits from the safety that concealed weapons provide, homicides of women,[21] blacks,[22] and children[23] decline the most. Not surprisingly, single black women living in high-crime urban areas are most likely to buy a firearm for self-protection.[24] Guns are the great equalizer in homes as well as on the street, enabling those of smaller stature or strength to defend themselves against those who are bigger and stronger.

Luckily for Jacqueline Roland, her six-year-old son Jimmy knew how to handle the family firearm. She told Jimmy to get the gun when she went outside to investigate a strange noise. When Jimmy came outside with his .22-caliber

Every day, 550 rapes, 1,100 murders, and 5,200 other violent crimes are prevented just by showing a gun. In less than 0.9% of the time is the gun ever actually fired.

—Guy Smith
GUN FACTS

Chapter 16

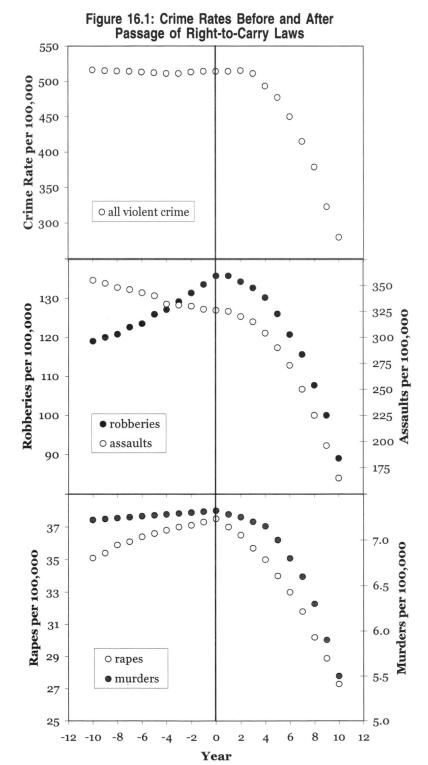

Figure 16.1: Crime Rates Before and After Passage of Right-to-Carry Laws

Data reprinted with permission from J. Lott, *More Guns, Less Crime* (Chicago: University of Chicago Press, 2000), pp. 170–174.

rifle, a masked man was holding a knife at his mother's throat. Aiming at the attacker, Jimmy demanded his mother's release. When the man told Jimmy to put the gun down, he cocked it instead. The terrified assailant fled. He was later captured, along with his two accomplices. All were career criminals. The sheriff told Jimmy that he had probably saved the lives of his mother and five siblings.[25]

Nine-year-old Ashley Carpenter and her seven-year-old brother John William were not so lucky. Their 14-year-old sister Jessica had been taught how to handle the family firearms. She ran to get a gun when Jonathan David Bruce went wild and began stabbing her siblings with a pitchfork. Unfortunately, because California has safe storage laws, the guns were locked up. Bruce had cut the phone lines, so Jessica couldn't call the police. She ran to a neighbor's house, begging for a gun, but the neighbor offered her only a phone. By the time the police arrived, Ashley and John William were dead. Another sister was wounded. Bruce rushed the police, and they shot him dead. Had Jessica been allowed to do the same, her siblings might be alive today.[26]

Rather than corrupting children, guns teach them to behave responsibly. Boys given guns by their fathers are less likely to use drugs or commit crimes than boys who carry no guns or have obtained them illegally.[27]

How Gun Bans Kill

Accidents with guns are rare. In 1999, only 88 children under 14 years of age lost their lives in firearm accidents, while 971 died from drowning. In the entire United States, 824 people died in firearm accidents in 1999,[28] while the defensive use of guns saved approximately 400,000 lives.[29] *A national gun ban would kill 400 people for every one that it saved!*

Do family firearms turn ordinary arguments into deadly shootouts? Rarely! Although 81% of handgun victims are relatives or acquaintances of the killer,[30] some 80% of the killers have prior arrest records, frequently for crimes of violence.[31] The average domestic killer is not a model citizen corrupted by guns, but a violent

Instead of suing gun manufacturers, I am of the opinion that it is our lawmakers who need to be sued. It was you who created the laws that kept my grandchildren from being able to defend themselves with any weapon greater than their bare hands.

　　　—Mary Carpenter
　　　grandmother of Ashley

The police can only get to a crime scene after the crime has been committed. A citizen must be able to stop a crime.

　　　—Fred Prasse
　　　former police officer

offender who has attacked before. Put another way, two-thirds of the people who die each year from gunshot wounds are criminals shot by other criminals, usually with illegally obtained weapons. Gun bans do little to reduce such killings.

Gun bans have often been considered after the tragic shootings in schools and other public places. After all, the deterrent effect of concealed weapons would most likely be ignored by "rampage" killers, who clearly have serious mental problems. However, *the average state experienced an incredible 78% reduction in the number of multiple, public "rampage" shootings after adopting right-to-carry laws.*[32] The only killing sprees in right-to-carry states occur in public schools and other "gun-free zones."[33] States with the fewest gun-free zones experience the greatest reduction in killings, injuries, and attacks when they adopt right-to-carry laws.[34]

Clearly, rampage killers are deterred by the possibility of armed defenders. Indeed, in two public school shootings (in Pearl, Mississippi, and Edinboro, Pennsylvania), the killers were stopped by adults who held the shooters at bay until police arrived.[35] If we want to protect our children from killers, we must arm their defenders.

Because the police are not always available when killers strike, we must be prepared to defend ourselves. During the Los Angeles riots of 1992, public police abandoned whole neighborhoods in the wake of widespread arson, looting, and violence. Law-abiding citizens rushed into the gun shops to buy some protection but were stopped by the 15-day waiting period. When the smoke cleared, dozens of people had been killed and thousands injured.

Luckily, Korean merchants were already armed and kept rioters at bay with warning shots. Without guns, the merchants would likely have been killed. Angry blacks targeted the Korean merchants because of an earlier shooting of a black woman, allegedly a shoplifter.[36]

When the police can't or won't help us, we need to be able to defend ourselves. Perhaps that's why over 90% of police officers want citizens to be able to buy firearms for defense as well as sport.[37]

In spite of the compelling evidence that an armed citizenry dramatically decreases crime, Britain and Australia instituted nationwide gun bans in 1996. *Gun crime in Great Britain rose 40%[38] in the next six years, but tripled in urban areas.[39] In Australia, armed robberies doubled in the first few years.[40]* Clearly, people who are willing to steal and kill think nothing of disobeying the gun laws too.

The Fruits of Aggression: "Seizure Fever"

In recent years, a new class of criminal has become a threat to our person and property. Some of the government law enforcers that we have hired to protect us from thieves and murderers have begun to take our lives and our money themselves without due process. Usually, sovereign immunity protects them from righting their wrongs.

For example, the Internal Revenue Service (IRS) seizes property, often without notice and usually without a trial, when it *thinks* that people owe back taxes.[41] The IRS assumes that people are guilty until proven innocent. Naturally, once the IRS takes their life savings, these unfortunates have no money to hire an attorney and fight a court battle. They are literally left without a defense!

Running afoul of the law is easy because the tax code is so complicated. Even accountants don't always prepare a return the way that the IRS says it should be done. *Money Magazine* held an annual contest for many years, giving a number of top accounting firms a dummy return. In 1993, 95% did it incorrectly.[42] The regulations are so complex that even professionals can't get it right, yet we could lose our property to seizure as a consequence.

In recent years, other branches of government have caught "seizure fever." In Chicago suburbs, automobiles are confiscated on the spot for blaring radios. The city of Detroit seized 3,000 cars in 1995 because they were allegedly used to solicit prostitutes.[43] Alternative health care practitioners have been raided by armed Food and Drug Administration agents, who hold both patients and health care personnel at gunpoint

Between 1997 and 1999, there were 429 murders in London, the highest two-year figure for more than 10 years—nearly two-thirds of those involved firearms—in a country that has banned private firearm ownership.
—Guy Smith
GUN FACTS

The IRS's managers pressure employees to seize taxpayers' property so they can win "merit pay," bonuses, according to testimony before the Senate Commerce Committee. Agents in a San Francisco IRS office even posted a notice on the bulletin board that said: "Seizure fever. Catch it."
—Steve Dasbach
LIBERTARIAN PARTY NEWS,
March 1997

while they seize computers, medicine, and patient records.[44] In most cases, the "crimes" upon which these seizures are based involve peaceful people, not aggressors.

Even when aggression is alleged, the seized property can be worth many times the amount the legal fine would be if the case ever went to trial. Kathy and Mark Schrama, for example, were accused of taking United Parcel Service packages valued at $500 from a neighbor's porch. If they had been tried and found guilty, they would have probably paid a fine and been put on probation, because this was their first offense. (Ideally, of course, they would have compensated their neighbors.) Instead, their cars and home— valued at $150,000—were seized.

Property is considered "guilty" simply for holding stolen goods or being connected with illegal activities.[45] Property has no rights, so presumably it can be declared guilty and seized without a trial. The courts have endorsed this practice, known as "civil asset forfeiture," but most Americans are unaware of it until their property is seized.

People carrying "excessive" cash are now *presumed* to be carrying proceeds from illegal drug sales, and the cash is routinely confiscated. In 1989, 49-year-old Ethel Hylton was stopped in Houston's airport because a drug-sniffing dog had scratched at her luggage. Ethel had her life savings inside, along with an insurance settlement, totaling a little more than $39,000. Ethel had worked hard to save her money as a hotel housekeeper and hospital janitor. She could document the source of her money, but even four years later, it still hadn't been returned.[46]

Like Ethel, some 80% of the people whose cash or property is seized are never even charged with a crime.[47] Being able to prove innocence, even at great legal cost, does not guarantee return of the property, which is frequently damaged during the search.[48] Even if the property is returned, a "storage" fee is often deducted by the government agency holding it.[49]

Our courts have ruled that property has no rights under the law, so it can be seized when a crime is simply "suspected."[50] When sick people grow marijuana for personal use, our police "suspect" them of drug-dealing. Naturally, taking their assets makes defending themselves even more difficult. Steve Kubby, Todd McCormick, and Peter McWilliams found themselves deprived not only of medical marijuana (see Chapter 15), but also of their possessions.

Russian immigrant Sam Zhadanov came to the United States as an engineer and inventor to escape the Russian police state. He manufactured plastic bottles, often used for perfume samples. He was designing a special syringe that would have protected health care workers from accidental infection with AIDS and hepatitis during blood draws. His factory and life savings were seized because drug dealers bought his bottles.

Sam was charged with conspiracy to transport two and a half tons of cocaine, the amount that his bottles could have held had they been all filled with the substance. He pled guilty after the prosecutor threatened to charge his family as well and was sentenced to five years in prison. Had the government not seized Sam's factory and savings, worth between $1.5 million and $2 million, he could have defended himself and his family.[51]

Had Sam been acquitted and marketed his new product, health care workers might now enjoy better protection against AIDS and hepatitis. Instead, our taxes are used to keep Sam in prison, thereby increasing the spread of these lethal diseases. A violent criminal no doubt gained early release so that Sam, who had not aggressed against anyone, could occupy his cell.

Rental properties are especially vulnerable to seizure, because any crime committed on the premises makes the properties "guilty." In Milwaukee, the owner of a 36 unit apartment building gave the police a master key so they could arrest some of his drug-using tenants. The city seized the "guilty" building, rather than arresting the tenants who committed the "crime."[52]

Our law enforcers have good reason to seize our property. The departments involved keep part of the proceeds. Budgets can be increased without raising taxes or haggling for a greater share of tax revenue. States that allow police to keep

... my father says he came to this country thinking he was going to escape the gulag, and he ended up in the gulag. You come here and you sort of relax, you say, " Oh, they'll see it's a mistake, its not the KGB, it's the federal government."

—Eli Zhadanov
son of Sam Zhadanov

part of the booty from raids also have more "seizure fever."[53]

People who "snitch" get rewarded as well. If the informant is serving time, his or her sentence can be reduced. Rewarding informants inevitably leads some people to lie.[54] Indeed, prison inmates routinely study newspapers in the hopes of concocting an appropriate tale. If they are able to convince the courts that another person (or property) is guilty, they can often negotiate a reduced sentence.[55]

The Fruits of Aggression: Murdering Innocents

Donald Scott at Trail's End Ranch

The rewards that enforcers and informants receive for seizure set the stage for abuse. Millionaire Donald Scott, for example, lived on a 200-acre ranch adjacent to the Santa Monica Mountains National Recreation Area near Malibu, California. The National Park Service wanted to buy his property, but Donald Scott wouldn't sell.

On the morning of October 2, 1992, two dozen law enforcement agents, including representatives from the U.S. Forest Service and National Park Service, broke into his home early in the morning. They were presumably looking for marijuana plants. His wife started screaming, "Don't shoot me, don't kill me!" Donald Scott awakened and grabbed his revolver to protect her—and was shot to death.[56] No drugs or marijuana plants were ever found.

Such "no knock" raids are becoming more common, often with deadly consequences. Innocent people are killed because they go for their guns or baseball bats when rudely awakened by heavily armed men. Other victims die of heart attacks. Sometimes the police raid the wrong home.[57] Even when innocent people are killed, prosecutors rarely go after the law enforcers, who are protected by sovereign immunity.

The official report of District Attorney Michael Bradbury claimed that the raid on Scott's home was based on a search warrant "that was not supported by probable cause" and that was "motivated, at least in part, by a desire to seize

For every bust, the law allows the DEA to pay the informer a commission of up to 25 percent of seized assets, with a ceiling of $250,000. Some career informants have become millionaires.

—Cynthia Cotts
REASON MAGAZINE

and forfeit the ranch for the government."[58] The members of the National Park Service were included in the raid so that they could lay claim to part or all of the seized property.

Donald's wife, Frances, who survived the raid, and his adult children filed suit against the government. While the suit was in progress, the house, which Frances still lived in a year later, caught fire. The county fire fighter told her that a National Park Service agent had denied the fire department permission to dig a firebreak that might have saved the house because "It violates our rules to disturb the natural beauty of the land."[59] Because the government officials who had tried to take the ranch were still employed, they simply kept on with their quest.

The Scott family finally managed to get a $5 million settlement. However, taxpayers had to pick up the tab. Sovereign immunity protected the government agents who killed Donald Scott from restitution claims and criminal prosecution.

The Scott family prevailed because they could afford high-powered attorney Johnny Cochran. Most people, however, don't have the money to fight city hall. Even when the raid is made at the wrong address or no illegal activities are uncovered, the *victims are rarely compensated, even when an innocent person is killed.*

The Weaver Family at Ruby Ridge, Idaho

Donald Scott lost his life because he chose not to sell his ranch. Former Green Beret Randy Weaver lost his wife and son when he refused to turn informant. Randy was "befriended" by a paid undercover Bureau of Alcohol, Tobacco and Firearms (ATF) informant, Ken Fadley. Ken prodded Randy to sell him two sawed-off shotguns. Because the barrels were one-quarter inch too short to be legally sold, Randy refused. However, several months later, Randy decided that he needed the money and agreed to the sale.

When the law enforcers arrested Randy for his nonaggressive "crime," he was told that he wouldn't be prosecuted if he agreed to spy on Aryan Nation groups. Randy refused and was indicted for manufacturing, possessing, and selling illegal firearms. The shotguns were "illegal" because they were about a quarter inch too short and the tax stamp ($200) had not yet been paid. Like the IRS regulations, those which govern firearms have become so complex that many people unwittingly violate them.[60]

The court date was moved from February 19 to February 20. The letter from the court, however, indicated that the new date was March 20. When Randy didn't come to court on February 20, a bench warrant was issued for his arrest. Understandably, Randy feared that he wouldn't get a fair hearing by a system that had spent so much effort setting him up. He had been told that if he lost the case, his house would be seized, leaving his family destitute while he was in prison. Randy stayed close to his cabin because law enforcers rarely go out of their way to arrest people who miss their court date.

In Randy's case, however, federal agents were more determined. Instead of knocking on Randy's door to serve the warrant or contacting him by mail or through the neighbors who visited, the ATF and the U.S. Marshals Service set up an elaborate *16-month* surveillance of the Weaver property. They even sent agents, pretending to be potential buyers of the neighboring property, to Randy's door. Vicki Weaver sometimes invited them in for coffee. Clearly the opportunity for peaceful discussion was available for well over a year. The U.S. marshals who were involved wanted to talk with Randy, but the deputy U.S. attorney, Ron Howen, would not permit it.

The tragedy at Ruby Ridge began when Randy's 14-year-old son Sammy and the teen's friend Kevin Harris, ran into the armed agents while out looking for game on the property. Sammy was shot in the back and killed, along with his dog. One of the agents was injured when Kevin returned fire. The family barricaded themselves in the cabin.

The next day, when Randy went to the shed where his son's body lay, he was shot in the back by FBI (Federal Bureau of Investigation) snipers. His wife, holding their 10-month-old baby in her arms, was killed by a sniper when she came outside to investigate her husband's cries.

Marshall service witnesses told about a series of pre-siege scenarios to root Weaver out of his cabin. But when pressed by the defense, they said they never considered simply knocking on the door and arresting him.

—Jim Oliver
THE RANDY WEAVER CASE

I was appalled at the extremely vicious attitude of Dick Rogers. ... The unit was the same as combat commando teams I have led. They were there to hurt instead of help their quarry.

—Colonel "Bo" Gritz
speaking of the FBI
team at Ruby Ridge

Kevin was injured as well. With the help of former Green Beret Col. James "Bo" Gritz, Kevin, Randy, and the three Weaver girls surrendered peacefully.

The Weavers were acquitted of all charges surrounding the shootout. Eventually, the Weaver children recieved a $3 million settlement from the taxpayers for the wrongful death of their mother.[61] The agents who did the killing and their superiors who authorized it were not required to pay a penny of this restitution.

The Branch Davidians at Waco, Texas

After a tragedy like Ruby Ridge, we might expect that the agents involved would be taken off cases with explosive potential, at least until investigations could be completed. However, two of the key players, Dick Rogers and Larry Potts, received praise instead of reprimand. They went on to become instrumental in the deaths of dozens of men, women, and children at the Branch Davidian complex in Waco, Texas.

Nearly 130 adults and children lived at the Davidian community near Waco. David Koresh, their charismatic leader, was a polygamist who favored teenage brides. Because of allegations of child abuse by a former member of the community, Child Protective Services visited with Koresh and the children on several occasions. In April 1992, the investigation was closed because no evidence of abuse had been found.

As they did at Ruby Ridge, the ATF began round-the-clock surveillance of the community at great taxpayer expense. Agents moved into a neighboring farmhouse. Aircraft with infrared radar cameras flew by, looking for the heat signature of a methamphetamine lab.

Unlike the Weavers, Koresh and his companions maintained positive relationships with local deputies and the children's social workers. Several members of the Davidian community were licensed gun dealers and kept an inventory for gun shows. Local law enforcers sometimes practiced at the Davidians' shooting range.

David Koresh frequently left the community, sometimes jogging by the farmhouse where the agents were living. The ATF could have stopped

What happened to Randy Weaver can happen to anybody in this country.
—Gerry Spence
Randy Weaver's defense attorney

... three ATF agents went on a friendly shooting trip with Davidian leader David Koresh just nine days before the initial ATF assault.
—Jon E. Dougherty
WORLD NET DAILY

Koresh during one of his outings, knocked on his door to serve the warrant, asked one of the local officers acquainted with Koresh to approach him, or inquired if the social workers would check on the children.

Instead, the ATF, armed with a warrant alleging child abuse, firearms violations, and drug trafficking, sent dozens of armed agents to the community's door preparing for a "dynamic entry." Shooting broke out, killing four ATF agents and six Davidians.

Why did ATF agents attempt a commando-style raid in a community with women and children, especially when their warrant named only David Koresh? If the purpose was to protect the children supposedly being abused, why did the ATF risk provoking an armed confrontation with so many other means at its disposal? Had the ATF become so accustomed to aggressive tactics that it didn't consider other options?

After the shooting, the ATF and The FBI surrounded the community. During the next month of the siege, 35 men, women, and children left. The adults were immediately handcuffed, separated from their children, and jailed, presumably because they had been accomplices in the "murder" of the four federal agents who were killed. Most people chose to stay rather than be jailed and separated from their children.

Koresh kept up negotiations, hoping for a peaceful resolution. Meanwhile, the federal agents turned off the community's electricity, flooded the area with glaring lights, and set up blaring loudspeakers to supply a continuous barrage of noise. Those unkind acts, as well as the jailing of the people who left the community, did not inspire trust in the remaining Davidians.

On April 19, 1993, the ATF attacked using a tear gas composed of orthochloro-benzal-malononitrile (CS) dissolved in methylene chloride, a central nervous system depressant. This gas, which creates poisonous fumes when it burns, was banned by the Chemical Weapons Convention, signed by the United States and 103 other countries. The gas causes disorientation, skin burns, severe vomiting, and convulsions when used in a restricted area. Consequently,

Law enforcers insist that the magnitude of the menace justifies the military metaphors and the use of military methods. But the methods create the reality that they are supposed to address.

—THE NATION
May 10, 1993

the manufacturer warns that CS grenades should not be used indoors.

This deadly gas was injected into the Davidians' buildings, even though the methylene chloride solvent was highly flammable. Fires broke out, probably from the kerosene lanterns and heaters used to replace the electric power that had been cut off. Twenty-one men, 32 women (two of whom were pregnant), and 21 children, were killed.[62]

Why did the agents attack when negotiations were ongoing? Why did they use a deadly, banned tear gas on innocent children? Surely, sending tanks and tear gas into closed buildings endangered agents and Davidians alike. The guns of government quite literally killed the very people they were supposed to protect—innocent and helpless children.

Several of the Davidian survivors were put on trial for the murder of the four ATF agents killed in the initial attack on their community. The jury found them not guilty of murder, attempted murder, or conspiracy to murder. As jury forewoman Sarah Bain put it, "We mistakenly found several of them guilty of the linked charge of using firearms during the commission of a crime—a crime of which they were innocent. That was a totally inconsistent verdict."[63]

In a letter to Judge Walter Smith Jr., Bain asked that most of the defendants be put on probation. "Even five years is too severe a penalty for what we believe to be a minor charge," Bain wrote. Despite the inconsistent verdict, however, Judge Smith sentenced the defendants as if they had been found guilty. Five were given 40 years in prison. The others received sentences of 20, 15, 5, and 3 years.[64]

Judge Smith was also chosen to preside over the $675 million wrongful death lawsuit brought by survivors and relatives of the Davidians killed at Waco. When asked that he recuse (excuse) himself from the case, Judge Smith refused. After hearing the evidence, he ruled that the government agents acted properly when they injected CS gas into the buildings and that the Davidians committed mass suicide by setting the complex on fire.[65]

Any time you start the day by gassing women and children, you have to expect it to end badly.
—Wesley Pruden
WASHINGTON TIMES editor

The militia movement in this country became highly active only after the federal killings at Ruby Ridge, Idaho and Waco, Texas. The fact that no federal officials have been held legally responsible for the deaths at Ruby Ridge and Waco made people presume, not surprisingly, that the government was out of control and a dire threat to their rights and safety.
—James Bovard
FREEDOM IN CHAINS

Would people who had access to firearms really choose such a painful suicide for themselves and their children?

Clearly, Waco was a law enforcement effort gone awry. The only crime of aggression that David Koresh was charged with was child abuse. (The other two charges dealt with nonaggressive firearms and drug violations.) Any enforcement effort should have protected, not endangered, the children. However, almost every step that the government agents took increased the risk that armed confrontation would break out.

Why didn't the agents use better judgment? Perhaps the enforcement agents were so accustomed to aggressive tactics that they knew nothing else. Aggression sets the stage for more aggression. The aggression of taxation used to support our law enforcers teaches them that they must "steal for their supper."

When law enforcers harm innocents, sovereign immunity usually protects them from righting their wrongs. Any restitution that the victims receive comes from the further aggression of taxation.

The "criminals" that our law enforcers track down are often peaceful people living their lives differently than we prefer (e.g., drug users). When we permit, even encourage, our law enforcers to violate the Good Neighbor Policy for our benefit, we should not be surprised that they increasingly adopt aggression as their means. Indeed, aggression may be all that they know. Under these conditions, more tragedies like Waco and Ruby Ridge are all but inevitable. We are reaping what we have sown.

Jury Tampering

Clearly, our courts will not stop government agents. The prosecutors, courts, and law enforcers all belong to related tax-subsidized monopolies. As part of what we call "government," they all enjoy a great deal of sovereign immunity. They are not obligated to serve us, even though our taxes pay their salaries. A prosecutor does not have to take on our case, but we will be stopped—at gunpoint, if necessary—from prosecuting without his or her help.

... anywhere between six to eight million people in this country enjoy some sort of immunity, including the absolute immunity granted to prosecutors. ... some five percent of the American population end up being above the law in one way or another.

—Rodolphe de Seife
HOFSTRA LAW REVIEW

I consider trial by jury as the only anchor ever yet imagined by man, by which a government can be held to the principles of its constitution.

—Thomas Jefferson,
1789

The judge can help prosecutors by excluding evidence in pretrial motions. For example, in Peter McWilliams's case, the judge ruled that Peter could not tell jurors about his medical condition or remind them that California's Proposition 215 allowed patients to use marijuana with a doctor's prescription. The judge destroyed Peter's case before it even got to trial.

The authors of the U.S. Constitution recognized that public judges and prosecutors would be predisposed to favor the government's case (prosecution) over that of a citizen (defendant). To ensure that lawmakers and enforcers didn't tyrannize the very people who had empowered them, writers of the Constitution made sure that guilt or innocence would be decided by a citizen jury, as it had been in colonial days. If the law was too harsh, inapplicable, or simply bad law, the jury could find defendants "not guilty" even if they had actually committed the crime.

Until the 20th century, juries in the United States were routinely instructed by the court to judge the law as well as the facts of a case. Jurors could ask questions and had access to all the information, not just what the judge wanted them to see.

Juries sabotaged alcohol Prohibition by refusing to convict 60% of the defendants. When they did convict, they often reduced the charges.[66] Juries ended the Fugitive Slave Laws by refusing to convict those who helped runaway slaves to safety.[67] Although jurors informed of their right to judge the law are more likely to convict aggressors who endanger others, they are less likely to convict nonaggressors whose behavior may be peaceful but illegal.[68]

Ultimately, however, aggression cannot be held in check by rules alone. The only way to control aggression is to abandon it ourselves. Eventually, judges stopped instructing juries of their rights. Later, judges told juries that they must convict the guilty, even if the law violated all they held dear. Finally, the judge decided through pretrial decisions what evidence the jury could see. Members of the jury pool who indicate that they know of their power to judge the law are routinely excluded from serving.[69]

The jury has the right to determine both the law and the facts.
—Samuel Chase
U.S. Supreme Court
Justice, 1796

The jury has the power to bring a verdict in the teeth of both law and fact.
—Justice Oliver Wendell Holmes
U.S. Supreme Court
Justice, 1920

The jury has a right to judge both the law as well as the fact in controversy.
—John Jay
U.S. Supreme Court
Justice, 1794

The jury has an unreviewable and irreversible power ... to acquit in disregard of the instructions on the law given by the trial judge. The pages of history shine upon instances of the jury's exercise of its prerogative to disregard instructions of the judge; for example, acquittals under the Fugitive Slave Law.
—U.S. v. Dougherty, 1972

Clearly, the aggression of exclusive licensing (monopoly) has corrupted our justice system. To fix it, we need only become Good Neighbors once again.

A Better Way

Target Aggressors, Not Good Neighbors
The first job of our justice system should be the apprehension of aggressors. However, diluting our policing efforts by trying to bend our peaceful neighbors to our will ultimately means that fewer violent criminals are captured. Focusing enforcement effort on aggressors, on the other hand, means that more of them will be brought to justice. When would-be aggressors know that they are likely to be captured, they wisely choose to live more peaceably.

Our police currently arrest as many pot smokers as violent criminals. *Simply by ending drug prohibition, we could double the law enforcement effort directed at rapists, murderers, kidnappers, child molesters, and thieves.*

Police also spend a great deal of their time giving out speeding tickets to safe motorists who drive above the speed limit. When they start chasing aggressors instead, arrests of violent criminals go up. For example, in the 1980s, Houston reassigned most of its traffic officers to felony divisions. Arrests doubled and homicide rates dropped.[70] If Houston is a typical example, we could *double* the time our police spend chasing aggressors simply by limiting traffic citations to drivers who pose a true threat of bodily harm to others. By ending drug prohibition and speeding tickets for safe drivers, we'd quadruple the law enforcement effort directed at violent criminals.

Wouldn't we have more accidents, especially fatal ones, if we didn't enforce speed limits? Evidently not. Although an accident is more likely to be fatal at high speeds, speed variation, rather than high speeds themselves, cause more accidents. Faster drivers change lanes, pass often, or tailgate to avoid slower drivers.

Artificially low speed limits *increase* speed variation (and accidents) because some drivers exceed the limit, while others hold back to avoid

When Congress abolished the 55-mile per hour speed limit, the experts at the National Highway Traffic Safety Administration predicted an additional 6,400 traffic fatalities annually from the higher speed limits. Yet both fatality and accident rates declined. 1997 had the lowest traffic fatality rate in the nation's history.

—Edmund Contoski
HAVE GOVERNMENT
REGULATIONS MADE YOUR
CAR SAFER—OR MORE
DANGEROUS?

tickets. When speed limits are high or nonexistent, less speed variation occurs, because no one drives slowly just to avoid a traffic ticket.

Although reckless driving, such as going the wrong way down a one-way street, poses an obvious threat of bodily harm to others, driving above posted speeds may not threaten anyone at all. *When the speed limits are raised, the decrease in speed variation, the reassignment of police resources from speeders to reckless and drunk drivers, and the shift in traffic from more dangerous local roads to the safer interstates result in a 3–5% decrease in the fatality rate.*[71] As always, we reap what we sow!

Keeping Our Streets Safe Through Privatization

Privatizing the highways would improve road safety further while freeing our police to catch violent criminals. *Private commercial roads operated by members of the International Bridge, Tunnel, and Turnpike Association have an accident rate one-third lower than the U.S. interstate system.*[72]

Private road owners have a profit incentive to make drivers safe and comfortable. Better attention to design features, good maintenance, easy access to rest areas, and more vigilance in removing reckless drivers are some of the ways in which private roads improve safety. Electronic toll booths now enable cars to drive by without stopping.[73] Making roadways safer through privatization means fewer accidents and less work for the police, who could increase their focus on aggressors. Because an increased risk of apprehension deters criminals, giving police more time to catch aggressors stops crime before it starts.

Keeping your streets safe is easier if you own them. In St. Louis, more than 1,000 city streets have been privatized. Residents own the streets jointly through a neighborhood association established for that purpose. They may then close off the street, patrol it, or hire private security to keep their street safe.[74] Over 50% of the street mileage in two of St. Louis's municipalities are private. In four other municipal areas, large numbers of the streets have been privatized.[75]

Most condominium and gated communities build and retain ownership of their roads. Buyers voluntarily agree to maintain them as part of the sale. Design features help reduce crime and are sometimes supplemented by private policing. For example, Starrett City, a 153-acre private complex in Brooklyn, employs private security and has one-seventh as much crime as the surrounding area.[76] The combination of private streets and private security is a powerful crime deterrent.

Stopping Crime Before It Starts

Private security deters crime even on public streets. Crime was so bad and public policing so poor that 85% of Georgetown neighborhood in Washington, D.C., pooled their money and hired private security. As a result, the robbery rate dropped 36% between 1992 and 1995.[77]

San Francisco's private patrols date from 1851. Although officially members of the city's police department, officers bid for one or more of the 65 beats and are paid by the businesses and individuals whom they serve. Each property owner has a separate contract with the patrolling officer according to the level of service that the property owner prefers.[78]

Private security, although focused primarily on prevention, successfully brings criminals to trial as well. Private companies that provide bail for criminals awaiting trial must recover any runaways to avoid losses. Their "bounty hunters" are so successful that only 1% of privately bonded defendants ultimately fail to show up for their court dates. In comparison, 8–10% of defendants supervised by public pretrial release agencies end up missing.[79]

In the early 20th century, the U.S. government gave the private railroad security officers full police powers. The number of arrests per reported crime was almost three times that of public police.[80] *Clearly, private police can do everything the public police do, but they do it better and at a lower cost.*

Moreover, private police are not paid through taxation. Lacking sovereign immunity, they right their wrongs. Consequently, their focus is to stop aggression, rather than acting as aggressors themselves.

If we privatized our law enforcement, we'd be less likely to repeat the tragedies at Ruby Ridge and Waco. Private police would be held accountable for their actions. No one would hire an enforcement agent whose reckless actions killed innocent victims.

Privatizing for Fairness

Instead of funding our court system through taxation, court costs could be added to an offender's restitution. The guilty would have incentive to settle with their victims out of court, because a trial and repeated appeals would only increase their restitution. (As we saw in Chapter 13, Japan uses such pretrial settlements already.) *With fewer cases coming to trial, justice would be swifter than it is today and would be paid for, in most cases, by the aggressor.*

When the accused was not able to convince the victim of his or her innocence, or a mutually agreeable resolution could not be found, the disputing parties might turn to a private court. In California and several other states, court judges are no longer part of a subsidized government monopoly. Anyone who is qualified for jury duty can now render a legal judgment.[81]

In addition to California's independent judges, companies such as Civicourt; Washington Arbitration Services, Inc.; Judicial Mediation, Inc.; Resolution, Inc.; Judicial Arbitration and Mediation Services;[82] and EnDispute, Inc., offer quick, inexpensive justice. Judicate, founded in Philadelphia, has been referred to as the "national private court," with offices throughout the United States.[83]

The rapid and reasonably priced trials these private courts provide are obviously considered a good deal by both parties because mutual agreement is required to take the case from the public courts to a private one. In addition, litigants must pay the private court costs. Clearly, private courts must provide superior service to thrive under those conditions.

What keeps private courts more honest than public ones? Unfair decisions by private courts result in a loss of business, because people don't want their cases to be heard by a biased judge. To stay in business, private courts must maintain high integrity. When the western American states were territories, for example, private miners' courts, which were commonly used to resolve criminal and civil disputes, were considered unbribable.[84]

Unlike private courts, public courts are often biased toward the prosecution. Forensic DNA testing over the past decade has discovered more than 60 death row inmates who were innocent of the crimes of which they were convicted. In 52 of these cases, mistaken identity was part of the reason; however, 57 instances of prosecutorial or police misconduct were also factors. In 15 instances, informants gave unreliable testimony in exchange for lighter prison sentences or cash.[85] *Clearly, our current system of public courts is so corrupt that many innocent people are sentenced to death.*

Private courts would not be predisposed toward either party, so their judgments would not favor the prosecution. Indeed, to maintain its reputation, a private court would have to base its decisions on truthful information. Thus, a private judiciary would serve as an integrity check on both litigants. In a restitution-based system, prosecutors would have no power to offer prison inmates reduced time to provide tailored testimony. Without sovereign immunity, police and prosecutors would be held liable for misconduct or perjured testimony. *Thus, private courts would be less likely to convict wrongfully.*

Today, even when people have been wrongly imprisoned, sovereign immunity usually limits the state government's liability.[86] In a society of Good Neighbors, a false accuser would be held liable for restoring his or her victim.

Private courts using nonaggression as their guide are likely to render more uniform judgments than the jumbled jurisdictions of current city, county, state, and federal courts. Today, judgments, laws, and penalties differ from state to state. Justice would be more uniform and predictable in a restitution-based society that focused on crimes of theft, bodily harm, and fraud.

A real-life example of such a system was the court system in the American western territories before they became states. As many as four courts shared a jurisdiction, yet "appeals were taken from one to the other, papers certified up or down and over, and recognized criminals delivered and judgments accepted from one court by another."[87] Judges had the best motive in the world for making their decisions clear and consistent: litigants would not hire them otherwise.

Private justice systems of the western U.S. territories illustrate the practicality and effectiveness of private courts. Contrary to the Hollywood portrayal of the "wild, wild West," crime, especially property crime against individuals, was low.[88] The legacy of effective private justice lives on in the unlocked doors and low murder rates still found in the rural western states.

Protecting the Poor

The poor would especially benefit from a justice system based on nonaggression. Indeed, police brutality, most often directed at the disadvantaged, would be rare in a fully privatized police system. Private police would not be able to invoke sovereign immunity and could be held *personally* liable for any brutality toward those whom they apprehended.

Discrimination in prosecuting the poor would also end. Today, poor victims have no recourse when the prosecutor chooses to work with high-profile victims instead. The prosecutor has an exclusive, tax-subsidized government monopoly on bringing criminal charges. Without this exclusive license, victims could hire lawyers of their choice to prosecute or could prosecute the case personally. Victims would not be forced to pay taxes for a prosecutor who wouldn't help them.

Even a poor victim would have little trouble attracting competent counsel to sue, because the anticipated restitution could cover legal fees and court costs. However, prosecutions made to intimidate or bankrupt a poor defendant are less likely when false accusers must make up for the damage that they do.

Today's poor live in slums where crime created by drug prohibition runs rampant. Ending

The union contract is so strong in Bridgeport, Connecticut, that an officer who pleaded guilty to police brutality not only remained on the force, but was promoted. ... even when a police brutality victim wins a civil suit against the officer or the department, it is rare for the officer to lose as much as one day of work, much less his job.

—Peter Davis
Massachusetts Institute
of Technology

this aggression will make poor neighborhoods much safer. The poor, of course, can rarely afford private security, because they must pay taxes, directly or indirectly, for public police. When we end the aggression of tax subsidies for the public police, the poor will be able to use that money for security systems, firearms, guard dogs, or private police. *The poor in a society of Good Neighbors will have greater wealth than they do today, making the purchase of security easier.*

Today, the poor often patrol their own neighborhoods, usually on a voluntary basis.[89] Even when done by unarmed citizens, "walking the beat" is an effective crime preventative.[90] However, public police often resist patrol assignments, especially when they are in low-income neighborhoods.[91] Private security firms, however, are likely to encourage and train voluntary patrollers, because their contribution to crime prevention makes the private officers' jobs easier and more profitable. Because of the win-win nature of citizen patrols, private security firms might even provide their training as a community service.

Even if the poor cannot afford to spend a penny on private protection, they would live more securely in a society that reduced crime with the reforms described previously. In essence, *the poor become "free riders" who are protected by the neighbors who carry firearms, hire private security, or patrol their streets.* In essence, by buying private protection tailored to our needs, we are also helping the needy.

People often shun private options for security because they resent the gain that free riders make at their expense. However, we are all free riders in some areas and not in others. People who buy concealed firearms deter crime, saving their neighbors as well as themselves from aggression. People who abhor guns might contribute their time to a voluntary patrol benefiting their gun-toting neighbors as well. People who simply protect their own property vigilantly create an environment that discourages would-be thieves.

... concealed handguns are the most cost-effective method of reducing crime. ... they provide a higher return than increased law enforcement or incarceration, other private security devices, or social programs like early educational intervention.

—John Lott Jr.
MORE GUNS, LESS CRIME

We take turns being providers and free riders. *When we honor our neighbor's choice, the
free rider problem is no problem at all.*

Chapter 16: Policing Aggression

In Summary ...

- Private police cost half as much as public police, yet deliver up to seven times faster response times. Crime drops as much as 95% because of their preventive procedures.

- Private police have no sovereign immunity, are not funded by taxation, and focus on aggressors. Because they themselves are Good Neighbors, they are less likely than government agents to create tragedies like Waco and Ruby Ridge.

- Guns save 400 times more people through self-defense than they accidentally kill.

- In Orlando, Florida, rape plummeted 87% when women were encouraged to train with firearms.

- Homicides dropped 30% and rampage shootings fell 78% when states permitted concealed weapons.

- In Britain and Australia, gun crime increased 40–300% when firearms were banned.

- Under U.S. civil asset forfeiture laws, property can be confiscated on suspicion alone.

- American juries have the right to judge the law as well as the guilt or innocence of the defendant. However, judges often tell juries otherwise.

- If police stopped chasing pot smokers and speeders, they could spend four times as much time apprehending violent criminals.

- Private highways have one-third fewer accidents than the U.S. interstates.

- The poor benefit the most from private justice.

Chapter 17
Healing Our World Is Inevitable

The Good Neighbor Policy not only sets the stage for societal harmony and abundance but also for our own personal health and happiness.

Putting It All Together

In Part II, we learned how using aggression to make a better world backfires every time. When we honor our neighbor's choice, however, the marketplace ecosystem limits the damage that selfish others do. Wealth creation flourishes, and abundance becomes the norm.

In Part III, we've seen how the second principle of the Good Neighbor Policy, righting our wrongs, heals the damage caused by aggression. When the societal norm becomes restoration of the victim rather than punishment of the wrongdoer, crime doesn't pay. Consequently, the incentive for crime disappears.

Deterrence is especially important in areas where victims can't be adequately restored, such as murder, rape, and pollution. As violence ebbs, peace flows naturally.

Today, sovereign immunity allows individuals employed by government to literally get away with murder. We have created a privileged class that increasingly abuses those it has sworn to protect. When everyone, including our government officials, must right their wrongs, everyone becomes equal under the law.

Taken together, the principles of the Good Neighbor Policy, honoring our neighbor's choice and righting our wrongs, create harmony and abundance. However, practicing the Good Neighbor Policy also has a profound impact on our minds and bodies. Consequently, Good Neighbors live longer, healthier, and happier lives.

How Aggression Promotes Heart Disease

We choose aggression as our means when we become *suspicious* of other people. For example, we fear that drug manufacturers might sell us a dangerous, untested drug just to make a few dollars. The people who benefit from pharmaceutical regulation encourage our hostility by focusing our attention on a few unscrupulous in-

We have strong evidence that hostility alone damages the heart. ... The kind of person at risk is someone who generally feels that other people are not to be trusted, that they'll lie and cheat if they can get away with it. ... Trusting hearts may live longer because for them the biologic cost of situations that anger or irritate is lower.

—Redford Williams
Duke University

dividuals. We forget about the many dedicated researchers trying to discover cures for our diseases and begin to view pharmaceutical manufacturers as shysters. When aggressive regulations that we enact cause the price of drugs to skyrocket, we blame drug makers for "exploiting" us. We become cynical as our own original suspicions are validated by "proof" that we ourselves unwittingly create. Our self-destructive spiral continues as we demand more aggression-through-government.

Suspiciousness, hostility, cynicism, and blame, which "justify" our aggression-through-government, also constitute the toxic core of the Type A personality. These negative judgments about others, rather than the fast pace favored by Type A individuals, alter the body's biochemistry in a way that accelerates cardiovascular disease.[1] Perhaps heart disease is the number one killer in the United States because we judge our neighbors so harshly and therefore try to control them through aggression.

How Aggression Predisposes Us to Cancer

As we've seen in previous chapters, the poor are hurt most by our well-meaning aggression. The lower rungs on the Ladder of Affluence are destroyed, preventing the disadvantaged from beginning their climb. Unable to legally create wealth, some steal it instead. Others simply give up in sheer frustration, succumbing to the seeming helplessness of their situation. Caught in the poverty trap, they give up and resign themselves to their fate. The disenfranchised put up only a token struggle, believing that they can't fight city hall. Consequently, their helplessness becomes a self-fulfilling prophecy.

These attitudes of frustration, helplessness, giving up, and resignation are Type C traits that predispose our body's biochemistry to cancer.[2] Aggression-through-government predisposes its victims to Type C thinking, perhaps explaining why cancer is the number two killer in the United States.

How We Get Caught in the A/C Loop

Because of our Type A beliefs, we may blame selfish employers for the plight of the poor.

When our lobbying results in minimum wage laws that destroy jobs held by the disadvantaged, we don't see our role in creating their distress. Instead, in typical Type A fashion, we blame their frustration and helplessness (Type C reactions) on the "selfish" rich and lobby for forcible redistribution. Of course, more aggression creates more poverty and helplessness (Type C reactions). We are caught in a destructive A/C loop. Our Type A aggression creates more victims with Type C attitudes. The growing number of "victims" justifies even more aggression. The end result, if this pattern remains unhealed, is universal poverty.

In real life, individuals often alternate between Type C and Type A thinking as they first become victims, then aggressors. For example, we may feel hostile toward employers, because our paychecks seem too small. As a result, we might lobby for living wages (Type A). We may feel helpless (Type C), however, when employers compensate by taking away benefits.

As a result, we become angry and hostile toward our employers once again. This Type A thinking drives us to lobby for laws that force employers to maintain benefits. When employers react with layoffs, we once again revert to Type C helplessness and frustration.

When we engage in Type A and Type C thinking, we focus on the impact that others have in our lives, rather than what we can personally control. Type A attitudes of blame and hostility are used to justify attacking selfish others with the guns of government. Type C attitudes of helplessness and despair justify our victimhood.

Why Good Neighbors Live Longer

Unlike Type A and C thinking, Type S (self-actualized) thinking focuses on how we can change our situation by changing ourselves. For example, if we want to be paid more, we can work harder or get training in a more lucrative field. When we stop looking toward others to fulfill our dreams, we automatically turn to strategies that make us less dependent them. We have greater control over our own lives when we stop trying to control others.

There was a significant decrease in Type-A behavior in the people who go to counseling. But more important, this group had half as many heart attacks as those in the other group. No other therapy— not diet, drugs, surgery, or exercise—has ever achieved such remarkable results. We had demonstrated that Type-A behavior isn't just associated with heart disease, but helps cause it.

—Meyer Friedman
PREVENTION MAGAZINE,
1987

When we become Good Neighbors, we break out of the destructive A/C loop, healing our world and healing ourselves. As we practice Type S thinking, we become disease resistant and live longer. *People who get counseling to change their Type A or Type C beliefs to Type S beliefs can cut their chance of heart disease or cancer in half.*[3]

Type S thinking has some additional benefits. When we come from Type A or Type C perspectives, our focus on what others do causes us to blame or resent them. When we come from a Type S perspective, it's easier to have goodwill toward all. In dealing with others, Type A thinkers generally attack; Type C people generally submit; people with Type S attitudes generally do neither. Because of their fear-based strategies, people with Type A or Type C attitudes often feel isolated from others, while Type S personalities are most likely to feel connected.

Why Good Neighbors Are Happier

The importance of feeling connected was revealed to me by a man involved in convincing the American public to accept aggression-through-government. I asked him what he wanted out of life, and he quickly replied, "Power and money." He already had both, so I next asked what he thought would make him happy. Despite his apparent success, he felt disconnected and apart from the rest of humanity. Happiness, he believed, required this connection.

Years later, I finally recognized how profound this gentleman's insight had been. With his "propaganda" campaigns, he regularly deceived the public. Before we can deceive people, steal from them, or assault them, we must first separate ourselves from them internally. We feel justified in bending them to our will because we consider ourselves wiser, nobler, or stronger. In other words, we feel that we are somehow better than they are; we are different, separate, apart. *Aggression is the physical manifestation of our judgment of others.*

Even with the best of intentions, trying to control others creates the layers that form the Pyramid of Power. At its apex, we look down at the rest of humanity and are very much disconnected and alone.

Ironically, we aggress to gain something for ourselves or for others, believing that our happiness or theirs will increase. *However, in using aggression as our means, we have destroyed the connectedness (goodwill toward all) that appears to be a necessary precondition of the happiness we seek.* In using aggression as our means, we sabotage our ends.

The power broker acknowledged that the special interests he served could easily be foiled by ordinary people, if they ever realized the power that they possess. If people ever shifted from Type A and Type C thinking to Type S thinking, they would reject aggression as their means. The licensing laws that form the Pyramid of Power would never be enacted. We have empowered the conglomerates and other special interests that control us. Consequently, we can also disempower them.

How "Meanies" Become Good Neighbors

The power broker described above was just beginning to learn the importance of goodwill toward all. Likewise, John D. Rockefeller discovered the importance of connectedness. Consequently, he gained more than money and power—he saved his own life.

When Rockefeller began his career, he greatly helped the poor by making kerosene affordable (Chapter 7). As Standard Oil grew, however, Rockefeller seemed to give more attention to obtaining a monopoly than serving customers. He focused on destroying competitors, even using aggression-through-government against other companies, such as Tidewater Pipeline. Pennsylvania workers, disgusted at his tactics, hanged him in effigy. By the time Rockefeller was 53, he was guarded day and night by bodyguards, an outward symbol of his inner separation from the rest of humankind.

Rockefeller's health began failing. His digestion was so poor that he could eat only milk and crackers. His hair began falling out, and he had chronic insomnia. The attending physicians told him that he wouldn't live another year.

Shortly after this gloomy prediction, Rockefeller shifted his focus again. Virtually on

Center your country in the Tao and evil will have no power. Not that it isn't there, but you'll be able to step out of its way.

—Lao tsu
TAO TE CHING

his deathbed, Rockefeller decided to involve himself in the charitable works that he had supported for many years.

Along with this shift from destruction to service, his enthusiasm for life returned. He began to feel connected to those around him as he directed his foundation to distribute hundreds of millions of dollars to hospitals, universities, missions, and individuals. Rockefeller's generosity helped researchers discover cures for tuberculosis, malaria, and diphtheria. His research grants contributed to the discovery of penicillin.

Rockefeller's inner shift from grasping to giving healed his body as well. He was finally able to eat and sleep normally. In becoming service-oriented again, Rockefeller connected with humankind and lived to the ripe old age of 98.[4]

Rockefeller's experience is not unique. Studies show that feelings of love and connectedness enhance our immune systems and decrease destructive stress hormone levels. Loving, caring, and connecting are important for our physical and mental well-being.[5]

Must we give away our hard-earned money in order to feel good, mentally and physically? Not at all! The compassion that drives us to help others is itself a manifestation of an already-established connection with them. The passion that drives a business person to give customers superior service is also evidence of this connection. The customers' wants and needs cannot be anticipated without it.

Serving, giving, or simply silently appreciating others enhances our connection with them further. Which specific action creates this enhancement differs for each individual.

For example, Rockefeller seemed to connect with others both through passion and compassion. He was passionate about oil refining, efficiency, and giving his customers a low-priced, quality product. In his early years, he was in alignment with humankind and prospered.

When Rockefeller started seeing competitors, not as part of the landscape, but as targets to destroy, he shifted from peaceful win-win interactions to aggressive lose-lose tactics. He seemed to realign with humankind later in his

---

The mandate to "Love your neighbor as you love yourself" is not just a moral mandate. It's a physiological mandate. Caring is biological. One thing you get from caring for others is you're not lonely. And the more connected you are to life, the healthier you are.

—James Lynch
THE BROKEN HEART: THE
MEDICAL CONSEQUENCES
OF LONELINESS

And ye shall know the truth, and the truth shall set you free.

—THE HOLY BIBLE
John 8:32

life by once again anticipating the needs of others. Had he been so inclined, he probably could have achieved the same healing for himself by starting another business, as long as he stayed passionately focused on giving customers a quality product or service, rather than aggressively snuffing out competitors.

When we truly care for others, we do not attack them, steal from them, or defraud them, regardless of whether we call them customers, competitors, friends, or family. *Honoring our neighbor's choice and righting our wrongs are the political manifestations of loving our neighbor as ourselves.*

Of course, Good Neighbors eventually grow old, get sick, and die too. However, we are likely to live a longer and happier life if we are connected to the rest of humankind by goodwill rather than separated from others with thoughts of aggression.

Why Healing Our World Is Virtually Inevitable

In earlier chapters, we learned that using aggression as our means boomeranged back to us, hurting those it was intended to help. Even when we are convinced that *our* aggression must be abandoned, we're not so sure that selfish others will change their ways. After all, they may not care if others are hurt as long as they benefit. We despair that healing can ever come to our world.

However, now we see that the thoughts used to justify aggression also keep us from health and happiness. Even those who have succeeded in acquiring power and money suffer until they learn this lesson. As the stories of Rockefeller and the power broker illustrate, the question is not *if* they will abandon aggression, but *when*. Their own quest for happiness will drive them to become Good Neighbors.

But won't many aggressors die before they learn that nonaggression serves them? Certainly! However, as the importance of abandoning aggressive thoughts becomes more prevalent in our culture, the benefits of becoming Good Neighbors will become more obvious. More people will learn; fewer will aggress. Finally, aggression will become a cultural aberration, rather than being accepted as a necessary evil.

As individuals become more aware of the benefits of becoming Good Neighbors, their nations will be transformed as well. My home, the United States, has a history that is reminiscent of Rockefeller's story. Although the United States was never a perfect practitioner of the nonaggression principle, in its early years it was a better example than most other nations.

Just as Rockefeller began seeing smaller competitors as enemies to be destroyed, so too did the United States began to view other developing nations as a threat. As we'll see in the next few chapters, my homeland used its great wealth destructively and aggressively.

As tragic and heart-rending as these next few chapters are, they are not the end of the story. Like Rockefeller and the power broker, Americans are beginning to realize that we may have lost our way. Once we recognize that we are going down the wrong path, we can choose differently. Like Rockefeller in his later years, we can embrace the Good Neighbor Policy with even more awareness to restore and even improve our societal well-being.

The desire to end our own suffering and experience health and happiness drives each of us to become Good Neighbors. Truly, it can be—and will be—a win–win world!

The Good Neighbor Policy Creates a Win–Win World!

Chapter 17: Healing Our World Is Inevitable

In Summary ...

- The Good Neighbor Policy, honoring our neighbor's choice and righting our wrongs, creates harmony and abundance in our city, state, and nation.

- Becoming Good Neighbors promotes our own individual health and happiness as well.

- Suspiciousness, hostility, cynicism, and blame—Type A or aggressor behavior—alter our body's biochemistry, predisposing us to cardiovascular disease.

- Similarly, Type C or victim behavior—frustration, helplessness, giving up, and resignation—predispose us to cancer.

- Much of our society is caught in a destructive A/C loop, alternately becoming victims and aggressors through the guns of government.

- Type S or self-actualized people focus on changing themselves rather than others. They are neither victims nor aggressors and reject aggression-through-government. Type S individuals live longer than Type A or Type C individuals.

- The thoughts that precede aggression estrange us from the rest of humankind, sabotaging the happiness that we hope to gain from our actions.

- Even those who gain money and power through the guns of government eventually recognize that aggression sabotages their own health and happiness and reject it.

- Because our health and happiness depend on our becoming Good Neighbors, we will all abandon aggression one day. Healing our world is virtually inevitable.

Part Four

Lead Us Not into Temptation:

Foreign Policy

Chapter 18

Beacon to the World

The best way to help poor nations is to be Good Neighbors.

In Parts II and III, we learned how we create poverty and strife in the developed world, using the United States as our example. In Part IV, we'll examine how this aggression ripples outward to less developed nations, further impoverishing them. We'll also discover how our aggressive acts are reflected back to us as threats to our national security.

We'll begin our journey by examining why Third World nations never experienced the leap in wealth creation that developed ones did (Figure 2.2). Simply put, poor nations never rid themselves of aggression-through-government to the degree that the United States, Great Britain, and Europe did.

How Poverty Is Created in the Third World

Aggression-through-government is the primary cause of poverty in developing nations just as it is in developed ones. The Third World today staggers under a smothering burden of licensing laws (first- and second-layer aggression). For example, licenses that take hours to obtain in Hong Kong and weeks in New York City take years in India, with no guarantee of success.[1] *Because licensing laws are so restrictive, 50–80% of people in Third World nations, including former Soviet states, create their wealth illegally.*

Underground entrepreneurs cannot openly advertise or get help from the police and courts if they are robbed or cheated. They live in fear that government enforcers will stop them from creating enough wealth to feed their families. *In Peru, the informal (illegal) manufacturers pay around 15% of gross income in bribes just to soothe the authorities.*[2]

In Third World countries, homesteading claims are rarely acknowledged by governments (third-layer aggression). People settle on the available land but can be driven off at any time.

In the American West, people settled on the available land too. Like the people of Third World

Massive extralegality is not a new phenomenon. It is what always happens when governments fail to make the law coincide with the way people live and work.

—Hernando de Soto co-author of THE OTHER PATH

*The Americans, not al-
ways eagerly or con-
sciously, gradually
legitimized extralegal
property norms and ar-
rangements created by
the poorest Americans
and integrated them into
the law of the land.*
          —Hernando de Soto
    THE MYSTERY OF CAPITAL

nations, they worked out boundaries among themselves. However, when the western territories became states, government granted formal titles according to these commonly accepted boundaries. This final step was never completed in Third World nations. Indeed, Japan only went through this process in the mid-1900s.[3]

In contrast, legalizing title to land in Peru requires 728 bureaucratic steps. Building a house on state-owned land is a seven-year process requiring 207 steps in 52 government offices. In Egypt, taking title to a homesteaded lot takes 5 to 14 years. In Haiti, a person can spend two years just getting a five-year lease on land he or she wants to buy. An additional 12 years and 111 bureaucratic hurdles are necessary for its purchase.[4]

Consequently, most houses in Third World countries are built without clear or formal title. In Peru, Egypt, and Haiti, more than 80% of rural dwellers are in legal limbo.[5] As a result, homes cannot easily be sold, used as collateral, or mortgaged. "Squatters" can be evicted at a moment's notice. People hesitate to build more than a shack or invest in other improvements.

Secure property rights mean the difference between poverty and affluence, as illustrated by two neighboring Peruvian settlements on the Rimac River. The residents of one settlement persevered for six years and finally "formalized" their claims. Because they felt secure in their property rights, they built their homes with bricks and added shops, sidewalks, and gardens. The neighboring settlement without formal title remained a shantytown of cardboard and mud.[6] When homesteading and ownership are thwarted, only poverty is possible.

The real estate held, but not formally owned, by the world's poor has been conservatively valued at a whopping $9.3 trillion. This figure is almost twice the U.S. money supply and more than 93 times the aid given to the Third World between 1989 and 1999.[7] *The world's poor are sitting on a pot of gold that they cannot spend because of aggression-through-government.*

Subsidized state-run monopolies (third-layer aggression) are more prevalent in poor nations as well. However, in the last decade of the 1990s, many of these state enterprises were privatized, especially in Chile, Mexico, and Malaysia. Privatizing even half of the subsidized monopolies increases the annual rate of wealth creation in developing nations by 2.5%.[8] *At this rate, India would have more than doubled its wealth creation in the first half of the 1990s simply by privatizing all of its subsidized monopolies.*[9]

Massive inflation (fourth-layer aggression) also plagues the Third World. Since 1968, poor countries have suffered 27 cases of decade-long inflation in excess of 40% per year. *In Peru and Brazil, the average annual inflation rate for one decade even exceeded 200%!*[10] Because inflation hurts those without land or assets the most, the poor became even poorer.[11]

The aggression that stifled the world's wealth creation for so long is still keeping Third World nations destitute. When developing nations cut government spending, privatize government monopolies, lower inflation, and respect private property rights, wealth creation soars (Figure 2.3). The Third World has only to adopt the Good Neighbor Policy to free itself from poverty.

How Our Aid Enslaves the Third World

Unfortunately, most of the "help" that Third World nations receive from the developed countries is based on the aggression of taxation. Consequently, it often backfires, hurting the very people we wish to help.

Most U.S. foreign aid goes for "security assistance" to underdeveloped nations.[12] Heads of state receive this tax-subsidized aid primarily on the basis of their support for U.S. foreign policies, even if they brutally oppress their own people. As a result, our aid ends up supporting dictators such as Ferdinand Marcos (Philippines), Sergeant Samuel Doe (Liberia), Mobutu Seko (Zaire), and Zia ul-Haq (Pakistan), to name a few.[13] Almost three-fourths of U.S. aid to El Salvador during the early 1980s went to support the government's war against protesting civilians.[14] The former Shah of Iran's cruel Savak and Idi Amin's "public safety unit" for internal security were trained with our help.[15] In Latin

... the subsidies do not go to the pathetic figures pictured in aid propaganda. They go to their rulers, who are often directly responsible for the hardship of their subjects. ... the more damaging the policies, the more acute becomes the need, the more effective become the appeals for aid.

—Peter Bauer
FROM SUBSISTENCE TO EXCHANGE AND OTHER ESSAYS

In the 1990s, there is consensus on the left and right that government-to-government aid funneled into the statist development approach has failed to help the poor. ... By fostering the growth of government, the development banks became one more obstacle for countries to overcome in order to progress economically.
— Paul C. Roberts and
Karen L. Araujo
THE CAPITALIST
REVOLUTION IN LATIN
AMERICA

... it's impossible to go through the powerful to reach the powerless.
— Frances Moore Lappe
et al.
BETRAYING THE NATIONAL
INTEREST

America in the 1970s, U.S. foreign aid was given to nations with the worst human rights violations.[16] Our tax-funded aid even helped establish Saddam Hussein[17] and the Taliban.[18]

The aggression of domestic taxation ripples out to create aggressors abroad. When these aggressors turn on us, we reap what we sow.

How Our Aid Creates Hunger in the Third World

Our tax-funded humanitarian aid often ends up supporting more aggression. Western nations often subsidize their agricultural products and then use additional taxes to buy up the surplus.[19] The food is given to Third World governments or purchased with tax-subsidized loans from the donor nations.[20] With so much aggression involved, the results are readily predictable.

For example, during the famine of the mid-1980s, the government of Bangladesh sold the "free" food at market prices to its people. The military, which kept the government in power, paid only one-fifth as much.[21] Somalia allocated 80% of its food aid to the military and government employees.[22] During the famine in Ethiopia, the rulers sold the donated food and refused to feed the hungriest provinces as punishment for harboring rebels.[23] Haiti's Jean Claude Duvalier simply liquidated supplies from donor countries and kept the money for himself.[24] Because poverty and starvation in poor countries are often caused by the aggression of those in power, we should not be surprised that such rulers use our aid to enrich themselves rather than help their people.

How Our Aid Destroys the Environment

Many sincere Third World governments borrow money from the World Bank for roads, dams, and other public works in the hope that prosperity will follow. Because these projects evolve from bureaucratic decree, they often are not what the country needs most. The inevitable inefficiency of bureaucratically selected and managed projects usually consumes wealth, rather than creating it. Aid to such countries does not increase wealth creation,[25] but it does saddle them with a debt to the World Bank that cannot be repaid.

In addition, many of the dams and agricultural projects destroy rainforests, threaten the native people who populate them, and leave thousands homeless.[26] Poorly managed irrigation projects result in millions of hectares becoming flooded, waterlogged, and salinated.[27]

In the early 1970s, Tanzania, which received more aid than any other nation, drove the poor from their land and into government villages or communes.[28] Generous loans to the governments of Vietnam,[29] Indonesia,[30] Ethiopia,[31] and Guatemala[32] funded similar resettlement programs. The communes were seldom productive.[33] Land snatched from the helpless farmers was awarded to political favorites.

In Indonesia and Brazil, the poor who were robbed of their farms were often resettled on cleared rainforest land.[34] Sometimes people made homeless by foreign aid projects cleared the forests so that they could farm. Because the rainforest soil is unsuited to intensive cultivation, it was quickly exhausted. Farmers had to clear more rainforest to survive. The Brazilian government encouraged rainforest destruction by giving ownership only when plots were cleared.[35] Natives who wished to use the forest sustainably were effectively banned from owning rainforest.

Governments in developing nations claim the rainforests as their own, just as the U.S. government claims much of the western rangeland. Just as the U.S. government once drove Native Americans onto reservations, Third World militaries often drive indigenous rainforest people from their homes. The government then rents the forest to loggers so that payments can be made to the World Bank. Because neither the loggers nor the politicians "own" the land, both groups have every incentive to exploit it—and they do!

In the 1990s, concerned conservationists attempted to stop the devastation of the rainforests with "debt for nature" swaps. Instead of paying back their loans to the World Bank, poor nations could "swap" some of their debt for a pledge to turn rainforest acreage into preserves or parks. Although the plants and animals were

... the World Bank has contributed as much to agricultural disaster in Ethiopia as the governments themselves.
—Yonas Deressa
president, Ethiopian
Refugees Education
and Relief Foundation

The World Bank, rather than consistently aiding in alleviating Third World poverty, in reality has contributed to the marginalization and devastation of hundreds of thousands of tribal and indigenous people and rural poor in India, Indonesia, and Brazil.
—Lori Udall
Environmental Defense
Fund

Without consulting us, you have traded our land for a debt we did not incur.
—Evaristo Nugkuag
Aguaruna Indian leader,
Peru

protected, the native people often were not. They were forced from their homes, even though they are an integral part of the forest's biodiversity— and its rightful owners.[36]

Even when the indigenous people were allowed to stay, they no longer took care of the forest. Because they knew that they could be evicted at any time, they could profit only by exploiting it. When the Philippine government recognized how the natives had gone from caretakers to destroyers, it wisely decided to return the rainforests to native ownership. Once the forest became theirs again, the natives protected it.[37] *Landowners make better caretakers of the environment than renters and politicians.*

Kicking Them When They're Down

The damage done by aggression-through-government and foreign "aid" is so immense that many Third World nations create little wealth at all. Our aggression of tariffs, quotas, and other trade restrictions knock out the lower rungs on the Ladder of Affluence, making weath creation even more difficult.

Tariffs are taxes imposed on imported goods. Consumers ultimately pay for tariffs in the form of higher product prices. Quotas are limits enforced—at gunpoint, if necessary—on the quantity of a product that can be imported. Demand for these imports usually exceeds the supply, which means consumers pay higher prices than they otherwise would.

Bangladesh, one of the world's poorest nations, has received billions in foreign aid since 1980 to make it self-sufficient. By 1985, Bangladesh had built enough garment factories to multiply the nation's output 30-fold. By creating a viable export industry Bangladesh had taken its first step on the Ladder of Affluence.

However, textile and apparel manufacturers in the United States, Great Britain, France, and Canada successfully lobbied for quotas on Bangladeshi products to limit imports. The new factories in Bangladesh had to close down.[38] The developed world is almost schizophrenia with its focus on aid, but little trade.[39]

Are we rich enough that we can afford to give Eastern Europeans shiploads of handouts—yet so poor and fragile that we cannot allow them a chance to earn a few dollars honestly? Charity is no substitute for opportunity.

—James Bovard
PERPETUATING POVERTY

A Lose–Lose Situation

Developed nations justify the aggression of trade restrictions as "protecting" their workers from foreign competition. As usual, however, our aggression backfires, hurting the very people we are trying to help. For example, in the early 1980s, when the average American worker in the clothing manufacturing industry made less than $7 per hour,[40] trade restrictions cost U.S. consumers $700,000 in higher prices for every job "saved"![41]

Such costs are not atypical.[42] Tariffs and quotas cost a family of four an average of $2,000 in 1989.[43] That amount represents 32% of the purchasing power of families classified as poor.[44] For the $7-per-hour textile workers, the very restrictions that "protected" their jobs cost them about one-seventh of their paycheck. Tariffs only made poor workers poorer.

When U.S. apparel and textile workers were laid off, they found jobs that, on average, paid more than they had made previously.[45] Tariffs and quotas may actually prevent U.S. workers from getting ahead!

The $700,000-per-job-saved that Americans paid in higher clothing costs meant that they couldn't buy other domestic products. Jobs in industries that were more competitive globally thus grew more slowly. *For every job protected in the textile or apparel industry, at least one other American job was lost in another sector.*[46]

Sometimes the jobs that we are trying to protect are the very ones that are lost. In the 1980s, trade restrictions "saved" the jobs of 22,000 auto workers and boosted the price of a new car from 36% to 48% of the median household's annual income. Because of the higher prices, Americans bought one million fewer new cars, causing 50,000 layoffs. Auto workers ended up worse off, not better.[47]

In the United States, approximately 11,000 sugar farmers are "protected" by high tariffs on imported sugar. Industries dependent on sugar, which employ over 77,000 people, lost at least 16,000 jobs in the 1980s because of the higher sugar prices. Nevertheless, the tariff was not

... according to the U.S. Department of Labor's own statistics, "protectionism" destroys eight jobs in the general economy for every one saved in a protected economy.

—Vincent Miller and James Elwood
FREE TRADE VS. PROTECTIONISM

abandoned. Candy companies are now leaving the country so that they can buy sugar at a fraction of the U.S. price.[48]

Tariffs, quotas, and other trade restrictions, like other forms of aggression, destroy jobs and limit wealth creation.[49] Indeed, the Fordney-McCumber Tariff of 1922 and the Smoot-Hawley Tariff of 1930 started international retaliation that devastated U.S. agriculture, forcing rural banks to close. Such trade restrictions, coupled with the Federal Reserve's manipulation of the money supply, helped create the Great Depression.[50] As always, we reap what we sow.

A Better Way

Creating Prosperity

The economic progress of Third World nations depends on the degree to which they reject aggression-through-government as their means. The widespread privatization that many developing countries are undertaking is an excellent start.

Poor countries can also eliminate the regulations that inhibit wealth creation. In Costa Rica, the corruption caused by licensing laws has been targeted by the Movimiento Libertario (Libertarian Movement), whose slogan is "Donde hay permiso hay chorizo." This Spanish idiom, loosely translated, means "Where a license is needed, so is a bribe."[51] Because poor countries usually have more licensing laws than rich ones, the bribery and corruption associated with them are much more problematic as well, especially for the poor. Licensing laws and the corruption they create limit a country's wealth creation.[52]

In 1998, Harvard graduate Otto Guevara became Movimiento Libertario's first elected congressman. Guevara successfully petitioned the Constitutional Court to stop the confiscation of gypsy cabs and to return them to their owners. In 2002, Movimiento Libertario won six seats and is continuing to promote nonaggressive solutions to the country's problems.[53]

Costa Rica, like many Latin American countries, began lowering tariffs and other trade barriers in the mid-1980s.[54] Indeed, the only developing nations that are actually catching up

When buying and selling are controlled by legislation, the first things to be bought and sold are the legislatures.
—P. J. O'Rourke
Cato Institute's
Mencken research
fellow

Genuine development cannot be imported or imposed; it can only be achieved by a people for themselves.
—Frances Moore Lappe
et al.
BETRAYING THE NATIONAL
INTEREST

to the rich countries are the ones that have practiced trade openness by both lowering tariffs and increasing their trading volume (Figure 18.1).[55]

Trade openness is so important that it explains 55% of the differences in the rate of wealth creation among countries. By factoring in the inflation rate and the respect for property rights to this statistical analysis, we can explain 78% of the difference in the wealth creation rate among the nations of the world.[56] Looking at this another way, factors other than the Good Neighbor Policy (e.g., geography, culture, or resources) contribute at most only 22% to a nation's wealth-creating ability.

Poor nations are now beginning to adopt the Good Neighbor Policy. For example, Hernando de Soto and his Institute for Liberty and Democracy are helping hundreds of thousands of Peruvians obtain formal title to their homes and businesses.[57] Market values of legally recognized property double overnight![58]

In summary, we find no cases to support the frequent worry that a country might open and yet fail to grow. ... We find that the open economies grow, on average, by 2.45 percentage points more than the closed economies.

—Jeffrey Sachs and
Andrew Warner
Harvard University

Figure 18.1: Trade Openness Increases Wealth Creation

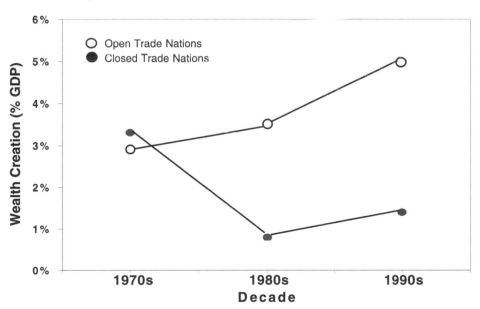

Data from D. Dollar and A. Kraay, "Trade, Growth, and Poverty," *Working Paper 2615* (Washington, DC: World Bank, 2001), p. 2. The "open trade" countries are the top third of 72 developing nations in terms of increased trade volume, compared to GDP. The "closed trade" countries are the remaining two-thirds of developing nations, and % GDP is the average rate of wealth creation for the decade indicated.

Openness to international trade accelerates development: this is one of the most widely held beliefs in the economics profession, one of the few things on which Nobel prize winners of both the left and the right agree.
                                    —David Dollar
                                    and Aart Kraay
                                    World Bank

Inequality tends to decrease as the level of development increases. As there are no societies ... which have both a low level of inequality and a low level of development, neither are there any with a high level of inequality and a high level of development.
                                    —Michael Ward
                              THE POLITICAL ECONOMY
                                  OF DISTRIBUTION

When child labor is prohibited by law, the law cannot protect the child workers since they legally do not exist.
                                    —William Knight
                              THE WORLD'S EXPLOITED
                                        CHILDREN

Reducing the Gap Between Rich and Poor

Recognizing homesteading claims puts a nation's poor on the road to income equality. In poor nations, land is the only safe haven for savings and capital, because currency is continuously eroded by high rates of inflation. Because of the hurdles that the poor face in owning land in Third World nations, the gap between the rich and poor is wide. Even when these countries start creating more wealth, inequality remains, because the hurdles to formal title are so steep.[59]

By protecting homesteading rights, Third World nations close the gap between the "haves" and "have-nots." When land distribution is more equitable, wealth creation is greater.[60] Less aggression means more wealth.

Although China still does not acknowledge homesteading rights, it did establish temporary "ownership" by giving farmers long-term leases in return for a share of their crop.[61] Once farmers felt secure, they turned China from a net *importer* of corn and soybeans to the third largest *exporter* of both crops.[62] A little less aggression goes a long way.

Letting Children Be Children

One of the tragedies of Third World poverty is that 250 million children must work or go hungry.[63] In preindustrial England, where poverty was as prevalent as in Third World nations today, children under 12 years of age supplied about 13% of a family's income. In poor nations such as Peru, children today provide a similar level of family support. The children of Paraguay earn almost one-quarter of their families' income. In contrast, in developed nations, child labor accounts for less than 1% of family income.[64]

However, outlawing child labor doesn't end it. Faced with a choice between working and starving, children continue to work even when the law forbids it. However, young workers have no legal recourse if their employers refuse to pay them or otherwise abuse them. The aggression of child labor laws ends up hurting the very people they were supposed to help.

In 1993, Senator Tom Harkin proposed that the United States ban imports from countries using child labor. As a result, factories in Bangladesh stopped hiring children. The displaced children ended up in worse jobs, such as prostitution, or ended up on the streets with no means of support at all.[65]

We institute child labor laws to stop cruel parents from forcing children to work long, hard hours unnecessarily. However, as familes move up the Ladder of Affluence, most parents send their children to school instead of work. In some countries, children continue to work so that they can afford to go to school.[66] Finally, families make enough to keep their children in school and child labor is no longer necessary.

The only way to end child labor is to create universal abundance by being Good Neighbors. One of the ways in which developed countries can help the poor children of the Third World is to end the aggression of tariffs, quotas, and bans that put both them and their parents out of work and onto the streets.

Using Rainforests' Sustainability

The rainforests are populated by indigenous natives who create wealth in a manner that preserves the ecosystem. Peruvian Amazon dwellers, for example, cultivate the rainforest profitably and sustainably by harvesting its fruit, rubber, and timber. They make up to three times as much as they would if they cleared the forest for cattle ranching.[67] Most native people, like 12,000 rubber-tapping families of Brazil,[68] are much more careful in managing their homeland than distant politicians are.

A number of indigenous people have, in theory at least, gained recognition as the owners of their rainforests during the 1990s. However, national governments still look the other way when gold miners, loggers, and trespassers plunder rainforest.[69] *To save the rainforests, we must protect the homesteading rights of the indigenous people.*

Some people fear that the native people will simply sell their lands to loggers and other commercial interests when they have formal title to their rainforest lands. Certainly some of them will. However, when a business has to buy the

It is a distortion of facts to say that the factories carried off the housewives from the nurseries and the kitchen and the children from their play. These women had nothing to cook with and to feed their children. These children were destitute and starving. Their only refuge was the factory. It saved them, in the strict sense of the term, from death by starvation.
—Ludwig von Mises
HUMAN ACTION

Farmers with secure title to land are more likely to invest in soil conservation, sustainable cultivation techniques, and other environmental practices. Vested with ownership rights, local communities have reforested degraded lands in India and Nepal.
—Vinod Thomas et al.
THE QUALITY OF GROWTH

property, rather than simply bribe a government official, logging often becomes unprofitable. Much of the exploitation of rainforest land would be prohibitively expensive if companies had to buy the land they wished to plunder.

Conservation organizations could prevent many commercially viable sales simply by paying the native people an annual fee not to sell. Nature lovers could also buy portions of the rainforests themselves. *Many people in the developed nations would enthusiastically buy a plot in order to preserve the rainforest.*

If companies had to purchase rainforest land in competition with conservationists and native people, the cost of rainforest land would be high. Only a few commercial needs would justify this expense, so logging, for example, would be more limited. In this way, the marketplace ecosystem balances the needs of the native people, commercial interests, and conservationists.

Setting the Example

Hong Kong provides an excellent model of how the poor of the Third World can become rich. In Chapter 2, we learned how this tiny nation overcame numerous obstacles to attain one of the highest per capita rates of wealth creation in the world.

Hong Kong didn't get much of the tax-supported "aid" that increases Third World indebtedness without promoting development. However, Hong Kong did have low taxes, low inflation, and low government spending. Because regulations or trade restrictions were few, corruption was low too. Such freedom from aggression is necessary for development.[70]

When a developing nation abandons aggression, private investors provide the capital necessary for expansion. Throughout the 1990s, private investment in Hong Kong has dwarfed tax-supported "aid."[71] With little "help" from the tax-supported World Bank or the International Monetary Fund,[72] Hong Kong went from rags to riches in just half a century. Countries wishing to share in Hong Kong's success need only embrace the Good Neighbor Policy.

... our greatest contribution to the cause of freedom and development overseas is not what we do over there, but what we do right here at home.
—Frances Moore Lappe et al.
BETRAYING THE NATIONAL INTEREST

The United States was once a shining example of freedom from aggression, a beacon to the world. Perhaps a developing nation will have to take up the torch of liberty and continue to light the way!

Chapter 18: Beacon to the World

In Summary ...

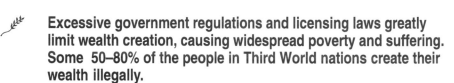

- ✎ Excessive government regulations and licensing laws greatly limit wealth creation, causing widespread poverty and suffering. Some 50–80% of the people in Third World nations create their wealth illegally.

- ✎ Legally owning a home in Third World countries is virtually impossible. For example, in Peru, obtaining legal title to land requires 728 steps. Consequently, most houses in poor nations are built without clear or formal title.

- ✎ The land and homes of the world's poor are worth almost $10 trillion, but because they don't have legal title, they cannot access this equity.

- ✎ Most U.S. foreign aid is squandered by Third World despots. Rather than using the money to help the poor or build their economies, they use it to increase their own wealth, power, and prestige.

- ✎ Because bureaucratically managed loan funds are usually wasted, borrowing leaves only crushing debt in Third World Nations.

- ✎ High tariffs and import restrictions in developed countries keep poor nations from becoming self-sufficient.

- ✎ Trade barriers designed to protect jobs in developed countries backfire to destroy jobs instead.

- ✎ The only poor nations that have grown rich in the past few decades are those that have lowered tariffs and increased their trading volume.

- ✎ To become wealthy, poor nations need only follow the example of Hong Kong and become Good Neighbors. By getting rid of stifling regulations, formalizing the property of the poor, and ending tariffs and import restrictions, they can go from abject poverty to First World affluence in a few short generations.

Chapter 19

Is Communism Really Dead?

Communism tries to provide for the common good by using aggression-through-government as its means. Every time we violate the Good Neighbor Policy to do good, we take our nation one step closer to the horrors experienced by the former Soviet Union.

Most people believe that communism died with the breakup of the Union of Soviet Socialist Republics (USSR). However, China, with a fifth of the world's population, still espouses its principles, as do North Korea, Cuba, Cambodia, Vietnam, and others. Communism is an extreme form of aggression-through-government.

In the first 87 years of the twentieth century, Communist nations killed more than 100 million of their own people. The Communist Khmer Rouge was responsible for the deaths of 31% of the Cambodian population in its four-year rule. The USSR and Communist China were the two biggest mega-murderers of the 1900s.[1]

Communism sabotaged its noble ends by using aggression-through-government as its means. Every time we use aggression for the common good, we come one step closer to creating the poverty, strife, and mass murder that communism promotes.

Is there a difference between communism and socialism, or for that matter, fascism? All these terms refer to nations where aggression-through-government predominates, perhaps with somewhat different emphasis. Communism, as used in this book, refers to the extreme form of aggression-through-goverment practiced in the former Soviet Union.

In theory at least, capitalism is a system where aggression-through-government is quite limited. As we've seen from earlier chapters, however, the United States can hardly claim to be capitalistic, even though it still bears that label. Consequently, the word capitalism, as it is used today, means different things to different people. Consequently, I rarely refer to it.

As this chapter will demonstrate, most developed nations are well on their way to embracing communism without even knowing it!

No one can be at the same time a sincere Catholic and a true socialist.
—Pope Pius XI
Roman Catholic pope
from 1921 to 1939

It is wrong to demand that the individual subordinate himself to the collectivity or merge into it, because it is by its most advanced individuals that the collectivity progresses and they can really advance only if they are free. ... The individual is indeed the key of the evolutionary movement.
—Sri Aurobindo
THE FUTURE EVOLUTION OF MAN

... violence is the cornerstone of socialism's existence as an institution.
—Hans-Hermann Hoppe
A THEORY OF SOCIALISM AND CAPITALISM

Creating Selfishness

Communists believe that individuals should give according to their ability and receive according to their needs. In this way, communists hope to achieve an even distribution of wealth so that no one will be poor, hungry, or miserable. Communists see selfish others, who won't voluntarily share the wealth they have created, as the primary obstacle to their goal. The communist solution is to force selfish others—at gunpoint, if necessary—to redistribute their wealth.

Communists want us to share with strangers just as we share with family members. Often we sacrifice our own goals to satisfy the needs of our family members. Parents, for example, might forgo recreation or new clothes to give their children the best education. Such acts are usually spontaneous and driven by the love parents have for their offspring.

Communists believe that we should all be family to one another. If we won't voluntarily give to others outside our family until the available wealth is evenly distributed, then we must be forced to do so.

Forcing people to be generous, however, quickly destroys the love that normally inspires such giving. For example, we might help a family member in need, even if the need is frequent. But, if that family member ordered us to help him or her and attacked us if we didn't, we'd angrily resist. Aggression inhibits spontaneous giving, encouraging resentment and hoarding instead. Aggression sets the stage for the very selfishness we are trying to eradicate.

Creating Animosity

Traveling by train through Poland and East Germany in the early 1980s, I always knew which side of the border I was on by the temperament of the customs officials. Those from the so-called free nations (i.e., free from aggression) were courteous and friendly; those from the Eastern Bloc seemed miserable and eager to take out their frustrations on the passengers. A society based on the belief that selfish others are to blame for the world's woes is a society in which those who have more are seen as enemies.

One person's gain is seen as another's loss. Communism teaches hate instead of love.

I visited the former East Berlin again in the mid-1990s several years after the Berlin Wall had been demolished. The hostility that communism had bred into people was still prevalent. "Service with a smile" was notably absent. Indeed, the people who sold train tickets seemed to take pride in giving the customer a difficult time.

The win–win practice of serving others to serve ourselves only occurs when we honor our neighbor's choice. A person whose choice is not honored will thwart the choices of others out of spite. Instead of promoting love, aggression-through-government creates resentment.

Creating Poverty

Most of the wealth in Communist countries was taken from its creators and distributed by a handful of government officials. People who created wealth seldom benefited by having more for themselves or their loved ones. As a result, wealth creation slowed to a tiny fraction of what it otherwise would have been.

A Soviet experiment in the late 1980s illustrates the consequences of ownership of wealth creation. Soviet citizens were allowed to keep the food grown in their gardens. Although these plots were only about 2% of the total farmland, they produced 25% of the food![2] When Soviets kept the wealth they created, they produced almost 16 times more than when it was taken from them![3] Communist China had a similar experience (Chapter 18).

In 1913, under Czar Nicholas II, Russia was the world's largest food exporter. In 1989, it was the world's largest food importer.[4] Clearly, the creation of wealth in Russia has been dampened tremendously by communism, even when compared to a czarist regime that could hardly be considered free from aggression.

A smaller Wealth Pie means fewer goods and services for everyone. In 1987, less than three-fourths of the Soviet housing had hot water; 15% of the population had no bathrooms; 20% of urban residents breathed air that was dangerously

Soviet citizens have a worse diet than did Russians under Czar Nicholas II in 1913.

—Mortimer B. Zuckerman
editor-in-chief
U.S. News & World Report, 1989

... capitalism organizes the material affairs of humankind more satisfactorily than socialism.

—Robert Heilbroner
The New Yorker

Measured by the health of its people, the Soviet Union is no longer a developed nation.
—Nicholas Eberstadt
THE POVERTY OF
COMMUNISM

polluted.[5] One out of three Soviet hospitals had no indoor toilets; some didn't even have running water.[6] Needles for intravenous injections were used repeatedly, spreading hepatitis and AIDS.[7] Most hospitals had no elevators; the ill had to drag themselves up several flights of stairs.[8] While the life expectancy in Western nations rose, in Soviet countries it declined. Alcoholism ran rampant as people tried to forget their plight.[9] Poverty was aggression's bitter fruit.

Americans learned the folly of wealth redistribution early in their history. The Pilgrims settled in Plymouth in 1620 and farmed collectively, much as the Soviets would do three centuries later. All produce, fish, and game were held in common and divided among the settlers.

Just as in the Soviet Union, people worked less when they could not keep the fruits of their labor. As a result, the Pilgrims were soon faced with starvation. In desperation, Gov. William Bradford assigned each family a plot of land and let them keep what they grew. As a result, the people worked hard and prospered. The governor began the tradition of the Thanksgiving holiday to celebrate the bountiful harvest that resulted when the Pilgrims rejected communism and became Good Neighbors.[10]

Creating Class Distinctions

Socialists feel that wealth should be forcibly redistributed so that everyone will be equal. However, Communist countries end up with greater extremes of wealth distribution than capitalistic ones. Individuals who created goods and services that the government considered critical (e.g., military officers, Olympic athletes) were rewarded with the best food and housing.

Under Communism, the average Soviet waited in long lines at state stores for poor-quality produce and occasional meat. In contrast, high-ranking party officials and political favorites could buy high-quality food in exclusive stores and restaurants that were off limits to the average Soviet.[11]

Medical care likewise depended on one's status. High-ranking party members and members of the power elite were able to get Western-style care in special hospitals.[12] In spite of the high-sounding rhetoric, top-level Communists enjoyed a lifestyle that the average Soviet had no chance of attaining, no matter how hard he or she was willing to work.

To understand how politicians dedicated to an even distribution of wealth could let this happen, put yourself in their shoes. Imagine that you are a concerned head of state who wants everyone in the country to enjoy the same standard of living. You have the guns of government at your disposal, so you start by forcing everyone to work for the same wage.

Because doctors are paid the same amount no matter how many patients they see, they work at a leisurely pace, and lines outside their offices grow. To counter this behavior, you consider paying doctors according to how many patients they see. Because doctors respond to incentives like everyone else, they see as many people as possible, giving all patients cursory exams and sending them on their way. Soon the doctors are making more than the workers they treat. Through aggression, you have created a privileged class!

Instead of paying the doctors per patient, you set a quota for each doctor and send someone to make sure that the doctor spends the allotted time with each patient. The monitors are paid the same regardless of what their reports on the doctors contain. Knowing this fact, doctors will suggest that the monitors look the other way while they maintain a leisurely pace. In return, the doctor will put a monitor's family member at the front of the line if that member needs treatment. This "medical insurance" costs the monitors nothing, so they have every reason to accept it. If the doctor lets some patients bribe their way to the head of the line, some of this money might also be split with the monitor. Monitors, like doctors, become a privileged class.

You could have a second monitor check on the first, but what prevents the new monitor from accepting bribes too? The more monitors you have, the less wealth is created, because monitors produce no new goods and services. You have less wealth to redistribute.

The use of force to achieve equality will destroy freedom, and the force, introduced for good purposes, will end up in the hands of people who use it to promote their own interests.
— Milton Friedman
Nobel Prize winner,
Economics

When man interferes with the Tao, the sky becomes filthy, the earth becomes depleted, the equilibrium crumbles, creatures become extinct.
— Lao-tsu
TAO TE CHING

The ecological situation in Czechoslovakia is, in a word, disastrous. ... It's nothing short of catastrophe.
— Dr. Bedrich Moldan
Czechoslovakian
Environmental Minister

You could ask the police to torture any monitor who takes bribes, but the monitors might bribe the police. If you threatened to torture police who accepted bribes, you would incur the animosity of an armed elite skilled in violent action—not a good idea if you wanted to live very long. To make your police unbribable, you would have to pay them more than anyone else. You will have created one more privileged class. Equality cannot be achieved through aggression.

Destroying the Environment

In a marketplace free from aggression, the desire for more profit encourages conservation. Companies gain more business by cutting energy costs and offering consumers lower prices. Consequently, by 1989, the cost of energy used to produce a dollar's worth of goods in the United States was about half what it had been in the late 1920s.

In Communist countries, however, no one profits by conserving energy, so manufacturing continues to be wasteful. Communist economies use almost three times as much energy as the so-called free nations for every dollar of goods produced.[13]

In Communist countries, the only choices that were honored were those that the government officials made for the entire nation. If government control were the solution to pollution, the Eastern European countries would have been pristine. Instead, pollution ran rampant to an extent seldom seen in the Western world. For example, in CopÕa Mic|, Romania, carbon spewed nightly from a nearby tire factory, literally coating everything and everybody in black powder.[14] In Leipzig, East Germany, more than 90% of the population suffered health problems because of the high level of sulfur dioxide.[15] Polish economists estimate that pollution destroyed 10% to 15% of their nation's annual GNP.[16]

The Czechoslovakian Environment Ministry estimated that 5% to 7% of that country's annual wealth creation was similarly wasted.[17] Two-thirds of the forests were actually dying from the pollution and half of the water supply was undrinkable. One allergy specialist in the

Bohemian city of Most blamed pollution for the 10-year reduction in the residents' already low life span.[18]

The plight of Eastern Europe reminds us that aggression-through-government makes pollution worse, not better. When aggression prevents individuals from owning the environment, they profit only by exploiting it.

Turning Adults into Children

The greatest tragedy of communism is not poverty, animosity, or environmental destruction, but the devastation of the human spirit.

A medical colleague returning from Finland in the 1980s told me that Russian men were marrying Finnish women so they could move to Finland. Once the men arrived, however, the decisions that the average citizen had to make concerning housing, shopping, and so on were just too much for many of them to bear. Overwhelmed by the task of taking responsibility for their lives, the men went back to Russia, where scarcity and aggression make choice a rarity. This destruction of the questing human spirit, of the confidence in one's ability to cope with the world, is the most devastating effect of the extreme aggression of communism.

Like overprotective parenting, aggression-through-government hinders normal psychological development. Most of the time, individuals know their situation, strengths, and limitations best, so they make the best choices for themselves. Even when they choose poorly, the lessons they learn enable them to make better choices later on. As each individual optimizes his or her own well-being without aggression, the whole society benefits. Looking out for Number One is nature's way of ensuring that we optimize the whole. If each cell maintains its health without harming the others, the body becomes vibrantly healthy.

A little bit of communism is like a little bit of disease. Mixing aggression with nonaggression isn't a happy medium; it's the beginning of societal ill health: poverty, environmental destruction, hostility, and mass murder are the results. As the developed nations embrace

Our power does not know liberty or justice. It is established on the destruction of the individual will.
—Vladimir I. Lenin
Bolshevik revolutionary leader

Socialism of any type leads to a total destruction of the human spirit.
—Alexander Solzhenitsyn
Soviet dissident and defector

Moderation in temper is always a virtue; but moderation in principle is always a vice.
—Thomas Paine
COMMON SENSE

aggression-through-government "for the common good," they start down the path to communism. The architects of communism understood that convincing the free nations to undertake aggression in the name of compassion would lead them to socialism.

Is It Happening Here?

In 1848, Karl Marx and Friedrich Engels proposed 10 steps to convert the Western nations to Communist countries without firing a shot.[19] Most of these ideas have been successfully implemented, even in the United States, the so-called land of the free.

One of the 10 steps called for *"centralization of credit in the hands of the state, by means of a national bank with state capital and an exclusive monopoly"* just like the Federal Reserve! As described in Chapter 9, a central bank transfers the wealth of the average person to the well-to-do through inflation.

Another of the 10 steps called for instituting *"a heavy progressive or graduated income tax"* just like the federal income tax of many Western nations!

Another step proposed by Marx and Engels was *"abolition of all right of inheritance,"* which we come ever closer to as inheritance taxes increase. (In the United States, federal inheritance tax is being phased out.) Taking wealth that one person has created and has given to another person is theft. Whether the wealth creator is alive or dead makes no difference.

Another step was *"free education for all children in public schools."* Although many developed nations, including the United States, still have private schools, most children attend the public ones. Because much of the content in both public and private schools is controlled by aggression-through-government, the schools teach aggression covertly and overtly.

Marx and Engels also recommended the *"extension of factories and instruments of production owned by the state,"* such as exclusive, subsidized government monopolies (e.g., garbage collection, water distribution, mass transit, etc.). Thankfully, many countries are now seeing the

Lenin is said to have declared that the best way to destroy the Capitalist system was to debauch the currency.

—John Maynard
Keynes
THE ECONOMIC
CONSEQUENCES OF THE
PEACE

Give me four years to teach the children and the seed I have sown will never be uprooted.

—Vladimir I. Lenin
Bolshevik revolutionary
leader

folly of paying more for less and are privatizing! However, the increase in regulations dictating work conditions, pay, and so on are simply imposing a different form of aggression on these businesses.

Marx also called for the *"centralization of the means of communications and transport in the hands of the state."* In the United States, television and radio stations are licensed by the Federal Communications Commission, so aggression controls ownership. Most other developed nations have similar constraints.

As always, licensing favors the rich and creates cartels. Three-fourths of the stock of the major U.S. television networks is controlled by a few large banks. Radio stations have an elite ownership as well.[20] Those who benefit from aggression-through-government have no incentive to tell the public that licensing is a tool of the special interests!

The Internet is not, as yet, highly regulated in most developed nations. As long as it remains free from aggression, this plank cannot be fully implemented.

The U.S. government owns most of the roads and regulates trucking, air travel, and railroads. The partial deregulation in the last quarter of the twentieth century is currently being offset by new regulations that have been established in the wake of the September 11, 2001, terrorist attacks.

Another of the 10 steps calls for *"confiscation of the property of all emigrants and rebels."* As we learned in Chapter 16, our law enforcement agents can seize the wealth of anyone *suspected* of crimes without a trial!

In addition, Marx and Engels called for *"abolition of property in land and application of all rents of land to public purposes."* In other words, land would not be privately owned. No homesteading would be permitted.

Our federal and local governments already claim approximately 40% of the land mass of the United States.[21] Landowners, furthermore, cannot do what they wish with "their" property without the approval of zoning, building, and environmental regulators.

The control of the production of wealth is the control of human life itself.

—Hilaire Belloc
THE SERVILE STATE

There is no such thing, at this date of the world's history, in America as an independent press. ... If I allowed my honest opinions to appear in one issue of my paper, before twenty-four hours my occupation would be gone. The business of journalists is to destroy truth. ... We are the tools and vassals of rich men behind the scenes.

—John Swinton
about 1880
journalist
NEW YORK TIMES and
NEW YORK SUN

The right of private property in land is forever abolished. All Land owned by the Church, by private persons, by peasants, is taken away without compensation.
—Vladimir I. Lenin
November 8, 1917

The American people will never knowingly adopt Socialism, but under the name of Liberalism, they will adopt every fragment of the Socialist program until one day America will be a Socialist nation without knowing how it happened.
—Norman Thomas
Socialist Party
presidential candidate
from 1928 to 1948

It is a known fact that the policies of the government today, whether Republican or Democratic, are closer to the 1932 platform of the Communist Party than they are to either of their own party platforms in that critical year.
—Walter Trohan
CHICAGO TRIBUNE
October 5, 1970

Homeowners must pay property taxes to the local government, making them renters in their "own" homes. When campaigning for the Kalamazoo, Michigan, City Commission in 1983, I met many older people who were moving from "their" homes because the property taxes had risen so much. Even though many of those people owned their homes free and clear, they couldn't afford the escalating property taxes on a retiree's income! Having worked all their lives to pay off their homes, they found they could no longer keep them.

Governments frequently evict individuals from properties they "own" if a proposed project construction is considered for "the common good." For example, Donald Trump convinced a state agency to use its "eminent domain" power to take Vera Coking's home from her. Trump wanted to build a parking lot on the site. Vera Coking, however, didn't want to sell her home of 30 years. The New Jersey Casino Reinvestment Development Authority condemned her property so that Vera wouldn't get market price for it and Trump could have it at a bargain basement price. As always, aggression that is supposed to aid the common good becomes a tool of the rich.

Luckily for Vera, the Institute for Justice, which helps people harmed by aggression-through-government, took her case to court and won![22] Unfortunately, most stories of eminent domain don't have such happy endings.

Owners can do what they please with their property; renters hold it subject to the consent of their landlords. Eminent domain and property taxes have made a mockery of the American dream of home ownership. Individuals no longer truly "own" their property!

At least 8 of the 10 steps designed to convert industrialized nations to communism have already been substantially implemented in the United States and most other developed nations! The progress of the remaining planks, *"establishment of industrial armies"* and *"equal obligation of all to work, especially for agriculture,"* is less obvious.

Clearly, the United States and other developed nations have let communism in the back door. The people clamoring for aggression-through-government, the foundation of socialism, wear the familiar face of our neighbors and ourselves!

We've spent much time, money, and effort fighting communism throughout the world because we didn't want it destroying our way of life. We didn't want others controlling our lives. In trying to dictate to selfish others, however, we walk the road toward communism of our own volition! The real Communist threat begins with our belief that aggression serves us. It starts in our own minds and hearts. Our tanks, bombs, and armies cannot save us from ourselves.

A Better Way

Does the failure of communism mean that we can never experience the communist ideal of universal sharing where we are all family to each other? Not at all! The goal was admirable; only the means used to attain it were flawed.

Sharing with others happens spontaneously when we love them as ourselves. Indeed, family members share wealth with each other because they identify with each other's joy and sorrow. Sharing follows love, which cannot be forced.

When we love others as ourselves, we treat their choices with the same respect that we give our own. Our willingness to honor our neighbor's choice is our first step in creating the universal love that sets the stage for sharing.

We sometimes resist this conclusion because we don't want to wait for a better world. However, we need not wait. If we believe that sharing our wealth is appropriate, we can set the example by sharing what we ourselves have created.

Perhaps an even better way to establish the communist ideal is possible. However, aggression is not that better way. While we may be frustrated because our chosen methods have not worked, we truly should rejoice: if aggression were an effective means to our goals, we would use it often. A world where first-strike force,

The United States will eventually fly the Communist Red flag. ... The American people will hoist it themselves.
—Nikita Khrushchev
Soviet premier
November 16, 1956

fraud, or theft is commonplace would be a world of eternal war. To achieve the common good, we would have to kill, cheat, or steal.

Isn't it wonderful that we need not do any of those things to create a world of universal harmony and abundance?

Chapter 19: Is Communism Really Dead?

In Summary ...

- Communism has killed more than 100 million people in the twentieth century, all in the name of compassion.
- Many people view communism as obsolete, even though it is openly practiced in a variety of countries, including China.
- Communism is simply aggression-through-government taken to its ultimate extreme.
- The communist vision is the whole of humankind sharing like one happy family—at gunpoint, if necessary.
- Because communists use aggression as their means, poverty results. People who can't keep the wealth they create don't create much. Shortages of food and medicine were so common in the Soviet Union that life expectancy there declined while it rose in other nations.
- Communism encourages resentment, hate, and animosity. Psychological development is hindered. The environment is destroyed.
- The Communist Manifesto of 1848 outlines a 10-step plan for converting the developed nations to socialist states. The United States and other Western nations have implemented at least 8 of these 10 planks.
- The real communist threat stems from our belief that aggression serves us. Our military might cannot protect us from ourselves.
- When we recognize that love must precede sharing, we realize that honoring our neighbor's choice is the first step to implementing the ideals of communism without its horrors.

Chapter 20

Making Our Nation Safe and Secure

The best defense against foreign aggression is to stop aggression at home.

Early chapters have described how aggression decreases our wealth both locally and globally. In this chapter, we'll discover how our aggression ripples outward into the world to create war, humankind's greatest tragedy.

War is devastating. We not only kill each other, but also destroy wealth (buildings, food, utilities, roads) and the infrastructures (manufacturing plants, farms) that produce it. War, with its loss of life and livelihood, is the ultimate and bitter fruit of aggression.

In Chapter 18, we learned how Third World dictators and even terrorists are funded by our foreign aid programs. Not surprisingly, such aggressors not only oppress their own people, but frequently make war on other nations as well.

While we are not responsible when tyrants, dictators, and terrorists choose to attack others, we often extend their reach with our aid and amplify the harm that they do.

How much has our domestic aggression contributed to the wars of the 20th century? The following examples, especially that of the Soviet Union, suggest that our contribution can be substantial enough to turn petty tyrants into a worldwide threats.

When this happens, our domestic aggression can be reflected back to us as seemingly unprovoked attacks. Until we learn how to stop empowering our enemies, they will continue to appear strong and menacing. However, to the extent that our actions have contributed to past wars, their cessation creates peace.

This chapter may be uncomfortable. It may even seem unpatriotic or even treasonous. However, true patriots are not those who blindly support their country "right or wrong," but those who make sure that their country always remains right. As such patriots, let's examine how our aggression at home helped create the Soviet threat overseas. Although the Soviet Union has

Voice or no voice, the people can always be brought to the bidding of the leaders. That is easy. All you have to do is to tell them they are being attacked, and denounce the pacifists for lack of patriotism and exposing the country to danger.
—Hermann Goering
Nazi leader

Beware the leader who bangs the drums of war in order to whip the citizenry into a patriotic fervor, for patriotism is indeed a double-edged sword. It emboldens the blood, just as it narrows the mind.
—Julius Caesar
dictator of the Roman Empire

*Those who cannot
remember the past are
condemned to repeat it.*
　　　—George Santayana
　　　　　1863–1952

been disbanded, the process by which we empowered it helps us better understand how we
might disable the aggressors of today before they
strike again.

Communism Makes the Rich Richer

Have you ever wondered how the former
Soviet Union, so unproductive that it could barely
feed its own people, managed to become a military power second only to the United States?
How did a nation based on aggression manage
to develop a world-class military with nuclear
weapons targeted at thousands of cities in Western nations? Ironically, the Soviet military
buildup was made possible by our own domestic
Pyramid of Power!

*It was common knowledge in the early 1900s
that U.S. and other Western banks helped establish communism in Russia (Figure 20.1).* In a
1911 cartoon from the *St. Louis Post Dispatch*,
Robert Minor showed Karl Marx welcomed to
Wall Street by representatives of several prominent banking firms. John D. Ryan (National City
Bank) and John D. Rockefeller (Chase National
Bank and Standard Oil), as well as J.P. Morgan
and his partner George W. Perkins (Guaranty
Trust Co. and Equitable Life), were pictured
along with Andrew Carnegie and President
Theodore Roosevelt. Why did America's wealthy
support communism, which portrayed them as
selfish capitalists who should be forced to give
up their wealth?

Those men did not become rich through stu-
pidity. They knew that aggression-through-government always favors the rich while fostering
the illusion of helping the poor. Many of them
had profited greatly from the aggression of licensing laws. The bankers had done especially
well, even before the Federal Reserve was created. Banks created more money than they
would have in a marketplace ecosystem free
from aggression. The extra dollars, subsidized
by the American public primarily through inflation, were loaned or given to the Communists
to aid them in their rise to power.[1]

In 1917, the Communists (Reds), those loyal
to the czar (Whites), and a group championing

*... we are conducting a
mass annihilation of de-
fenseless men together
with their wives and
children.*
　　　—Nikolai Bukharin
　　　　　Bolshevik leader

Figure 20.1: "DEE-LIGHTED"

The Soviet government has been given United States Treasury funds by the Federal Reserve Board and the Federal Reserve Banks acting through the Chase Bank and the Guaranty Trust Company and other banks in New York City.

—Louis McFadden
chairman, U.S. House of
Representatives
Banking Committee

... for the period 1917 to 1930 Western assistance in various forms was the single most important factor, first in the sheer survival of the Soviet regime and secondly in industrial progress to pre-revolutionary levels.

—Antony Sutton
WESTERN TECHNOLOGY AND
SOVIET ECONOMIC
DEVELOPMENT

the Good Neighbor Policy (Greens) struggled for power.[2] Of the three groups, only the Communists favored the aggression of central banking. Not surprisingly, the banking and business elite gave substantial support to the Communists, knowing that they would be rewarded with exclusive monopolies once socialism triumphed.

The huge Russian reserves of oil, which threatened Rockefeller's worldwide monopoly (Chapter 7), were forcibly seized. Standard Oil was given exclusive control.[3] *By supporting communism, Rockefeller was able to escape the regulation of the marketplace ecosystem and to destroy his international competition.*

Chase National Bank and Kuhn, Loeb & Company supplied the Soviets with a steady stream of credit.[4] Without the massive creation of money made possible through the Federal Reserve System (Chapter 9: "Banking on Aggression"), the loans probably never would have been made. By allowing domestic aggression to create the money monopoly and the Pyramid of Power, Americans unwittingly laid the yoke of communism on the backs of the Russian people. In the process, they saddled themselves with burdensome inflation and taxation, while empowering the elite.

How Our Aggression Sustained Communism

The Communists repaid loans from the U.S. banks by plundering the czar's treasury and seizing the nation's crops for exportation.[5] So much food was sold on the world market that the Russian people went hungry. In 1922, Herbert Hoover, then secretary of commerce, sent the Russians famine relief, subsidized by the U.S. taxpayer.[6] *Without American tax-funded aid, the Soviet Communist regime would probably have collapsed in the 1920s.*

In hopes of defeating Hitler, President Franklin D. Roosevelt empowered the Soviets with the taxpayer-financed Lend-Lease programs.[7] By 1944, Stalin acknowledged that two-thirds of Soviet heavy industry had been built with U.S. help. The rest came from other Western nations or was seized in conquered countries. Entire factories were dismantled, moved to Russia, and reassembled there.[8] Without U.S. assistance, Soviet technology would have remained primitive, most likely without nuclear capabilities.[9]

During World War II, helping the Soviets was regarded as essential to defeating Hitler. The price of Stalin's help, however, was the enslavement of Eastern Europe for almost 50 years. World War II simply substituted one European tyrant (Hitler) for another (Stalin).

Communism Is Its Own Worst Enemy

Innovation and the creation of wealth are so greatly stifled in Communist societies (Chapter 19) that the Soviet nations, once agricultural exporters, were never able to even feed themselves. American loans assisted the Soviets in financing food purchases after the poor 1972 harvest. In Poland, such credits added over 10% to the national income in 1974![10]

In the long run, aggression defeats itself. Without "humanitarian" aid from the United States, the Soviet system would have collapsed decades before it did. *Neutralizing the Soviet threat would have been as easy as allowing it to reap what it sowed.*

How Aggression Begets Aggression

Even when American aid to the Soviets was provided through private banks, taxpayers were usually at risk. Loans were often guaranteed by the tax-financed Export-Import Bank,[11] so taxpayers ended up making up any defaults.

Even without such guarantees, U.S. taxpayers could be liable. Loans that are not repaid can bankrupt lending institutions. In such cases, taxpayers, not the bankers who took foolish chances with their depositors' money, are usually expected to make up the loss if the Federal Deposit Insurance Corporation (FDIC) is short on funds.

The aid that created and maintained Communist Russia and the Soviet Union would not have been possible without the aggression of taxation and inflation. *The Soviet threat was a direct reflection of our own domestic aggression as it rippled outward into the world.*

Our whole slave system depends on your economic assistance. When they bury us alive, please do not send them shovels and the most up-to-date earth-moving equipment.
—Alexander Solzhenitsyn
Soviet historian

How Our Aggression Creates Endless Enemies

It's somewhat disheartening to discover that we were responsible for creating the superpower that we feared for so many years. However, if this formidable foe was only a paper tiger dependent on us for its very existence, maybe the world is only as dangerous as we make it!

When we look closely at the history of U.S. interventions, we see that we make our world very dangerous indeed. We empower endless enemies throughout the world in the same way that we created the Soviet threat.

Hitler's funding, for example, came from German banks and the American elite, and it was ultimately guaranteed by taxpayers of several nations.[12] Manuel Noriega, the drug lord, assisted the U.S. effort to aid the Nicaraguan Contras and was on the tax-supported payroll of the Central Intelligence Agency (CIA) for many years.[13]

Similarly, Saddam Hussein was given money, arms, biological and chemical weapons, courtesy of Western taxpayers. We empowered Hussein so that he would attack the Ayatollah Khomeini. The ayatollah gained popular support in reaction to the repressive shah of Iran, who maintained his political position with the help of tax-supported aid from the developed nations.[14]

Even Osama bin Laden and the Taliban were supported by tax-funded aid from Western nations to fight the Soviet invasion of Afghanistan. Afghans were supplied with both weapons and training and were encouraged to recruit fighters from other Muslim nations.[15] The Taliban received $114 million in 2000 and $124 million in 2001 from the United States.[16] This humanitarian aid, like earlier gifts to the Soviets, enabled the Taliban to maintain its hold on the Afghan people.

Through its domestic aggression, the United States has empowered virtually every threat to its own national security in the past 50 years. If we had consistently been Good Neighbors, our enemies would be fewer in number and not as well-supplied. Without our aid, global tyrants might have remained petty dictators.

In addition, a significant portion of the $6 billion in covert U.S. arms and training that went to Afghan rebel groups in the 1980s was funneled to right-wing Islamic fundamentalist forces that have utilized these resources to attack U.S. allies and U.S. citizens.

    —William D. Hartung
    World Policy Institute

... as recently as 1999, U.S. taxpayers paid the entire annual salary of every single Taliban Government official.

    —Ted Rall
    San Francisco
    Chronicle
    November 2, 2001

Do We Train Terrorists?

We not only supplied tyrants with money, but we trained them to be terrorists.

Many modern-day terrorists received much of their training from our own CIA. For example, the CIA showed the Contras how to blow up bridges and attack health clinics, hospitals, and schools,[17] just as the CIA had trained East Germans to do in the 1950s.[18] Consequently, the Contras engaged in well-documented terrorist acts against civilians that included killing, kidnapping, raping, torturing, and mutilating them.[19]

Why would the CIA encourage such tactics? The Reagan administration wanted to oust the Sandinistas, but it did not have enough congressionally authorized funding to mount a military campaign. Most likely, deciding that the ends justified the means, the CIA relied on "dirty tricks" to accomplish its goal.

For similar reasons, the U.S. and British governments helped Saddam Hussein develop chemical and biological weapons to use against the numerically superior Iranians.[20] State Department officials even violated normal visa procedures so that bin Laden's followers could come to the United States and receive CIA terrorist training to fight the Soviets in Afghanistan.[21]

When Americans are kidnapped, bombed, tortured, or killed by terrorists, are we simply reaping what we have sown?

Does Uncle Sam Deal Drugs?

The CIA agents who trained terrorists probably thought that pitting them against America's enemies was an effective defense. When we don't understand how we reap what we sow, we often believe that aggression serves us.

For the same reasons, the CIA appears to recruit and support international drug dealers as well as terrorists. For example, in 1984, after the socialist Sandinistas were fairly elected in Nicaragua,[22] Congress cut off funding for the Contras who opposed them.[23] While Nancy Reagan toured the United States asking our youth to say "Just say 'No!' " to drugs, the Contras

Sometimes terror is very productive. This is the policy: keep putting on pressure until the people cry "uncle."

—Edgar Chamorro
Contra leader

Two of the terrorists convicted in the 1993 World Trade Center bombing received weapons training in Afghanistan under the direction of fundamentalist Islamic forces that were armed and trained by the CIA

—William D. Hartung
World Policy Institute

U.S. military sources have given the FBI information that suggests five of the alleged hijackers of the planes that were used in Tuesday's terror attacks received training at secure U.S. military installations in the 1990s.

—NEWSWEEK
September 15, 2001

In my 30-year history in the Drug Enforcement Administration and related agencies, the major targets of my investigations almost invariably turned out to be working for the CIA.
—Dennis Dayle
former chief of an elite
DEA unit

Cocaine trafficking was a major source of funding for CIA covert operations. Using drug money instead of funds appropriated from Congress allowed the CIA to operate without having to account to the U.S. government for its actions or expenditures.
—Michael Levine
25-year DEA veteran
and author of BIG WHITE
LIE and DEEP COVER

The illegal drug trade is the financial engine that fuels many terrorist organizations around the world, including Osama bin Laden.
—Dennis Hastert (R-Ill.)
Speaker, U.S. House

supported themselves through profitable drug sales. A great deal of evidence suggests that many of those deals were facilitated by our own CIA.[24]

Costa Rica's Nobel Peace Prize–winning president actually banned the Americans connected with the Contras (Oliver North, U.S. Ambassador Lewis Tambs, National Security Advisor Admiral John Poindexter, Presidential Advisor Richard Secord, and CIA Station Chief José Fernandez) from his country because, he alleged, they were all drug runners![25]

As incredible as it might seem, funding overseas covert operations with "protection money" from drug lords also appears to be common practice.[26] The Drug Enforcement Administration (DEA) claims that the CIA has attempted to interfere with at least 27 prosecutions of drug dealers acting as CIA informants.[27]

Drug-running Panamanian military dictator Manuel Noriega was even on the CIA's payroll for several years as noted earlier.[28] In return, Noriega provided a base of operations from which the United States could support the Contras in Nicaragua.[29] Most likely, Noriega helped the Contras broker their drug deals too.

Apparently, our CIA even helped drug traffickers oust the elected president of Bolivia, Lidia Gueiler, and take control of the country.[30] In 1990, General Guillen and his Venezuelan National Guard were caught smuggling a ton of cocaine through the Miami Airport. Guillen claimed he was operating under CIA orders, which the CIA reluctantly confirmed.[31]

No government agents were charged, tried, or imprisoned for their role in those drug deals. Indeed, public employees are rarely prosecuted for drug "crimes" that would send you or me to prison for decades. Instead, our CIA appears to profit from the War on Drugs and to fund covert operations without congressional consent.

The War on Drugs empowered the Taliban and al Qaeda as well. When it gained power, the Taliban encouraged farmers to increase opium production, so that the country could profit from black market prices.[32] *The profits created by the Drug War help fund organized crime, terrorist organizations, and rogue CIA operations.* Ending the War on Drugs would do much to stop the money that now flows into hidden bank accounts of all three groups.

Killing Innocents to Topple Tyrants

When we try to replace the dictators, drug runners, and thugs whom we've empowered, thousands of innocent people are often killed in the crossfire.

For example, in December 1989, the U.S. military invaded Panama to capture Noriega, who had been indicted in a Florida court for drug trafficking. U.S. taxpayers paid both to fund Noriega and to catch him. A couple of dozen Marines lost their lives in the invasion. In addition, 2,500–4,000 Panamanian civilians were killed in the bombing and the fighting, while more than 20,000 lost their homes. Entire neighborhoods were obliterated.[33]

Most Americans are unaware that many atrocities, such as the killing of thousands of innocent Panamanians, have been committed in their name. The U.S. press gives a rather sanitized version of events overseas. Few journalists risk reporting on such issues. Censorship is becoming so common that journalists have even named it the "buzzsaw." Those who encounter the buzzsaw usually end up "radioactive" or unemployable. News organizations that run politically incorrect stories are excluded from the government briefings on which most stories are based.[34]

Even when we do hear about civilian deaths caused by U.S. military intervention, our leaders justify trading Third World lives and livelihoods in order to protect America. CBS reporter Leslie Stahl noted that the embargo to punish Saddam Hussein was blamed for the deaths of a half-million Iraqi children.[35] "Is the price worth it?" she asked Madeleine Albright, U.S. ambassador to the United Nations. Ms. Albright replied, "I think this is a very hard choice, but the price—we think the price is worth it."[36]

Of course, as noted earlier, our tax dollars empowered Saddam Hussein in the first place. Can we really protect ourselves by putting the

The reporters are making too much money, and have too much invested in the stock market, to possess the inclination to raise fundamental questions about the government's exercise of power.
—Philip Weiss
INTO THE BUZZSAW

The Americans are educated people. They can see that these [my neighbors] are not terrorists. Why do they target them?
—Haji Awal Khan Nasr
Afghan survivor of U.S. bombing raids

Before the bombing, the Taliban was always saying that Americans were enemies of Muslims and of Islam, and we did not believe that. But when [they] are killing innocent people, we believe that what the Taliban was saying about America is true: They are trying to kill Muslims and finish Islam.
— Sardar Bibi Khan
Afghan farmer

Now people are angry at America because they have destroyed our houses and they are forcing us to leave and come here to Pakistan as refugees. I brought my family, but I couldn't bring any of my belongings. I have nothing now.
— Abdul Audar
Afghan hotel manager

There are some things the general public does not need to know and shouldn't. I believe that democracy flourishes when the government can take legitimate steps to keep its secrets and when the press can decide whether to print what it knows.
— Katharine Graham
chair of the board
WASHINGTON POST

Iraqi people at the mercy of a tyrant and then killing *their* children to punish *him*?

Ousting our former allies, the Taliban and Osama bin Laden, has cost innocent lives as well. News reports indicate that between 3,100 and 3,500 Afghan civilians were killed and another 4,000–6,500 were injured in the first 20 weeks of U.S. bombing.[37] The loss of civilian lives in Afghanistan has already surpassed that of the terrorist attacks of September 11, 2001. One researcher estimated that 133 civilians perished for every Taliban leader killed in Afghanistan.[38]

War refugee deaths from hunger, disease, and exposure probably numbered about 20,000.[39] The Afghan economy, already poor, was further devastated. As much as 80% of the urban population left their homes to avoid being killed by bombs. Electrical power plants and infrastructure were damaged, making clean drinking water scarce. Escape became difficult, because so many roads and bridges were destroyed.[40]

Starvation threatened the Afghan people even before September 11, but U.S. bombing made the situation worse. Little food aid could be delivered during the bombing. Food drops from U.S. planes were woefully inadequate. The food packets looked like the cluster bombs that were dropped in the same area; many of the bombs killed the hungry people who picked them up. Even when the packets were full of food, it was often spoiled after splitting open during the air drop.[41] When the so-called "smart bombs" went astray, refugee camps, Red Cross warehouses (twice), and World Food Programme facilities were hit, resulting in further misery.[42]

In the United States, the news media downplayed civilian casualties. A memo to the staff of Florida's *Panama City News Herald* in October 2001 read: "DO NOT USE photos on Page 1A showing civilian casualties from the U.S. war on Afghanistan. ... DO NOT USE wire stories which lead with civilian casualties. ... If the story needs rewriting to play down the civilian casualties, DO IT."[43]

Ignorance is not bliss. Bin Laden's representatives delivered the message that if Afghan homes were destroyed in the bombing, there would be "consequences."[44] Because bombing Afghanistan will not destroy the terrorist network that has tentacles throughout the world,[45] we should take that threat seriously.

In destroying the Taliban, the United States empowered the Northern Alliance, a group of warlords with an even bloodier history of rape and torture.[46] When Taliban forces surrendered and were disarmed, many were taken to prison in closed metal containers. They were given no water, and hundreds, perhaps thousands, suffocated and were thrown into mass graves. Drivers who tried to ventilate the containers by punching holes in them were beaten by Alliance soldiers, so "death by container," was clearly done on purpose. Indeed, this form of execution had been practiced some years before the war.[47]

Are we substituting one group of tyrants in Afghanistan for another? Only time will tell. Some of the Afghanistan people will profit from the change and be grateful for U.S. intervention. Those who lost loved ones in the bombing, however, may resent or even hate us. Perhaps, in their sorrow, they will become terrorists to avenge their loved ones.

The devastation wrought by our intervention in Iraq, Nicaragua, Bolivia, Panama, and Afghanistan are not rare, isolated examples. When we follow the history of developing nations, it is difficult to find one where our CIA has not left its mark. The U.S. Senate's Church Committee documented 900 major and thousands of smaller covert operations undertaken by the CIA between 1960 and 1975.[48] Sometimes, as in Korea, Vietnam, Cambodia, Laos, Angola, and Nicaragua, U.S. intervention instigated or prolonged civil war.[49] Our intervention often creates trauma, heartbreak, and incredible loss of life in the Third World. None of those nations attacked or even threatened to attack us first.

Shortly after the terrorist attacks of 9/11, Pakistani demonstrators held up a sign saying "Americans, think! Why you are hated all over the world."[50] In our name, atrocities are committed as our attempts to control our neighbors in domestic matters ripple out to intensify war and poverty in the rest of the world. I no longer

It is, of course, richly ironic that the first achievement of the war on terrorism has been to install in Kabul the Northern Alliance, for whom terrorism has been the entire line of business and way of life for more than 20 years.

—Andrew Murray
THE GUARDIAN,
November 16, 2001

President Bush has authorized continued bombing of innocent people in Iraq. President Clinton bombed innocent people in the Sudan, Afghanistan, Iraq, and Serbia. President Bush Senior invaded Iraq and Panama. President Reagan bombed innocent people in Libya and invaded Grenada. And on and on it goes. Did we think the people who lost their families and friends and property in all that destruction would love America for what happened?

—Harry Browne
Libertarian Party
presidential candidate
1996 and 2000

wonder why so many hate us. What surprises me is that so many don't.

The Rich Get Richer—with Our Help!

Why does our CIA run covert operations in the Third World, train terrorists, empower dictators, manipulate governments, and protect drug dealers?

When in doubt, follow the money. If the CIA had pulled out of Nicaragua when Congress ended the funding, the Contras would not have been able to fight the Sandinistas for any length of time. Without conflict, peace would reign.

However, if the Contras continued their fight, the arms manufacturers could sell to both sides. Weapons could be bought with drug deals or with taxpayer-guaranteed loans. Eventually, sending U.S. troops in to "settle" the conflict would mean even more arms purchases.

Eternal war means continual profits for the banks and the military-industrial complex. Our CIA, like most government agencies, works for special interest groups that can reward it with a share of the profits. Through frequent military conflicts, the wealth of the average American, through inflation or direct taxation, is transferred to the CIA, rogue agents, weapons contractors, and banks without much resistance.

After the War on Terrorism ends, especially if Iraq is also vanquished, Saudi and American oil interests will control virtually all Middle Eastern oil. *Protecting oil interests with our tax-supported military allows war to be made in our name for the benefit of special interests.*

Indeed, 14 families of 9/11 victims are suing the Bush administration, claiming that his connection with the oil industry clouded his judgment and compromised national security. They allege that terrorist investigations in Saudi Arabia, which would have uncovered the 9/11 terrorists, were stopped to protect oil interests. The suit claims that several FBI agents will testify in support of these charges.[51]

Indeed, the Saudis have funded many Islamic terrorist groups over the years.[52] Fifteen of the 19 hijackers involved in the September 11, 2001 terrorist attack were from Saudi Arabia[53] as is

---

We must guard against the acquisition of unwarranted influence by the ... military-industrial complex.

— President Dwight D. Eisenhower, January 1961

I spent 33 years ... in active service ... most of my time as a high-class muscle man for Big Business, for Wall Street, and the bankers. Thus, I helped make Mexico, and especially Tampico, safe for American oil interests in 1914. I helped make Haiti and Cuba a decent place for the National City Bank boys to collect revenue in. I helped in raping of half-a-dozen Central American republics for the benefit of Wall Street. ... I helped purify Nicaragua for the international banking house of Brown Brothers and Co. in 1909. I helped make Honduras "right" for American fruit companies in 1903.

— General Smedley D. Butler, Marine Corps, two-time recipient of the Congressional Medal of Honor

the bin Laden family and the alleged 9/11 mastermind, Osama bin Laden.

However, because of their partnership with U.S. oil companies, the Saudis were protected from close scrutiny,[54] just as Noriega's drug deals were ignored when he was on the CIA payroll. The FBI's John O'Neill, who had evidence to implicate Osama bin Laden in the attack on the *USS Cole,* was stopped by American diplomats when his investigation led him into Saudi Arabia.[55]

A president can hardly avoid such conflicts of interest, however, when our global businesses expect U.S. foreign policy to aid and defend them overseas. No matter how sincerely President Bush tries to serve the American public, his motives will be questioned as long as his decisions have a profound impact on his family's finances. In "A Better Way," we'll discover how to protect American interests abroad without putting our presidents into this no-win position.

Even war itself provides a conflict of interests for our presidents. None are so beloved as those who have led us in war (e.g., Washington, Lincoln, Franklin D. Roosevelt).

Indeed, the War on Terrorism increased President Bush's popularity dramatically. On September 9, 2001, only 55% of Americans approved of the president's work in office. In the month after the attacks, the president's approval ratings soared to an incredible 92%![56]

Because Americans stand behind their president in times of war, engaging in armed conflict is a sure way to gain public support. (The entertaining 1997 Warner Bros. movie *Wag the Dog* is based on this concept.) Clearly, our current system gives our presidents a great deal of motivation to make war.

Unprovoked Attacks or Blowback?

Indeed, President Franklin D. Roosevelt apparently did trick Americans into war, probably believing that his deceit was necessary to rid the world of Adolf Hitler. Roosevelt knew 88% of the American public wanted to stay out of World War II.[57] Roosevelt, however, did not honor their choice.

All of the answers, all of the clues allowing us to dismantle Osama bin Laden's organization, can be found in Saudi Arabia.
—John O'Neill
former head of FBI's antiterrorism division who died in the 9/11 attacks

What is undeniable is that corporations close to the administration have directly benefited from the increased defense spending arising from the aftermath of September 11.
—U.S. Representative Cynthia McKinney (D-Ga.)

Declassified files recently revealed that FDR was even more cunning than the "conspiracy theorists" believed. He not only let the Japanese attack Pearl Harbor—he first executed an 8-point plan to provoke and lure them, ensuring that they saw no alternative to attack.
— Nafeez Mosaddeq Ahmed
THE WAR ON FREEDOM

When goods don't cross borders, armies will.
— Frederic Bastiat
French economist
1801–1850

Arabs see the U.S. as an accomplice of Israel, a partner in what they believe is the ruthless repression of Palestinian aspirations for land and independence. The most provocative issues: Israel's control over Islamic holy sites in Jerusalem; the stationing of U.S. troops in Saudi Arabia near some of Islam's holiest sites; and economic sanctions against Iraq, which have been seen to deprive children there of medicine and food.
— Jim Wooten
WORLD NEWS TONIGHT
September 12, 2001

A 1940 memorandum, hidden until 1995, describes a program to provoke Japan into an overt act of war. This eight-point plan, designed by the head of the Far East desk of Naval Intelligence, Lt. Commander Arthur H. McCollum, can be summarized as follows: (1) giving aid to Japan's enemy, China; (2) establishing, along with the United Kingdom and the Netherlands, a trade embargo against Japan; and (3) mounting a military, naval, and submarine presence in the Pacific, in order to overtly threaten Japan's territorial waters.[58]

Japan was especially incensed in July 1941 when the United States government would no longer allow it to use the Panama Canal; tightened a preexisting embargo so that Japan could no longer purchase oil, iron, and steel; and seized Japanese assets in the United States. In the same month, one of the Honolulu newspapers described the possible retaliation—an attack on Pearl Harbor to clear the way for Japan's invasion of the oil-rich Dutch East Indies.[59] Clearly, the possible consequences of the American sanctions were well understood by many people.

All of the steps in the eight-point plan taken to provoke Japan contained elements of aggression. U.S. aid to China came from taxes, and the trade embargo stopped willing traders from buying and selling. The trespass of U.S. naval vessels into Japanese waters and the military build-up in the area were naturally perceived as a threat of first-strike force. Clearly, these tactics were successful in provoking a Japanese attack on Pearl Harbor.

Osama bin Laden, the alleged mastermind of the 9/11 terrorist attack, had similar reasons for declaring war on the United States. They include (1) U.S. aid to Islam's enemy, Israel; (2) the U.S. attacks and embargo on Iraq, alleged to have subjected hundreds of thousands to death by starvation or disease; and (3) U.S. military bases and naval presence in the Middle East.[60] Had we learned from past history, we would have recognized the parallels between bin Laden's complaints and the provocative strategies that led to Pearl Harbor.

Pearl Harbor and 9/11, the only two attacks on U.S. soil in the past hundred years, apparently have been "blowback" from America's own foreign policy. *A nation of Good Neighbors would not have undertaken these aggressive actions. The Japanese attack at Pearl Harbor almost certainly would not have occurred. The terrorist attack on September 11, 2001, might also have been avoided.*

Of course, some killers will seek out targets without much provocation. Perhaps Osama bin Laden is one of them. However, when Arabs see their loved ones killed because of U.S. trade embargoes or arms subsidies, their anger makes them easier targets for fanatical leaders.

Prudent people don't wave a red flag in front of a bull and then express surprise and outrage when he charges. Refusing to recognize that the color red aggravates an angry bull puts us in danger of our life.

Similarly, we should not be surprised that aiding one side of a war, erecting trade embargoes, or setting up military bases in or around a nation's borders evokes fear, resentment, and even hatred. America is not to blame for the violent choices of the 9/11 terrorists. However, we should have been aware that our actions were extremely provocative.

Prolonging the War with Germany

Many people believe that the U.S. entry into World War II was necessary to save Europe from Hitler. They therefore excuse, or even applaud, Roosevelt's ploy to get the United States into the war.

As we learned earlier, World War II simply replaced one tyrant with another. Western Europe was saved from Hitler by sacrificing Eastern Europe to the equally bloodthirsty Stalin.[61] In addition, President Roosevelt's demand for unconditional surrender greatly prolonged the war and cost millions of lives.

Germany had an active resistance, which called itself the Front of Decent People. The Front was greatly frustrated by Roosevelt's policy of unconditional surrender. By 1943, many

Even small children know that Israel is nothing without America and here America means F-16, M-16, Apache helicopters, the tools Israelis use to kill us and destroy our homes.

—Shikh Abdul Majeed Atta Palestinian preacher

Many opinion-makers deride the idea that the September 11 terrorist attacks could have been somehow linked to American foreign policy. To seek such connections may be seen as adding insult to injury, or unpatriotic.

—Nafeez Mosaddeq Ahmed THE WAR ON FREEDOM

*There never was a good
war or a bad peace.*
—Benjamin Franklin,
1783

*The first casualty when
war comes is truth.*
—U.S. Senator Hiram
Johnson, 1917

*Insistence on "uncondi-
tional surrender" thus
aids the hostile regime
in keeping control of its
people, and convincing
them that they have no
alternative than to sink or
swim with the regime.*
—Anne Armstrong
UNCONDITIONAL
SURRENDER

prominent German military officers were ready
to join the resistance to overthrow or assassinate Hitler. However, because Germany's surrender to the Allies was sure to follow, the
military wanted assurances that they and the
German people would not be punished for Hitler's
crimes.

The Front tried to approach Roosevelt repeatedly through different mediators, for acknowledgment, support, and reconsideration of
his demands for unconditional surrender, but the
president harshly turned away its overtures.[62]
He even forbade the press to mention the Front
of Decent People or talk favorably about the German resistance.[63]

Determined to succeed without the support
of Roosevelt or German military officers fearful
of unconditional surrender, the Front tried on
several occasions to assassinate Hitler. Many of
their members were eventually caught and executed. Roosevelt's control over the press was
so firm that these brave Germans were vilified
rather than lauded.[64]

Just as Nazi officers continued to support
Hitler rather than surrender unconditionally, so
too did German soldiers fight even when they
knew the war was hopelessly lost. American war
correspondent John Thompson interviewed 130
German prisoners and found that 120 of them
were still in the field because they would rather
die in battle than face prolonged suffering at
enemy hands. Insistence on unconditional surrender was interpreted by the average fighting
man as a desire to see Germany and her people
totally obliterated.[65]

Roosevelt may have tricked America into war
for the noblest of reasons. However, by permitting our executive branch to use aggressive foreign policy (trade sanctions, tax-supported foreign
aid, armed invasion of sovereign territory), we
set stage for an unscrupulous administration to
trick us into war for the benefit of the special
interests that support them.

Prolonging the War with Japan

The demand for unconditional surrender also
prolonged the war with Japan. It was behind the

devastating attacks on Nagasaki and Hiroshima. An estimated 400,000 people, about 85% of them civilians, were either killed instantly or died from radiation poisoning.[66] These attacks are widely credited with saving millions of lives by ending World War II quickly.

However, shortly after President Truman took office in 1945, former president Herbert Hoover advised him that the Japanese were ready to surrender.[67] Tokyo's Foreign Office had been sending out peace probes since April of that year.[68] The biggest obstacle was the unusual insistence by both former president Roosevelt and then-president Truman that surrender be unconditional. Advisors to both presidents largely opposed this stance.[69] Pope Pius XII even went so far as to call unconditional surrender "incompatible with Christian doctrine."[70]

The Japanese wanted only the assurance that their emperor would remain on his throne.[71] Instead of accepting these terms and ending the war, Truman issued the Potsdam Declaration on July 26, repeating the inflammatory demand for "unconditional surrender." The Japanese continued fighting. Consequently, two atomic bombs were dropped, on August 6 and August 10.[72]

Even after these devastating attacks, the Japanese stood firm. They would surrender only if "the prerogatives of his Majesty as a Sovereign Ruler" were retained. To the Japanese, the Emperor was divine and should be protected even if Japan had to be annihilated in the process. Rather than continuing the war, Truman wisely allowed Emperor Hirohito to remain.[73]

The war was prolonged by the demand for unconditional surrender and ended only when Truman agreed to Japan's terms. *Dropping the first atomic bombs did not influence the Japanese position, but it did convince President Truman to accept the surrender that Japan had already offered.* What a shame that it took the deaths of 400,000 people, many of them children, for Truman to accept the olive branch that the Japanese had extended earlier!

The war might have been shortened by the brave Americans who fought in World War II, but it was also lengthened by the demand for

If we add all the dead and wounded since 1943, when unconditional surrender was promulgated, destroying the German resistance's hope of overthrowing Hitler, that figure [is] 8 million. Unquestionably, this ultimatum was written in blood.
—Thomas Fleming
THE NEW DEALERS' WAR

unconditional surrender. We can never know what would have happened if the United States had not entered World War II. However, the German resistance, unhampered by Roosevelt's policy of unconditional surrender, might have been able to recruit key military officers and successfully eliminate the führer as early as 1943. The atomic bomb would probably not have been developed or dropped. A shorter war might have even kept much of Eastern Europe from Stalin's grasp. Some of the millions Stalin killed in conquered countries might have lived full and happy lives.

Unconditional Surrender Lives On

Echoes of World War II could be heard in President Bush's demand for the unconditional surrender of Osama bin Laden after the 9/11 terrorist attacks. In the past, negotiating for the extradition of terrorists has enjoyed some success. The Sudan turned the terrorist known as Carlos the Jackal over to the French in 1994. In 1998, Libya gave the Dutch the two men charged with the bombing of the Pan Am airliner over Lockerbie, Scotland.[74]

The president of the Sudan, Omar Hassan Ahmed Bashir, had met with President Clinton's representatives between 1996 and 1998. Bashir actually offered to arrest bin Laden, who was wanted at the time for attacks on American embassies. Bashir would have also supplied intelligence on terrorist networks, which would have led to two of the 9/11 hijackers. In return, Bashir wanted the terrorism sanctions against the Sudan lifted. Instead of accepting the offer, Clinton told the Sudan to expel bin Laden, who then moved to Afghanistan.[75]

Clearly, Arab nations are willing to work with other nations in bringing terrorists, including bin Laden, to justice. No wonder a Gallup poll conducted in September 2001 indicated that countries other than the United States and Israel preferred negotiated extradition of bin Laden rather than bombing or other military actions against Afghanistan![76]

Nevertheless, when the Taliban tried to negotiate, as a condition of extradition, where bin

In this case, the Taliban's offer to detain bin Laden and try him before an Islamic court, while unacceptable, was a serious initial negotiating position and would have merited a serious counteroffer—unless one had already decided to go to war.

—Rahul Mahajan and
Robert Jensen
A WAR OF LIES

Laden would be held and tried, Bush continued to demand his unconditional surrender.[77] Bush answered the Taliban's requests for terms with an extensive bombing of Afghanistan. When the smoke from the bombing cleared, bin Laden was still at large.

We'll never know if the Taliban would have given up bin Laden in exchange for some reasonable guarantees of due process, because we weren't even willing to talk about it.

Destroying Our Freedoms

Many people believe that the terrorist attacks of September 11, 2001, came from hatred and jealousy of America's freedom and prosperity. If so, the actions taken by the U.S. government in the wake of 9/11 are playing right into al Qaeda's hands. Our freedoms are being destroyed in the name of protecting them.

Shortly after the bombing began, 15-year-old Katie Sierra wore a T-shirt to school that proclaimed, "When I saw the dead and dying Afghani children on TV, I felt a newly recovered sense of national security. God Bless America." She was promptly suspended and the court upheld the principal's decision, even when challenged on First Amendment grounds.[78]

The USA Patriot Act (HR 3162), passed shortly after the 9/11 terrorist attacks, essentially nullifies Fourth Amendment protections against unreasonable search and seizure. Government agencies can search your home without notice and without a warrant. Software can secretly be installed on your computer to monitor your e-mail and Internet activity without telling you.[79]

Attorney General John Ashcroft has even proposed constructing camps for indefinite detention of any U.S. citizens he labels as "enemy combatants."[80] In Chapter 15, we learned how the Tucker family was sent to prison for selling gardening equipment that someone else might use to grow marijuana. Perhaps some Americans will eventually be considered "enemy combatants" or "conspirators" for selling box cutters or other common household items that can be used by terrorists.

Critics both left and right are saying it [the USA Patriot Act] not only strips Americans of fundamental rights but does little or nothing to secure the nation from terrorist attacks.
—Insight Magazine
December 9, 2001

They came for the Communists, and I didn't object, for I wasn't a Communist; they came for the Socialists, and I didn't object, for I wasn't a Socialist; they came for the labor leaders, and I didn't object, for I wasn't a labor leader; they came for the Jews, and I didn't object, for I wasn't a Jew; then they came for me, and there was no one left to object.
—Martin Niemoller
German Protestant
pastor,1945

... fascism will come to America in the name of national security.
— Jim Garrison
district attorney

It is quite remarkable that they have detained so many people and have refused to give their identities. The secret detention is frighteningly close to the practice of "disappearing" people in Latin America.

—Kate Martin
Center for National
Security Studies

What we've seen, since Sept. 11, if you add up everything ... is a coup d'etat against the United States Constitution.

—Francis A. Boyle
professor of
international law,
University of Illinois

And when the drums of war reached a fever pitch and the blood boils with hate and the mind has "closed," the leader will have no need in seizing the rights of the citizenry. Rather, the citizenry, infused with fear and blinded by patriotism, will offer up all their rights unto the leader and gladly so.
How do I know? For this is what I have done. AND I AM CAESAR.

—Julius Caesar
dictator of Rome

Shortly after the 9/11 terrorist attacks, more than 1,000 people were detained without legal counsel or access to their families. Their names and details of their citizenship have not been revealed.[81] Secret military tribunals, rather than trial by jury, may ultimately determine their fate.[82] Some have even been sent to countries where interrogation by torture is legal.[83]

Don't we need to give up some of our freedoms for our security? Such a question is akin to asking for a square circle or a barking cat. Freedom and security are two sides of the same coin and can't be separated. *Freedom from aggression, including aggression-through-government, is the definition of security. Every loss of freedom is ultimately a loss of security.*

Where is your security when a bureaucrat can throw you into prison indefinitely or destroy your belongings to see if you have terrorist connections? If our antiterrorist task force finds interrogation-by-torture useful, how long will it be before it becomes routine for all suspects? If politically incorrect speech loses the protection of the First Amendment, how will we know the truth? If we believe that our innocence will protect us, we need only remember how well innocence protected the Jews once the Nazis convinced the Germans to give up their freedom for security.

Americans are making the same mistake that the vast majority of the German people made in the 1930s and 1940s. In the name of national security and patriotism, we are destroying the very thing we are trying to protect.

Our government did not fail to prevent the 9/11 attacks because of too much freedom in our society The attacks were virtually inevitable because we had too much aggression-through-government. If we want fewer attacks, we need less aggression, not more. If we want more security, we need more freedom, not less.

Wealth creation, as well as security, depends on freedom from aggression-through-government. As we lose our liberty, we'll lose our prosperity as well. If the terrorists who attacked America wanted to destroy our freedom and abundance, we are playing right into their hands!

A Better Way

Our historical review indicates that war is often caused by our domestic aggression rippling out into the world. Our aggression empowers some tyrants and provokes others. We've been largely unaware of our role in creating war because the special interests that profit from it go to great lengths to obscure our vision. If we wish to be free from aggression, both domestic and foreign, we need to do things differently.

Ending Support for Future Enemies

Clearly, the best defense against aggressors is not to empower them in the first place. Virtually every modern tyrant came to power through loans and aid generated through the aggression of banking regulations and taxes. Without the aggression of banking regulations (Chapter 9) and tax-funded foreign aid (Chapter 18), Saddam Hussein and Osama bin Laden would probably never have come into power. *If we forsake aggression, most tyrants would never become worldwide threats.*

Ending Drug Prohibition

The War on Drugs creates black-market profits for Third World dictators and rogue CIA operators. Ending drug prohibition would disempower these groups, ending their human rights violations as well.

If the CIA had not been so busy attempting to topple or support dictators throughout the world, it might have told the FBI that they had tracked two of Osama bin Laden's trusted followers from an al Qaeda meeting to San Diego in early 2000. The FBI could have tracked them as they enrolled in flight schools. "There's no question that we could have tied all 19 hijackers together," an FBI official claimed when he found out about the CIA's oversight.[84]

The FBI was negligent as well. Two flight schools, one in Minneapolis and one in Phoenix, notified the FBI that their Arab students wanted to learn how to fly jets, but not how to land them. Minneapolis FBI agents took Zacarias Moussaoui, who may have been slated to be one of the 9/11 hijackers, into custody on August 15,

Indeed, I tremble for my country when I reflect that God is just.
—Thomas Jefferson
Notes on the State of Virginia

Without U.S. bumbling and stumbling around the Middle East ... malevolent criminals like bin Laden would never have been able to gain influence. He did so by ... blaming the U.S. for all the misery there.
—James Ostrowski
Ludwig von Mises Institute

While Osama bin laden and his al-Qaida minions were diligently preparing for their murderous mission ... more than twice as many FBI agents were assigned to fighting drugs (2,500) than fighting terrorism (1,151).
—Arianna Huffington
Did the Drug War Claim Another 3,056 Casualties on 9/11?

The illegal drug trade is the financial engine that fuels many terrorist organizations around the world, including Osama bin Laden.

> —Dennis Hastert
> Speaker of the U.S.
> House

Let us not kill our enemies, but kill their desire to kill.

> —Mohandas Gandhi
> father of modern nonviolent resistance

but FBI headquarters would not approve a request for a search warrant. As Minneapolis FBI Chief Counsel Coleen Rowley states in her May 21, 2002, letter to FBI Director Robert Mueller, she and other agents had "connected the dots" but were not allowed to pursue their implications.[85] Had our FBI been less dedicated to tracking drugs and more focused on finding terrorists, the tragedies of 9/11 might never had happened.

Creating Friendship Through Trade

During World War II, Japan and the United States were bitter enemies. In the last few decades, however, trade between the two nations has flourished, even though it has not been totally free from aggression (Chapter 18). War now is totally unthinkable, because our economies are so entwined economically.

Free trade lets each nation specialize in what it does best, so wealth creation is maximized. However, each nation becomes dependent upon the other for its particular specialty. The hidden benefit of trade-generated interdependence is the strong incentive to keep the peace. *Open trade between nations may be the single most effective peace strategy ever devised. If all the nations of the world traded freely with each other, war might quickly become obsolete.*

Winning the Game—Even in a World of Aggressors

As we learned in Chapter 18, nations with open and unregulated trade grow faster than countries with closed economies. Good Neighbors do so well trading with each other that they thrive—even in a world of aggressors.

In Chapter 13, we learned that TIT FOR TAT, a computer program that simulated the Good Neighbor Policy, won the tournament by converting aggressors into nonaggressors. *Further competition suggested that even if only 5% of the players (nations) are Good Neighbors who practice TIT FOR TAT, they will outperform the other 95% who practice aggression.*[86] In real life, "outperforming" means growing in wealth. Even if other nations remain steeped in aggression (e.g., trade barriers), Good Neighbors still come out ahead by trading with each other.

Trading with the Enemy?

Should we then trade freely even with dictators, selling them arms so that they can oppress their people? What would a Good Neighbor do?

A Good Neighbor wouldn't fight aggression with aggression because it would only make a bad situation worse. If we stop merchants from selling food, medicine, and other commodities to an aggressor nation, only the poor are deprived. The dictators like Saddam Hussein simply buy up the scarce supplies for themselves.

Outlawing arms sales to dictators only drives them to purchase weapons on the black market. The way to stop arms sales to dictators is to impoverish them so that they can't make purchases by ending taxpayer-guaranteed loans and aid. Furthermore, when we stop the War on Drugs, would-be tyrants will no longer receive black market profits that supply them with quick cash. *Without that cash or loan guarantees, most weapon deals simply won't be made.*

Tyrants wishing to rise to power will have a more difficult, and perhaps impossible, struggle. Indeed, the best way to help Third World nations free themselves from tyrants is to end the aid that allows them to pay their soldiers and buy arms.

Protecting Our Interests Abroad

Using taxes to protect "American" interests abroad leads to corruption and waste. For example, the United States purchases $11 billion worth of oil per year from the Persian Gulf, but taxpayers spend a whopping $40 billion to $50 billion to protect oil interests there.[87] Surely we don't need to spend four to five times as much as a commodity is worth to "protect" it.

If our fuel bills reflected the money that we actually spend on protecting American interests in the Middle East, we'd quickly find ways to conserve by insulating our buildings, increasing auto engine efficiency, and so on. In a marketplace ecosystem free from aggression, high prices warn us that a resource is scarce and should be conserved. When prices are kept artificially low through higher taxes, we still overpay for a resource, but aren't aware of it. Because we think that the resource is cheap, we may use it wastefully.

If oil companies and other overseas American companies paid for their own security services, the cost would be passed on to consumers. Conservation would then occur naturally.

Of course, private security for American interests abroad is likely to be less expensive than tax-supported military protection. Like private police in our cities, independent security firms working for American oil companies would find ways to keep costs down. Because they would profit most by preventing attacks, rather than defending against them, private protection agencies would be more likely than politically motivated bureaucrats to promote peaceful interactions with Arab nations.

Private firms would not establish military bases that desecrate Arab hold ground by leaking toxins into the groundwater and leaving behind dangerous munitions (Chapter 14). In all likelihood, security would be established at the drilling rigs and on transport ships. Thus, in addition to cutting costs, private firms would stop engaging in activities that fuel resentment in and motivate terrorists like bin Laden.

Just as our public police are not obligated to come when we call (Chapter 16), tax-supported military and diplomats don't have to help us either. Ross Perot learned that harsh reality in 1978 when two of his top executives were taken hostage in Iran. Frustrated by government disinterest in rescuing the captured Americans, Perot asked Col. Arthur "Bull" Simons to save them. The successful rescue, executed two months later with a team of seven of Perot's corporate executives and a young Iranian, was completed without casualties.[88]

In contrast, after five months of planning, the elite Delta Force was unsuccessful in rescuing the U.S. embassy personnel taken hostage by the Iranians in November 1979. The rescue had to be aborted almost immediately because three of the eight helicopters developed mechanical problems. A refueling aircraft and one of the helicopters collided while preparing to return home, killing both crews in the explosion.[89]

Although these cases are isolated examples, they do illustrate some important points. Our tax-supported defense can fail miserably at times. In addition, *the private sector can be remarkably effective at protection and even rescue.* Indeed, private companies staffed by ex-military personnel now offer a variety of such services.[90]

In addition to lower cost, *private security tends to be entrepreneurial and result driven.* Perot hired the best man for the job (Bull Simons) and then let him use his expertise to solve the problems at hand. Some of the participants in the American embassy rescue believe that political decisions had compromised it.[91] The brave men and women of our armed forces can die needlessly in such cases.

Private security for American interests abroad avoids the aggression of taxation, is more economical with its emphasis on prevention, and is more likely to keep relations with foreign nations peaceful. Private security can be a viable alternative to public defense.

Protecting the Home Front

Even if we can protect our interests overseas without taxation, how can we provide domestic security without forcing people to contribute? We have no real-life examples of nonaggressive defense in modern times. However, with a little imagination, we can readily see how the marketplace ecosystem might provide more economical and effective defense than our tax-subsidized defense monopoly.

Switzerland, although historically neutral, has one of the strongest defenses against armed invasion of any modern nation. Every man is a member of the army and is required to keep his military weapon in his home. An invading force would literally have to subdue every household to conquer the Swiss.

In both World Wars, when Germans threatened to invade, the Swiss dissuaded them by inviting key enemy officers to witness their preparedness. During World War II, the Nazis considered a shortcut through nonmountainous regions of the tiny country. The Germans, however, wisely decided against invading "the little

A Swiss publication states, "The Swiss do not have an army; they are the army."
—Benedict LaRosa
Freedom Daily, July 1994

A militia when properly formed are in fact the people themselves ... and include all men capable of bearing arms.
—Richard Henry Lee
Additional Letters from the Federal Farmer

If every Jewish and anti-Nazi family in Germany had owned a Mauser rifle and twenty rounds of ammunition and the will to use it, Adolf Hitler would be a little-known footnote to the history of the Weimar Republic.
—Aaron Zelman
Jews for the
Preservation of Firearm
Ownership

No free man shall ever be de-barred the use of arms. The strongest reason for the people to retain their right to keep and bear arms is as a last resort to protect themselves against tyranny in government.
—Thomas Jefferson
third president of the
United States

Americans need never fear their government because of the advantage of being armed, which the Americans possess over the people of almost every other nation.
—James Madison
fourth president of the
United States

porcupine."[92] *A heavily armed populace discourages invaders just as it discourages criminals.*

A nation of Good Neighbors could easily and affordably develop a Swiss-style defense, without the aggression of taxation or a universal draft. Indeed, the American colonies defeated the elite fighting forces of the British Empire with a voluntary militia defense!

Immediately after the 9/11 attacks, premier training academy Front Sight offered free firearms training to every commercial pilot in the world—an estimated $150 million gift! However, the major television networks refused to run ads with Front Sight's generous offer. Arming pilots was simply not politically correct.

However, many pilots are military veterans, who could be rapidly trained to thwart terrorists. Special bullets that will not puncture aircraft could be used to stop would-be hijackers.[93] Had pilots been armed on 9/11, the Twin Towers might still be standing.

Terrorists prefer to prey on the helpless, just as rampage shooters do (Chapter 16). Allowing people to carry firearms would make it difficult, if not impossible, for a small group of terrorists to control large numbers of people. Had airlines allowed passengers with concealed-carry permits to bring their firearms on board, the 9/11 terrorists might have been stopped.

When citizens are armed, the most common threat to their security—aggression by their own government—is usually thwarted. Throughout history, tyrants who have invaded other nations have first practiced their aggression at home, killing many more of their own citizens than the foreigners they later attempt to conquer.[94] With stealth and a simple handgun, weapons with more firepower can be captured and turned against a more powerful enemy. The failed Soviet invasion of Afghanistan illustrated this fact quite well.

Crisis Creates Opportunity

In the week following the 9/11 terrorist attacks, applications for gun permits soared.[95] People were ready and eager to participate in their own defense. Had this energy been put into community militias, private defense would be well on its way to becoming a reality.

Businesses and prominent citizens would have contributed money for weapons, training, and the hiring of skilled leadership. Churches and other community groups would have offered clerical help, storage facilities, food, and other training necessities. Local physicians and nurses would have helped train militia medical teams. Communities would have come together in a common, unifying cause.

Americans were ready, able, and willing to volunteer time, money, and effort. Blood donors rushed unsolicited to the American Red Cross and stood in line for hours to give blood. Almost $1 billion in donations poured in spontaneously to help the victims' families. Tradespeople traveled hundreds of miles to volunteer their expertise in clearing the debris. So many New Yorkers wanted to help that they had to be turned away.[96] The community spirit is alive and well throughout the nation and can readily be channeled into an effective private defense.

Of course, some weaponry, such as fighter planes and ships, are too expensive for most communities to fund. However, just as companies sponsor race cars, so too might businesses, separately or together, sponsor private military airplanes and ships, especially if training exercises included national and even international competition. Such "Military Olympics" would inspire rapid innovation, intensive training, and avid fans. Like professional sports, private defense might even become self-supporting.

The Military Olympics would warn off aggressors, just as Switzerland's military exercises convinced the Germans to leave the Swiss alone. International competition would likely include armed services supported voluntarily by Good Neighbors and those supported by taxation. Most likely, the better showing by private forces would discourage aggressor nations.

Since the Military Olympics would provide opportunities for honor and glory, the military would not feel the need to provoke a war to gain status. A restless army is one of the biggest threats to domestic security.

Today, we need a nation of Minutemen, citizens who are not only prepared to take arms, but citizens who regard the preservation of freedom as the basic purpose of their daily life and who are willing to consciously work and sacrifice for that freedom.
—John F. Kennedy
U.S. president,
1961–1963

I ask, sir, what is the militia? It is the whole people, except for few public officials.
—George Mason
supporter of adding a
Bill of Rights to the U.S.
Constitution

What, sir, is the use of a militia? It is to prevent the establishment of a standing army, the bane of liberty.
—Elbridge Gerry
during floor debate over
the Second Amendment,
1789

The United States should get rid of its militias.
—Joseph Stalin
communist dictator, 1933

For example, Kennedy's Joint Chiefs of Staff wanted to stage terrorist attacks *on Americans* to provoke a war with Cuba. Their plan "Operation Northwoods" included, among other things, blowing up a U.S. ship, orchestrating terrorist attacks in U.S. cities, and killing John Glenn during the first attempt to put a man in orbit. Evidence would be fabricated so that the strikes would be blamed on Fidel Castro. Bribing Cuban forces to attack the U.S. military base at Guantanamo Bay was even considered!

President Kennedy's administration rejected these written and signed recommendations made by the Joint Chiefs of Staff, which were uncovered only recently by investigative reporter James Bamford.[97] Clearly, a fighting force will want to do what it is trained to do: fight. The Military Olympics would, in part, provide that release in a way that honors the dedicated men and women of our armed services.

Private Defense Is Better and More Economical

Like most tax-supported monopolies, our public defense is expensive and inefficient. The U.S. military ordinarily pays extraordinary prices for the simplest products: $435 for an ordinary hammer, $243 for vise grip pliers, $2.04 for a common threaded nut, and $437 for a 12-foot tape measure![98]

Even with all of this expense, our military can't protect itself! Navy Seal Commander Richard Marcinko was asked to infiltrate key Naval bases. Commanders of the target installation were given notice that Marcinko's raiders were coming. Nevertheless, seven of Marcinko's fake terrorists easily planted dummy demolition charges on nuclear submarines, captured the women and children living on the base, and even gained access to Air Force One as it was being refueled! The Naval commanders were outraged when the chinks in their armor were exposed and demanded that these "infiltrations" stop.[99]

The commanders were more concerned about defending their reputations than defending their country. Because the military is a subsidized monopoly, the taxpayer cannot fire these indifferent service providers and hire others. *If our armed forces can't protect the bases that they control from terrorists, how are they going to protect us?*

Focusing on Defense, Not Offense

Focusing on defense alters our national security program. Switzerland, for example, has no nuclear weapons. However, it requires bomb shelters to be part of every building's structure. People in homes that don't have a shelter pay an annual tax that gives them access to a community facility.[100]

The goal of the Swiss shelters is to protect its entire population against attack by nuclear, biological, or chemical weapons. Their shelters could be especially effective against "dirty bombs" (e.g., radioactive material dispersed by conventional explosives) easily constructed by terrorists. In contrast, other developed nations provide little protection against such devices. If the nuclear weapons that serve as a deterrent fail in their task, we have no protection.

A nation of Good Neighbors could easily create a Swiss-style shelter system without the use of aggression. Even a Star Wars defense against nuclear weapons might be developed. A company or group of companies could expect to discover profitable products along the way, much as the space program did. Once a Star Wars defense was functional, its protective umbrella could be profitably extended to nations that would rather buy missile defense than nuclear weaponry.

Focusing on defense moves us away from weaponry that incurs large civilian casualties. Because nuclear weapons can be used in a first-strike capacity, the U.S. build-up of nuclear weapons instigated an arms race in the second half of the twentieth century. As a schoolgirl, I remember feeling that the Soviets were being foolish spending their money on nuclear weapons; after all, the United States would never attack them first!

Apparently, the United States is now considering using first-strike nuclear force. President Bush has recently asked for plans to deploy nuclear weapons, including smaller, "battlefield" nuclear bombs, against countries that can hold out against nonnuclear attacks; in retaliation for attack by nuclear, biological, or chemical weapons; or "in the event of surprising military developments." The countries specifically targeted are China, Iran, Iraq, Libya, North Korea, Russia and Syria.[101]

The *perceived* threat of this first-strike force will, at the very least, cause another arms race. At worst, it could trigger a preemptive first strike against the United States, killing millions of people. Nuclear fallout, even from a halfhearted exchange, could seriously contaminate the environment. The Swiss have wisely chosen to spend their money on protecting themselves from the folly of other nations rather than on participating in it. A nation of Good Neighbors could do likewise.

Are Free Riders a Problem?

If we don't force people to pay taxes for national defense, won't we have free riders who don't contribute? Probably. Some people might feel that taking care of the poor is more important than practicing militia drills. Others might want to put every extra dollar into their children's education rather than spend it on handguns. We don't need every person to contribute to national defense for it to be effective. Each of us needn't minister to the poor to ensure their care. For some of us, taking care of our family is so overwhelming that we have no energy left for community activities. Each of us puts our time, money, and effort into what we personally believe is most important. In doing so, we take care of our entire spectrum of needs.

In the past, we've spent a great deal of our time, money, and effort trying to force contributions from our neighbors, usually in the form of taxes or military service. We try to defend ourselves against war by making war on neighbors who don't agree with our priorities. The cost of this force is steeper than the cost of simply joining with others of like mind and doing what needs to be done. As a community, we will address all of our needs by honoring our neighbor's choice.

An added benefit of private defense is the resurrection of community spirit. Most people

Men are afraid that war might come because they know that they have never rejected the doctrine which causes wars ... the doctrine that it is right or practical or necessary for men to achieve their goals by means of physical force (by initiating *the use of force against other men) and that some sort of "good" can justify it.*

—Ayn Rand
CAPITALISM: THE
UNKNOWN IDEAL

will be inspired to participate in some small way, recreating the sense of camaraderie that was so prevalent in the communities of bygone days. Perhaps it's no accident that as aggression-through-government has grown, we have grown apart from each other.

Rescuing the Oppressed

Community spirit resulted in one of the most incredible rescues of all time. During World War II, concerned Europeans tried to shelter the persecuted Jews. However, few countries would lower their immigration barriers to take them in. The Netherlands, Belgium, and Great Britain welcomed more than 10,000 child refugees in the late 1930s.[102] President Roosevelt, however, would not support the Child Refugee Bill, proposed in 1939, which would have allowed 20,000 youngsters to come to the United States over a two-year period. Four thousand U.S. families offered to adopt the youngsters just a day after the Child Refugee Bill was proposed![103] Americans who were ready and eager to help the displaced children were stopped from saving their lives.

Roosevelt even turned away the ocean liner *St. Louis,* which arrived from Europe in the summer of 1939 with more than 900 Jewish escapees. Although 734 of them had immigration quota numbers, allowing them to take up residence in the United States 3 to 36 months later, Roosevelt refused them early entry when Cuba retracted its invitation for temporary residence. As the ill-fated ship sailed along the coast of Florida, a U.S. Coast Guard escort made sure that anyone trying to swim to the United States would be stopped—at gunpoint, if necessary. The *St. Louis* had little choice but to return to Europe, where Belgium, England, the Netherlands, and France took the refugees in. Almost half of these unfortunates were killed when Hitler's troops invaded the Western European nations.[104]

By October 1943, the Nazis were on the verge of rounding up the Danish Jews and sending them to concentration camps.[105] Neutral Sweden made the historic decision to end refugee immigration restrictions. On October 2, it boldly

We are saying openly that we don't want the Jews, while the democracies keep on claiming that they are willing to receive them—and then leave the guests out in the cold! Aren't we savages better men after all?
—Adolf Hitler
August 1939

The failure to take any steps whatever to assist these distressed, persecuted Jews in their hour of extremity was one of the most disgraceful things which has happened in American History and leaves a stain and brand of shame upon the record of our nation.
—Bishop James Cannon Jr.
RICHMOND TIMES DISPATCH

The Danes formed a human wall of daring and silence around the rescue operation. Only a few informers succeeded in penetrating the organization, although a large part of its activities were conducted in broad daylight and lots of people were privy to its secrets. The majority were people without any experience in conspiratory or clandestine work.

—Herbert Pundik
THE RESCUE OF THE
DANISH JEWS

announced that all Danish Jews who could reach its shores would be welcome.

Sweden's compassion triggered what may have been the largest rescue of all time. The Danish people, under German occupation, smuggled more than 90% of their Jewish population (7,200 Jews and 686 Gentile spouses) to the shores of Sweden in a matter of weeks.[106]

What made this rescue remarkable is that almost the entire population of Denmark participated spontaneously without much of a plan or preexisting organization. Taxi drivers went through phone books looking for the addresses of people with Jewish names and drove them to the coast. The Academic Rifle Club searched the forests where Jews were hiding to escort them to the shore. Hospitals became a holding center for Jews until an escort to the beach could be arranged. Each person simply did what he or she was inspired to do!

Once at the coast, Jews hid in nearby homes until Danish fishermen and other boat operators were able to take them across the sea to Sweden. The Danish coast guard and police protected the refugees instead of arresting them.

The cost of feeding the refugees, buying bigger boats, bribing a few reluctant officials, and paying for ocean passage were financed by private contributions. No Jew was left behind for lack of money.[107]

Once the refugees arrived on Swedish soil, they were welcomed and allowed to work. They were not forced into refugee camps.[108] When the Jews finally returned to Denmark after the war, many found that their Gentile neighbors had taken care of their homes and businesses for them.[109]

The Danish Jews were saved by Sweden's willingness to end the aggression of immigration restrictions and the Danes' determination to protect their neighbors. If such an amazing rescue could be accomplished spontaneously on a national scale, with each person choosing his or her contribution, what could we expect from a private defense built over time by the same means?

Using the Power of Public Opinion

The Germans in Denmark were successful in capturing 464 Jews and some of the Danish rescue workers. Even then, the Danes would not forsake their neighbors. Danish King Christian X sent a delegation to Theresienstadt, where his subjects languished in the concentration camp. The delegation supplied the prisoners with food, medicine, and hope.

Eventually the Danes negotiated the release of the 425 survivors to Sweden.[110] How did they convince the Germans to let their prisoners go?

The Danes had kept the occupation forces from harming their Jewish population for years by holding the Germans to their politically motivated assurances that they would not threaten the "independence of the Kingdom of Denmark."

Whenever the Germans sought the Danish government's assistance in passing laws that discriminated against the Jews, Danes closed down discussion with the curt statement, "There is no Jewish problem in Denmark."[111] By insisting that the Germans live up to their own propaganda, the Danes were able to protect their Jewish population for a couple of years.

Even tyrants will yield to the pressure of public opinion. A determined populace can rarely be controlled, even by armies. *The almost bloodless rescue of the Danish Jews demonstrates our power to thwart aggression. Had other nations protected their Jewish inhabitants with as much vigor, far fewer Jews would have been slaughtered during World War II.*

Promising Sanctuary

In January 1944, the U.S. government, possibly shamed into action by the dramatic rescue of the Danish Jews, created the War Refugee Board. The board was given $1.15 million in tax money to aid the victims of Nazi persecution. However, the board used less than half that amount. Most of its efforts were funded with almost $20 million in private donations.[112]

Consequently, the projects funded by the board were entrepreneurial and relatively unhampered by political considerations. It supplied the Red Cross with food and medicine for refugees and prisoners. By funding the underground and bribing German guards, rescuers smuggled thousands of Jewish prisoners into Switzerland or Sweden. In areas where rescues would be too dangerous, Jews in hiding and their protectors were supplied with food, medicine, and many other necessities.[113]

One of the boldest moves by the War Refugee Board was to work with Swedish diplomat Raoul Wallenberg. Wallenberg issued "protective passports" to Jews threatened by the Nazis. These passports stated that the bearer was awaiting emigration to Sweden and was protected in the interim by that nation. To reinforce the protection afforded by these passports, Wallenberg flew the Swedish flag from homes where passport bearers lived.

The Germans did not want neutral Sweden drawn into the war and left most of the Jews that Sweden claimed alone. Even when Wallenberg boldly gave passports to Jews in railroad cars bound for Auschwitz, he received only verbal threats as he single-handedly led them off the train. The International Red Cross began mimicking Wallenberg's strategy, giving out its own protective passports, which the Germans reluctantly honored.[114]

Could saving the six million Jews who perished under Hitler have been as simple as accepting them as immigrants? Clearly, the lives saved when Sweden opened her borders suggests the possibility.

Today, desperate Cubans jump aboard flimsy rafts and try to reach Florida. Sometimes cruise ships save the refugees, who often die from thirst or exposure otherwise. However, the U.S. government fines such Good Samaritans up to $3,000 for each undocumented immigrant brought into the port cities of Florida. To avoid such penalties, some ship crews simply ignore the refugees' plea for help and leave them to die.[115]

The aggression of immigration laws is still a death sentence for many seeking to flee from tyranny. They are the new Fugitive Slave Laws that force those shackled by oppression to be sent back to their "owners." We could choose instead to be modern abolitionists, providing a haven to these unfortunates.

Putting Our Fears to Rest

Those of us in developed nations have great resistance to welcoming refugees and immigrants. We fear that hordes will "invade" our cities, taking our jobs from us or living off welfare that our taxes supply. Our fears, logical though they may seem, are largely groundless.

Many people want to come to developed nations because of the poverty and strife in their own. Moving to a strange country, especially one with a different language or new customs, is difficult. Most Third World immigrants leave their native land only in desperation.

However, as we have seen, a great deal of the war and poverty in Third World nations is actually created by the developed nations (Chapter 18). *If we stopped funding the dictators who oppress their own people and ended the trade barriers that keep the poor from entering the global marketplace, fewer people would feel the need to leave their homeland.*

A common belief in developed nations is that immigrants are a drain on the economy. In the United States, however, immigrants pay more in taxes than natives do because immigrants tend to be healthy, young adults of working age rather than juveniles or retired dependents. For the same reason, immigrants use fewer tax-subsidized programs (i.e., welfare, health services, and social security) as well. The average immigrant puts $1,300 more per year into the "system" than he or she takes out.[116]

Of course, a drain on "public" resources would not be an issue if such services were private (Chapter 11). People would help refugees to the extent that they chose to do so. No one would be forced to support someone else.

But do immigrants take jobs away from the native population? Apparently not! Numerous studies have shown that immigrants do not cause native unemployment, even among low-paid minorities. Wages for natives do not decrease either.[117]

Immigration is the sincerest form of flattery.
—Graffiti®
UNITED FEATURE SYNDICATE

... the bosom of America is open to receive not only the opulent and respectable stranger, but the oppressed and persecuted of all nations and religions, whom we should welcome to a participation of all our rights and privileges.
—George Washington, first U.S. president

The most concentrated immigration influx in modern U.S. history is often referred to as the Mariel boatlift. In 1980, Castro announced that he would allow anyone wishing to go to the United States to leave by boat. Within a couple of months, 125,000 refugees had flooded Miami, increasing the city's workforce by 6–7%. However, Miami's unemployment rate did not increase more rapidly than other areas of the country. Wages for natives, even for low-skilled blacks, were unaffected.

Most of the refugees had few skills and little English. In addition, about 5% were violent criminals or mentally unstable. Some of these "undesirables" were slated for deportation and held in detention camps. However, the Miami economy quickly absorbed the rest of this "wretched refuse."[118]

Like other immigrants, most Cuban boat people created jobs for Americans by becoming consumers and created jobs for themselves by doing things that Americans wouldn't. For example, immigrants often start their climb up the Ladder of Affluence by picking produce—hard, backbreaking work—all day in the sun. Americans might take these jobs if the pay were better, but costs would be so high that most farmers would mechanize. More produce would be imported from Mexico or Chile. Without the immigrants, grocery bills in the United States would increase dramatically, harming every consumer.

California gardeners, New York garment makers, and live-in nannies are predominantly immigrants. Without them, Californians would likely have fewer gardens, New York would lose the garment industry to overseas competition, and many career women would find child care so expensive that they couldn't afford to work.[119]

As immigrants move up the Ladder of Affluence, they create jobs for native-born Americans. Foreign-born immigrants are more likely to be self-employed[120] and hire others. Many immigrants excel in the technical and engineering sciences and have been key players in the U.S. dominance of the computer industry, which creates jobs for thousands upon thousands of Americans. U.S. immigrants help their employers interface with companies in other nations, giving American companies a competitive edge in foreign trade over nations without a diverse cultural base.[121]

Immigrants often have to work harder because they must overcome employer aversion to their accents and customs. They are less likely to be hired for public relations, telephone, and sales jobs than native-born applicants. Consequently, they substitute hard work in the fields or long hours in the laboratory to create a niche for themselves in the marketplace ecosystem. They create wealth in arenas that workers from the developed world are abandoning. As exploitive as this may seem, immigrants generally feel that working hard in the United States is a much better opportunity than they could get in their native land. They wouldn't relocate otherwise!

More than 40% of Hong Kong's population consists of refugees, yet Hong Kong boasts one of the highest rates of wealth creation in the world.[122] Indeed, in a poll of top economists, 81% agreed that immigration is "very favorable." Another 19% claimed immigration was "slightly favorable." None said that immigration was "slightly" or "very" unfavorable or that they didn't know.[123]

Without the aggression-through-government that prevents homesteading, all land would be privately owned. Immigrants could only enter with the permission of the owners, who would defend against trespassers. In such a society, churches and other charitable groups would provide a point of entry for new immigrants.

These way stations would probably care for the newcomers until they could support themselves or receive help from sponsor families. Without tax-supported welfare, immigrants could only receive aid that was freely given.

If the charities didn't turn away people looking only for a handout, their facilities would soon be filled to capacity. Thus, the charity stations would have incentive to welcome only those who could find support or provide their own.

Wouldn't terrorists be able to easily enter our country if we don't have a national system of screening? We have such a system now, but it

The United States would not be remotely dominant in high-technology industries without immigrants. ... And at every important high-tech company in America, the crucial players, half of them or more, are immigrants.

—George Gilder
author of WEALTH AND POVERTY

failed to keep the 9/11 terrorists out. The alleged lead hijacker Mohamed Atta entered the United States three times on an expired tourist visa in 2001, even though officials were aware that he had violated its terms by taking flight lessons![124]

Terrorists will be able to enter our country no matter how many restrictions we place on immigration. No border is so tight that some people won't get through. Terrorists who are capable of planning an operation as complex as the 9/11 attacks will easily find a way of getting into the country.

In the meantime, we waste our wealth by investigating each and every person who sets foot in our country. Instead, our resources would be better spent keeping track of terrorists and other people who represent a clear and present danger.

Joining the Fight

Today, if we want to take sides in other people's wars, we must do so as a nation. In a society of Good Neighbors, however, people would decide individually what to do about international conflicts, just as they do when witnessing a mugging. Some people might choose to join the fray; others would call the police; some might choose not to get involved at all.

If we chose to help, we wouldn't first force other bystanders to join us. The time, money, and effort that we would spend trying to force someone to join us would take those resources away from vanquishing the aggressor! In our communities, we wisely honor our neighbor's choice.

In other people's wars, just as in other people's fights, each of us might respond differently. For example, in the Vietnam conflict, many people might have voluntarily contributed time, money, effort, and military service to help the South Vietnamese. In the early days of the war, the public supported it to save the Vietnamese from communism. In a nation of Good Neighbors, with a network of local militia and widespread military games, equipment and personnel would be readily available to answer such a call for assistance. The war effort would be financed by those who believed the cause to be worthy.

If, as time went on, people changed their minds about the worthiness of the conflict, as they did in Vietnam, support would dwindle. The people, not the president, would decide.

The conflict between Israel and the Palestinians would be handled similarly. Both sides could try to convince the developed nations that their cause was worthy of support. People could donate time, effort, or money to the side of their choice or stay out of the conflict entirely.

Such a nonaggressive approach would have been less likely to provoke bin Laden. Only a fraction of Americans would have donated to Israel; some might have even supported the Palestinians. Most Americans would probably have remained neutral. Consequently, bin Laden would have been less likely to have looked on the majority of Americans as supporters of Islam's enemy, even though the donations to Israel might dwarf those given to the Palestinians. More likely, his strategy would have been to publicize what he believes to be terrorist acts by Israel, in an attempt to persuade people to stop contributing to that nation.

When government gives Israel our tax dollars, we all contribute, willingly or unwillingly, to bankrolling the Israeli army. When we honor each other's choices, however, we act separately and are less likely to be blamed for actions that we don't personally fund.

Indeed, if we honored our neighbor's choice, the United States would not, as a nation, have instituted an embargo on Iraq, given aid to Israel, or stationed troops in the Middle East to protect oil interests. Without these provocations, cited repeatedly by bin Laden, the Twin Towers might still stand proudly against the New York skyline.

Terrorists harm civilians in an attempt to change aggressive government policy.[125] *If we had no aggressive government policy, we would no longer be such a convenient scapegoat for anyone wanting to whip up hatred. Indeed, we might not be a target for terrorism at all!*

Suppose they gave a war, and no one came?
—Leslie Parrish-Bach, actress, Vietnam protestor

Historical data show a strong correlation between U.S. involvement in international situations and an increase in terrorist attacks against the United States.
—Defense Science Board, U.S. Department of Defense

What would we do as a nation of Good Neighbors if terrorists did attack? Clearly, we should track them down, just like any other aggressors. One possible strategy, which doesn't create more enemies by bombing innocents, would be to offer a reward for their capture or hire private security forces to bring in the terrorists. The Rewards for Justice Program has been instrumental in the past in apprehending terrorists such as Ramzi Ahmed Yousef, convicted for his participation in the 1993 World Trade Center bombing.[126]

After the 9/11 attacks, a group of American Businessmen volunteered to launch a reward program for the capture of bin Laden.[127] Indeed, if all the effort put into bombing Afghanistan had been devoted to such efforts, bin Laden might even now be languishing in prison awaiting trail.

Al Qaeda has infiltrated many nations of the world. We certainly can't go around bombing every country in the hopes of destroying them. Indeed, the very act of bombing, which is virtually assured to kill innocents, only creates the emotional foundation for more terrorism.

Creating the Best Defense

Ideally, if we are Good Neighbors, few nations will want to attack us. However, in the event that we do need to defend ourselves against foreign aggressors, wealth and technical expertise become important tools in our defensive arsenal. Because nonaggressive nations create more wealth than aggressive ones, Good Neighbors have the edge in any conflict.

In addition, Good Neighbors don't waste their wealth on prohibiting drugs or defending special interests overseas (e.g., the oil industry). They don't pay taxes to subsidize their enemies. The value of their money is not lost through inflation. Thus, in addition to creating wealth rapidly, Good Neighbors don't waste their wealth. They don't spend billions of dollars developing offensive technology. Consequently, they have more time and "disposable income" with which to support a private defense. A nation of Good Neighbors will have fewer enemies and will be

... people want peace so much that one of these days governments had better get out of their way and let them have it.
—President Dwight D. Eisenhower, 1959

better prepared to deal effectively with the ones remaining.

The only perfect defense is to create a world without enemies. The Good Neighbor Policy comes closest to achieving this ideal.

Chapter 20: Making Our Nation Safe and Secure

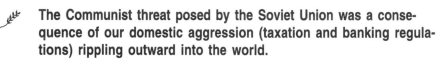

In Summary ...

- The Communist threat posed by the Soviet Union was a consequence of our domestic aggression (taxation and banking regulations) rippling outward into the world.

- By similar means, we have helped to empower virtually every threat to U.S. national security in the past 50 years, including terrorists Saddam Hussein and Osama bin Laden.

- U.S. intervention in the Third World often causes a great deal of death and suffering. The result: animosity toward Americans.

- Because of biased reporting, Americans are often unaware of what is done in their name.

- New findings suggest that both Pearl Harbor and the 9/11 attacks were provoked by aggressive U.S. foreign policy.

- Because the military-industrial complex profits from war, it encourages conflict. As President Eisenhower warned us, we need to be vigilant.

- If the 9/11 terrorists wanted to destroy our freedoms, we are playing right into their hands with the USA Patriot Act, secret military tribunals, and torture of suspects.

- By ending foreign aid and the drug war, we can deplete the cash flow to would-be dictators and terrorists.

- Trade turns enemies into allies by increasing the wealth of both nations (e.g., Japan). Trade with every nation may be the best deterrent of all!

- Privatizing defense can be an effective, economical, and innovative alternative to a tax-supported military.

- Good Neighbors make few enemies. In the rare instances when defense becomes necessary, their superior wealth-creating abilities give them a strategic advantage over their adversaries.

Part Five

But Deliver Us from Evil:

Our Choices Make Our World

Chapter 21

A New Age or a New World Order?

Once we understand how global peace and prosperity are created, we cannot be easily fooled.

In the previous chapter, we learned how our domestic aggression-through-government ripples out to create a warring world. Many people believe that unification through world government would end these horrific conflicts.

Unification can be achieved in one of two ways: by choice (nonaggression) or by force (aggression). The result we get is very different depending on the means we use.

For comparison, consider the difference between forced and consensual sexual union. The physical and emotional joining that occurs between lovers who come together voluntarily differs dramatically from the forced union of rape. Likewise, global unity that is achieved or maintained by aggression won't create the harmony of universal love, but the nightmare of violence and violation.

If a world government resembled the governments of today, it would most likely be an instrument of aggression. Let's examine several problems that we hope world government (sometimes referred to as the New World Order) would solve and see if its consummation would be an act of love or rape.

Controlling Population Growth

Many people are concerned that overpopulation will create poverty, famine, and "standing room only" living conditions. Don't we need global government to force people to have fewer children to prevent such problems?

As we learned in Chapter 2, population density has little effect on a country's wealth. Hong Kong, for example, has a population density almost 50 times that of the rest of China, yet creates about 6.5 times as much wealth each year. South Korea has 2.5 times as many people as North Korea, yet creates almost 23 times as much wealth. How can this be?

Fears of overpopulation have sprung from the belief that wealth is limited. However, as

We shall have world government whether or not you like it—by conquest or consent.

—James Warburg
testimony before Senate
Foreign Relations
Committee, 1950

... the need of a growing solidarity with our fellow and a growing collective soul in humanity is not in dispute. But the loss of the self in the State is not the thing these high ideals mean, nor is it the way to their fulfillment.

—Sri Aurobindo
SOCIAL AND POLITICAL
THOUGHT

we now know, wealth is limitless. Scarcity in modern times is a direct result of restricting wealth creation usually by aggression-through-government, not from too many people.

The "carrying capacity" of the earth depends on the type of society it sustains. The earth has a lower carrying capacity for hunting and gathering populations than for farming societies. Improved farming techniques regularly increase the yield per acre and the earth's carrying capacity along with it.[1]

Additional space in densely populated areas can be provided by multilevel buildings. Clearly, the carrying capacity of the earth changes with how we use the space that we have. The high standard of living enjoyed in densely populated Japan suggests that the earth can support many times more people than it does now.

In all likelihood, the earth's carrying capacity will never be reached. As societies become wealthier, the number of births drops dramatically.[2] In most industrialized economies, manual labor, especially child labor, creates little wealth relative to the work of experienced, skilled adults. In rural economies, however, children contribute substantially to family income (Chapter 18). Consequently, in rural economies, children are a financial asset; in industrialized countries, children consume more wealth than they create. As countries become more industrialized, the financial incentive to have children declines.

Indeed, developed countries now have a birthrate so low that they can no longer maintain their population levels without immigration. In the next 50 years, for example, Italy expects to have 28% fewer people.[3]

Even the birthrates in developing countries are slowing as the Third World becomes more industrialized. Consequently, by 2055, world population should stabilize at about 9 billion.[4]

Although the earth can easily sustain these numbers, they are likely to decline as the Third World becomes even more affluent. Indeed, the best way to limit population growth is to pursue policies that maximize wealth creation. The Good Neighbor Policy does exactly that!

Protecting Endangered Species

On Land

Some conservationists see a global government as a way to enforce worldwide bans on hunting endangered species, such as the elephant and rhinoceros. Such bans threaten first-strike force against those who create wealth by "harvesting" these unclaimed animals. Homesteading of wild herds is forbidden just as homesteading of land is. Environmentalists support such bans to preserve endangered species.

However, this aggression is backfiring, hurting the very creatures it's supposed to help, as the following examples show. In Kenya, the elephant population dropped from 65,000 to 19,000 between 1979 and 1989, even though elephant hunting was forbidden. Farmers and ranchers consider elephants a dangerous nuisance, so they destroy the elephant habitat, kill the elephants secretly, or look the other way when poachers hunt them.

But, in Zimbabwe, natives can claim (homestead) elephants living on their lands. Natives can legally sell permits to hunt the elephants on their land. When animals that are old or injured are culled from the herd, their meat and hides can be legally sold as well. Naturally, the natives protect their valuable elephants from poachers and provide habitat so that the elephants can reproduce.

In the same 10 years that the elephant herds were ravaged in Kenya, Zimbabwe's elephant population grew from 30,000 to 43,000.[5] By 1998, the Zimbabwe elephant herds boasted 70,000 animals.[6] *People will protect the environment when they own it and profit from it.*

Namibia and South Africa give private landowners control over the animals on their land. Consequently, many ranchers have switched from raising cattle to supporting wildlife. Neighboring ranchers have banded together to form conservancies for roaming species. The ranchers profit from both hunts and photo safaris.

Thirst for profits and love of nature have encouraged ranchers to protect and propagate

Making elephants valuable to Africans by allowing them to own the animals and trade in their products is the best way to ensure the species' sustainable existence.
—Roger Bates
Institute of Economic Affairs

Privatization of control over the use of wildlife has had more success in promoting biodiversity in the southern African region than any other policy measure.
—Robert H. Nelson and Kay Muir-Leresche
Competitive Enterprise Institute

In fact, there are more scimitar-horned oryx on the private game ranches in Texas than in their native territories in Africa, where they are under government protection. And the Y.O. Ranch alone boasts more blackbuck antelope than are left in their native territories of India and Pakistan.

—Edmund Contoski
MAKERS AND TAKERS

the endangered southern white rhino and the threatened black rhino. Both species were brought back from the brink of extinction largely through private efforts.[7] Other species, such as eland, kudu, giraffe, cheetah, sable, and impala, are thriving on privately owned wildlife ranches.[8] Owners charge tourists for photo safaris and, in some cases, hunting permits. *When owners can profit from wildlife, they protect it and help it propagate.*

Exotic wildlife ranching has become popular in the United States too. The North American buffalo and tule elk have been brought back from near extinction through the efforts of private ranchers.[9]

One of these individuals, David Bamberger, single-handedly preserved 29 of the 31 remaining bloodlines of a rare antelope known as the scimitar-horned oryx, saving yet another species from extinction.[10] Individuals and small groups are often able to propagate endangered animals. Magicians Siegfried and Roy, for example, breed white tigers and lions at their Las Vegas ranch. They not only use them in their stage performances, but supply zoos throughout the world with these delightful creatures.[11]

However, not all animals can be saved in captivity. Nevertheless, determined individuals have managed to save migrating species from extinction as well. Edward Avery McIlhenny brought eight snowy egret chicks back to his home on Avery Island, Louisiana. After he raised and released them, the egrets returned to Avery Island and now number in the tens of thousands.[12] Private conservation involving thousands of people brought back the peregrine falcon when overuse of DDT interfered with its reproduction (Chapter 14).[13]

We never worry that cows and horses will become extinct. Because we own them and profit from their use, we have motivation to make sure they propagate. When we encourage ownership of wildlife, we make it more plentiful.

How do we protect animals when they are destructive and can't be used commercially? Environmentalists concerned about snow leopards have found a way.

Snow leopard habitat is unsuitable for farming. People living in snow leopard habitat raise livestock instead for meat, milk, and transportation. Losing even one animal to a hungry snow leopard can be a great hardship. Consequently, the community kills the snow leopards and destroys their habitat whenever possible. Banning such activities simply means that the activities are done clandestinely. For the natives in snow leopard country, killing these fine animals is a matter of their own life or death.

Concerned environmentalists sought a nonaggressive way to help both the snow leopard and the people who shared its habitat. The representatives of the Seattle-based International Snow Leopard Trust used donations to help a Mongolian community develop better security for its livestock so that snow leopard attacks would not deplete its meager herds. The organization gave the community food, clothing, irrigation systems, and fencing, which provided a buffer if a snow leopard occasionally breached the improved defenses and killed livestock.

In northern Pakistan, the trust paid one community to protect the snow leopard's traditional prey, the ibex, a horned goat. The program was so successful that the community can now sell permits to hunt the ibex for $5,000 each. The community, the ibex, and the snow leopard are all thriving.[14]

The snow leopard, ibex, elephant, and rhino are making their comebacks through the Good Neighbor Policy. When we try to save endangered species with aggression, however, we actually harm the animals we wish to help.

The story of Ben Cone Sr. and his son illustrate this point. In the 1930s, Ben Cone Sr. purchased more than 7,000 deforested acres in North Carolina. He cultivated the barren land until it became a well-managed forest. His son, Ben Cone Jr., continued in his father's footsteps, harvesting timber carefully to maintain the forest's abundance of songbirds, deer, quail, and wild turkey, as well as 29 endangered red-cockaded woodpeckers.

The Cones should have been applauded for creating a habitat that promoted biodiversity and

We needed a clear strategy to win the hearts and minds of the people involved.

—Helen Foreman
founder, International
Snow Leopard Trust

propagation of an endangered species. Instead, the U.S. Fish and Wildlife Service told Ben Cone Jr. that it would stop him from cutting timber—at gunpoint, if necessary—on more than 1,500 acres of his property. For Ben Cone Jr., the woodpeckers became a multimillion dollar liability. He could not harvest much of his timber, but was still taxed as if he could.

Cone did the only sensible thing. He quickly cut timber around the perimeter of the 1,500 acres that contained the woodpeckers. He changed his rotating harvest schedule from 80 years to 40 so that his woods would no longer have the old growth that attracted the birds. His neighbors, fearful that Cone's fate would become theirs, cleared their old-growth forests before any woodpeckers could be discovered on their lands.[15]

Aggression backfires every time. Forcing people to protect the woodpecker habitat resulted in its destruction!

On Sea

Aggression harms marine life just as it harms animal life. In waters where homesteading of ocean plots or ocean fish is honored, fish thrive. Other areas, however, are over-fished and marine life is threatened.

For example, in some states, homesteading of oyster beds is permitted. Private oyster beds are more prolific and profitable than public ones. The owners, who profit when the oysters thrive, have incentive to invest money in caring for the beds and harvesting them sustainably.[16]

The ocean fishing industry does not own the oceans, however, and thus has little incentive to fish sustainably. Fish stocks become dangerously depleted. However, when ocean fisheries are even partially privatized, depleted fish stocks have recovered in Alaska, Australia, British Columbia, Greenland, Iceland, the Netherlands, and New Zealand.[17]

Partial privatization usually occurs with a government entity or fishing cooperative determining what the sustainable catch will be for a particular year. Fishing companies either buy or are assigned a share of the allowable catch.

The "deed" to the fish, most often called an Individual Transferable Quota (ITQ), can be sold or traded. If a fishing company catches too much fish or the wrong species, it must purchase the appropriate ITQ from another owner.[18]

Not only do such arrangements prevent overfishing, they also encourage research to enhance fish stocks. More fish mean more profit, so fishing companies jointly fund research to encourage their propagation. Consequently, by 1996, harvest of 29 out of 32 ITQ species in New Zealand had increased from 1986 levels.[19]

Many fish thrive around artificial reefs, which are relatively inexpensive to construct and sink. Only Japan recognizes the ownership by those who construct such reefs.[20] As other nations stop claiming the fish attracted to artifical constructs, more will be built and fish stocks will increase.

Research suggests that the ocean can be fertilized to increase phytoplankton, the bottom of the fish food chain. Experiments suggest that continuous fertilization could give each square mile of ocean about 1,000 tons of catchable fish each year. Even a modest increase in phytoplankton might be expected to enhance fish populations.[21] However, people won't undertake the cost of ocean fertilization unless they are allowed to own the ocean plot or the fish it contains.

Clearly, ocean "ownership" could be broad enough to include everything in a particular "plot" or could be narrowed to simply a claim on single species of marine life in a given area. To date, the marketplace ecosystem appears to be evolving in favor of the latter. Shipping lanes, for example, are so plentiful that no one bothers to homestead them. Of course, if a tanker leaked oil that contaminated a claimed fishery, the oil company would have to compensate fish owners for any damage to their stocks. Just as fishing rights in Britain are enforced by their owners, ocean fisheries would be fiercely protected by those who owned and profited from them. Would world government encourage homesteading of the earth's creatures on land and sea? Probably not, since most of today's governments are claiming more land, not less.

Controlling the Greenhouse Effect

In addition to controlling population and saving endangered species, we often believe that only world government can deal with global phenomena, such as warming caused by the greenhouse effect.

The media treat global warming as if it were established fact. Ironically, our meteorologists can hardly predict tomorrow's temperature accurately, yet somehow predictions of a few degrees of global warming over the next century are supposed to be possible! I don't need my Ph.D. in biophysics to know that this kind of logic just doesn't add up.

Is the earth warming? The answer depends on which measurements you believe. Warming is only apparent in surface temperature measurements, but does not appear in NASA's satellite readings, except for the transient El Niño effect in 1998.[22] Satellite readings provide a more global temperature measurement over both sea and land, but most of the sampling points for surface measurements are on land and cover less than 20% of the earth's area.[23] Some regions, like the United States, show no warming at all.[24] Surface temperatures rise in urban areas from the storage of heat in pavement and other structures.[25] *Because coverage by rural measuring stations has dropped 65% between 1970 and 1998,[26] the 0.7°C increase in global surface temperatures in the twentieth century may simply be a sampling bias.* According to the satellite measurements, we have no significant warming trends at all!

Let's assume, however, that the surface temperatures are correct and that the earth's temperature increased slightly over the past century. Is this warming part of a normal variation, or are we causing it? To answer that question, we need to look at temperatures over the past several centuries. During the Medieval Warm Period, about 1,000 years ago, the Vikings settled in Greenland because global temperatures were 2–3°C warmer then. However, between 1400 and 1900, the "Little Ice Age" arrived, with temperatures 0.4–0.8°C[27] colder than today. *Thus, the warming observed in the twentieth century (about*

... the temperatures we measure from space are actually on a very slight downward trend since 1979. ... the trend is about 0.05 degrees Celsius per decade cooling.
—Roy Spenser
meteorologist and team leader, NASA/Marshall Space Flight, 1997

The climate issue is not "settled"; it is both uncertain and incomplete.
—Bert Bolin
chairman,
Intergovernmental Panel on Climate Change, 1997

The trend is statistically significant and it's downward. ... Two of the three methods we use to measure planetary temperature show cooling, and one shows nothing at all.
—Robert Balling
director of the Office of Climatology, Arizona State University, 1997

0.7°C) could result from natural variations, a re-covery from the unusually cold centuries that preceded it.

We simply don't understand enough about the factors that contribute to the planet's temperature to predict future warming. *The computer models are refined each year as real temperatures consistently fall short of projections.* For example, in 1990, the "best guess" for 2100 was 3.2°C; in 1992, it was 2.6°C; in 1995, it had dropped to 2.0°C. Other adjustments, based on improved estimates of carbon dioxide and methane contributions, have taken the "best guess" down to 1.25°C.[28]

Would such shifts be dangerous even if they did happen? Note that most of the temperature changes under discussion are somewhat less than the 2.4–3.8°C difference observed between the Little Ice Age and the Medieval Warm Period. Written records show no catastrophic events accompanying these shifts. *Changes happened slowly, allowing even these premodern cultures to adapt.*

Indeed, normal temperatures, measured over the past 20 years by satellite, routinely fluctuate 0.7°C within a year.[29] It's difficult to imagine that doubling or even tripling such variation would have much effect if the change were to be spread over the next century, giving us plenty of time to adapt. If warming were to happen slowly, which even surface temperature measurements would suggest, rising seas would inch forward year after year, providing ample time to build dikes and sea walls.

Indeed, adaptation (e.g., putting up sea walls) is less expensive than trying to control carbon dioxide emissions through cutbacks in fossil fuel use. *One estimate puts the cost of stabilizing global CO_2 emissions at $8.5 trillion in lost wealth creation, but the damage done by global warming to crops, coastal property, and so on would be substantially less—about $5 trillion.*[30] To actually cut back CO_2 emissions enough to nullify the projected warming of 1.25°C would require us to stop burning almost all fossil fuels by 2035, shutting down the world as we know it.[31] In other words, the proposed cure for global warming is

Over 17,000 scientists have signed a petition saying, in part, "there is no convincing scientific evidence that human release of carbon dioxide, methane, or other greenhouse gas is causing or will, in the foreseeable future, cause catastrophic heating of the Earth's atmosphere and disruption of the Earth's climate." ... Over one hundred climate scientists signed the 1996 Leipzig Declaration, which stated in part, "there does not exist today a general scientific consensus about the importance of greenhouse warming from rising levels of carbon dioxide. On the contrary, most scientists now accept the fact that actual observations from Earth satellites show no climate warming whatsoever." ... A remarkable 89 percent of state climatologists agreed that "current science is unable to isolate and measure variations in global temperatures caused only by man-made factors."

—Joseph Bast
THE QUESTIONABLE
SCIENCE BEHIND THE
GLOBAL WARMING SCARE

worse than the disease. *We are better off doing nothing than trying to stabilize or cut back on emissions!*

The cost of cutting fuel use will hurt the economies of the developed nations, but devastate the already troubled economies of developing countries. More poverty means less food, less medicine, and a lowered life expectancy. Poverty quite literally kills.

Thus, before we take actions that will cost lives, shouldn't we be sure that warming is occurring, that human activity is causing it, and that serious problems will result if we do nothing? At present, none of these conditions has been met.

Indeed, Dr. James Hansen, whose testimony to Congress in 1988 triggered concerns about global warming, has changed much of his own thinking. *He noted that in the past two decades of the twentieth century, carbon dioxide levels didn't change much, despite a 30% increase in fossil fuel use.*[32] In addition, Hansen's own data show that most of the surface temperature increase observed over the past century occurred from 1880 to 1940,[33] long before the heaviest industrial activity. If warming is occurring, something other than fossil fuels is likely responsible. Indeed, Hansen himself now claims that "Non-CO_2 greenhouse gases are probably the main cause of observed global warming."[34] If the "experts" have been wrong about the relationship between energy use and the amount of carbon dioxide in the atmosphere, we clearly don't know enough to take action.

However, Mother Nature knows just what to do. Carbon dioxide acts like a fertilizer to stimulate plant growth, especially trees. Plants convert the carbon dioxide into biomass and oxygen. Thus, they help stabilize atmospheric carbon dioxide by growing faster when CO_2 goes up and by growing slower when it decreases.[35]

What would happen if this stabilizing feedback were overcome by too much carbon dioxide and the earth began to warm? As temperatures rose, plant growth would be stimulated further. The tropics are lush because most of the earth's flora prefer warmer temperatures.

Nearly the entire observed rise of 0.5 degrees Centigrade occurred before 1940. However, most of the man-made carbon dioxide entered the atmosphere after 1940. ... Furthermore, from 1940 to 1970, carbon dioxide built up rapidly ... [and] the temperature actually dropped.

—Robert Jastrow
NASA Goddard Institute
of Space Science

Thus, if plants were unable to stabilize atmospheric carbon dioxide and a greenhouse effect truly began, plants would grow even faster, consuming more carbon dioxide and at least partially restoring the balance.

More plants and better crop yields that would accompany a world with more carbon dioxide and slightly higher temperatures would be beneficial rather than detrimental. Such gains would at least partially offset any damage that global warming might cause. Indeed, lives might be saved as food became more abundant. Because people tend to die more from cold winters than hot summers, global warming might save other lives too.

Clearly, we know too little about earth's temperature cycles to throw millions of people into life-threatening poverty by cutting back on use of fossil fuel. *The dangers of global warming pale in comparison to the wealth-shattering proposals that seek to prevent it by slashing our fossil fuel use.*

Why do we care so much about wealth? Do we really need faster cars, fancier food, more lavish entertainment? Probably not. However, wealth also means better medical care, healthier lifestyles and more innovative treatments. The number of years that we live is highly dependent on how wealthy we are (Figure 21.1). Wealth is literally a matter of life or death!

Any proposal to cut fossil fuel use or, for that matter, any form of aggression-through-government, limits wealth creation. Less wealth creation means that the life of you and your loved ones will almost certainly be shortened. That's a steep price to pay for flawed government policy!

How then would a world of Good Neighbors prevent a problem like global warming if it did indeed endanger life on earth? If a specific chemical (e.g., chlorofluorocarbons or CFCs) or specific products (e.g., fossil fuels) threatened to cause damage, insurance companies that protected the sellers of CFCs or fossil fuels would raise their liability rates. This added cost would be passed on to consumers, who would then be motivated to find a substitute that would enable them to buy less of these harmful products.

If the threat was high, insurance rates would be high too. The harmful items would be used only sparingly, and more benign substitutes would be found. Damage, if it occurred at all, would be minimized. Any victims would be fully compensated through the seller's liability insurance. The marketplace ecosystem would balance the needs of the producers, consumers, and the environment without aggression—or the need for a world government!

What would make companies buy liability insurance? As discussed in Chapter 13, corporate owners and executives might have to compensate victims personally. Investors and decision makers would not be likely to become involved in businesses that didn't protect them with liability insurance.

Figure 21.1: How Life Expectancy Increases with Wealth

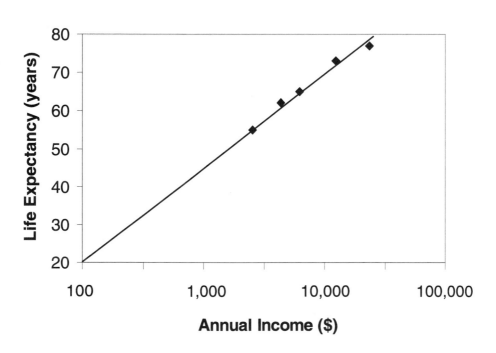

Data taken from J.D. Gwartney and R.A. Lawson, *Economic Freedom of the World 2002 Annual Report* (Vancouver, BC: Fraser Institute, 2002), p. 20. Countries (n = 123) were divided into five groups on the basis of their Economic Freedom Index. Each data point compares the life expectancy for 1999 births and the gross national income per capita in 2000 U.S. dollars of one quintile.

A world of Good Neighbors would have additional options. Rather than slowing or stopping the use of problem-causing substances, Good Neighbors might find a way to simply stop the damaging effects. For example, let's assume that carbon dioxide did indeed turn out to be warming the world. Instead of cutting back on emissions, fossil fuel suppliers might be able to increase the carbon "sinks," such as plants, that extract carbon dioxide from the atmosphere.

For example, the oceans' phytoplankton are a large portion of the world's carbon sink. By fertilizing the oceans and increasing the plankton, we might not only increase the fish population but stabilize the atmosphere's carbon dioxide also.[36] Another possibility would be to genetically engineer plants that consume more carbon dioxide to restore the balance. In a world where we have enough wealth to support such research, multiple solutions are likely.

Issuing Global Currency

A single, global currency sounds heavenly to world travelers who are constantly exchanging one type of money for another. However, these different currencies are an important part of the self-regulating marketplace ecosystem. Each country's central bank has the power to inflate the currency, which transfers buying power from the average person into the hands of bankers, governments, and other well-to-do special interests (Chapter 9). The presence of other central banks, however, limits the extent of this transfer.

For example, if our Federal Reserve starts creating more dollars while the Japanese central bank does not inflate the yen, savvy investors exchange their dollars for the more valuable yen. The more the Fed increases the money supply, the more people fearfully convert their dollars to something else. The U.S. banks can't profit as much if people won't keep their savings in dollars. Currencies compete just as service providers do. Creating a monopoly on currency eliminates all customer control.

If everyone were forced to use a single global currency, these checks and balances would be destroyed. The sole central bank could manipulate the money supply at will. Through inflation, wealth would be transferred from those who had no property and savings to those who did. Alternating inflation with deflation would bankrupt those who failed to accurately predict the timing of the cycles and invest their resources accordingly (see Chapter 9 for a review of this process). Those who controlled the money supply would get richer at the expense of the less fortunate. Without other central banks to keep money creation in check, the transfer of wealth from the rich to the poor could happen virtually overnight.

A global currency would allow those who control it to have more power than any ruling elite has ever known. Clearly, we do not need world government to create such an exploitive monopoly!

Keeping the Peace

One of the largest benefits expected from a global government is that it would put an end to war. World government would unite nations much as the U.S. Constitution joined states into a united country. Let's take a closer look at U.S. history to determine what might be expected from a world government patterned after the reorganization of the United States in 1788.

Each state ratified the U.S. Constitution with the understanding that joining was voluntary. The ultimate check on the federal government was the ability of each state to secede from the union.

However, by 1860, Southern states were dissatisfied with the union. The North and the South were divided on several issues, including slavery, a tariff structure that harmed the South, and a shift in the congressional balance of power to the more populated Northern states. South Carolina formally withdrew in December, and other southern states followed in early 1861.

The bitter Civil War that followed was fought primarily to preserve the Union. The Emancipation Proclamation was not issued until September 1862, when the Union lost hope that the Southern states would return to it voluntarily.

Freeing the slaves was a tactic; the goal of the war was to keep the Southern states in the union—at gunpoint, if necessary.

The Southern states held a bitter grudge for more than a century. In the mid-1970s, as an industrial scientist hiring an assistant, I called a woman doctor working nearby. "The gentleman I want to hire once worked for you," I explained. "How does he feel about reporting to a female?" In those days, many men still objected to women in the workplace, especially in the sciences.

"He won't mind that you're a woman," she explained with a gentle Southern drawl. "It's more likely that he won't want to work with a Yankee." The aggression of Northern states remained a bitter memory and, over a century later, still poisoned interactions between the North and the South.

My story ended happily. I hired the gentleman from Tennessee, who became my indispensable teammate for almost two decades. However, the forcible domination of the member states by the federal government continues.

For example, as we learned in Chapter 15, seven states have passed legislation allowing the sick to use medical marijuana with a doctor's recommendation. However, the Drug Enforcement Administration continues to prosecute doctors who prescribe marijuana, patients who use it, and suppliers, violating the will of the people. What can the states do against the more powerful federal government? Clearly, very little—unless they are ready to take on the might of the U.S. military.

In the United States, the federal government maintains the Union by force, not by consent. A world government is almost certain to do the same.

What Would World Government Do?

We can see how global government might operate by watching the European Union (EU), which is in the process of uniting most European nations under a supra-regional government. Currently, members can "opt out" of some of the more controversial dictates—but for how long?

My paramount object in this struggle is to save the Union, and is not either to save or destroy slavery. If I could save the Union without freeing any slave I would do it, and if I could save it by freeing some and leaving others alone I would also do that. What I do about slavery, and about the colored race, I do because I believe it helps to save the Union; and what I forbear, I forbear because I do not believe it would help save the Union.

—President Abraham Lincoln, 1862

... once having joined the One-World federated Government, no nation could secede or revolt ... because with the Atom Bomb in its possession the Federal Government would blow that nation off the face of the earth

—Cord Meyer Jr. first president of the United World Federalists

A well-known result of the union is the establishment of the euro, which replaced the currency in most member nations in January 2002.[37] Instead of promoting competing currencies, the European Union has fostered the transfer of wealth from the average European to the banking and political elite.

In 1999, EU antitrust investigators raided the London offices of Coca-Cola, searching e-mails, computers, and confidential files. They had no warrant and were subject to no judicial review. Their supervisor, Mario Manit, is seeking the authorization to interrogate employees of suspect companies like Coca-Cola without giving them access to legal counsel.[38]

A British greengrocer, Steven Thoburn, became one of five "Metric Martyrs" when he sold his customers bananas by the pound instead of by the kilogram. The European Union demands conformance to the metric system, but many of Thoburn's customers want to buy produce in weights that they understand. Another trader, Colin Hunt, was ordered to pay a UK£4,500 fine for pricing vegetables by the pound.[39] The Metric Martyrs are appealing to the European Court of Human Rights in Strasbourg to retain their right to give their customers what they want.[40]

On February 28, 2002, leaders of the European Union started a constitutional convention. Proposals include a minimum wage for all of Europe.[41] Clearly, Europe is heading toward a regional version of global government. EU actions described above suggest that the EU will increase in aggression-through-government.

The United Nations (UN) also has many of the characteristics of a world government. At its 2002 Monterrey summit, a variety of global taxation schemes were discussed, including a carbon tax, ostensibly to discourage fossil fuel use to prevent global warming. Other proposals include taxes on e-commerce, aviation fuel, use of oceanic shipping lanes, and use of outer space for orbiting satellites. Outer space and ocean use would be taxed because these areas are considered "global public goods."[42] Clearly, the United Nations does not believe in recognizing homesteading claims by individuals.

How would the United Nations enforce global taxes? Most likely, nations of the world would allow their troops to report to a UN commander. In fact, it is already happening.

In 1995, before U.S. troops were dispatched to Macedonia, they were told to wear a UN patch on their uniform, don blue UN headgear, and report to a commander whose oath of allegiance was to the United Nations rather than the United States. One career soldier, Specialist Michael G. New, had studied the UN charter and concluded that it was incompatible with the U.S. Constitution he had sworn to support. New was asked to be given written justification for the change in uniform or a transfer to a unit that was not required to wear the UN insignia. He even offered to accept an honorable discharge rather than act against his conscience.

New's superiors did not answer his queries for information. Instead, the Army court-martialed him and gave him a dishonorable discharge. New appealed his discharge to the Supreme Court, which refused to hear his case. New believes that the order to don the UN uniform and report to a UN commander is illegal under current law, and he is continuing litigation solely on these issues.[43]

The United Nations and the European Union are not (yet) global governments, but their mode of operation is clear. They practice aggression just like the governments of today, through taxation, regulation, antitrust prosecutions, and prohibition of oceanic and outer space homesteading. They have empowered the banking elite with the euro. They have dragged hard-working greengrocers through the courts simply for giving customers weights they can understand. They have thrown a young soldier out of the Army for trying to make sure that he honored his word.

Global government does not solve our problems, but simply makes them worse. The United Nations and European Union are simply smaller versions of what we could expect from global government. Without a better example, world government will simply duplicate the mistakes of national ones.

But, the world is more sophisticated and prepared to march towards a world government. The supernational sovereignty of an intellectual elite and world bankers is surely preferable to the national autodetermination practiced in past centuries.
—David Rockefeller
chairman and CEO of
Chase Bank
1969–1980

Still if you will not fight for the right when you can easily win without bloodshed, if you will not fight when your victory will be sure and not so costly, you may come to the moment when you will have to fight with all the odds against you and only a precarious chance for survival. There may be a worse case. You may have to fight when there is no chance of victory, because it is better to perish than to live as slaves.
—Winston Churchill,
1874–1965

If you want to be a great leader, you must learn to follow the Tao. Stop trying to control. Let go of fixed plans and concepts and the world will govern itself.

—Lao-tsu
Tao Te Ching

As usual, global representatives, whose decisions may cause great harm, will not be liable for the damage that they do. Sovereign immunity will protect them from liability and prevent their victims from gaining compensation.

If we wished to assert our independence from the global government, we could not, in all likelihood, defend ourselves against the combined weaponry of the world. We would reap what we have sown: eternal enslavement by the master we had created to control others.

An even worse fate might befall us, however. With no country permitted to try different ways of relating to others, we might never know that a world of masters and slaves is not our only option. We might not know that interactions can be win–win instead of win–lose. Just as a rape victim loses sight of how beautiful physical union can be, so too might we lose sight of the unlimited harmony and abundance that can be ours. We might remain in another Dark Age where our only hope of salvation is to take on the role of master instead of slave. We might not ever learn of a better way to create a world without borders.

A Better Way

When we are Good Neighbors, borders simply dissolve. Without the aggression of immigration restrictions, we aren't stopped—at gunpoint, if necessary—from visiting our friends in other countries. Without the aggression of trade restrictions or customs duty, our products aren't stopped—at gunpoint, if necessary—from entering stores in other nations. *Without aggression to erect and maintain them, there are no borders.*

It really is that simple!

Chapter 21: A New Age or a New World Order?

In Summary ...

- A world government would resemble the governments of today and thus would most likely be an instrument of aggression.

- The things that we want global government to do (prevent overpopulation, protect endangered species, prevent global warming, create a single global currency, and end war) are best accomplished by simply becoming Good Neighbors.

- As countries grow in wealth, their birthrate declines. Because the Good Neighbor Policy enhances wealth creation, it both destroys poverty and controls population naturally.

- Private ownership of the world's fauna promotes biodiversity and protection of endangered species on land or in the sea much better than governmental bans on hunting or habitat destruction.

- Global temperature and its measurement are so complex that we can't be sure that warming is occurring or what might cause it. Even if global warming becomes a problem, restitution would reduce the use of harmful products.

- Multiple currencies provide an important check on inflation by central banks. A single, global currency would give the people who control it more power than any ruling elite has ever known.

- World government is more likely to be a forced union than a voluntary one. Consequently, its consummation will more closely approximate rape than love.

- The Good Neighbor Policy is more effective in creating a world without borders than global government is. Indeed, there are no borders without aggression to erect and maintain them.

Chapter 22

How to Get There from Here

If we each work on the piece of the puzzle that appeals to us most, the final picture will reflect the composite of our dreams.

If you've reached this chapter, you've probably come to at least three conclusions. First, universal peace and plenty are within our reach. Second, the Good Neighbor Policy can help take us to that end. Third, we seem to be going down the opposite path!

Teaching by Example

Of course, appearances can be deceiving. In 1750, less than 300 years ago, few people would have predicted that the monarchs of the world would soon be stripped of their power. Even making such a claim would likely have been considered evidence of insanity!

Indeed, the founders of the United States were ridiculed for ever dreaming that a country could thrive without a king or queen at the helm. Yet, within a few decades, European nations began dethroning their royalty or vastly limiting its power.

The European nations were not *forced* to adopt the American way. On the contrary, they were eager to imitate the United States in the hopes that they too would prosper. In those days, the United States came closest to living the Good Neighbor Policy and became a shining example of what could be. The idealists won the day because they had the more practical philosophy!

If we want to catalyze change, we should simply set an example. Success attracts imitators. We don't need to wait for everyone to see things our way. We can manifest the dream of universal harmony and abundance in our corner of the world and others will follow. We may have created a world of war and poverty, but *because* it is our creation, we have the power to change it.

Reaping What We Sow: What a World of Good Neighbors Would Look Like

Good Neighbors enjoy the twin benefits of prosperity and peace. Wealth creation is likely

I wonder if we in the United States were to concentrate ... on making ourselves the best possible society we can be, whether the nations of the world might once again, without any pressure except the influence of example, begin to emulate us.

—M. Scott Peck
THE DIFFERENT DRUM

to be multiplied 3–18 times. Imagine what you could have if your paycheck tripled! Put this book down for a moment and imagine what you could do if it quadrupled or more!

Most people's lives would change so dramatically that even imagining them is difficult. However, more wealth is only the beginning.

Part of the greater wealth would be better health. "Better" doesn't mean only more of what we have now, but new cures for disease and a better understanding of how to prevent it. Good Neighbors live longer lives.

Indeed, most new wealth consists of discovery of better ways to live and work. For example, instead of simply harvesting the bounty of the sea, we'd learn how to cultivate it, as we do on land. Instead of depleting the resources we have, we'd find ways to use the virtually inexhaustible supply of energy offered by the sun, wind, and atom. Greater wealth allows us to be kind to our environment, rather than simply ravishing it to meet the needs of our immediate survival.

Greater wealth means more leisure to reflect on what we want our life to be and more time to spend with our loved ones. Greater wealth allows us to be generous to others who have less than we do. Good Neighbors have more than enough wealth to share.

The great wealth that Good Neighbors enjoy is a product of honoring our neighbor's choice. In other words, tolerance and respect for others and their property come first and the wealth follows. Peaceful relations promote prosperity, not vice versa.

When we can't force people to our will, we must persuade them to it. Persuasion requires that we understand others' needs and wants so that we can best make our appeal. When we understand others, we are most likely to respond with compassion, and less likely to respond with prejudice.

Becoming Good Neighbors won't make us perfect neighbors. A nonaggressive world won't be a perfect one. However, honoring our neighbor's choice and righting our wrongs is the only path pointed toward perfection. The path of aggression takes us further away.

Clarifying Our Goals

What changes do we need to create a world without first-strike force, theft, or fraud by individuals or governments?

In honoring our neighbor's choice, we say "No!" to licensing laws and regulations that stop voluntary exchange between consumers and suppliers, employers and employees. We encourage deregulation.

Instead of maintaining *centralization* of power through the guns of government, we promote decentralization by honoring the peaceful choice of each individual. Instead of providing services through regulated government monopolies, we keep the marketplace free from aggression so that small businesses can flourish.

We reject the idea of forcibly taking our neighbor's hard-earned wealth as taxes for government-run programs. We choose voluntary, private services, which lower costs and improve quality. We do away with subsidies and encourage private ownership of land and animals to stop special interest groups from exploiting the public domain.

Our refusal to use aggression against our neighbors frees us from special-interest control. Indeed, without aggression-through-government, groups have no power. The international conglomerates thrive on the national regulations that put their small competitors out of business. Without such aggression, consumers are in control because they have alternatives.

We stop aggression before it starts and deter crime through restitution instead of punishment. In doing so, we set the stage for healing both the victim and the attacker.

When we end sovereign immunity, government officials will compensate their victims too. Nothing will reform government as quickly as making government officials personally liable for any damage that they do.

Winning an election or gaining an appointment does not exempt office holders from the universal law of cause and effect. The ends and means are still intimately intertwined. *Our belief that we can create peace and plenty with aggression-through-government has caused most*

... a next major step toward peace is the creation of an image of a future world of peace, an image that is widely credible and is ever-more-widely held.
—Richard Smoke and Willis Harman
PATHS TO PEACE

... the power system continues only as long as individuals try to get something for nothing. The day when a majority of individuals declares or acts as if it wants nothing from government, declares that it will look after its own welfare and interests, then on that day the power elites are doomed.
—Antony Sutton
author of THE BEST ENEMY MONEY CAN BUY

of the war and poverty that we see in the modern world. Without this belief, we would honor our neighbor's choice because to do otherwise would be counterproductive.

We need not choose between our welfare and that of others; both are served by the practice of nonaggression. We need not choose between the individual and the common good; both are served by the Good Neighbor Policy. We needn't choose between the environment and our standard of living; both are balanced when the marketplace ecosystem is free from aggression. *We need not choose between the ideal and the practical because they are simply two sides of the same coin.*

Resisting Temptation

As we begin to promote the Good Neighbor Policy, our resolve will be tested. For example, the serpent might whisper, "Yes, regulations and licensing laws are causing health costs to skyrocket. But until we're able to get rid of them, government needs to help by paying for health care. After all, government caused the problem, so shouldn't government pick up the tab?"

Of course, government can pay for health care only by first taking the wealth that others have created. Trying to solve problems caused by aggression with more aggression is a cure worse than the disease.

In Chapter 6, we learned that our medicines would cost at least 80% less without aggressive regulations. Other health care costs would plummet as well. Until these reforms are made, however, what happens if the aggression of taxation and inflation are used to pay for health care?

As we've learned, subsidies encourage waste. In every country with national health insurance, socialized medicine, or other subsidies, this waste results in rationing and long waiting lists. The cost of this waste is measured in lives.

For example, in Canada, a cardiac patient is 10 times as likely to die waiting (the average is 24–30 months) for surgery as on the operating table. In the United States, there is no wait.[1]

Consequently, thousands of Canadians go south to get immediate treatment—if they can afford it. When a former Quebec premier needed

A January 2000 poll found that 78 percent of Canadians believe that their health care system is "in crisis."

—Pharmaceutical Research and Manufacturers of America
Why Do Prescription Drugs Cost So Much?

a malignant tumor removed from his back, he went to the United States rather than wait his turn.[2] Canadians spend more than $1 billion a year for health care in the United States.[3]

The elderly are often simply turned away. When Canadian Donald Porter, 64, was told he was "too old" for an expensive bone-marrow transplant to fight his lymphatic cancer, he went to the United States, he was treated, and his cancer went into remission.[4] In Canada, your age influences your place in the waiting line and determines if you will get any care at all!

In Britain, people over 75 receive little medical attention. Lifesaving kidney dialysis is denied to those 65 or older at 45% of the treatment centers.[5] Each year, an estimated 9,000 Britons die prematurely when they are refused kidney dialysis; 15,000 die for lack of chemotherapy; 17,000 go without cardiovascular surgery; and more than 7,000 are refused hip replacements.[6]

The poor are neglected as well. In Britain, Canada, Sweden, and New Zealand, people with high social standing receive two to six times more health care than the less affluent.

Government-run health care in the United States has a similar record. The Veterans Health Administration (VHA) offers tax-supported health care to ex-military personnel. More than 90% of those eligible for this "free" care choose private alternatives instead.[7]

Medicare and Medicaid, government programs for elderly and poor Americans respectively, spend 66% more in overhead than private insurance does.[8] Because of such waste, doctors are paid just 59% of what they normally charge. Patients in most states are not allowed to make up the difference,[9] so many physicians refuse to see Medicare and Medicaid patients.

Subsidizing health care means long waiting lines, health care rationing, and premature death. Ultimately, aggression is a death sentence.

Deepening Our Awareness

The health care examples described above show us the importance of learning more about nonaggression so that we can easily identify what will harm us and what will help.

Canada spends less of its GDP on health care not because we have found a way to produce health care at lower unit cost but because we have found a way to limit the total supply of services made available. ... We ration the supply, denying treatment to some and making others wait.

—Michael Walker
executive director of the
Fraser Institute in
Vancouver

Nationalized health is synonymous with delays, waiting lists, rationing, and high taxes.

—Christopher
Lyon, M.D.
former British citizen

Of course, few people see things, including the Good Neighbor Policy, in exactly the same way. Instead, we each bring our own unique viewpoint. Such diversity ensures that we will see all possibilities and be more likely to arrive at the multifaceted diamond that we call "truth."

A number of groups throughout the world are actively promoting nonaggression or the Good Neighbor Policy, although they often don't use these labels. Most identify their viewpoint as "libertarian," from the word "liberty," as in free from aggression-through-government. Libertarians believe that such freedom is the most fundamental of all human rights.

Libertarian organizations have become so numerous that I can mention only a few here. More comprehensive listings can be found on the Web,[10] but new ones start up so often that the directories can't keep up!

Many of these organizations gather real-life examples of the application of the Good Neighbor Policy. Indeed, much of the research cited in this book came from the Cato Institute,[11] Competitive Enterprise Institute,[12] Fraser Institute,[13] Future of Freedom Foundation,[14] Heartland Institute,[15] Independent Institute,[16] Manhattan Institute for Policy Research,[17] National Center for Policy Analysis,[18] Pacific Research Institute for Public Policy,[19] and Reason Foundation.[20] These and other libertarian organizations promote true understanding that the ideal of liberty is the most practical political paradigm of all.

Most of the foundations listed above have a broad focus, but some organizations are issue oriented. For example, PERC, the Political Economy Research Center,[21] details the "New Resource Economics," the term given to the ecological applications of the Good Neighbor Policy. The Alliance for the Separation of School and State is dedicated to taking aggression out of education.[22] FEAR (Forfeiture Endangers American Rights) tries to reform the laws allowing government agents to confiscate a person's property without a trial or even charging him or her with a crime.[23] FIJA, the Fully Informed Jury Association reminds jurors of their time-honored role in judging the law as well as the facts of a case.[24]

In the libertarian view, all human relationships should be voluntary; the only actions that should be forbidden by law are those that involve the initiation of force against those who have not themselves used force—actions like murder, rape, robbery, kidnapping, and fraud. ... Libertarians believe this code should be applied to actions by governments as well as by individuals.
—David Boaz
LIBERTARIANISM: A PRIMER

It's not only a juror's right, but his duty, to find the verdict according to his best understanding, judgment and conscience, though in direct opposition to the direction of the court.

—John Adams
second president of the
United States

The *Journal of Libertarian Studies,* published by the Ludwig von Mises Institute, provides a scholarly format for continued research.[25] In addition to such publications, the institute conducts conferences on the workings of the free market. The Liberty Fund,[26] the Institute for Humane Studies,[27] and the Cato Institute[28] also conduct conferences and seminars on nonaggression and its benefits to society. A number of mail-order bookstores carry books and tapes put out by these organizations as well as others dedicated to the principle of nonaggression.[29]

Michigan's Mackinac Center, in addition to its research activities, briefs high school debate teams across the country on nonaggressive approaches to their annual topic.[30] Another Michigan institution, the privately funded Hillsdale College, is one of the few colleges in the country that takes no tax subsidies.[31]

Overwhelmed by all of these information sources? Check out Advocates for Self-Government.[32] The Advocates offer a variety of tools to promote easy understanding and sharing of libertarian solutions to today's problems. My Web column appears regularly in their complimentary e-zine.

The Advocates Website also boasts the World's Smallest Political Quiz, which helps you place yourself on the political diamond. A major polling firm found that 16% of Americans fall into the libertarian quadrant, although only 2% identified themselves with that label.[33] As a Good Neighbor, you are not alone!

This Portrait of America poll found that 21% of blacks were libertarians, making them much more likely than whites to favor nonaggressive relations. Having experienced aggression-through-government more often than any other racial group in the United States, more of them understand its true nature.

The disadvantaged of other nations often understand that nonaggression is their true savior. As we learned in Chapter 18, the Movimiento Libertario in Costa Rica sent six congressmen to the national assembly by appealing to the people hurt most by licensing laws, taxes, and inflation.

Legalize freedom—vote Libertarian!

    —slogan of the
Libertarian Party, U.S.A.

The country is a one-party country. Half of it is called Republican and half is called Democrat. It doesn't make any difference. All the really good ideas belong to the Libertarians.

    —Hugh Downs
ABC journalist

In the United States, the Libertarian Party challenges our two-party system.[34] Its founder, David Nolan, was recently named one of the "2,000 Outstanding Intellectuals of the Twentieth Century" by the International Biographical Centre in England. Tonie Nathan, the 1972 Libertarian vice presidential nominee, became the first woman to receive a vote from the Electoral College. In 1980, Ed Clark became the first Libertarian presidential candidate to be on the ballot in all 50 states.[35]

More than 500 Libertarians now hold public office.[36] Libertarians have been elected as state representatives, county sheriffs, and city mayors. What do Libertarians do when elected to office? They do away with aggression, especially taxation. The Libertarian mayor of Big Water, Utah, recently slashed property taxes in half and even repealed his own salary![37]

Libertarians reject the idea of taking money forcibly from their neighbors. For example, Libertarian presidential candidate Harry Browne qualified for federal campaign subsidies, called matching funds, in both 1996 and 2000. However, he refused them both times. Mr. Browne didn't want to force taxpayers to pay for his campaign, although he gratefully accepted voluntary donations. Libertarians clearly aren't interested in politics as usual!

Of course, Libertarians haven't waited to get elected to reduce taxes. They have been active in coalitions defeating tax increases throughout the country, repealing the Alaska state income tax, and putting an initiative on the 2002 ballot to repeal the Massachusetts state income tax.[38]

Because Libertarians support the nonaggression principle, special-interest control of our political system would dissolve if they were elected. Consequently, even when Libertarian presidential candidates are better qualified than their opponents, they are routinely excluded from the televised debates.

In the 1992 election, Libertarian presidential candidate Andre Marrou had served as a Libertarian state representative, but independent presidential hopeful Ross Perot had not held office. Nevertheless, millionaire Perot was invited to participate in the televised debates, while Marrou was not. Such resistance will dissolve as more people recognize the win–win rewards of being Good Neighbors.

Ron Paul, who had served as a Republican U.S. congressional representative, was the Libertarian presidential nominee in 1988. In spite of his qualifications, he too was excluded from the televised debates. Afterward, he returned to the U.S. Congress as a Republican, still upholding his libertarian ideals. He is also a member of the Republican Liberty Caucus,[39] which promotes the ideas of nonaggression from within the Republican Party.

Libertarian ideas are spreading throughout the world. The International Society for Individual Liberty (ISIL) networks them and sponsors annual conferences in different countries.[40]

In 1989, 1991, and 1992, Leon Louw and Frances Kendall, two South African ISIL members, were nominated for the Nobel Peace Prize. Their work demonstrated how a decentralized system of government would honor the choices of both white and black South Africans, thereby creating peace in their troubled country.[41] Their book, *South Africa: The Solution*, was also popular in the United States under a different title, *After Apartheid*.[42] When we use licensing laws and regulations in an attempt to stop individual aggressors, we slash our wealth creation. When we substitute restitution for these laws, we will deter individual aggressors more effectively and increase wealth creation once again. Its ideas were widely endorsed by both black and white South Africans, but unfortunately they have not been implemented.

Louw and Kendall found that the Swiss people enjoy one of the highest standards of living in the world because aggression-through-government there is kept in check. The Swiss national government posts are part-time positions. The Swiss pride themselves on their decentralized system in which the cantons (states), not the federal government, are the primary decision makers. Swiss per capita income is one of the highest in the world because nonaggression pays.[43]

How did the Swiss come to adopt a relatively nonaggressive constitution in an aggressive world? In the mid-1800s, they imitated the U.S. Constitution and managed to keep their federal government limited. However, several of my Swiss friends note that the canton governments move continuously toward more aggression. Should this trend continue, Switzerland may lose much of its prosperity.

Choosing Your Path

Clearly, people all over the world are becoming aware of the win–win nature of the Good Neighbor Policy. What still needs to be done to fully manifest a world of universal harmony and abundance?

The answer to this question is different for each of us. One leader, one idea, one strategy will not bring about global changes. Each of us in our uniqueness must apply what we know.

The founders of the Institute for Justice (Chapters 3, 4, and 11) are an example. They saw a need to protect disadvantaged entrepreneurs from aggressive regulations. They met that need by providing pro-bono legal services to fight city hall.

Research scientists Durk Pearson and Sandy Shaw, with the help of other interested individuals and groups, realized that the FDA's aggressive regulations were harming people. They successfully sued the FDA when it prohibited manufacturers from advertising truthful statements about nutritional supplements.[44] When the FDA still blocked such claims, the court reaffirmed its earlier ruling.[45]

Everyone contributes differently to the task. We are all educators, whether we tell others about the Good Neighbor Policy or simply teach by example.

Some activists are trying to set that example on a statewide basis. The Free State Project is gathering Good Neighbors together for a move to one of the less populated states. Once there, they hope to persuade others of the value of non-aggression. They seek to elect Libertarians to roll back aggression-through-government. As the Free State prospers, others will see the value of becoming Good Neighbors themselves and imitate the Free State's success.[46]

In Costa Rica, libertarians are attempting to convert the coastal city of Limón to a port free from the aggression of custom duties. They hope to show how peaceful and prosperous that an enclave of Good Neighbors can be by making Limon's laws much less aggressive than that of the rest of Costa Rica.[47]

Of course, we don't need to be part of a group to implement nonaggressive solutions. Guy Polhemus, founder of We Can and Kimi Gray, organizer of College Here We Come (Chapter 11) simply did what needed to be done. A spectrum of ideas and their implementation are needed to help others recognize that nonaggression is in everybody's best self-interest.

Our world is a joint creation. Each of us has the power to affect those around us profoundly. Each of us has his or her own wisdom to identify the piece of the puzzle that we can fit into the whole. *Never doubt that what you can do, however small it may seem, is crucial.*

Embrace whatever aspect of nonggression seems most appropriate to your unique talents and understanding. Whether you work behind the scenes or in the limelight, rest assured that your input will be felt.

Never doubt what one person can do. Throughout history, individuals such as Jesus Christ, Martin Luther King, Gandhi, and the prophet Muhammad have changed the direction of the world. However, most people who alter history are never remembered. Indeed, such people don't even realize the importance of their own contribution.

My favorite story illustrating this point is about a blacksmith in the Middle Ages, who began to believe that his contribution was unimportant. Discouraged, he no longer paid as much attention to his work and one day forgot to put the final nail in a horse's shoe.

For lack of that nail, the horse lost its shoe and went lame. The rider, who was carrying critical tactical information to the king's army, had to continue on foot. Without the timely arrival of the crucial information that the messenger

> *Do not wait for leaders. Do it alone, person to person.*
>
> —Mother Teresa
> beloved helper of the
> poor

The hottest places in hell are reserved for those who, in times of moral crisis, do nothing.
—Dante
medieval writer

Never doubt that a small group of committed, thoughtful citizens can change the world. Indeed, it's the only thing that ever has.
—Margaret Mead
American
anthropologist

carried, the king was defeated and the land fell to invaders.

The blacksmith, who never knew that his lack of effort had changed the course of history, lost his family when the invaders plundered his village. The blacksmith reaped what he had sown, but he was unaware of the connection. He did not see how war and destruction had come to his village through his own belief that his actions were unimportant.

The tiniest of contributions can ripple out to change the world. Had the blacksmith shod horses as if the kingdom depended on him, he would have saved both his country and his family. He would have been a hero, although no one, not even he, would have ever known.

Each of us plays a critical role in humankind's evolution. Never doubt the importance of your choices or your actions. They, quite literally, are the difference between a world of war and poverty and a world of universal harmony and abundance.

Thank you so much for helping make the world a better place!

Chapter 22: How to Get There from Here

In Summary ...

⚘ Although the world seems to be moving away from the Good Neighbor Policy, appearances can be deceiving. In 1750, no one thought nations could survive without monarchs. During the next two centuries, however, much of Europe began dethroning or disempowered their royalty.

⚘ Europe wanted the prosperity of the United States and so voluntarily imitated it. Catalyzing change can sometimes be as easy as setting an example.

⚘ By ending aggression-through-government, we can create a world of universal harmony and abundance. Nothing will reform government as quickly as making elected and appointed officials personally liable for any damage that they do.

⚘ When we are tempted to use taxation or regulation to temporarily relieve suffering caused by aggression, let us remember the devastating impact—long lines and rationing— that subsidies have on health care. Trying to solve the problems caused by aggression with more aggression is a cure worse than the disease.

⚘ A number of organizations actively promote the Good Neighbor Policy, usually under the label "libertarian," from the word "liberty," as in free from aggression-through-government.

⚘ You can use the research done by these organizations to increase your understanding of the Good Neighbor Policy or become actively involved in its promotion.

⚘ You are the best judge of how your talents can help create a nonaggressive world. No matter how small you think your contribution is, it most likely will have a major impact. Each link in the chain is vital.

⚘ Please accept my gratitude for helping make our world a better place!

Afterword

Martie's Journey

In December of 1991, the first edition of *Healing Our World* was completed. My younger sister, Martie, who served as my moral support and critical evaluator, glowed as she handed the last part of the manuscript back to me. "There's nothing more to change," she assured me. "It's finished."

Martie and I, along with our brothers and sisters, had returned to the family homestead in the Detroit area for Christmas, our first since our mother had died. Although the completion of *Healing* warranted a culinary celebration, Martie was hesitant to indulge in the ethnic foods that we loved. "Nothing spicy," she cautioned me as we planned our gourmet outing. "My stomach has been acting up lately. I probably have an ulcer."

When Martie returned to her home in San Diego after the Christmas holidays, her doctor gave her discouraging news. Martie's upper intestine was partially blocked by a tumor, possibly benign, possibly malignant. Many family members, including our mother, had died of the dread disease. We feared the worst.

"If this is cancer, I'm not going to force myself to suffer," 40-year-old Martie confided in me before the surgery. "I'm just going to call Dr. Kevorkian." With this declaration, Martie plunged us both into a real-life drama of healing and aggression-through-government.

At that time, Dr. Kevorkian had better name recognition than the U.S. president. This Michigan physician helped desperately ill people end their suffering by providing a humane suicide system for them to use.

The doctor made his work public, hoping to end suffering by ending the ban on physician-assisted suicide for the terminally ill. The local authorities dragged the doctor into court on several occasions, believing that people should be stopped—at gunpoint, if necessary—from taking their own lives. Instead of convicting Dr. Kevorkian of murder on these occasions, juries returned "not guilty" verdicts.

While I sat at Martie's bedside in San Diego, thoughts of Dr. Kevorkian were far from my mind. Martie had to wait for her surgery, because very few surgeons could perform the delicate operation that would remove the tumor and leave part of her pancreas. Without her pancreas, Martie would be a diabetic, a complication she wanted to avoid.

During the three-week wait, Martie was hospitalized, because she could no longer eat with the tumor blocking her stomach. She experienced the health care rationing created by the aggression of licensing laws. The overworked staff was not able to adequately attend to all the patients, even though Martie had deliberately chosen one of the premier hospitals in the San Diego area.

Indeed, to get Martie the care she needed, a family member had to be present all day and sometimes for part of the night. The staff was composed of wonderful, warm, and caring people, but they had too many patients under their care. Patients with on-site advocates, usually family members, ended up with more attention and better care. Martie's brothers, sisters, and friends took turns at her side.

The cancerous tumor was removed at surgery, and no evidence of its spread was found in Martie's lymph nodes. The doctor proposed chemotherapy, but Martie was reluctant. According to the doctor, all the tests suggested that the tumor had been caught in time. The chemotherapy regime was tough, and Martie had just undergone a complex surgery that had weakened her considerably. Never very strong, Martie decided that the chemo might do more harm than good and decided to do without it.

This pivotal decision may have been fatal primarily because it was based on faulty information. Martie's physician had not read the medical reports carefully enough. When Martie ordered copies of her tests and received them several weeks later, they clearly showed small growths on her ovaries. The radiologist had indicated that many women had such "cysts," but with Martie's history, he suggested further follow-up.

By the time she read the report, Martie's ovarian "cysts" had grown into grapefruit-size tumors. Had they been removed earlier, perhaps the cancer would not have spread to her abdomen, which was studded with tiny tumors. The operating surgeon who removed Martie's ovaries told me that she had only months to live.

Martie didn't blame her surgeon for this critical oversight, however. She knew that her surgeon, like the hospital staff members, was overworked because licensing laws limited the number of surgeons.

While recovering from her second surgery, Martie received intravenous medication to control her pain. Shortly before I took my dinner break, Martie was resting comfortably. The nurse came in and hung up a new bag of medication. By the time I came back from dinner barely an hour later, Martie was writhing in agony.

The pain control had been so successful in the preceding days that I strongly suspected that the new bag simply didn't have the right amount of medication. The nurses told me that government regulations didn't permit them to increase the prescription painkiller without specific instructions from Martie's physician. Since he was off duty, more than an hour went by before he could be reached, review the situation by phone, and authorize more of the drug.

The nursing staff was clearly competent enough to adjust Martie's dosage and put her at ease without waiting for a doctor to approve such relief. Because Martie had an intravenous catheter, the dosage could have been adjusted rapidly and carefully. As I watched Martie suffering needlessly, I could only fume in frustration at the replacement of common sense by bureaucratic decree.

In spite of her dismal diagnosis, Martie was not yet ready to give up. Before her surgery, she had visited the Gerson Clinic in Mexico. Dr. Max Gerson had combined an intensive fresh vegetable juice diet with coffee enemas, supplemental vitamins, and thyroid stimulation. Dr. Gerson had moved to Mexico because he felt threatened by the Food and Drug Administration and other regulatory bodies. Luckily for Martie, she could afford to go to Mexico for the treatment and instruction on how to continue it at home.

Martie, who had a background in the sciences, felt that Dr. Gerson's treatment was the most promising of nonstandard therapies. In addition, it was gentle enough that it wouldn't compromise the quality of her life. If death was imminent, Martie wanted her last weeks to be as pleasant as possible. Chemotherapy would have been rigorous. Published reports for similar cancers gave us little reason to hope that chemotherapy would provide a cure.

When we came home from the hospital, Martie was able to qualify for hospice care for the terminally ill, even though she was determined to keep fighting. Like all of Martie's health care providers, the hospice group had exceptional individuals on staff. They came directly to my home to assist Martie with her many needs.

Martie wanted to be sure that Dr. Kevorkian was standing by, just in case her therapies didn't work. When the hospice nurses assured her that they would help her in any way they could, Martie asked them to help her locate Dr. Kevorkian. Shocked, they told her that this request was one thing that they would not meet. Assisted suicide was not a politically correct option. As Dr. Kevorkian's experience showed, the state government would consider it murder. (We eventually found that good doctor's number could be had by simply calling directory assistance!)

In the interim, Martie continued the Gerson regime, adding among other things, Essiac tea. The tea is an herbal brew that many people feel has cured their cancers and other health problems. As Martie's cancer spread, she started vomiting up her meals. Essiac tea settled her stomach and allowed her to eat again, even when medication was ineffective.

As the cancer progressed, however, the nausea got increasingly worse. We continually juggled her medication, meals, and Essiac tea times to keep her from starving. Finally, we reached a point where we were running out of options: Martie vomited almost anything she ate or drank.

We knew that marijuana might be able to help. When our mother had suffered from chemotherapy-induced nausea, she had refused to even consider marijuana, for fear that her house and savings would be seized by the government and our father, just retired, would be left penniless. "I'd rather suffer than see that happen," she confided in us.

Martie was also concerned that my home and savings might be taken if she was found to be smoking marijuana, even for medicinal purposes. My job might also be in jeopardy because, as a research scientist, I handled controlled substances, such as opiates. Therefore, we went to Martie's physician in the hope of getting a prescription for Marinol, the registered trade name under which the active ingredient of marijuana is sold.

Marinol has many drawbacks. It is expensive, especially for chronic users. It must be taken orally, so the amount absorbed depends on the condition of a person's gastrointestinal health. Because Martie's cancer had spread to her intestines, she would have difficulty absorbing Marinol, making it difficult to give her the proper dose. Finally, a patient is likely to throw up the pills before they can be digested and absorbed. In spite of these drawbacks, however, we decided to try to obtain the only available legal option.

Martie's doctor immediately denied our request and offered Martie another surgery to put a drainage tube in her stomach instead. My feeling, as I watched his face, was that he feared the paperwork and possible professional repercussions that might occur from such a politically incorrect prescription. Such fears would not have been unfounded in the climate of the times.

Martie decided not to have an additional surgery, but to call Dr. Kevorkian. We had made contact earlier and had forwarded Martie's medical record to him. He was selective in the people that he agreed to help. After several conversations, perhaps moved by Martie's heartfelt pleas, the doctor promised to assist her late one evening.

After the call, Martie wanted to go back to bed. "I'm feeling pretty good," she assured me when I offered her more pain medication. "I don't think I need any more tonight." When we climbed into my king-sized water bed, I fully expected that we would awake every few hours, as we usually did, for pain medication, a small meal, or a soak in the tub, which often brought Martie some relief.

To my surprise, Martie slept through the night. When we awoke, Martie started ripping off her pain patches. "I'm overmedicated," she explained. "And I'm hungry!" Martie ate a small meal without any adverse reactions. As long as she kept the meals small, she was able to eat again. Her change was nothing short of miraculous.

I called Dr. Kevorkian and asked if he had seen this before. He claimed it was quite common. When he agreed to help people, they lost their fear that their death would be prolonged and agonizing. They were able to relax and sometimes died quietly in their sleep.

Clearly, making assisted suicide illegal put people into a state of fear so intense that it interfered with health and healing. For a person who teetered on the edge of healing or succumbing to their disease, this added fear and the stress associated with it could make the difference between life and death. Laws intended to save people from themselves created conditions that probably caused many more to die from their diseases.

Martie's cancer eventually reasserted itself. When she could no longer hold down even water, Martie asked Dr. Kevorkian to help end her suffering. He provided a carbon monoxide gas cylinder attached to a face mask by a tube. Surrounded by friends and family, Martie removed the clip on the tube, breathed a mixture of air and carbon monoxide, and fell quietly into her final sleep.

Martie's early death saved other lives. During the last few weeks of life, most of us use between 70% and 90% of the medical resources that we will consume in our lifetimes. When we honor the choice of those who wish to avoid these final weeks, we free up a great deal of rationed medical resources. Doctors and other health care providers have more time to spend with people who might otherwise die from a dangerous oversight. When we honor our neighbor's choice to take their own lives, we likely save many more. Conversely, forcing people to live, when they would rather not, consumes medical care that must then be denied to those whose life may depend on it. For those individuals, laws against assisted suicide are a death sentence.

I never intended to talk to anyone about my sister's death. However, when I returned home from Martie's deathbed, reporters had already begun calling.

"The families of the people Dr. Kevorkian helps never talk to us," one woman reporter explained. "That's why we never have anything good to say about him."

I could almost hear Martie's voice saying "Well, Mary, I can't talk anymore, but you can. Tell the world that Dr. Kevorkian was my angel, sent to me in my hour of need."

As I have fulfilled Martie's request over the years, it has healed the sorrow of her passing. Martie and I are partners still, even though we are separated by death's veil.

I have also come to realize, in telling Martie's story, that honoring our neighbor's choice in the realm of life and death is an issue of religious freedom. Martie believed that Dr. Kevorkian was sent to her by the Loving Principle of the Universe to relieve her suffering. Some people believe he is an instrument of Evil.

Many wars have been fought over such divergent beliefs. During the Spanish Inquisition, people were tortured—presumably for the good of their soul. Today, many of our beloved, denied assisted suicide, are forced to die in unbearable agony—presumably for the good of their soul. The Diety may have granted us free will but we aren't yet ready to grant it to each other.

Clearly, what we believe and how we live our lives—or choose to end them—are questions of religious freedom. If we fail to honor our neighbor's peaceful choices, they will not honor ours either. Religious wars will become commonplace once more.

Indeed, the war on assisted suicide eventually took Dr. Kevorkian prisoner. He was convicted of second-degree murder for aiding Thomas Youk, who suffered from Lou Gehrig's disease. He is serving 10–25 years in a Michigan prison, a virtual life sentence for the physician, who was 70 years old when he was convicted in March 1999.

Most likely, a child molester or rapist will serve a shorter sentence so that the Dr. Kevorkian can be kept behind bars. The man who relieves suffering is imprisoned, while the one who causes suffering is released to strike again.

Such suffering needn't continue, however. We've learned the secret of ending war and poverty, not just in theory, but in practice. Perhaps our world will never be perfect, but it can be made a great deal better. Universal harmony and abundance, for example, are easily within our grasp. Even in an age of aggression, we can heal our world!

About the Author

Mary J. Ruwart received her B.S. in biochemistry (1970) and Ph.D. in biophysics (1974) from Michigan State University. She left her position as Assistant Professor of Surgery at St. Louis University Medical School to join the Upjohn Co., where she was a senior research scientist for the next 19 years. Currently, Dr. Ruwart holds an adjunct faculty position at the Union Institute, Cincinnati, Ohio, and teaches communications courses to research scientists throughout the country.

An influential member of her local community, Dr. Ruwart has worked extensively with the disadvantaged through rehabilitation of low-income housing. She has been a member of the Kalamazoo Rain Forest Action Committee, served on the board of directors for the Heartland Institute's Michigan chapter, and been a member of the Libertarian Party National Committee. Currently, Dr. Ruwart serves on the board of directors for the Fully Informed Jury Association and the International Society for Individual Liberty. Her scientific, political, and community activities have been profiled in several prestigious biographical works, including *American Men and Women of Science, World's Who's Who of Women, International Leaders in Achievement,* and *Community Leaders of America.*

Chapter 1: Good Neighbor Policy

1. S. Milgram, *Obedience to Authority* (New York: Harper & Row, 1974), pp. 99–144.
2. Ibid., pp. 33–36.
3. Ibid., pp. 44–54, 73–88.
4. Ibid., pp. 27–31.

Chapter 2: Wealth Is Unlimited!

1. World Bank, *Attacking Poverty: World Development Report 2000/2001* (New York: Oxford University Press, 2001), p. 45.
2. T. Sowell, *The Economics and Politics of Race: An International Perspective* (New York: William Morrow, 1983), p. 214.
3. T.R. Dye and H. Zeigler, "Socialism and Equality in Cross-National Perspective," *Political Science and Politics* 21: 45–56, 1988; J.L. Cordeiro, *The Great Taboo: A True Nationalization of the Venezuelan Petroleum* (Caracas, Venezuela: Cedice, 1998), pp. 43–46.
4. For GDP/capita, see J. Gwartney and R. Lawson, *Economic Freedom of the World 1997* (Vancouver, BC: Fraser Institute, 1997), pp. 75, 109, 115, and 165. For population data see <http://www.overpopulation.com/faq/asic_information/population_density/asia.html>, accessed on June 11, 2002.
5. Colin Clark, *Population Growth: The Advantages* (Santa Ana, CA: R.L. Sassone, 1972), p. 84.
6. Michael Novak, *Will It Liberate? Questions About Liberation Theology* (New York: Paulist Press, 1986), p. 89.
7. Gwartney and Lawson, cf. p. 109 (Hong Kong) with p. 195 (United States).
8. A. Rabushka, *From Adam Smith to the Wealth of America* (New Brunswick, NJ: Transaction Books, 1985), p. 127.
9. Gwartney and Lawson, p. 27.
10. Ibid., p. 34.
11. V. Thomas, M. Dailami, A. Dhareshwar, et al., *The Quality of Growth* (New York: Oxford University Press, 2000), pp. 3–4; H. Li, L. Squire, and H. Zou, "Explaining International and Intertemporal Variations in Income Inequality," *The Economic Journal* 108: 26–43, 1998; A. Alesina and D. Rodrik, "Distributive Politics and Economic Growth," *Quarterly Journal of Economics* 109: 465–490, 1994; G.W. Scully, *Constitutional Environments and Economic Growth* (Princeton, NJ: Princeton University Press, 1992), pp. 196–197.
12. W.M. Cox and R. Alm, *Myths of Rich and Poor: Why We're Better Off Than We Think* (New York: Basic Books, 1999), pp. 69–78.

Chapter 3: Destroying Jobs

1. For a detailed description of the marketplace as an ecosystem, see M. Rothschild, *Bionomics: Economy As Ecosystem* (New York: Henry Holt, 1992).
2. M. Reynolds cited in D. Eric Schansberg, *Poor Policy: How Government Harms the Poor* (Boulder: Westview Press, 1996), p. 62; A.C. Freeman and R.B. Freeman, "Minimum Wages in Puerto Rico: Textbook Case of a Wage Floor?" *NBER Working Paper No. W3759* (Cambridge, MA: National Bureau of Economic Research, 1991).
3. P.H. Douglas and J. Hackman, "Fair Labor Standards Act of 1938. II," *Political Science Quarterly* 54: 29–55, 1939.
4. R. Vedder and L. Gallaway, "Should the Federal Minimum Wage Be Increased?" *NCPA Policy Report No. 190* (Dallas: National Center for Policy Analysis, 1995).
5. K.B. Leffler, "Minimum Wages, Welfare, and Wealth Transfers to the Poor," *Journal of Law and Economics* 21: 345–358, 1978.
6. G. Stigler, "The Economics of Minimum Wage Legislation," *American Economic Review* 36: 358–365, 1946; J.M. Peterson, "Employment Effects of Minimum Wages, 1938–50," *Journal of Political Economy* 65: 412–430, 1957; H.M. Douty, "Some Effects of the $1.00 Minimum Wage in the United States," *Economica* 27: 137–147, 1960; M. Colberg, "Minimum Wage Effects on Florida's Economic Development," *Journal of Law and Economics* 3: 106–117, 1960; Y. Brozen, "The Effect of Statutory Minimum Wage Increases on Teen-age Employment," *Journal of Law and Economics* 12: 109–122, 1969; T.G. Moore, "The Effect of Minimum Wages on Teenage Unemployment Rates," *Journal of Political Economy* 79: 897–902, 1971; M. Kosters and F. Welch, "The Effects of Minimum Wages on the Distribution of Changes in Aggregate Employment," *American Economic Review* 62: 323–332, 1972; D. Adie, "Teen-Age Unemployment and Real Federal Minimum Wages," *Journal of Political Economy* 81: 435–441, 1973; F. Welch, "Minimum Wage Legislation in the United States," *Economic Inquiry* 12: 285–318, 1974; H.F. Gallasch Jr., "Minimum Wages and the Farm Labor Market," *Southern Economic Journal* 41: 480–490, 1975; J. Mincer, "Unemployment Effects of Minimum Wages," *Journal of Political Economy* 84: S87–S104, 1976; E.M. Gramlich, "Impact of Minimum Wages on Other Wages, Employment, and Family Incomes," *Brookings Papers on Economic Activity* 2: 409–461, 1976; J.F. Ragan, "Minimum Wages and the Youth Labor Market," *Review of Economics and Statistics* 59: 129–136, 1977; F. Welch and J. Cunningham, "Effects of Minimum Wages on the Level and Age Composition of Youth Employment," *Review of Economics and Statistics* 60: 140–145, 1978; P. Linneman, "The Economic

Impacts of Minimum Wage Laws: A New Look at an Old Question," *Journal of Political Economy* 90: 443–469, 1982; D.S. Hammermesh, "Minimum Wages and the Demand for Labor," *Economic Inquiry* 20: 365–380, 1982; R.H. Meyer and D.A. Wise, "The Effects of the Minimum Wage on the Employment and Earnings of Youth," *Journal of Labor Economics* 1: 66–100, 1983; R.H. Meyer and D.A. Wise, "Discontinuous Distributions and Missing Persons: Minimum Wage and Unemployed Youth," *Econometrica* 51: 1677–1698, 1983; J.C. Cox and R.L. Oaxaca, "Minimum Wage Effects with Output Stabilization," *Economic Inquiry* 24: 443–453, 1986; D. Neumark and W. Wascher, "Employment Effects of Minimum and Subminimum Wages: Panel Data on State Minimum Wage Laws," *Industrial and Labor Relations Review* 46: 55–81, 1992; D. Deere, K. Murphy, and F. Welch, "Employment and the 1990–1991 Minimum Wage Hike," *American Economic Review* 85: 232–237, 1995.

7. D.R. Deere, "Don't Raise the Minimum Wage—The Bar Is Already Too High," *NCPA Policy Report No. 270* (Dallas: National Center for Policy Analysis, 1998).

8. M.D. Turner, "Does the Minimum Wage Help or Hurt Low-Wage Workers?" in *The Low-Wage Labor Market: Challenges and Opportunities for Economic Self-Sufficiency* (Washington, DC: Urban Institute, 1999).

9. Vedder and Gallaway, 1995, op. cit.

10. W. Williams, *The State Against Blacks* (New York: New Press, McGraw-Hill, 1982), pp. 43–44.

11. R.K. Vedder and L.E. Gallaway, *Out of Work: Unemployment and Government in Twentieth-Century America* (New York: New York University Press, 1997), p. 294.

12. D. Neumark, "Effects of Minimum Wages on Teenage Employment, Enrollment and Idleness," Employment Policies Institute, August 1995, <http://www.epionline.org/study_neumark_08-1995.html>, accessed January 5, 2002.

13. R.E. Smith and B. Vavrichek, "The Wage Mobility of Minimum Wage Workers," *Industrial Relations and Labor Review*, 46: 82–88, 1992; W. Even and D. Macpherson, "Rising Above the Minimum Wage," Employment Policies Institute, January 2000, <http://www.epionline.org/study_even-macpherson_01-2000.html>, January 15, 2002.

14. B. Wildavsky, "McJobs," *Policy Review*, Summer 1989: 30–37.

15. D. Neumark and W. Wascher, "Do Minimum Wages Fight Poverty?" *NBER Working Paper No. W6127* (Cambridge, MA: National Bureau of Economic Research, 1997).

16. R.K. Vedder and L.E. Gallaway, "Does the Minimum Wage Reduce Poverty?" Employment Policies Institute, June 2001, <http://www.epionline.org/study_vedder_06-2001.html>, accessed January 15, 2001.

17. W.M. Cox and R. Alm, *Myths of Rich and Poor: Why We're Better Off Than We Think* (New York: Basic Books), pp. 73–74.

18. U.S. Bureau of the Census, "Poverty in the United States: 1999," *Current Population Reports Series P-60, No. 210* (Washington, DC: Government Printing Office, 2000), p. 15.

19. J.E. Stiglitz, *Economics* (New York: W.W. Norton, 1993), pp. 130–133.

20. D. Bernstein, "The Davis-Bacon Act: Let's Bring Jim Crow to an End," *Cato Institute Briefing Paper No. 17* (Washington, DC: Cato Institute, 1993), p. 3.

21. S. Bullock and J. Frantz, "Removing Barriers to Opportunity: A Constitutional Challenge to the Davis-Bacon Act," Litigation Backgrounder for *Brazier Construction Co., et al. v. Robert Reich, et al.*, No. 93-2318 (D.D.C.), <http://www.ij.org/cases/economic/davisbk.shtml>, accessed April 21, 2002.

22. Nona M. Brazier, "Stop Law That Hurts My Minority Business," *Wall Street Journal*, January 12, 1994.

23. J. Bernstein and E. Houston, *Crime and Work: What We Can Learn from the Low-Wage Labor Market* (Washington, DC: Economic Policy Institute, 2000).

24. C. Bolick, *Transformation: The Promise and Politics of Empowerment* (Oakland, CA: Institute for Contemporary Studies, 1998), p. 88.

25. Ibid., p. 84.

26. D. Neumark and S. Adams, "Do Living Wage Ordinances Reduce Urban Poverty?" *NBER Working Paper No. W7606* (Cambridge, MA: National Bureau of Economic Research, 2000).

27. J. Serwach and R. Ankeny, "Salvation Army May Ax Contracts over Wage Law," *Crain's Detroit Business*, March 20, 2000.

28. *Association of Community Organizations for Reform Now vs. State of California, Department of Industrial Relations, Division of Labor Standards Enforcement*, Case No. AO 69744, Appellant's Opening Brief, in the Court of Appeal of California, First Appellate District, Division Five, August 1995, p. 10.

29. *Living Wage Policy: The Basics* (Washington, DC: Employment Policies Institute, 2000), p. 18.

30. Bullock and Frantz, op.cit.

31. U.S. Bureau of the Census, Statistical Abstract of the United States (Washington, DC: U.S. Government Printing Office, 2000), p. 439.

32. G. Robbins and A. Robbins, "Capital, Taxes, and Growth," *NCPA Policy Report No. 169* (Dallas: National Center for Policy Analysis, 1992), p. 7.

33. T. Sowell, *The Economics and Politics of Race: An International Perspective* (New York: William Morrow, 1983), pp. 174–175.

Chapter 4: Eliminating Small Businesses

1. W. Williams, *The State Against Blacks* (New York: New Press, McGraw-Hill, 1982), pp. 92–94.
2. Ibid., pp. 90–97.
3. C. Bolick, *Transformation: The Promise and Politics of Empowerment* (Oakland, CA: Institute for Contemporary Studies, 1998), p. 77.
4. Williams, p. 78.
5. C. Vidich, *The New York Cab Driver and His Fare* (Cambridge, MA: Schenkman, 1976), p. 146.
6. Williams, p. 82.
7. Ibid., p. 84.
8. Ibid., p. 81 (175 independent operators in Philadelphia); p. 86 (14 black owners). 14/175 = 0.08 = 8%.
9. "Monique in Tangles," *Wall Street Journal*, June 18, 1993.
10. D.G. Matias, "Judge Upbraids State Board of Barbering and Cosmetology: IJ Licks in Victory in First Round," *Liberty & Law*, June 1997, p. 5.
11. G.F. Will, "Can't Get the Government Out of Their Hair," *Washington Post*, August 3, 1997.
12. W.H. Mellor, "No Jobs, No Work," *New York Times*, August 31, 1996.
13. J. Kramer, "African Hairbraiders Seek to Untangle Regulations," *Institute for Justice Press Release*, November 16, 1998.
14. "Get Out of Her Hair," *Wall Street Journal*, September 4, 1998.
15. "Polishing Off the Homeless," *The Liberator*, Summer 1991, p. 2.
16. V. Postrel, "Who's Behind the Child Care Crisis?" *Reason*, June 1989, pp. 20–27.
17. J. Hood and J. Merline, "What You Should Know About Day Care," *Consumers' Research*, August 1990, p. 25.
18. W.H. Mellor, "Relax the Rules," *New York Times*, April 17, 1998.
19. Hood and Merline, p. 23.
20. Ibid., p. 26.
21. H. Baetjer, "Beauty and the Beast," *Reason*, December 1988, pp. 28–31.
22. J.H. Pratt, "Legal Barriers to Home-Based Work," *NCPA Policy Report No. 129* (Dallas: National Center for Policy Analysis, 1987), p. 31.
23. Ibid., p. 32.
24. Ibid., pp. 29–30.
25. L. Schweikart, *The Entrepreneurial Adventure: A History of Business in the United States* (New York: Harcourt College Publishers, 2000), p. 435.
26. C. Frenze, E. Gillespie, and N. Morgan, *Income Mobility and Economic Opportunity, 2nd ed.* (Washington, DC: U.S. Joint Economic Committee Republican Staff, 1995) as cited in "Moving On Up," *Executive Alert*, November/December 1995, p. 4.
27. B. Bartlett, "Wealth, Mobility, Inheritance and the Estate Tax," *NCPA Policy Report No. 235* (Dallas: National Center for Policy Analysis, 2000), p. 1.
28. V. Whitescarver, "TWM's 'Million Dollar Mission,'" *Tax Wise Money*, July 1998, p. 5.
29. H. de Soto, *The Other Path: The Invisible Revolution in the Third World* (New York: Harper & Row, 1989), pp. 134, 144–148.
30. J. Stossel, "Is America Number One?" *ABC News Special*, September 1, 2000.
31. H.G. Grubel, "Economic Freedom and Human Welfare: Some Empirical Findings," *Cato Journal* 18: 287—304, 1998.
32. T.R. Dye and H. Zeigler, "Socialism and Equality in Cross-National Perspective," *Political Science and Politics* 21: 45–58, 1988.
33. Williams, pp. 68–69; Pratt, pp. 1, 22, 34; S. Rottenberg, "The Economics of Occupational Licensing," in *Discrimination, Affirmative Action, and Equal Opportunity*, W.E. Block and M.A. Walker, eds. (Vancouver, BC: Fraser Institute, 1982), p. 4.
34. E. Bierhanzl and J. Gwartney, "Regulation, Unions, and Labor Markets: In OECD Countries, Higher Unionization Equals Higher Unemployment," *Regulation* 21: 40–53, 1998.
35. W.M. Cox and R. Alm, *Myths of Rich & Poor: Why We're Better Off Than We Think* (New York: Basic Books, 1999), p. 115.
36. "Small Business," *Executive Alert*, September/October, 1994, p. 2.
37. C. Oliver, "How Cities Keep the Poor Down: Red Tape Often Thwarts Their Efforts in Business," *Investor's Business Daily*, September 18, 1996.
38. Schweikart, p. 520.

Chapter 5: Harming Our Health

1. S.L. Carroll and R.J. Gaston, "Occupational Restrictions and the Quality of Service Received: Some Evidence," *Southern Economic Journal* 47: 959–976, 1981.
2. Ibid.
3. R. Hamoway, "The Early Development of Medical Licensing Laws in the United States, 1875–1900," *Journal of Libertarian Studies* 3: 73–75, 1979.
4. Ibid., p. 98.
5. E. Rayack, *Professional Power and American Medicine: The Economics of the American Medical Association* (Cleveland, OH: World Publishing, 1967), pp. 66–70.
6. Ibid., p. 79.
7. Hamoway, p. 103.
8. P. Starr, *The Social Transformation of American Medicine* (New York: Basic Books), pp. 391–392.
9. Rayack, p. 71.
10. Ibid., pp. 124–125.
11. Rayack, p. 71.
12. M.S. Blumberg, *Trends and Projections of Physicians in the United States 1967–2002* (Berkeley, CA: Carnegie Commission on Higher Education, 1971), p. 9.

13. *The World Almanac and Book of Facts 1991* (New York: World Almanac, 1991), p. 836.
14. Bill No. AB3203, introduced by Assembly Member J. Speier, February 26, 1990, State of California.
15. "New Action by Council on Medical Education and Hospitals," *Journal of the American Medical Association* 105: 1123, 1935.
16. Rayack, p. 6.
17. Ibid., pp. 7–10; J.C. Goodman, *The Regulation of Medical Care: Is the Price too High?* (San Francisco: Cato Institute, 1980), pp. 65–67.
18. Starr, p. 333.
19. *Wilk et al. v. American Medical Association et al.*, 76C3777, U.S. District Court, Northern District of Illinois, Eastern Division.
20. Ibid., pp. 36–37.
21. Ibid., pp. 155–158.
22. S.D. Young, *The Rule of Experts* (Washington DC: Cato Institute, 1987), p. 13.
23. Rayack, p. 113.
24. C.S. Lieber, L.M. DeCarli, and E. Rubin, "Sequential Production of Fatty Liver, Hepatitis and Cirrhosis in Sub-human Primates Fed Ethanol with Adequate Diets," *Proceedings of the National Academy of Sciences* 72: 437–441, 1975.
25. C.S. Lieber, L.M. DeCarli, K.M. Mak, C.I. Kim, and M.A. Leo, "Attentuation of Alcohol-Induced Hepatic Fibrosis by Polyunsaturated Lecithin," *Hepatology* 12: 1390–1398, 1990.
26. B. Barzansky, Division of Undergraduale Medical Education of the American Medical Association, personal communication, March 2, 1990.
27. K.G. Losonczy, T.B. Harris, and R.J. Havlik, "Vitamin E and Vitamin C Supplement Use and Risk of All-Cause and Coronary Heart Disease Mortality in Older Persons: The Established Populations for Epidemiologic Studies of the Elderly," *American Journal of Clinical Nutrition* 64: 190–196, 1996.
28. S. Liu, W.C. Willet, M.J. Stampfer, et al., "A Prospective Study of Dietary Glycemic Load, Carbohydrate Intake, and Risk of Coronary Heart Disease in U.S. Women," *American Journal of Clinical Nutrition* 71: 1455–1461, 2000. For comparison with the USDA Food Pyramid, see Dr. B. Sears's comments at <http://drsears.com/site/Tools/Research/ResearchHome.nsf/9f94524929694527852566cc0076418f/dca95cbfaf6ce88b85256905006ad2d0?OpenDocument>, accessed February 14, 2002.
29. J.E. Enstrom, L.E. Kanim, and M.A. Klein, "Vitamin C Intake and Mortality Among a Sample of the United States Population," *Epidemiology* 3930: 189–191, 1992.
30. E. Cameron and L. Pauling, *Cancer and Vitamin C* (Menlo Park, CA: Linus Pauling Institute of Science and Medicine, 1979), pp. 133–134.
31. T. Kealey, *The Economic Laws of Scientific Research* (New York: St. Martin's Press, 1996), p. 216.
32. Ibid., p. 159.
33. Office of Technology Assessment, *Addressing the Efficacy and Safety of Medical Technologies* (Washington, DC: Congress of the United States, 1978), p. 7.
34. M.B. Mock, "Lessons Learned from Randomized Trials of Coronary Bypass Surgery: Viewpoint of the Cardiologist," *Cardiology* 73: 196–203, 1986.
35. L. Tabachnik, "Licensing in the Legal and Medical Professions, 1820–1860: A Historical Case Study," in *Profession for the People: The Politics of Skill*, J. Gerstl and G. Jacobs, eds. (New York: Halsted Press, John Wiley, 1976), pp. 25–42.
36. H.S. Cohen, "Regulatory Politics and American Medicine," *American Behavioral Scientist* 19: 122–136, 1975.
37. Rayack, pp. 72–78; S. Reverby and D. Rosner, *Health Care in America* (Philadelphia: Temple University Press, 1979), pp. 188–200.
38. A. Maurizi, "Occupational Licensing and the Public Interest," *Journal of Political Economy* 82: 399–413, 1974.
39. Goodman, pp. 22–25.
40. Ibid., p. 36.
41. Ibid., p. 42.
42. Starr, pp. 124–125.
43. Goodman, pp. 30–31.
44. S.A. Blevins, "The Medical Monopoly: Protecting Consumers or Limiting Competition?" *Cato Policy Analysis No. 246* (Washington, DC: Cato Institute, 1995), p. 8.
45. Starr, p. 117; Reverby and Rosner, p. 194.
46. N.D. Campbell, "Replace FDA Regulation of Medical Devices with Third-Party Certification," *Cato Policy Analysis No. 288* (Washington, DC: Cato Institute, 1997), p. 7.
47. Ibid., p. 11.
48. Carroll and Gaston, op. cit.
49. P.B. Ginsburg and E. Moy, "Physician Licensure and the Quality of Care," *Regulation* 15: 32–39., 1992. See especially p. 35.
50. M. Haug, "The Sociological Approach to Self-Regulation," in *Regulating the Professions*, R.D. Blair and S. Rubin, eds., (Lexington, MA: Lexington Books, 1980), pp. 61–80.
51. G. Charles, D.H. Stimson, M.D. Maurier, and J.C. Good Jr., "Physician's Assistants and Clinical Algorithms in Health Care Delivery: A Case Study," *Annals of Internal Medicine* 81: 733–739, 1974; J.W. Runyan Jr., "The Memphis Chronic Disease Program: Comparisons in Outcome and the Nurse's Extended Role," *Journal of the American Medical Association* 231: 264–267, 1975; A.L. Komaroff, W.L. Black, Margaret Flatley, R.H. Knopp, B. Reiffen, and H. Sherman, "Protocols for

Physician Assistants: Management of Diabetes and Hypertension," *New England Journal of Medicine* 290: 307–312, 1974; M.O. Mundinger, R.L. Kane, and E.R. Lentz, "Primary Care Outcomes in Patients Treated by Nurse Practitioners," *Journal of the American Medical Association* 283: 59–68, 2000.

52. L. Pearson, "How Each State Stands on Legislative Issues Affecting Advanced Nursing Practices," *The Nurse Practitioner* 26: 7–16, 2001.

53. E. Charney and H. Kitzman, "The Child-Health Nurse (Pediatric Nurse Practitioner) in Private Practice," *New England Journal of Medicine* 285: 1353–1358, 1971; W.O. Spitzer, D.L. Sackett, J.C. Sibley, R.S. Roberts, M. Gent, D.J. Kergin, B.C. Hackett, and A. Olynich, "The Burlington Randomized Trial of the Nurse Practitioner," *New England Journal of Medicine* 290: 251–256, 1974.

54. *The World Almanac and Book of Facts 1991*, p. 836.

Chapter 6: Protecting Ourselves to Death

1. Personal communication with James Navarro; L. Green, "Six-Year-Old Thomas Navarro Dies," November 2001, CBN.com, <http://www.cbn.com/cbnnews%2Fnews%2Fthomas%5Fnavarro%5Fobit%2Easp>; P. Strand, "Capitol Hill Weighs Future of Cancer Patients," CBN.com, <http://www.christianity.com/CC/article/1,1183,PTID 2546%7cCHID%7cCIID133908,00.html>; J. Navarro, "Thomas Navarro: Still Fighting for Life," CBN.com, <http://www.christianity.com/CC /article1,1183,PTID 2546%7cCHID%7cCIID237300,00.html>, all accessed March 10, 2002.

2. CNN.com, "Battle over AIDS Drug in S. Africa," November 27, 2001, <http://www.cnn.com/2001/WORLD/africa/11/27/aids.drug>, accessed on January 15, 2002; D. Kraft, "Court Battle Begins over Drug Access," *Associated Press*, <http://ww2.aegis.org/news/ap/2001/AP011129.html>, accessed on January 15, 2002; C. Rickard, "State Routed in Constitutional Court's Nevirapine Judgment," *Sunday Times*, July 7, 2002, <http://www.suntimes.co za/business/legal/2002/07/08/carmel101.asp>, accessed October 4, 2002.

3. S. Sternberg, "Bottleneck Keeps Existing Vaccine off the Market," *Science* 266: 22–23, 1994.

4. S.D. Young, *The Rule of Experts* (Washington, DC: Cato Institute, 1987), p. 16.

5. H.F. Dowling, "The American Medical Association's Policy on Drugs in Recent Decades," in *Safeguarding the Public: Historical Aspects of Medicinal Drug Control*, J.B. Blake, ed. (Baltimore: Johns Hopkins University Press, 1968), p. 124; W.M. Wardell and L. Lasagna,

Regulation and Drug Development (Washington, DC: American Enterprise Institute for Public Policy Research, 1975), p. 13.

6. C.O. Jackson, *Food and Drug Legislation in the New Deal* (Princeton, NJ: Princeton University Press, 1970), p. 20; Dowling, pp. 123–124; J.G. Burrow, "The Prescription Drug Policies of the American Medical Association in the Progressive Era," in Blake, pp. 113–115; Glenn Sonnedecker, "Contribution of the Pharmaceutical Profession Toward Controlling the Quality of Drugs in the Nineteenth Century," in Blake, pp. 105–106.

7. Jackson, pp. 17–22.

8. S. Wilson, *Food and Drug Regulation* (Washington, DC: American Council on Public Affairs, 1942), p. 22–23.

9. Ibid., p. 27.

10. E.C. Lambert, *Modern Medical Mistakes* (Bloomington, IN: Indiana University Press, 1978), pp. 70–72.

11. Ibid., pp. 78–80.

12. Ibid., pp. 73–75; Wilson, p. 102.

13. D.L. Weimer, "Safe and Available Drugs," in *Instead of Regulation*, Robert W. Poole Jr., ed. (Lexington, MA: Lexington Books, 1982), p. 243.

14. *Journal of the American Medical Association* 109: 1531, 1937.

15. Weimer, pp. 243–244.

16. J.L. Schardein, *Drugs as Tetrogens* (Cleveland, OH: CRC Press, 1976), p. 5.

17. L. Meyler, ed., *Side Effects of Drugs* (New York: Elsevier, 1966), Vol. V, pp. 43–44.

18. S. Kazman, "The FDA's Deadly Approval Process," *Consumers' Research*, April 1991, p. 31.

19. Weimer, pp. 245–246.

20. S. Peltzman, *Regulation of Pharmaceutical Innovation* (Washington, DC: American Enterprise Institute for Public Policy Research, 1974), pp. 44–45.

21. Ibid., pp. 13–18; Wardell and Lasagna, pp. 57–59.

22. Arthur D. Little, Inc., *Cost-Effectiveness of Pharmaceuticals #7: Beta-Blocker Reduction of Mortality and Reinfarction Rate in Survivors of Myocardial Infarction: A Cost-Benefit Study* (Washington, DC: Pharmaceutical Manufacturers Association, 1984), p. I.

23. L. Lasagna, "Congress, the FDA, and New Drug Development: Before and After 1962," *Perspectives in Biology and Medicine* 32: 322–343, 1989; W.M. Wardell, "Rx: More Regulation or Better Therapies?" *Regulation* 3: 30, 1979.

24. H.I. Miller, *To America's Health: A Proposal to Reform the Food and Drug Administration* (Stanford, CA: Hoover Institution Press, 2000), pp. 41–42.

25. J.J. Pierce, "Dangerous Excesses: A Look at the Food and Drug Administration," *Issue Analysis No. 13*, Citizens for a Sound Economy Foundation, November 9, 1995.

26. Competitive Enterprise Institute, "A National Survey of Oncologists Regarding

the Food and Drug Administration"
(Washington, DC: Competitive Enter-
prise Institute, 1995); "A National Survey
of Cardiologists Regarding the Food and
Drug Administration" (Washington, DC:
Competitive Enterprise Institute, 1996);
"A National Survey of Neurologists and
Neurosurgeons Regarding the Food and
Drug Administration" (Washington, DC:
Competitive Enterprise Institute, 1998).
27. F. Andersson, "The Drug Lag Issue: The
Debate Seen from an International Per-
spective." *International Journal of Health
Science* 22: 53–72, 1992.
28. R.B. Roberts, G.M. Dickinson, P.N.
Heseltine, et al., "A Multicenter Clinical
Trial of Oral Ribavirin in HIV-Infected
Patients with Lymphadenopathy. The
Ribavirin-LAS Collaborative Group,"
*Journal of Acquired Immune Deficiency
Syndrome* 3: 884–892, 1990.
29. C. Pedersen, E. Sandstrom, C.S.
Petersen, et al., "The Efficacy of Inosine
Pranobex in Preventing the Acquired
Immunodeficiency Syndrome in Patients
with Human Immunodeficiency Virus
Infection. The Scandinavian Isoprinosine
Study Group," *New England Journal of
Medicine* 323: 1360, 1990.
30. W. Booth, "An Underground Drug for
AIDS," *Science* 241: 1279–1281, 1988.
31. P.M. Boffey, "F.D.A. Expands Earlier
Stand by Allowing Mailing of Drugs,"
Wall Street Journal, July 25, 1988.
32. Life Extension Foundation, "The FDA
Threatens Criminal Charges Against
Offshore Pharmacies," *FDA Raid Report:
The Insider's Guide to Illegal and Uncon-
stitutional Acts by the FDA* (Fort Lauderdale, FL: Life Extension Foundation,
1995), pp. 1–5.
33. G. Kolata, "Patients Turning to Illegal
Pharmacies," *New York Times,* November
4, 1991, p. A1; Elizabeth Larson, "Un-
equal Treatments," *Reason*, April 1992,
pp. 48–50; William Sherman, "Underground Medicine," *U.S. News & World
Report,* May 11, 1992, pp. 62–69.
34. FDA Antiviral Advisory Committee
Meeting, February 13–14, 1991. Personal
communication.
35. D.H. Gieringer, "The Safety and Efficacy
of New Drug Approval," *Cato Journal* 5:
177–201, 1985. On p. 196, Gieringer
states that 1,000 more people would have
died between 1950 and 1980 if the United
States had experienced the same death
rate as other nations with less regulation
(i.e., 33 people/year). He estimates that
the same aggressive regulations kill
21,000–120,000 per decade or 2,100–
12,000 per year. Thus, the regulations
kill 64–364 times as many people as they
save.
36. J. Kwitney, *Acceptable Risks* (New York:
Poseidon Press, 1992), pp. 349–350.
37. N.D. Campbell, "Replace FDA Regulation
of Medical Devices with Third-Party Certification," *Policy Analysis No. 288*
(Washington, DC: Cato Institute, 1997).

38. O.M. Bakke, Michael Manocchia, Francisco de Abajo, et al., "Drug Safety
Discontinuations in the United Kingdom,
the United States, and Spain from 1974
to 1993: A Regulatory Perspective." *Clinical Pharmacology & Therapeutics* 58:
108–117, 1995.
39. J.A. DiMasi, J.S. Brown, and L. Lasagna,
"An Analysis of Regulatory Review Times
of Supplemental Indications for Already-
Approved Drugs: 1989–1994," *Drug Information Journal* 30: 315–337, 1996.
40. W.L. Christopher, "Off-Label Drug Prescription: Filling the Regulatory
Vacuum," *Food and Drug Law Journal*
48: 247–262, 1993.
41. R.M. Goldberg, "Speak No Good: The
Tragedy of FDA Gag Rules," *Brief Analysis No. 214* (Dallas: National Center for
Policy Analysis, 1996).
42. Competitive Enterprise Institute, op. cit.
43. "Final Report on the Aspirin Component
of the Ongoing Physicians' Health
Study," *New England Journal of Medicine* 321: 131–135, 1989.
44. D. Pearson and S. Shaw, *Freedom of Informed Choice: FDA versus Nutrient
Supplements* (Neptune, NJ: Common
Sense Press, 1993), pp. 14–15.
45. Ibid., p. 83.
46. A. Keith, "Regulating Information About
Aspirin and the Prevention of Heart Attack," *American Economic Review* 85: 96–
99, 1995.
47. Ippolitio and Matios, 1990.
48. R. Ricardo-Campbell, *Drug Lag: Federal
Government Decision Making* (Stanford,
CA.: Hoover Institution Press, 1976),
p. 48.
49. M. Fridl Ross, "FDA Proposes Labeling
Aspirin for Use at Onset of Heart Attack," University of Florida News Release, June 14, 1996.
50. Pearson and Shaw, p. 12.
51. Gieringer, p. 196, estimated that the
drug lag caused 21,000–120,000 American deaths *per decade*, compared with
the 10,000–100,000 deaths *per year* attributed to lack of information on aspirin.
Thus, the lowest ratio of annual excess
heart disease deaths to drug lag deaths is
10,000/12,000 or 1 person; the highest
ratio is 100,000/2,100 or 48 people.
52. R.W. Smithells, S. Sheppard, C.J.
Schorah, et al., "Apparent Prevention of
Neural Tube Defects by Periconceptional
Vitamin Supplements," *Archives of Disease in Childhood* 56: 911–918, 1981;
D. Czeizel, "Prevention of the First Oc-
currence of Neural-Tube Defects by
Periconceptional Vitamin Supplementation, *New England Journal of Medicine*
327: 1832–1835, 1992; J. Palca, "Agencies
Split on Nutrition Advice," *Science* 257:
1857, 1992.
53. A.T. Tabarrok, "Assessing the FDA via
the Anomaly of Off-Label Drug Prescribing," *Independent Review* 1: 25–53, 2000.
54. Pearson and Shaw, p. 20.
55. D.S. Landes, *The Wealth and Poverty of*

Nations: Why Some Are So Rich and Some So Poor (New York: W.W. Norton, 1999), pp. xvii–xviii.

56. J.L. Simon, *The Ultimate Resource 2* (Princeton, NJ: Princeton University Press, 1996), p. 319.

57. M.J. Ruwart, B.D. Rush, N.M. Friedle, J. Stachura, and A. Tarnawski, "16,16-Dimethyl-PGE2 Protection Against Napthylisothiocyanate-Induced Experimental Cholangitis in Rat," *Hepatology* 4: 658–660, 1984; B.D. Rush, M.V. Merritt, M. Kaluzny, T. Van Schoick, M.N. Brunden, and M.J. Ruwart, "Studies on the Mechanism of the Protective Action of 16,16-Dimethyl PGE2 in Carbon Tetrachloride-Induced Acute Hepatic Injury in the Rat," *Prostaglandins* 32: 439–455, 1986; B.D. Rush, K.F. Wilkinson, N.M. Nichols, R. Ochoa, M.N. Brunden, and M.J. Ruwart, "Hepatic Protection by 16,16-Dimethyl Prostaglandin E2 (DMPG) Against Acute Aflatoxim-B1-Induced Injury in Rat," *Prostaglandins* 37: 683–693, 1989.

58. D. Pearson and S. Shaw, *Life Extension: A Practical Scientific Approach* (New York: Warner Books, 1982), p. 274.

59. J.E. Calfee, *Fear of Persuasion: A New Perspective on Advertising and Regulation* (Monnaz, Switzerland: Agora Association with AEI Press, 1997) as cited in Tabarrok, p. 43.

60. Phrma, *Why Do Medicines Cost So Much?* (Washington, DC: Phrma, 2001), p. 2, <http://www.phrma.org/publications/publications/brochure/questions/whycostmuch.phtml>, accessed April 2, 2002.

61. R.T. Robertson et al., "Aspirin: Teratogenic Evaluation in the Dog," *Tetrology* 20: 313–320, 1979; W.M. Layton, "An Analysis of Teratogenic Testing Procedures," in *Congenital Defects*, D.T. Janerich, R.G. Skalko, and I.H. Porter, eds. (New York: Academic Press, 1974), pp. 205–217.

62. W.M. Wardell, "Regulatory Assessment Models Reassessed," in *Regulation, Economics, and Pharmaceutical Innovation*, J.D. Cooper, ed. (Washington, DC: American University, 1976), p. 245.

63. P. Hewitt and P. Lowy, "Tufts Center for the Study of Drug Development Pegs Cost of a New Prescription Medicine at $802 Million," *Tufts Center for the Study of Drug Development News Release*, November 30, 2001, <http://www.tufts.edu/med/csdd/images/NewsRelease113001pm.pdf>, accessed January 15, 2002.

64. Boston Consulting Group, *The Contribution of Pharmaceutical Companies: What's at Stake for America* (Boston: Boston Consulting Group, 1993).

65. Time from submission of NDA to FDA approval was 7 months prior to 1962, according to J.M. Jadlow, "The Economic Effects of the 1962 Drug Amendments," Ph.D. dissertation, University of Virginia, 1970), p. 174; time for pre-NDA studies prior to the 1962 Amendments was 2 years, according to J.E. Schnee, "Research and Technological Change in the Ethical Pharmaceutical Industry" (Ph.D. dissertation, University of Pennsylvania, 1970), p. 77; both cited in Peltzman, pp. 17–18. The estimate that 80% of drug costs are due to excess regulation may be conservative. Similar comparisons of pre-1962 costs of development and 2000 costs ($802 million as per reference 63) suggest that 92% of drug development outlays are necessitated by excess regulation. The 1962 costs are estimated at $11 million on the basis of Weimer (p. 261); the 1976 cost of $54 million was five times that of pre-1962 development costs. Adjusted for inflation, pre-1962 development costs were approximately $63 million or 8% of $802 million.

66. J.A. DiMasi, M.A. Seibring, and L. Lasagna, "New Drug Development in the United States from 1963 to 1992," *Clinical Pharmacology & Therapeutics* 55: 609–622, 1992.

67. "Delayed Access in Europe," *National Center for Policy Analysis Executive Alert*, November/December 2000, p. 2, <http://www.ncpa.org/sub/ea/2000/ea00f.pdf>, accessed April 2, 2002.

68. Hewitt and Lowy, op. cit.

69. American Medical Association, *Drug Evaluations Annual* (Chicago: American Medical Association, 1995).

70. G.F. Roll, "Of Politics and Drug Regulation," *Publications Series PS-7701* (Rochester, NY: Center for the Study of Drug Development, 1977), p. 20.

71. R. Paul and P. Defazio, "Statement on Dietary Supplement Regulation and Research," March 20, 2001, <http://www.house.gov/paul/congrec/congrec2001/cr032001.htm>, accessed April 20, 2001.

72. S. Peltzman and G. Jarrell, "The Impact of Product Recalls on the Wealth of Sellers," *Journal of Political Economy* 93: 512–536, 1985.

73. Kwitney, op. cit.

74. Weimer, pp. 265–266.

75. N.D. Campbell, "Replace FDA Regulation of Medical Devices wit Third-Party Certification," *Policy Analysis No. 288* (Washington, D.C.: Cato Institute, 1997).

76. Wilkerson Group, "Forces Reshaping the Performance and Contribution of the U.S. Medical Device Industry," prepared for the Health Industry Manufacturers Association, 1995, cited in R.D. Tollison, "Institutional Alternatives for the Regulation of Drugs and Medical Devices," in R.A. Epstein, T.M. Lenard, H.I. Miller, et al., *Advancing Medical Innovation: Health, Safety, and the Role of Government in the 21st Century* (Washington, DC: Progress and Freedom Foundation, 1996), <http://www.pff.org/mip/fdatoc.html>, accessed December 15, 2001.

77. H.I. Miller and D. Longtin, "Herbal Dietary Supplements Hunger for

Regulation," *Food Today,* Winter 2001, pp. 17–21.

78. USANA Health Sciences, Inc., 3838 West Parkway Blvd., Salt Lake City, UT 84120-6336, <http://www.usana.com/ USMAINPAGE_11931.html>, March 15, 2002.

79. Contact information for the Life Extension Foundation is 1100 West Commercial Blvd., Fort Lauderdale, FL 33309, <http://www.lef.org/magazine/mag2000/ june00-qanda.html>, accessed April 15, 2002.

Chapter 7: Creating Monopolies That Control Us

1. W.C. Wooldrige, *Uncle Sam, the Monopoly Man* (Rochelle, NY: New Arlington House, 1970); M.J. Green, "Uncle Sam, the Monopoly Man," in *The Monopoly Makers: Ralph Nader's Study Group Report on Regulation and Competition,* M.J. Green, ed. (New York: Grossman, 1973), p. 1.

2. D.T. Armentano, *Antitrust Policy: The Case for Repeal* (Washington, DC: Cato Institute, 1986), p. 24; B.W. Folsom Jr., *The Myth of the Robber Barons: A New Look at the Rise of Big Business in America* (Reston, VA: Young America's Foundation, 1987), pp. 83–84.

3. Folsom, pp. 93–94; F. Lundberg, *The Rockefeller Syndrome* (Secaucus, NJ: Lyle Stuart, 1975), p. 132.

4. Folsom, p. 91.

5. D.F. Hawke, *John D.: The Founding Father of the Rockefellers* (New York: Harper & Row, 1980), p. 167.

6. Folsom, pp. 89–90.

7. A. Nevins, *Study in Power: John D. Rockefeller, Vol. I,* (New York: Charles Scribner's Sons, 1953), pp. 277–279, 555–556, 671–672.

8. Hawke, p. 175.

9. J.S. Robbins, "How Capitalism Saved the Whales," *The Freeman,* August 1992.

10. I.M. Tarbell, *The History of the Standard Oil Company, Vol. II* (New York: Macmillan, 1925), pp. 196–198.

11. R.W. Grant, *The Incredible Bread Machine: A Study of Capitalism, Freedom, and the State* (San Francisco: Fox & Wilkes, 1999), pp. 18–19.

12. Nevins, pp. 256, 296–297.

13. R. Cherno, *Titan: The Life of John D. Rockefeller, Sr.* (New York: Random House, 1998), pp. 139–141.

14. J. Abels, *The Rockefeller Billions* (New York: Macmillan, 1965), pp. 208–209.

15. Cherno, p. 209.

16. Hawke, p. 175.

17. Ibid., p. 177.

18. Armentano, p. 25.

19. Folsom, p. 90.

20. M. Copulos, "Natural Gas Controls Are No Bargain," *Consumers' Research,* March 1983, p. 17.

21. R.B. McKenzie, *Trust on Trial: How the Microsoft Case Is Reframing the Rules of Competition* (Cambridge, MA: Perseus, 2000), p. 64.

22. D.B. Kopel, *Antitrust After Microsoft: The Obsolescence of Antitrust in the Digital Era* (Chicago: Heartland Institute, 2001), pp. 42–43.

23. McKenzie, p. 56.

24. Ibid., p. 40.

25. Kopel (2001), p. 63.

26. McKenzie, pp. 58, 89; Kopel (2001), p. 72.

27. McKenzie, pp. 197–198; D.B. Kopel, "AOL Must Now Fight the Tiger It Once Rode," *Intellectual Ammunition* 9: 1–3, 2000.

28. Kopel (2001), p. 72.

29. McKenzie, pp. 151, 157.

30. Ibid., p. 203.

31. Kopel (2001), pp. 118–121; Grant, pp. 23–24.

32. Kopel (2001), p. 37.

33. E. Mansfield, "Patents and Innovation: An Empirical Study," *Management Science* 32: 173–181, 1986.

34. B.H. Baker, *The Gray Matter: The Forgotten Story of the Telephone* (St. Joseph, MI: Telepress, 2001).

35. B. Catania, "The United States Government vs. Alexander Graham Bell: An Important Acknowledgment for Antonio Meucci," based on the F. Ricciardi's translation of B. Catania, "Il Governo degli Stati Uniti contro Alexander Graham Bell—Un Importante Riconoscimento per Antonio Meucci," *Automazione, Energia, Informazione* 86S: 1–12, 1999, <http://www.esanet.it/ chez_basilio/us_bell.htm>, accessed October 16, 2002.

36. J.R. Meyer, R.W. Wilson, A. Baughcum, et al., *The Economics of Competition in the Telecommunications Industry* (Cambridge, MA: Oelgeschlager, Gunn & Hain, 1980), p. 31.

37. P. Samuel, "Telecommunications: After the Bell Break-Up," in *Unnatural Monopolies: The Case for Deregulating Public Utilities,* R.W. Poole, ed. (Lexington, KY: D.C. Heath, 1985), p. 180–181.

38. Ibid.; I. Walters, "Freedom for Communications," in *Instead of Regulation: Alternatives to Federal Regulatory Agencies,* R.W. Poole, ed. (Lexington, KY: D.C. Heath, 1982), p. 117–118.

39. Walters, p. 118.

40. Meyer, p. 29.

41. Ibid., pp. 120–123.

42. Ibid., p. 122.

43. Ibid., pp. 120–124.

44. P. Payson, "Why Your Phone Bills Keep Going Up," *Consumers' Research,* June 1989, p. 12.

45. Ibid., p. 10.

46. Ibid., p. 11.

47. Ibid., pp. 12, 14.

48. J. Ellig, "Consumers on Hold," *Reason,* July 1989, pp. 36–37.

49. Payson, p. 13.

50. W.J. Primeaux Jr., "Total Deregulation of Electric Utilities: A Viable Policy Choice," in Poole, ed. (1985), pp. 121–146; W.J.

Primeaux Jr., *Direct Electric Utility Competition: The Natural Monopoly Myth* (New York: Praeger, 1985), pp. 37–41; W.J. Primeaux Jr., "Competition Between Electric Utilities," in *Electric Power: Deregulation and the Public Interest*, John C. Moorhouse, ed. (San Francisco: Pacific Research Institute for Public Policy, 1986), pp. 395–423.

51. R. Stobaugh and D. Yergin, eds., *Energy Future* (New York: Random House, 1979), pp. 159–160; Y. Brozen, "Making Crisis, Not Energy," *Regulation*, March/April 1980, pp. 11–14.
52. Kopel (2000), op.cit.
53. McKenzie, pp. 159–160.
54. I. Vasquez, *Global Fortune* (Washington, DC: Cato Institute, 2000), pp. 80–81.
55. K.R. Sheets and R.F. Black "Generating Cash from Trash," *U.S. News & World Report*, August 22, 1988, pp. 38–40.
56. L. Kiesling, "Getting Electricity Deregulation Right: How Other States and Nations Have Avoided California's Mistakes," *Policy Study No. 281* (Los Angeles: Reason Public Policy Institute, 2000), p. 1.
57. Ibid.
58. Kiesling, p. 6.
59. M.W. Lynch, "California Scheming," *Reason Online*, January 4, 2001, <http://www.reason.com/ml/ml010401.shtml>, accessed January 15, 2002.
60. W.P. Kucewicz, "Too Much Regulation Keeps California in the Dark," *Wall Street Journal*, August 7, 2000.

Chapter 8: Destroying the Environment

1. T.E. Borcherding, "The Sources of Growth in Public Expenditures in the U.S.: 1902–1970," *Budgets and Bureaucrats: The Sources of Government Growth*, T.E. Borcherding, ed. (Durham, NC: Duke University Press, 1977), p. 62; J.T. Bennett and M.H. Johnson, *Better Government at Half the Price* (Ottawa, IL: Green Hill, 1981).
2. "Privatization in the U.S.: Cities and Counties," *NCPA Policy Report No.116* (Dallas: National Center for Policy Analysis, 1985), p. 17.
3. P. Fixler Jr., R.W. Poole Jr., L. Scarlett, and W.D. Eggers, "Privatization 1990" (Santa Monica, CA: Reason Foundation, 1990), p. 8; R. Fitzgerald, *When Government Goes Private: Successful Alternatives to Public Services* (New York: Universe Books, 1988), pp. 158–163.
4. R. Poole Jr., *Cutting Back City Hall* (New York: Universe Books, 1980), pp. 62–78.
5. Ibid., pp. 79–87.
6. Ibid., pp. 152–154; Fitzgerald, pp. 177–181.
7. L. Scarlett, "From Silent Waste to Recycling," *Privatization Watch*, July 1989, pp. 3–4.

8. L. Scarlett, "Managing America's Garbage: Alternatives and Solutions," *Policy Study No.115* (Los Angeles: Reason Foundation, 1989).
9. J. Marinelli, "Composting: From Backyards to Big Time," *Garbage*, July/August 1990, pp. 44–51.
10. R.R. Rucker and P.V. Fishback, "The Federal Reclamation Program: An Analysis of Rent-Seeking Behavior," in *Water Rights*, T.L. Anderson, ed. (San Francisco: Pacific Research Institute for Public Policy, 1983), pp. 62–63.
11. T.L. Anderson and D.R. Leal, *Free Market Environmentalism: A Property Rights Approach* (San Francisco: Pacific Research Institute for Public Policy, 1990), pp. 55–56.
12. J. Baden, "Destroying the Environment: Government Mismanagement of Our Natural Resources," *NCPA Policy Report No. 124* (Dallas: National Center for Policy Analysis, 1986), pp. 20–21.
13. Ibid., p. 38.
14. R.M. Latimer, "Chained to the Bottom," in *Bureaucracy vs. Environment*, J. Baden and R.L. Stroup, eds. (Ann Arbor, MI: University of Michigan Press, 1981), p. 156.
15. Baden, p. 18.
16. G.D. Libecap, *Locking Up the Range* (San Francisco: Pacific Research Institute for Public Policy, 1981), p. 27.
17. Ibid., p. 46.
18. Ibid., p. 76.
19. M. Rothbard, *For a New Liberty* (New York: Macmillan, 1973), p. 264.
20. P. Kirby and W. Arthur, *Our National Forests: Lands in Peril* (Washington, DC: Wilderness Society and the Sierra Club, 1985), p. 4.
21. Baden, p. 10.
22. T. Barlow, G.E. Helfand, T.W. Orr, and T.B. Stoel Jr., *Giving Away the National Forests* (New York: Natural Resources Defense Council, 1980), Appendix 1.
23. Baden, p. 14.
24. E. Contoski, *Makers and Takers: How Wealth and Progress Are Made and How They Are Taken Away or Prevented* (Minneapolis: American Liberty Publishers, 1997), p. 305.
25. K. Barton and W. Fosburgh, *Audubon Wildlife Report 1986* (New York: National Audubon Society, 1986), p. 129.
26. Contoski, p. 302.
27. T.L. Anderson and D.R. Leal, "Rekindling the Privatization Fires: Political Lands Revisited," *Federal Privatization Project, Issue Paper No. 108* (Santa Monica, CA: Reason Foundation, 1989), p. 12.
28. Contoski, p. 302.
29. "Special Report: The Public Benefits of Private Conservation," *Environmental Quality: 15th Annual Report of the Council on Environmental Quality Together with the President's Message to Congress*, (Washington, DC: U.S. Government Printing Office, 1984), pp. 387–394.
30. Ibid., pp. 394–398.

31. T. McNamee, "Yellowstone's Missing Element," *Audubon* 88: 12, 1986.
32. A. Chase, *Playing God in Yellowstone: The Destruction of America's First National Park* (New York: Atlantic Monthly Press), pp. 123–124.
33. Ibid., pp. 12, 28, 29.
34. Ibid., pp. 155, 173.
35. T. Blood, "Men, Elk, and Wolves," in *The Yellowstone Primer: Land and Resource Management in the Greater Yellowstone Ecosystem*, J.A. Baden and D. R. Leal, eds. (San Francisco: Pacific Research Institute for Public Policy Research, 1990), p. 109.
36. "Special Report: The Public Benefits of Private Conservation," op. cit., p. 368.
37. R.L. Stroup and J.A. Baden, *Natural Resources: Bureaucratic Myths and Environmental Management* (San Francisco: Pacific Research Institute for Public Policy Research, 1983), pp. 49–50.
38. Anderson and Leal, pp. 51–52.
39. P. Young, "Privatization Around the Globe: Lessons for the Reagan Administration," *NCPA Policy Report No. 120* (Dallas: National Center for Policy Analysis, 1986), pp. 1–23.
40. D. Yergin and J. Stanislaw, *The Commanding Heights: The Battle Between Government and the Marketplace That Is Remaking the Modern World* (New York: Simon & Schuster, 1998), pp.119–124.
41. W.L. Megginson, R.C. Nash, and M. van Randenborgh, "The Financial and Operating Performance of Newly Privatized Firms: An International Empirical Analysis," in *The Privatization Process: A Worldwide Perspective*, T.L. Anderson and P.J. Hill, eds. (Lanham, MD: Rowman & Littlefield, 1996), pp. 115–154; I. Vogelsang, L. Jones, and P. Tandon, *Welfare Consequences of Selling Public Enterprises: An Empirical Analysis* (New York: World Bank, 1994); W.L. Megginson and J.M. Netter, "From State to Market: A Survey of Empirical Studies on Privatization," *Journal of Economic Literature* 39: 321–389, 2001; S. Kikeri and J. Nellis, "Privatization in Competitive Sectors: The Record So Far," October 29, 2001, <http://rru.worldbank.org/Documents/Privatization_%20paper.doc>, accessed January 15, 2002.
42. J. Crutcher, "Free Enterprise Delivers the Mail," *Consumers' Research*, September 1990, pp. 34–35.
43. Marinelli, op. cit.
44. Yergin and Stanislaw, op. cit.
45. S. Barnett, "Evidence on the Fiscal and Macroeconomic Impact of Privatization," *IMF Working Paper WP/00/130*, July 2000, <http://www.imf.org/external/pubs/ft/wp/2000/wp00130.pdf>, accessed March 15, 2002.
46. Megginson and Netter, op.cit.
47. W.C. Dunkelberg and J.Skorburg, "How Rising Tax Burdens Can Produce Recession," *Policy Analysis No. 148* (Dallas: National Center for Policy Analysis, 1991); W.T. Brookes, *The Economy in Mind* (New York: Universe Books, 1982), pp. 187–195; G.W. Scully, "How State and Local Taxes Affect Economic Growth," *NCPA Policy Report No. 106* (Dallas: National Center for Policy Analysis, 1991).

Chapter 9: Banking on Aggression

1. D.R. Streifling, "Inflation," *International Forum* 4: 3–4, 2001.
2. R.J. Barro, *Determinants of Economic Growth: A Cross-Country Empirical Study* (Cambridge, MA: MIT Press, 1999), pp. 93–101.
3. L.H. White, *Free Banking in Britain: Theory, Experience and Debate, 1800–1845* (New York: Cambridge University Press, 1984), pp. 23–49; C.A. Conant, *A History of Modern Banks of Issue* (New York: Augustus M. Kelley, 1969), pp. 142–170.
4. K. Dowd, *Laissez-faire Banking* (New York: Routledge, 1993), p. 52.
5. K. Dowd, *The State and the Monetary System* (New York: St. Martin's Press, 1989), p. 122.
6. Ibid., p. 124.
7. G. Selgin, *Bank Deregulation and Monetary Order* (New York: Routledge, 1996), pp. 24–26, 30–32; Dowd (1993), pp. 149–175.
8. Ibid., pp. 195–200.
9. White, p. 41.
10. C.A. Phillips, T.F. McManus, and R.W. Nelson, *Banking and the Business Cycle: A Study of the Great Depression in the United States* (New York: Arno Press and New York Times, 1972), pp. 23, 25, 79, 82–84.
11. Ibid., p. 25.
12. Ibid., p. 30.
13. Ibid., p. 82.
14. Ibid., p. 84.
15. Ibid., p. 81.
16. R. Paul and L. Lehrman, *The Case for Gold* (Washington, DC: Cato Institute, 1982), p. 125.
17. Phillips et al., p. 167.
18. Paul and Lehrman, pp. 126–128; M. Friedman and A.J. Schwartz, *A Monetary History of the United States, 1867–1960* (Princeton, NJ: Princeton University Press, 1963), p. 332.
19. Selgin, pp. 25, 205.
20. Paul and Lehrman, p. 129.
21. G. Gorton, "Banking Panics and Business Cycles," *Working Paper 86–9*, Federal Reserve Bank of Philadelphia, March 1986, cited in K. Dowd (1989), p. 169.
22. B. Ely, "The Big Bust: The 1930–33 Banking Collapse: Its Causes, Its Lessons," in *The Financial Services Revolution: Policy Directions for the Future*, C. England and T. Huertas, eds. (Boston: Kluwer Academic Publishers, 1988), pp. 55–56.
23. Conant, pp. 448–479.
24. G.A. Selgin, *The Theory of Free Banking: Money Supply Under Competitive Note Issue* (Totowa, NJ: Rowman & Littlefield, 1988), pp. 11–12.

25. A.R. Epperson, *The Unseen Hand* (Tucson, AZ: Publius Press, 1985); L. Abraham, *Call It Conspiracy* (Seattle: Double A Publications, 1971); G. Allen, *Say "No!" to the New World Order* (Seal Beach, CA: Concord Press, 1987); G. Allen and L. Abraham, *None Dare Call It Conspiracy* (Rossmoor, CA: Concord Press, 1972); G.E. Griffin, *A Survival Course on Money* (Westlake Village, CA: American Media, 1985).

26. J.R. Adams, *The Big Fix* (New York: John Wiley, 1991), pp. 289–290.

27. R.V. Remini, *Andrew Jackson and the Course of American Democracy, Vol. III* (New York: Harper & Row, 1984), pp. 105–113.

28. For a description of how modern banking free from aggression might work, see Dowd (1993), pp. 23–113.

29. C.W. Calomiris, "Is Deposit Insurance Necessary? A Historical Perspective," *Journal of Economic History* 50: 283–295, 1990; C.W. Calomiris, "Deposit Insurance: Lessons from the Record," *Economic Perspectives* 13: 10–30, 1989.

30. Adams, p. viii.

31. e-gold, <http://www.e-gold.com>. (800) 909-6590 (USA); (321) 956-1200 (worldwide); fax (321) 951-0790.

32. E.S. Cahn, *No More Throw-Away People: The Co-Production Imperative* (Washington, DC: Essential Information, 2000); E.S. Cahn, *Time Dollars: The New Currency That Enables Americans to Turn Their Hidden Resource-Time-Into Personal Security and Community Renewal* (Emmaus, PA: Rodale Press, 1992), <http://www.timedollars.org>.

33. Universal Trade Hour Administration, P.O. Box 390979, Cambridge, MA 02139. (781) 925-5253; fax (781) 925-3906, <http://www.citizensjustice.com/uth/>.

Chapter 10: Learning Lessons Our Schools Can't Teach

1. A.J. Coulson, *Market Education: The Unknown History* (New Brunswick, NJ: Transaction Publishers, 1999), pp. 202–203.

2. National Commission of Excellence in Education, *A Nation at Risk: The Imperative for Educational Reform* (Washington, DC: U.S. Government Printing Office, 1983).

3. D.T. Kearns and D.P. Doyle, *Winning the Brain Race: A Bold Plan to Make Our Schools Competitive* (San Francisco: Institute for Contemporary Studies, 1988), p. 15.

4. "Illiterate U.S. Workers Drive Jobs Overseas," *School Reform News*, April 1998, p. 7.

5. J.T. Gatto, *The Underground History of American Education: A Schoolteacher's Intimate Investigation into the Problem of Modern Schooling* (New York: Oxford Village Press, 2001), p. 54.

6. Ibid., p. 52.

7. M.L. Gross, *The Conspiracy of Ignorance: The Failure of American Public Schools* (New York: HarperCollins, 1999), pp. 1–2.

8. Coulson, pp. 140–141; The California version of the teacher's test is available at <http://www.heartland.org/education/feb97/teachers.htm>, accessed March 15, 2002.

9. M. Lieberman, "Market Solutions to the Education Crisis," *Cato Policy Analysis No. 75*, (Washington, DC: Cato Institute, 1986), p. 2.

10. R. Fitzgerald, *When Government Goes Private: Successful Alternatives to Public Services* (New York: Universe Books, 1988), p. 141, R.W. Poole Jr., *Cutting Back City Hall* (New York: Universe Books, 1980), p. 184; H.J. Walberg, "Should Schools Compete?" *Heartland Perspective*, September 29, 1987, p. 3.

11. For a review of these studies and their critics, see Coulson, pp. 207–209.

12. J. Bishop, "Is the Test Score Decline Responsible for the Productivity Growth Decline?" *American Economic Review* 79: 178–197, 1989.

13. S.L. Blumenfeld, *Is Public Education Necessary?* (Boise, ID: Paradigm, 1985), pp. 68, 126; S.L. Blumenfeld "Why the Schools Went Public," *Reason*, March 1979, p. 19.

14. Gatto (2001), p. 57.

15. J.T. Gatto, "Our Prussian School System," *Cato Policy Report* 15: 2, 1993.

16. B.W. Poulson, "Education and the Family During the Industrial Revolution," in J.R. Peden and F.R. Glahe, eds., *The American Family and the State*, (San Francisco: Pacific Research Institute for Public Policy, 1986), p. 138.

17. S.K. Schultz, *The Culture Factory: Boston Public Schools, 1789–1860* (New York: Oxford University Press, 1973), pp. 32–33.

18. R.W. Grant, *The Incredible Bread Machine* (San Francisco: Fox & Wiles, 1999), pp. 178–179.

19. Blumenfeld (1985), p. 42.

20. Schultz, p. 25.

21. C.F. Kaestle, *The Evolution of an Urban School System: New York City, 1750–1850* (Cambridge, MA: Harvard University Press, 1973), p. 89.

22. T. Cowen, *The Theory of Market Failure* (Fairfax, VA: George Mason University Press, 1988), pp. 374–377.

23. J. Spring, "The Evolving Political Structure of American Schooling," in *The Public School Monopoly*, R.B. Everhart, ed. (San Francisco: Pacific Research Institute for Public Policy, 1982), pp. 89–92.

24. C. Bolick, *Transformation: The Promise and Politics of Empowerment* (Oakland, CA: Institute for Contemporary Studies, 1998), p. 74; S. Mariotti, "Solving the Problem of Poverty," <http://www.amigospais-guaracabuya.org/oagim007.html>, accessed March 15, 2002.

25. L.B. Stebbins, R.G. St. Pierre, E.C. Proper, R.B. Anderson, T.R. Cerva, and

M.M. Kennedy, *Education as Experimentation: A Planned Variation Model, Volume IV-A, An Evaluation of Follow-Through* (Cambridge, MA: Abt Associates, 1977).

26. Poole, pp. 175–176.
27. (no author given), Heartland Institute, *Intellectual Ammunition,* March/April 1996, p. 14.
28. G.A. Clowes, "Voucher Initiatives Crushed in Michigan and California," *School Reform News,* January 2001, p. 1.
29. G.A. Clowes, "New Education Journal Launched: A Mother's Graduation Wish," *School Reform News,* March 2001, p. 5.
30. M. Valverde, "Is Government Drugging to Blame for Wave of School Violence?" *Freedom Network News,* August/September/October 1999, p. 9; D. Montero, "'I Was Told to Dope My Kid,'" *NYPost.com,* August 7, 2002, <http:/www.nypost.com/news/regionalnews/54243.htm>, accessed August 11, 2002.
31. D. Kelly, "Kids' Scores for Reading 'In Trouble,'" *USA Today,* April 28–30, 1995, p. 1A; "U.S. Students Make Progress in Math," *Dallas Morning News* February 28, 1997, p. 6A, as cited in Bolick, p. 36.
32. Fitzgerald, pp. 143–144; Poole, pp. 184–186.
33. T.W. Vitullo-Martin, "The Impact of Taxation Policy on Public and Private Schools," in *The Public School Monopoly*, R.B. Everhart, ed. (Cambridge, MA: Ballinger, 1982) pp. 445–458.
34. T. Sowell, *Education: Assumptions versus History* (Stanford, CA: Hoover Institution Press, 1986), p. 103.
35. Coulson, p. 268.
36. A.S. Bryk, V.E. Lee, and P.B. Holland, *Catholic Schools and the Common Good* (Cambridge, MA: Harvard University Press, 1993), pp. 262–263.
37. Ibid., pp. 246–247; L. Reed and H. Hutchinson, *Educational Choice for Michigan* (Midland, MI: Mackinac Center for Public Policy, 1991), p. 49.
38. J. Coleman, "Predicting the Consequences of Policy Changes: The Case of Public and Private Schools," in *Equality and Achievement in Education,* J. Coleman, ed., (Boulder, CO: Westview Press, 1990), pp. 255–256.
39. J.P. Greene, "Private Schools Promote Better Civic Values," *Intellectual Ammunition,* September/October 1998, p. 15.
40. J.P. Greene, "Integration Where It Counts: A Study of Racial Integration in Public and Private School Lunchrooms," paper presented to the American Political Science Association, Boston, September 1998, <http://www.schoolchoices.org/roo/jay1.htm>, accessed February 10, 2002.
41. Vitullo-Martin, p. 444.
42. Greene, "Private Schools Promote Better Civic Values," op. cit.
43. "Cleveland Catholic, Public Schools Compared," *Intellectual Ammunition,* November/December 1993, p. 22.
44. Bryk et al., p. 286; J.G. Cibulka, T.J.

O'Brien, and D. Zewe, *Inner-City Private Elementary Schools: A Study* (Milwaukee, WI: Marquette University Press, 1982), p. 137.
45. J.R. Beales and T.F. Bertonneau, "Do Private Schools Serve Difficult-to-Educate Students?" Mackinac Center for Public Policy, October 1997, <http://www.mackinac.org/361>, accessed December 10, 2001.
46. C. Lochhead, "A Lesson from Private Practitioners," *Insight,* December 24, 1990, pp. 34–36; D.W. Kirkpatrick, "Choice, Charters, and Privatizations," <http://www.schoolreport.com/schoolreport/articles/choicecharter_9_96.htm>, accessed February 10, 2002.
47. "A Canadian's Perspective on Milwaukee's Choice Program," *School Reform News,* June 1999, p. 7.
48. T. Hetland, "Learning Thrives at Westside Prep," *Heartland Perspective*, January 15, 1993, p. 2.
49. Sylvan Learning Center, <http://www.educate.com/homepage.html>, accessed January 15, 2002.
50. "Court: Public Schools Not Accountable to Parents," *School Reform News,* May 2000, p. 5.
51. N.H. Shokraii, "How Members of Congress Practice School Choice," *FYI* 147, September 9, 1997, <http://www.heritage.org/library/categories/education/fyi147.html>, accessed December 9, 2001.
52. Bolick (1998) , pp. 44–45.
53. Shokraii, op.cit.
54. Coulson, pp. 277–279.
55. Ibid., p. 272.
56. Ibid., p. 206.
57. D. Lindsay, "PepsiCo Backs Off Voucher Plan in Jersey City," *Education Week*, November 15, 1995, p. 3.
58. L. Sternberg, "Lessons from Vermont: 132-Year-Old Voucher Program Rebuts Critics," *Briefing Paper No. 67* (Washington, DC: Cato Institute, 2001).
59. F. Heller, "Lessons from Maine: Education Vouchers for Students Since 1873," *Briefing Paper No. 66* (Washington, DC: Cato Institute, 2001).
60. C. Bolick, "The March Toward Educational Choice," *Intellectual Ammunition,* November/December 1996, pp. 1–3.
61. "Voucher Schools Keep Costs Low: Private Schools Return Unused Tax Dollars," *School Reform News*, July 2000, p. 4.
62. J.P. Greene, P.E. Peterson, J. Du, L. Boeger, and C.L. Frazier, *The Effectiveness of School Choice in Milwaukee: A Secondary Analysis of Data from the Program's Evaluation* (Cambridge, MA: Harvard University, John F. Kennedy School of Government, 1996), <http://www.ksg.harvard.edu/pepg/op/evaluate.htm>, accessed March 15, 2002; P.E. Peterson, W.G. Howell, and J.P. Greene, *An Evaluation of the Cleveland Voucher Program After Two Years* (Cambridge, MA: Harvard University John F. Kennedy School of Government, 1999).

63. E.F. Toma, "Public Funding and Private Schooling Across Countries," *Journal of Law & Economics* 39: 121–148, 1996.
64. J.P. Greene, "2001 Education Freedom Index," *Civic Report No. 24* (New York: Manhattan Institute for Public Policy, 2002).
65. Sylvan Learning Center, op. cit.
66. For a good review of the *juku* system, see Coulson, pp. 226–229.
67. L.M. Rudner, "Scholastic Achievement and Demographic Characteristics of Home School Students in 1998," *Education Policy Analysis Archives,* March 23, 1999, <http://epaa.asu.edu/epaa/v7n8/>, accessed February 8, 2002.
68. I. Lyman, *The Homeschooling Revolution* (Amherst, MA: Bench Press International, 2000), pp. 33–44; Coulson, pp. 119–122.
69. Lyman, p. 28; G. Clowes, "More Growth Ahead for Home Schooling," *Intellectual Ammunition,* July/August 1999, p. 5.
70. Lyman, p. 61.
71. Rudner, op. cit.
72. L.E. Shyers, "Comparison of Social Adjustments Between Home and Traditionally Schooled Students," (Ph.D. dissertation, University of Florida, 1992), p. 199, as cited in Lyman, pp. 52–53.
73. Lyman, pp. 54–55.
74. Sylvan Learning Center, <http://www.educate.com/homepage.html>, accessed March 10, 2002.
75. W. Tucker, "Foot in the Door," *Forbes,* February 3, 1992, pp. 50–51.
76. Lewis J. Perelman, "Closing Education's Technology Gap," *Briefing Paper No. 111* (Indianapolis, IN.: Hudson Institute, 1989); W.E. Halal and J. Liebowitz, "Telelearning: The Multimedia Revolution in Education," *The Futurist,* November/December, 1994, pp. 21–26.
77. Coulson, p. 207.
78. Gross, p. 51.
79. Ibid., p. 115.
80. H.J. Walberg, "How to Make Students and Teachers Want to Succeed," *Intellectual Ammunition,* April/May 1998, pp. 18–19.
81. Sylvan, op .cit., uses this technique.
82. Walberg, op.cit.
83. Because Sylvan, Ombudsman, and Hope are all able to cut learning time at least in half, this estimate is probably conservative.
84. S. Pyane, "A School with a Money-Back Guarantee," *The Freeman,* June 1992, pp. 226–227.
85. Coulson, p. 376.
86. For some examples, see Lyman, pp. 64–68.
87. "Class.com Offers High School Diploma over the Internet: University of Nebraska Starts For-Profit Company," *School Reform News,* July 1999, p. 14.
88. "Virtual High School Now on the Internet: Round-the-Clock School Seen as Boon for Resource-Poor Rural and Small Schools," *School Reform News,* February 1998, p. 13.
89. Dave Meleney, "Private TV Channel Catches On in 4,000 High Schools," *Privatization Watch,* 164, August 1990, p. 6.
90. "Private Vouchers: Demonstration Projects for School Choice," *School Reform News,* January 2001, <www.heartland.org/education/jan01/private.htm>, accessed January 7, 2002.
91. *Education at a Glance* (Paris: Organization for Economic Cooperation and Development Publications, 1995), p. 135.

Chapter 11: Springing the Poverty Trap

1. K.B. Leffler, "Minimum Wages, Welfare, and Wealth Transfers to the Poor," *Journal of Law and Economics* 21: 345–358, 1978; B.R. Bartlett, "Statement on Impact of Federal Minimum Wage Increase on Small Business," Committee on Small Business, U.S. House of Representatives, May 15, 1996, <http://www.ncpa.org/hotlines/min/bartmw6.html>, accessed February 10, 2002.
2. National Commission of Jobs and Small Business, *Making America Work Again: Jobs, Small Business, and the International Challenge* (Washington, DC: National Commission on Jobs and Small Business, 1987), p. 13.
3. R.K. Vedder and L.E. Gallaway, *Does the Minimum Wage Reduce Poverty?* (Washington, DC: Employment Policies Institute, 2001), pp. 4–5, <http://www.epionline.org/study_vedder_06-2001.html>, accessed March 10, 2002.
4. "Welfare and Poverty," *NCPA Policy Report No. 107* (Dallas: National Center for Policy Analysis), pp. 4–5
5. M. Tanner, S. Moore, and D. Hartman, "The Work vs. Welfare Trade-Off," *Policy Analysis No. 240* (Dallas: National Center for Policy Analysis, 1995), p. 4.
6. R.E. Rector and W.F. Lauber, *America's Failed $5.4 Trillion War on Poverty* (Washington, DC: Heritage Foundation, 1995).
7. V. Burke, "Cash and Non-Cash Benefits for Persons with Limited Income: Eligibility Rules, Recipient, and Expenditure Data, FY 1982–1984," *Congressional Research Source Report No. 85-194 EPW,* September 30, 1985, p. 52, as cited in J.C. Goodman and M.D. Stroup, "Privatizing the Welfare State," *NCPA Policy Report No. 123* (Dallas: National Center for Policy Analysis, 1986), p. 23.
8. L. Dash, *When Children Want Children: An Inside Look at the Crisis of Teenage Parenthood* (New York: Penguin Books, 1990).
9. D.W. Allen, "Welfare and the Family: The Canadian Experience," *Journal of Labor Economics* 11: 5201–5223, 1993; R. Rector, "The Impact of New Jersey's Family Cap on Out-of-Wedlock Births and Abortions," *FYI* 59, September 6, 1995; S. Lundberg and R.D. Plotnick, "Adolescent Premarital Childbearing: Do Opportunity Costs Matter?" Revision of

paper presented at the May1990 Population Association of America Conference in Toronto, Canada, cited in R. Rector, "Welfare Reform," in *Issues '96: The Candidates Briefing Book,* S. Butler and K. Holmes, eds. (Washington, DC: Heritage Foundation, 1996), p. 211.

10. M.A. Hill and J. O'Neill, *Underclass Behaviors in the United States: Measurement and Analysis of Determinants* (New York: Baruch College, City University of New York, 1993).

11. "One Child in Eight on Welfare," *Intellectual Ammunition* November/December, 1993, p. 14.

12. "An Evaluation of the 1981 AFDC Changes: Initial Analysis," General Accounting Office, April 2, 1984.

13. R.K. Vedder and L.E. Gallaway, *The War on the Poor* (Lewisville, TX: Institute for Policy Innovation, 1992).

14. R.K. Vedder and L.E. Gallaway, "The New Poverty: Consequence of Past Policy," *Policy Study No. 11* (Chicago: Heartland Institute, 1986).

15. C. Bolick, *Transformation: The Promise and Politics of Empowerment* (Oakland, CA: Institute for Contemporary Studies, 1998), p. 19.

16. T. Sowell, "Dems, GOPers, and Blacks," *Jewish World Review,* September 28, 2000, <http://www.jewishworldreview.com/cols/sowell092800.asp>, accessed March 13, 2002.

17. "Welfare and Poverty," p. 3.

18. Ibid.

19. S. Thernstrom and A. Thernstrom, *America in Black and White: One Nation, Indivisible* (New York: Simon & Schuster, 1997), p. 239.

20. W.J. Wilson, *When Work Disappears: The World of the New Urban Poor* (New York: Alfred A. Knopf, 1996), p. 195.

21. R.E. Rector, "Why Congress Must Reform Welfare," *Heritage Backgrounder No. 1063* (Washington, DC: Heritage Foundation, 1995).

22. C. Murray, *Losing Ground: American Social Policy 1950–1980* (New York: Basic Books, 1984), pp. 148–153.

23. Ibid., p. 152.

24. P. Craig, "Big Government Still the Problem," *Naples Daily News* <http://www.naplesnews.com/01/10/perspective/d679258a.htm>, accessed January 7, 2002.

25. J.C. Goodman and M. Matthews Jr., "Does Welfare Reform Cost More Money?" *NCPA Brief Analysis No. 210* (Dallas: National Center for Policy Analysis, 1996).

26. L.E. Gallaway and R.K. Vedder, "Paying People to Be Poor," *NCPA Policy Report No. 121* (Dallas: National Center for Policy Analysis, 1986).

27. R.K. Rector and S. Youssef, "Welfare Case-load Declines: It's the State Policies, Stupid," *Intellectual Ammunition,* May/June 1999, p. 14.

28. B. Barron, "Welfare to Work in Pennsylvania," *Allegheny Institute Report No. 99-04,* March 1998, p. 3.

29. T. Thompson and W.J. Bennett, "The Good News About Welfare Reform: Wisconsin's Success Story," *Heritage Lecture Series No. 593* (Washington, DC: Heritage Foundation, 1997), pp. 8–9.

30. R.E. Rector, "Despite Recession, Black Child Poverty Plunges to All-Time Historic Low," *Backgrounder No.1595* (Washington, DC: Heritage Foundation, 2002).

31. J.C. Goodman, G.W. Reed, and P.S. Ferrara, "Why Not Abolish the Welfare State?" *NCPA Policy Report No. 187* (Dallas: National Center for Policy Analysis, 1994), p. 3.

32. R.L. Woodson, "Breaking the Poverty Cycle: Private Sector Alternatives to the Welfare State," (Harrisburg, PA: Commonwealth Foundation for Public Policy Alternatives, 1988), p. 63.

33. N. Dunford, "N.Y.C., True to Form," *New York Times,* April 10, 1990, p. A21.

34. S.A. Kondratas, "A Strategy for Helping America's Homeless," as cited in Goodman, Reed, and Ferrara, p. 26.

35. J. Stossel, "Who Hears the Children?" *ABC News Special,* December 28, 1999.

36. W. Tucker, *The Excluded Americans: Homelessness and Housing Policies* (Washington, DC: Regnery Gateway, 1990); W. Tucker, "How Rent Control Drives Out Affordable Housing," *Policy Analysis No. 274* (Washington, DC: Cato Institute, 1997).

37. P.K. Howard, "Common Sense and the Law," <http://www.christianityinternational.com/commonsense.html>, accessed April 21, 2002.

38. M. Olasky, The Tragedy of American of Compassion (Washington, DC: Regnery Gateway, 1992), p. 82.

39. Ibid., p. 75.

40. For a partial list of these organizations, see Olasky, pp. 80–98; M. Magnet, ed., *What Makes Charity Work? A Century of Public and Private Philanthropy* (Chicago: Manhattan Institute, 2000), pp. 43–46, 78–79, 83–88.

41. J.L. Payne, *The Befriending Leader: Social Assistance Without Dependency. Essays by Octavia Hill* (Sandpoint, ID: Lytton, 1997).

42. "Guy Polhemus," *Noetic Sciences Review,* Summer 1989, p. 32; Grossman Jill, "Can We Can Go On?" *City Limits Weekly,* August 26, 2002.

43. Magnet, pp. 217–230.

44. For a summary of these and other findings related to U.S. government job programs, see J. Bovard, "The Failure of Federal Job Training," *Policy Analysis No. 77* (Washington, DC: Cato Institute, 1986).

45. Payne, pp. 136–139.

46. M. Bragin, "Moving Social Services Back

to Our Communities," *Policy Issue* (San Francisco: Pacific Research Institute for Public Policy Research, 2001), <http://www.pacificresearch.org/pub/sab/health/delancey.html>, accessed January 7, 2002.

47. D. Reinhard, "Something to Believe In," *The Oregonian*, July 20, 1997.
48. C. Bolick, pp. 120–121.
49. Ibid., pp. 114–115.
50. R. Fitzgerald, *When Government Goes Private: Successful Alternatives to Public Services* (New York: Universe Books, 1988), pp. 127–129.
51. Ibid., pp. 33–35; D. Whitman, "More Moral," *New Republic*, February 22, 1999; J.C. Goodman, G.W. Reed, and P.S. Ferrara, "Why Not Abolish the Welfare State?" *NCPA Policy Report No. 187* (Dallas: National Center for Policy Analysis, 1994).
52. R.B. McKenzie, "America: What Went Right," *Policy Analysis No. 172* (Washington, DC: Cato Institute, 1992), pp. 19–20.
53. D.T. Oliver, "Helping the Needy: Lessons from the Chicago Fire," *Alternatives in Philanthropy*, July 1999, <http://www.capitalresearch.org/publications/alternatives/1999/july.htm>, accessed January 3, 2002.
54. M. Kasindorf, "$1.5B of 9/11 Donations Distributed," *USA Today*, September 19, 2002.
55. "South Carolina Students Repay Old NYC Kindness," *Associated Press*, November 14, 2001, <http://ww.elvisthefish.com/fishy/sc_promise.shtml>, accessed January 14, 2002.
56. E.T. Devine, "Pensions for Mothers," *Survey* 30: 458–459, 1913; F. Almy, "The Relation Between Private and Public Outdoor Relief," *Charities Review* 7: 22, 1899, as cited in D.T. Beito, *From Mutual Aid to the Welfare State: Fraternal Societies and Social Services, 1890–1967* (Chapel Hill, NC: University of North Carolina Press, 2000), pp. 19–20.
57. For a thorough treatment of this subject, see Beito.
58. Beito, pp. 28, 43.
59. Ibid., pp. 30–31.
60. Ibid., p. 117.
61. Ibid., p. 213.
62. Ibid., pp. 124–128, 213–215, 231.
63. Ibid., pp. 195–201.
64. Ibid., pp. 223–230.
65. Ibid., pp. 140, 207.

Chapter 12: By Their Fruits You Shall Know Them

1. J.D. Gwartney, R.A. Lawson, and R.G. Holcombe, "Economic Freedom and the Environment for Economic Growth," *Journal of Institutional and Theoretical Economics* 155: 643–663, 1999.
2. R.J. Keating, "The State Tax-Cut Revolt," *Investor's Business Daily*, October 23, 1994.

3. S. Moore and D. Stansel, "The Myth of America's Underfunded Cities," *Policy Analysis No. 188* (Washington, DC: Cato Institute, 1993).
4. J.D. Gwartney, R.G. Holcombe, and R.A. Lawson, "The Scope of Government and the Wealth of Nations," *Cato Journal* 18: 163–190, 1998.
5. Gwartney, Lawson, and Holcombe, pp. 654–655.
6. Gwartney, Holcombe, and Lawson, op. cit.
7. Gwartney, Lawson, and Holcombe, p. 650, indicate that countries that increased their EFI by one unit (on a scale of 1 to 10) between 1980 and 1985 enjoyed a 0.8% increase in % GDP/capita from 1980 to 1995. If the United States, which had an EFI of 7.9 in 1995 (J.D. Gwartney and R.A. Lawson, *Economic Freedom of the World 1997* (Vancouver, BC: Fraser Institute, 1997), p. 195)) were to increase its EFI to 10, its wealth creation would experience an average increase from 1% (both the 1995 value and the average value for 1990 to 1995 as per Gwartney and Lawson, p. 195) to 2.7% (2.7 times) over the next 15 years. Because the EFI measures only a portion of aggression-through-government, this estimate is probably a conservative one.
8. W.C. Dunkelberg and J. Skorburg, "How Rising Tax Burdens Can Produce Recession," *NCPA Policy Analysis No. 148* (Dallas: National Center for Policy Analysis, 1991), p. 6, indicate that every 1% rise in the federal tax burden reduces real aggregate GNP growth by 1.8%. At 0% tax rate, real aggregate GNP growth is 37% (extrapolated by author). In 1995, and for the years 1990 to 1995, real aggregate GNP averaged 2% (Gwartney and Lawson, p. 195). The theoretical increase is an 18.5-fold increase in wealth creation.
9. In theory at least, lowering taxes might have less of an impact on GNP once taxes are reduced to single-digit levels. People move out of the black market when the cost of evading taxes is high compared with the tax itself, as is true at lower tax rates. Wealth creation might therefore become more efficient, partially compensating for the continued aggression of taxation. Low-tax governments would presumably be more defensive than offensive and thus inhibit wealth creation to a lesser extent.

Chapter 13: The Other Piece of the Puzzle

1. B.L. Benson, *To Serve and Protect: Privatization and Community in Criminal Justice* (Oakland, CA: Independent Institute, 1998), pp. 69, 320.
2. *Wall Street Journal*, March 21, 1989.
3. R. Axelrod, *The Evolution of Cooperation* (New York: Basic Books, 1981), pp. 27–54.

4. Ibid., pp. 5, 40–41.
5. M.O. Reynolds, *Crime by Choice: An Economic Analysis* (Dallas: Fisher Institute 1984,) p. 6.
6. Ibid., p. 9.
7. J.O. Haley, "Confession, Repentance, and Absolution," in *Mediation and Criminal Justice: Victims, Offenders, and Community*, M. Wright and B. Gallaway, eds. (London: Sage, 1989), pp. 195–211 as cited in Benson, p. 254.
8. Benson, pp. 251–254.
9. Haley, op. cit.
10. W.M. Evers, *Victim's Rights, Restitution, and Retribution* (Oakland, CA: Independent Institute, 1994) as cited in Benson.
11. Ibid.
12. M.S. Umbreit, "Restorative Justice Through Victim-Offender Mediation: A Multi-Site Assessment," *Western Criminology Review* (Online)1:16, 1998, <http://wcr.sonoma.edu/v1n1/umbreit.html>, accessed April 29, 2002.
13. Ibid., p. 20.
14. E.J. Pollock, "Victim-Perpetrator Reconciliations Grow in Popularity," *Wall Street Journal*, October 28, 1993, pp. B1, 8.
15. Umbreit, p. 18.
16. Ibid., pp. 18–19.
17. Ibid., p. 21.
18. Ibid., pp. 22–24.
19. M.S. Umbreit, *Victim Meets Offender: The Impact of Restorative Justice & Mediation* (Monsey, NY: Criminal Justice Press, 1994).
20. Reynolds, p. 68.
21. Benson, p. 28.
22. Ibid., p. 37.
23. P.E. Fixler Jr., "Can Privatization Solve the Prison Crisis?" *Fiscal Watchdog*, April 1984, p. 1.
24. J.W. Johnston, ed., "The Missouri State Penitentiary," *Illustrated Sketchbook of Jefferson City and Cole County* (Jefferson City, MO: Missouri Illustrated Sketchbook, 1900), pp. 250–251.
25. Benson, p. 300.
26. J.K. Stewart, letter to *Wall Street Journal*, July 26, 1989.
27. T.A. Roe, "A Guide to Prison Privatization," *Heritage Foundation Backgrounder No. 650*, May 24, 1988, pp. 3–4.
28. T. Gest, "Why More Criminals Are Doing Time Beyond Bars," *U.S. News & World Report*, February 26, 1990, pp. 23–24.
29. J. Shedd, "Making Goods Behind Bars," *Reason*, March 1982, pp. 23–32.
30. R.E. Barnett, "Restitution: A New Paradigm of Criminal Justice," *Ethics* 87: 293, 1977; Benson, p. 309.
31. B.M. Fleisher, *The Economics of Delinquency* (Chicago: Quadrangle Books, 1966), pp. 68–85.
32. M.A. Hill and J. O'Neill, *Underclass Behaviors in the United States: Measurement and Analysis of Determinants* (New York: Baruch College, City University of New York, 1990).

33. J. Wu and R. Axelrod, "Coping with Noise: How to Cope with Noise in the Iterated Prisoner's Dilemma," in R. Axelrod, ed. *The Complexity of Cooperation: Agent-Based Models of Competition and Collaboration* (Princeton, NJ: Princeton University Press, 1997), pp. 33–39.
34. I. Kim, B.L. Benson, D.W. Rasmussen, and T.W. Zuehlke, "An Economic Analysis of Recidivism among Drug Offenders," *Southern Economic Journal* 60: 169–183, 1993.

Chapter 14: The Pollution Solution

1. J.S. Shaw and R.L. Stroup, "Gone Fishin'," *Reason*, August/September 1988, pp. 34–37.
2. E. Zuesse, "Love Canal: The Truth Seeps Out," *Reason*, February 1981, pp. 16–33.
3. R. Blumenthal, "Fight to Curb 'Love Canals,'" *New York Times*, June 30, 1980, pp. B-1, B-11.
4. Zuesse, op. cit.
5. H. Browne, *The Great Libertarian Offer* (Great Falls, MT: LiamWorks, 2000), p. 159.
6. E.M. Whelan, *Toxic Terror* (Ottawa, IL: Jameson Books, 1985), pp. 94–98.
7. Browne, p. 160.
8. F. Smith Jr., "Superfund: A Hazardous Waste of Taxpayer Money," *Human Events*, August 2, 1986, pp. 10–12, 19; Whelan, pp. 102–105.
9. "Court Rules U.S. Not Liable in Deaths from Atom Tests," *San Francisco Examiner*, January 11, 1988, p. A-1.
10. For a narrative review of this evidence, see J.G. Fuller, *The Day We Bombed Utah: America's Most Lethal Secret* (New York: New American Library, 1984); reference to the congressional subcommittee investigation, p. 233.
11. J.L. Lyon, M.R. Klauber, J.W. Gardner, and K.S. Udall, "Childhood Leukemias Associated with Fallout from Nuclear Testing," *New England Journal of Medicine* 22: 397–402, 1979.
12. E.S. Weiss, R.E. Olson, G.D. Thompson, and A.T. Masi, "Surgically Treated Thyroid Disease Among Young People in Utah, 1948–1962," *American Journal of Public Health* 57: 1807–1814, 1967.
13. Fuller, p. 248.
14. Ibid., p. 213.
15. Ibid., pp. 257–258.
16. M. Wald, "Thousands Have Thyroid Cancer from Atomic Tests," *New York Times*, August 2, 1997.
17. For a partial list of the worst U.S. sites see S. Shulman, *The Threat at Home: Confronting the Toxic Legacy of the U.S. Military* (Boston: Beacon Press, 1992), pp. 171–188.
18. Smith, pp. 10–12, 19.
19. J. St. Clair, "The Military's Toxic Timebombs," *InTheseTimes.com*, May 28, 2001, <http://www.inthesetimes.com/web2513/stclair2513.html>, accessed June 7, 2001.

20. "The Biggest Cleanup in History," *Nucleus*, Winter 1989, p. 5; "Regulate Thyself," *Dollars & Sense*, July/August 1988, p. 16.
21. For examples, see Shulman, pp. 61–104.
22. Shulman, pp. 107–112.
23. J. Lewis, "Nuclear Power Generation: Cut the Cord!" *National Gazette*, September 1987, p. 1.
24. B. Ames, "Too Much Fuss about Pesticides," *Consumers' Research*, April 1990, pp. 32–34.
25. "Pesticide Residues in Our Food," *Consumers' Research*, June 1990, pp. 33–34.
26. Whelan, pp. 120–125.
27. I.M. Goklany, "Economic Growth and the State of Humanity," *Policy Series No. PS-21* (Bozeman, MT: Political Economy Research Center, 2001), p. 28.
28. A. Attaran, D.R. Roberts, C.F. Curtis, and W.L. Kilama, "Balancing Risks on the Backs of the Poor," *Nature Medicine* 6: 729–731, 2000, <http://www.nature.com/cgi-taf/DynaPage.taf?file=/nm/journal/v6n7/full/nm0700_729. html&filetype=pdf>, accessed May 2, 2002.
29. P.K. Driessen, "Is the DDT Ban Intended to Control Global Population?" *Environment & Climate News*, April 2001, p. 12.
30. F.D. McCarthy, H. Wolf, and Y. Wu, "The Growth Costs of Malaria," December 1999, <http://www.malaria/org/Wolf_Wu_McCarthy.pdf> accessed May 2, 2002.
31. World Bank, *World Development Report: Investing in Health* (New York: Oxford University Press, 1993) as cited in Goklany, op. cit.
32. E. Contoski, *Makers and Takers: How Wealth and Progress Are Made and How They Are Taken Away or Prevented* (Minneapolis: American Liberty Publishers, 1997), p. 235.
33. Ibid., pp. 235–236.
34. Ibid.
35. Attaran et al., op. cit.
36. Driessen, op. cit.
37. Ibid.
38. Attaran et al., op. cit.
39. Committee on Diet and Health, Food and Nutrition Board; and Commission on Life Sciences, National Research Council, *Diet and Health: Implications for Reducing Chronic Disease Risk* (Washington, DC: National Academy Press, 1989), pp. 593-614, <http://www.nap.edu/books/0309039940/html/index.html>, accessed November 8, 2001.
40. K.J. Helzlsouer, A.J. Alberg, H.-Y. Huang, et al., "Serum Concentrations of Organochlorine Compounds and the Subsequent Development of Breast Cancer," *Cancer Epidemiology, Biomarkers, & Prevention* 8: 525–532, 1999. In addition to presenting original data, this paper reviews a number of earlier studies with similar findings.
41. "Not All Risks Are Equal,"*Detroit News*, February 26, 1990, p. 3.
42. R. Doll and R. Peto, "Proportions of Cancer Deaths Attributed to Various Factors," *Journal of the National Cancer Institute* 66: 1194, 1981.
43. "Assessing the Asbestos Risk," *Consumers' Research*, July 1990, pp. 10–13.
44. M. Ross, "Did Risk Reduction Backfire in Space?" *Washington Times,* January 28, 1996, <http://www.sepp.org/space/riskmross.html>, accessed on May 2, 2002.
45. W.T. Brookes, "How the EPA Lauched the Hysteria About Alar," *Detroit News*, February 25, 1990, pp. 9-11.

Chapter 15: Dealing in Death

1. B.L. Benson, *To Serve and Protect: Privatization and Community in Criminal Justice* (Oakland, CA: Independent Institute, 1998), p. 53; J.R. Lott Jr., *More Guns, Less Crime: Understanding Crime and Gun Control Laws* (Chicago: University of Chicago Press, 2000), p. 18.
2. Reuters, "U.S. Marijuana Busts Remained High in 1998," October 17, 1999, <http://www.mpp.org/news/rts101799.htm>, accessed May 6, 2002.
3. T.M. Coffey, *The Long Thirst: Prohibition in America, 1920–1933* (New York: W.W. Norton, 1975), pp. 196–198.
4. J.A. Miron, "Violence and the U.S. Prohibitions of Drugs and Alcohol," *American Law and Economics Review* 1: 78–114, 1999.
5. S. Ehlers, "How American Women Repealed Prohibition," *Drug Policy Letter*, Winter 1998, pp. 23–24, reviewing K.D. Rose's *American Women and the Repeal of Prohibition* (New York: New York University Press, 1996).
6. Miron (1999), op. cit.
7. E. Nadelman, "Prohibition in the United States: Costs, Consequences, and Alternatives," *Science* 245: 945, 1989.
8. J. Ostrowski, *Thinking About Drug Legalization* (Washington, DC: Cato Institute, 1989) p. 8.
9. Drug Policy Foundation, *The Bush Drug War Record: The Real Story of a $45 Billion Domestic War* (Washington, DC: Drug Policy Foundation, 1992), p. 5
10. "Warehouse of Addiction," *New York Times,* July 2, 3, and 4, 1995.
11. Ostrowski, p. 14.
12. R.F. Service, "Closing in on a Stomach-Sparing Aspirin Substitute," *Science* 273: 1660, 1996.
13. Author's calculations by the method of Ostrowski. Data from U.S. Department of Justice (homicides), U.S. Department of Health and Human Services (drug-induced deaths), and Statistical Abstract of the United States (new AIDS cases from drug use).
14. J.P. Kassirer, "Criticizing the Clinton Administration for Its Stance on Medical Marijuana," *New England Journal of Medicine* 336: 366–367, 1997.

15. About, Inc. "Alcohol-Related Deaths 1979–1996," <http://www.alcoholism.about.com/library/narmort01.htm>, accessed August 3, 2002.
16. M.J. Thun, L.F. Apicella, and S.J. Henley, "Smoking vs. Other Risk Factors As the Cause of Smoking-Attributable Deaths," *Journal of the American Medical Association* 284: 706–712, 2000.
17. D. Pearson and S. Shaw, "The Hardest Drug," *Life Extension Newsletter* 1: 55, 1988.
18. Ostrowski's note 140: personal communication from Dr. Regan Bradford of the National Heart, Lung, and Blood Institute in which he said he believes that 90% of the one million cardiovascular deaths in the United States each year could be prevented by low-fat diets.
19. Ostrowski, p. 14.
20. Ibid., p. 11; D. Pearson and S. Shaw, *Life Extension: A Practical Scientific Approach* (New York: Warner Books, Inc., 1982), p. 715.
21. Drug Policy Foundation, p. 20.
22. A.S. Trebach and K.B. Zeese, *Drug Prohibition and the Conscience of Nations* (Washington, DC: Drug Policy Foundation, 1990), p. 142, from the World Health Organization's "AIDS Surveillance in Europe," December 31, 1989.
23. N.D. Kristof, "Hong Kong Program: Addicts Without Aids," *New York Times*, June 17, 1987, p. A-1.
24. Ostrowski, p. 23
25. P.J. Goldstein, "The Drugs/Violence Nexus: A Tripartite Conceptual Framework," *Journal of Drug Issues* 15: 493–506, 1985; P.J. Goldstein, H.H. Brownstein, P.J. Ryan, and P.A. Bellucci, "Crack and Homicide in New York City, 1988: A Conceptually Based Event Analysis," *Contemporary Drug Problems* 16: 651–687, 1989.
26. Miron, (1999) op. cit.; J.A. Miron, "Violence, Guns, and Drugs: A Cross-Country Analysis," *Journal of Law and Economics*, in press 2002; D.W. Rasmussen, B.L. Benson, and D.L. Sollars, "Spatial Competition in Illicit Drug Markets: The Consequences of Increased Drug Law Enforcement," *Review of Regional Studies* 23: 219–236, 1993; P. Fajnzylber, D. Lederman, and N. Loazya, *Determinants of Crime Rates in Latin America and the World: An Empirical Assessment* (Washington, DC: World Bank, 1998); B.L. Benson and D.W. Rasmussen, *Illicit Drugs and Crime* (Oakland, CA: Independent Institute, 1996), pp.16–18; H.J. Brumm and D.O. Cloninger, "The Drug War and the Homicide Rate: A Direct Correlation?" *Cato Journal* 14: 507–517, 1995.
27. B.L. Benson, I. Kim, D.W. Rasmussen, and T.W. Zuehlke, "Is Property Crime Caused by Drug Use or Drug Enforcement Policy?"*Applied Economics* 24: 679–692, 1992; D.L. Sollars, B.L. Benson, and D.W. Rasmussen, "A Drug Enforcement and Deterrence of Property Crime Among Local Jurisdictions," *Public Finance Quarterly* 22: 22–45, 1994; B.L. Benson and D.W. Rasmussen, "The Relationship Between Illicit Drug Enforcement Policy and Property Crimes," *Contemporary Policy Issues* 9: 106–115, 1991.
28. Benson and Rasmussen, (1996), p. 8.
29. E. Blumenson and E. Nilsen, "Policing for Profit: The Drug War's Hidden Economic Agenda," *University of Chicago Law Review* 65: 35–114, 1998.
30. Ibid., note 12.
31. Ostrowski, pp. 14–15, finds that the War on Drugs kills about 8,250 people per year (from drug-related AIDS, overdose due to black-market side effects, homicide), whereas cocaine- and heroin-related deaths would be about 600 people per year in the absence of drug prohibition. The ratio of deaths caused by the War on Drugs vs. deaths due to drugs is 13.75:1.
32. In 1999, U.S. drug users were estimated to be 14.8 million ("Drug Use in the United States," U.S. Department of Justice, Drug Enforcement Administration, 2000, <http://www.ericcass.uncg.edu/virtuallib/subabuse/1010.html>, accessed October 27, 2002). Adjusting this number for an average underreporting rate of 36% (A.R. Morral, D. McCaffrey, and M.Y. Iguchi, "Hardcore Drug Users Claim to Be Occasional Users: Drug Use Frequency Underrreporting," *Drug and Alcohol Dependence* 57: 2000), brings users to 20.1 million. In 1999, the U.S. population over 13 years of age was 218.3 million (*Statistical Abstract of the United States* (Washington, DC: U.S. Census Bureau, 2000). Drug users constitute about 9.3% of teenagers and adults.
33. B.Freking, "Ivory Tower Meets the Streets: Ex-Gang Member Shocks Academics into Reality," *Kalamazoo Gazette*, July 25, 1993.
34. O. Bikel, "Snitch," *Frontline*, January 12, 1999, <http://www.pbs.org/wgbh/pages/frontline/shows/snitch/etc/script.html>, accessed May 7, 2002.
35. M. Norris, C. Conrad, and V. Resner, *Shattered Lives: Portraits from America's Drug War* (El Cerrito, CA: Creative Xpressions, 1998), p. 101.
36. H. Browne, *The Great Libertarian Offer* (Great Falls, MT: LiamWorks, 2000), p. 99.
37. Ibid., pp. 97–98.
38. Norris, Conrad, and Resner, p. 14.
39. Ibid., p. 15.
40. Ibid., p. 42.
41. Benson (1998), p. 137.
42. Nadelman, p. 942; L. Grinspoon and J.B. Bakalar, "Medical Uses of Illicit Drugs," in *Dealing with Drugs*, R. Hamowy, ed. (San Francisco: Pacific Research Institute for Public Policy for Researchers, 1987), pp. 183–220; S.E. Sallan, N.E. Zinberg, and E. Frie III, "Antiemetic Effect of Delta-9-Tetrahydrocannabinol in Patients Receiving Cancer Chemotherapy," *New England Journal of*

Medicine 293: 785–797, 1975; AMA Council on Scientific Affairs, "Marijuana: Its Health Hazards and Therapeutic Potentials," *Journal of the American Medical Association* 246: 1823–1827, 1981; R. Robinson, *The Great Book of Hemp* (Rochester, VT: Park Street Press, 1996), pp. 44–54.

43. S.B. Duke and A.C. Gross, *America's Longest War: Rethinking Our Tragic Crusade Against Drugs* (New York: G.P. Putnan's Sons, 1993), p. 186–187; Norris, Conrad, and Resner, p. 90.

44. "Kentuckian Living in Exile," *Libertarian Party of Kentucky News*, April 1998, p. 3.

45. "Peter McWilliams Files Medical Marijuana Lawsuit," *Libertarian Party of Kentucky News*, December 1998, p. 17.

46. J. Stossel, "Give Me a Break," June 9, 2000, <http://abcnews.go.com/onair/2020/2020_000609_gmab_marijuana_feature.html>, accessed May 5, 2002.

47. "Death of a Crusader," Freemarket.net, <http://www.free-market.net/spotlight/mcwilliams/>, accessed May 5, 2002.

48. B. Bridges, "Clear As the Rising Sun: The Sentencing of Todd McCormick," <http://www.fairlaw.org/toddtodds_ sentencing.htm>, accessed May 5, 2002.

49. "Kubby Faces Marijuana Charges in Canada," *Auburn Journal*, April 21, 2002, <http://www.mapinc.org/sknews/v02/n765/a03.html?101>, accessed May 5, 2002.

50. S. Kubby, personal communication, May 8, 2002. For updates, see <http://www.kubby.org>.

51. Associated Press, "Judge Dismisses Cannabis Program," *San Jose News*, May 4, 2002, <http://www.bayarea.com/mld/mercurynews> accessed May 7, 2002.

52. Browne, p. 101.

53. J. Herer, *Hemp and the Marijuana Conspiracy: The Emperor Wears No Clothes* (Van Nuys, CA: HEMP Publishing, 1995), p. 5.

54. Ibid., p. 2.

55. Ibid., p. 26.

56. Ibid., p. 22.

57. Ibid., p. 2.

58. Ibid., p. 8.

59. Ibid., pp. 25–27.

60. "DEA Bans Hemp Products,"*Sierra Times*, October 15, 2001, <http://www.sierratimes.com/archive/files/oct/15/ardea101501.htm>, accessed October 15, 2001.

61. For a fuller discussion of this topic, see R. Carr, "Industrial Hemp: The Hidden Agenda Behind the War on Drugs." <http://www.raycarr.net/nss folder/folders/NC_hemp3.doc>, accessed July 2, 2001.

62. C.F. Thies and C.A. Register, "Decriminalization of Marijuana and the Demand for Alcohol, Marijuana, and Cocaine," *Social Science Journal* 30: 385–399, 1993.

63. Trebach and Zeese, p. 49.

64. Ibid., p. 49.

65. Ibid., p. 58.

66. Ibid., p. 49.

67. Browne, p. 89.

68. U.K. Department of the Environment, Transport, and the Regions, "Cannabis and Driving: A Review of the Literature and Commentary," <http://www.roads.detr.gov.uk/roadsafety/cannabis/index.htm>, accessed May 12, 2002; G.B. Chesher, H. Dauncey, J. Crawford, and K. Horn, "The Interaction Between Alcohol and Marijuana: A Dose Dependent Study of the Effects on Human Moods and Performance Skills," <http://www.druglibrary.org/schaffer/hemp/mjdriv1.htm>, accessed May 12, 2002; H.W.J. Robbe and J.F. O'Hanlon, "Marijuana and Actual Driving Performance," <http://www.druglibrary.org/schaffer/hemp/general/mjdrive.htm>, accessed May 12, 2002; A. Smiley, "Marijuana Not a Factor in Driving Accidents," *University of Toronto* news release, March 29, 1999.

Chapter 16: Policing Aggression

1. T. Gage, "Cops Inc.," *Reason*, November 1982, p. 23.

2. B.L. Benson, *The Enterprise of Law: Justice Without the State* (San Francisco: Pacific Research Institute for Public Policy Research, 1990), p. 185.

3. A. Blumberg, *Criminal Justice* (Chicago: Quadrangle Books, 1970), p. 185.

4. Gage, p. 26.

5. P.E. Fixler Jr. and R.W. Poole Jr., "Can Police Be Privatized?" *Privatizing the United States Justice System: Police, Adjudication, and Corrections Services from the Private Sector*, G.W. Bowman, S. Hakim, and P. Seidenstat, eds. (Jefferson, NC: McFarland, 1992), pp. 27–41.

6. B. Benson, *To Serve and Protect: Privatization and Community in Criminal Justice* (New York: New York University Press, 1998), pp. 20–21.

7. For an easy-to-read review of relevant court cases, see R.W. Stevens, *Dial 911 and Die: The Shocking Truth about the Police Protection Myth* (Harford, WI: Mazel Freedom Press, 1999).

8. Benson (1998), p. 56.

9. J. Wright and P. Rossi, *Armed and Considered Dangerous: A Survey of Felons and Their Firearms* (New York: Aldine, 1986), p. 185; Bureau of Justice Statistics, "Firearm Use by Offenders," November 2001.

10. J.R. Lott Jr., *More Guns, Less Crime* (Chicago: University of Chicago Press, 2000), p. 3.

11. G. Kleck and M. Gertz, "Armed Resistance to Crime: The Prevalence and Nature of Self-Defense with a Gun," *Journal of Criminal Law and Criminology* 86: 150–187, 1995.

12. For a good review of the literature in this area, see Benson (1990), pp. 253–268; B.L. Benson, "Guns for Protection and Other Private Sector Responses to the

Government's Failure to Control Crime," *Journal of Libertarian Studies* 8: 92–95, 1986.

13. M. Lorenz Dietz, *Killing for Profit: The Social Organization of Felony Homicide* (Chicago: Nelson-Hall, 1983), Table A.1, pp. 202–203.

14. Lott (2000), pp.1–2.

15. P.J. Cook, "The Relationship Between Victim Resistance and Injury in Noncommercial Robbery, *Journal of Legal Studies* 15: 405–406, 1986.

16. G. Kleck, "Policy Lessons from Recent Gun Control Research," *Journal of Law and Contemporary Problems* 49: 35–47, 1986; A. Krug, "The Relationship Between Firearms Ownership and Crime: A Statistical Analysis," reprinted in *Congressional Record*, 99th Cong., 2nd Sess., January 30, 1968, p. 1496, n. 7.

17. C.R. Silver and D.B. Kates Jr., "Self-Defense, Handgun Ownership, and the Independence of Women in a Violent, Sexist Society," in *Restricting Handguns: The Liberal Skeptics Speak Out*, D.B. Kates, ed. (Croton-on-Hudson, NY: North River Press, 1979), p. 152.

18. G. Kleck and D. Bordua, "The Factual Foundation for Certain Key Assumptions of Gun Control," *Law and Policy Quarterly* 5: 271–298, 1983.

19. "Town to Celebrate Mandatory Arms," *New York Times*, April 11, 1987, p. 6.

20. For the details of these and related studies, see Lott (2000).

21. Lott (2000), p. 141.

22. Ibid., p. 63.

23. Ibid., p. 141.

24. D.T. Hardy, "Gun Control: Arm Yourself with Evidence," *Reason*, November 1982, pp. 37–41.

25. R.A. Waters, "Kids and Guns," <http://www.sierratimes.com/archive/waters/edrw122700.htm>, accessed January 21, 2001.

26. V. Suprynowicz, "Shouldn't We Repeal the Gun Laws ... If It'll Save a Single Child?" *The Libertarian*, September 24, 2000, <http://www.thelibertarian.net/2000/vs000924.htm>, accessed October 9, 2000.

27. U.S. Department of Justice, *Urban Delinquency and Substance Abuse: Initial Findings, Research Summary* (Washington, DC: Office of Juvenile Justice and Delinquency Prevention, 1994), p. 18, <http://www.ncjrs.org/pdffiles/urdel.pdf>, accessed June 2, 2002.

28. Centers for Disease Control, <http://www.cdc.gov/ncipc/wisqars/>, accessed June 2, 2002.

29. V. Suprynowicz, *The Ballad of Carl Drega: Essays Based on the Freedom Movement, 1994 to 2001* (Reno, NV: Mountain Media, 2002), p. 413.

30. D.B. Kopel, "Trust the People: The Case Against Gun Control," *Policy Analysis No. 109* (Washington, DC: Cato Institute, 1988), p. 7.

31. Ibid., p. 6.

32. J.R. Lott Jr. and W.M. Landes, "Multiple Victim Public Shootings," John M. Olin Law & Economics Working Paper No. 73 (Chicago: University of Chicago Law School, 2000), p. 9, <http://papers.ssrn.com/paper.taf?abstract_id=16137>, accessed May 23, 2002.

33. Ibid., p. 14.

34. Ibid., p. 18.

35. Ibid., p. 13.

36. R.A. Waters, "When Order Breaks Down," October 22, 2001, <http://www.keepandbeararms.com/information/XcIBViewItem.asp?id=2725>, accessed June 3, 2002.

37. National Association of Chiefs of Police, "13th Annual National Survey of Police Chiefs & Sheriffs, 2000," <http://www.aphf.org/survres.html>, accessed June 2, 2002.

38. J.R. Lott Jr., "Gun Control Misfires in Europe: What's Behind the Massacres in Germany, France, and Switzerland?" *Wall Street Journal*, May 4, 2002, <http://www.opinionjournal.com/extra/?id=105002026>, accessed May 23, 2002.

39. D. Bamber, "Gun Crime Trebles As Weapons and Drugs Flood British Cities," *telegraph.co.uk*, February 24, 2002, <http://www.telegraph.co.uk/news/main.jhtml?xml=/news/2002/02/24/nguns24.xml>, accessed May 12, 2002.

40. Lott (2002).

41. For some examples, see W.V. Roth Jr. and W.H. Nixon, *The Power to Destroy* (Boston: Atlantic Monthly Press, 1999); S.L. Davis and M. Matalin, *Unbridled Power: Inside the Secret Culture of the IRS* (New York: HarperCollins, 1998); D. Burham, *A Law Unto Itself: The IRS and the Abuse of Power* (New York: Vintage Books, 1991); J. Bovard, *Lost Rights: The Destruction of American Liberty* (New York: St. Martin's Press, 1994), pp. 259–292.

42. Bovard (1994), p. 275.

43. J. Bovard, *Freedom in Chains: The Rise of the State and the Demise of the Citizen* (New York: St. Martin's Press, 1999), pp. 26–27.

44. J.C. Hammel, "FDA Attacks Alternative Clinics: Cancer Patient Lives Threatened," *Life Extension*, April 2002, pp. 36–42; Life Extension Foundation, *FDA vs. the People of the United States* (Ft. Lauderdale, FL: 1995); see also various articles and updates at <http://www.lef.org>.

45. J. Wollstein, "How Police Confiscation Is Destroying America, Part I," *Freedom Daily*, October 1993, p. 22; for more details, see "Policing and Prosecuting for Profit: New Jersey Ex-Sheriff Fights Civil Forfeiture Abuse," *Litigation Backgrounder* (Washington, DC: Institute for Justice, no date given, <http://www.ij.org/media/private_property/new_jersey/background.shtml>, accessed June 1, 2002..

46. Wollstein (1993), p. 21.

47. A. Schneider and M.P. Flaherty, *Presumed Guilty: The Law's Victims in the War on Drugs* (Pittsburgh, PA: Pittsburgh Press, 1991), p. 18.

48. A. Schneider and M.P. Flaherty, "Drug Law Leaves Trail of Innocents: In 80% of Seizures, No Charges," *Pittsburgh Press*, August 11, 1991, pp. 1, 13; "The Outrageous Forfeiture Scandal," *Blue Duck*, October 1997, pp. 1–3.

49. R. Miniter, "Ill-Gotten Gains," *Reason*, August/September 1993, pp. 32–37; "The Outrageous Forfeiture Scandal," op. cit.

50. For more details on the legal basis for these procedures, see T.G. Reed, "American Forfeiture Law: Property Owners Meet the Prosecutor," *Policy Analysis No. 179* (Washington, DC: Cato Institute, 1992); J.B. Wollstein, "Calculated Hysteria: The War on Drugs," *Individual Liberty*, Summer 1989, p. 4; S.B. Herpel, "United States v. One Assortment of 89 Firearms," *Reason*, May 1990, pp. 33–36; "Policing and Prosecuting for Profit: New Jersey Ex-Sheriff Fights Civil Forfeiture Abuse," *Litigation Backgrounder* (Washington, DC: Institute for Justice, no date specified, <http://www.ij.org/media/private_property/new_jersey/background.shtml>, accessed May 14, 2002; E. Blumenson and E. Nilsen, "Policing for Profit: The Drug War's Hidden Economic Agenda," *University of Chicago Law Review* 65: 35–40, 1998.

51. J. Sullum, "Meet Sam Zhadanov, 68-Year-Old Plastic Molder and Drug-War Casualty," *Reason Online*, <http://reason.com/9505/JACOB.may.shtml>, accessed May 7, 2002.

52. Schneider and Flaherty (1991), p. 18.

53. B.L. Benson, "Predatory Public Finance and the Origins of the War on Drugs 1984–1989," *Independent Review* 1: 163–189, 1996.

54. Cotts, "Rat Race," *Reason*, May 1992, pp. 36–41.

55. Blumenson and Nilsen, op. cit.

56. J.D. Tucille, "Donald Scott: The $5 Million Man," *About.com*, January 24, 2000, <http://civilliberty.about.com/library/weekly/aa012400a.htm?once=true&>, accessed May 7, 2002.

57. M. Cooper, "Another Police Raid on a Home Yields No Drugs, but Much Trauma," *New York Times,* May 8, 1998.

58. Ibid.

59. Associated Press, "Don Scott Family Awarded $5 Million for Fatal Raid," January 12, 2000.

60. V. Suprynowiz, *The Ballad of Carl Drega: Essays on the Freedom Movement, 1994–2001* (Reno, NV: Mountain Media, 2002), pp. 349–351.

61. R. Weaver and S. Weaver, *The Federal Siege at Ruby Ridge: In Our Own Words* (Marion, MT: Ruby Ridge, 1998), especially pp. xiii, 92–93; A.W. Bock, "Ambush at Ruby Ridge: How Government Agents Set Randy Weaver Up and Took His Family Down," *Reason*, October

1993, pp. 22–28; Bovard (1994), pp. 224–227; J. Oliver, "The Randy Weaver Case," <http://www.land.netonecom.net/tlp/ref/weaver.shtml>, accessed June 2, 2002.

62. Bovard (1999), pp. 250–255; D. Thibodeau, *A Place Called Waco: A Survivor's Story* (New York: Public Affairs, 1999); T. Lynch, "No Confidence: An Unofficial Account of the Waco Incident," *Policy Analysis No 395* (Washington, DC: Cato Institute, 2001); "Judge Clears Government in Branch Davidian Case: Suit Dismissed; Koresh Blamed for Waco Deaths," September 21, 2000, <http://www.cnn.com/2000/LAW/scotus/09/21/waco.judgment.01/index.html>, accessed May 27, 2002.

63. Thibodeau, p. 314.

64. Ibid., p. 316.

65. "Judge Clears Government in Branch Davidian Case,"op cit.

66. C. Conrad, *Jury Nullification: The Evolution of a Doctrine* (Durham, NC: Carolina Academic Press, 1998); pp. 108–115.

67. Ibid., pp. 75–88.

68. Ibid., p. 133.

69. Ibid., pp.117–124; see also the Website of the Fully Informed Jury Association at <http://www.fija.org>, accessed July 10, 2001.

70. N. Fulcher and S. Moak, "A Tale of Two Cities," *AntiShyster* 6: 36–38, 1996.

71. For some reviews, see C. Lave and L. Lave, "Fuel Economy and Auto Safety Regulation: Is the Cure Worse Than the Disease?" in *Essays in Transportation Economics and Policy: A Handbook in Honor of John R. Meyer* J.A. Gómez Ibáñez, W.B. Tye, and C. Winston, eds., (Washington, DC: Brookings Institution, 1999), pp. 257–290, <http://brookings.nap.edu/books/0815731817/html/257.html#pagetop>, accessed May 25, 2002; Institute for Research in Public Safety, *A Study for the Selection of Maximum Speed Limits, Volumes 1–4* (Bloomington, IN: Institute for Research in Public Safety, 1970).

72. G. Roth, *Roads in a Market Economy* (Brookfield, VT: Ashgate, 1998), p. 55.

73. Ibid., pp. 124–125.

74. W.D. Eggers and J. O'Leary, "The Beat Generation: Community Policing at Its Best," *Policy Review* 74: 4–14, 1995, <http://www.policyreview.org/fall95/thegg.html>, accessed May 25, 2002.

75. F. Foldvary, *Public Goods and Private Communities: The Market Provision of Social Services* (Adlershot, England: Edward Elgar, 1994).

76. B. Benson, "Why Crime Declines," <http://www.independent.org/tii/news/000100Benson.html>, accessed May 26, 2002.

77. Bolick, pp. 140–141.

78. Fixler and Poole, p. 37.

79. Benson (1998), p. 59.

80. B. Benson, "The Countervailing Trend to FBI Failure: A Return to Privatized Police Services," May 29, 2001, <http://

www.independent.org/tii/news/ 010529Benson.html>, accessed May 26, 2002.

81. G. Pruitt, "California's Rent-a-Judge Justice," *Journal of Contemporary Studies* 5: 49–57, 1982.
82. Benson (1998), p. 115.
83. Benson (1990), pp. 223–224.
84. Benson (1998), p. 106.
85. B. Scheck, P. Newfeld, and J. Dwyer, *Actual Innocence: Five Days to Execution and Other Dispatches from the Wrongly Convicted* (New York: Doubleday, 1999), pp. xiv, 263; for updates, see <http:// www. innocenceproject.org/>, accessed May 15, 2002. See following reference for a typical case.
86. "Cotton's Wrongful Conviction: Cotton's Compensation," *Frontline's What Jennifer Saw*, 1998, <http://www.pbs.org/wgbh/ pages/frontline/shows/dna/cotton/>, accessed June 2, 2002.
87. J.H. Beadle, *Western Wilds and the Men Who Redeem Them* (Cincinnati, OH: Jones Brothers, 1878), p.477.
88. T.L. Anderson and P.J. Hill, "An American Experiment in Anarcho-Capitalism: The *Not* So Wild, Wild West," *Journal of Libertarian Studies* 3: 9–29, 1979.
89. Benson (1990), p. 208.
90. C. Bolick, *Transformation: The Promise and Politics of Empowerment* (Oakland, CA: Institute for Contemporary Studies, 1998), pp. 135–138.
91. Ibid., p. 140.

Chapter 17: Healing Our World Is Inevitable

1. H.J. Eysenck, "Prediction of Cancer and Coronary Heart Disease Mortality by Means of a Personality Inventory: Results of a 15-year-Follow-Up Study," *Psychological Reports* 72: 499-516, 1993; B.O. Hafen, K.J. Frandsen, K.J. Karren, and K.R. Hooker, *The Health Effects of Attitudes, Emotions, Relationships* (Provo, UT: EMS Associates, 1992), pp. 125–168, 181–202.
2. Eysenck, op. cit.; H.J. Eysenck, "Personality, Stress and Cancer: Prediction and Prophylaxis," *British Journal of Medical Psychology* 61: 57–75, 1988; Hafen et al., pp. 110–116, 176–177, 227–229.
3. Hafen et al., pp. 233–252.
4. S.I. McMillen, *None of These Diseases*, rev. ed. (Old Tappan, NJ: Fleming H. Revell, 1984), pp. 188–189.
5. Hafen et al., pp. 253-374.

Chapter 18: Beacon to the World

1. J. Stossel, "Is America Number One?" *ABC News Special,* September 1, 2000.
2. H. de Soto, *The Mystery of Capital: Why Capitalism Triumphs in the West and Fails Everywhere Else* (New York: Basic Books, 2000), pp. 69, 154–155.
3. de Soto, p. 53.
4. Ibid., pp. 20–21.
5. Ibid., pp. 32–33.
6. T. Bethell, *The Noblest Triumph: Property and Prosperity Through the Ages* (New York: St. Martin's Press, 1998), pp. 96–197.
7. de Soto, p. 35.
8. A. Galal and M. Shirley, *Does Privatization Deliver?: Highlights from a World Bank Conference* (Washington, DC: World Bank, 1994), Summary at <http://publications.worldbank.org/ ecommerce/catalog/product?context= drilldown&item%5fid=195286>, accessed April 23, 2002.
9. India's real aggregate GDP averaged 4.3% from 1990 to 1994, according to J. Gwartney and R. Lawson, *Economic Freedom of the World: 2001 Annual Report* (Vancouver, BC: Fraser Institute, 2001), p.115, <http://www.cato.org/ economicfreedom/>, accessed June 15, 2002.
10. R.J. Barro, *Determinants of Economic Growth: A Cross-Country Empirical Study* (Cambridge, MA: MIT Press, 1999), p. 99.
11. W. Easterly and S. Fischer, "Inflation and the Poor," *Working Paper No. 2335* (Washington, DC: World Bank, 1999).
12. F.M. Lappe, R. Schurman, and K. Danaher, *Betraying the National Interest: How U.S. Foreign Aid Threatens Global Security by Undermining the Political and Economic Stability of the Third World* (New York: Grove Press, 1987), p. 9.
13. Ibid., pp. 19–25.
14. Ibid., p. 40.
15. H. Burkhalter and A. Paine, "Our Overseas Cops," *Nation*, September 14, 1985, p. 197.
16. L. Schoultz, "U.S. Foreign Policy and Human Rights Violations in Latin America: A Comparative Analysis of Foreign Aid Distributions," *Comparative Politics* 13: 162, 1981.
17. R. Flick, "How We Appeased a Tyrant," *Reader's Digest,* January 1991, pp. 39–44.
18. N.M. Ahmed, *The War on Freedom: How and Why America Was Attacked* (Joshua Tree, CA: Tree of Life Publications, 2002), pp. 41–54; Associated Press, "Powell Announces Afghan Aid Program," May 17, 2001.
19. For a good review, see C. B. Luttrell, *The High Cost of Farm Welfare* (Washington, DC: Cato Institute, 1989).
20. Lappe et al., pp. 84–85.
21. Ibid., p. 85.
22. Ibid., p. 103.
23. D. Osterfeld, "The Tragedy of Foreign 'Aid,'" *Pragmatist*, June 1988, p. 6.
24. "Duvalier Accused of Graft on Food," *New York Times*, March 13, 1986, p. 18.
25. D. Dollar and L. Pritchett, *Assessing Aid: What Works, What Doesn't, and Why* (New York: Oxford University Press, 1998), p. 35.
26. J. Bovard, "The World Bank vs. the

World's Poor," *Cato Policy Analysis No. 92*, September 28, 1987, pp. 23–24.

27. Ibid., p. 24.
28. Agence France-Presse, "Tanzania Resettlement Described As 'Cruel,'" *Washington Post*, May 1, 1976, p. B8.
29. S. Scheibla, "Asian Sinking Fund: The World Bank Is Helping to Finance Vietnam," *Barron's*, September 3, 1979, p. 7.
30. Bovard (1987), p. 4.
31. Ibid., p. 5.
32. Lappe et al., p. 101.
33. Bovard (1987), p. 22; J. Bovard, "The World Bank: What They're Doing with Your Money Is a Crime," *Reason*, April 1989, pp. 26–31.
34. Bovard (1987), p. 22.
35. "How Brazil Subsidizes the Destruction of the Amazon," *The Economist*, March 18, 1989, p. 69.
36. Coordinating Body for the Indigenous Peoples' Organizations of the Amazon Basin, "To the Community of Concerned Environmentalists...," <http://www.wri.org/biodiv/b18-gbs.html>, accessed June 15, 2002.
37. F. Pearce, "Brazil, Where the Ice Cream Comes From," *New Scientist*, July 7, 1990, pp. 45–48.
38. J. Bovard, *The Fair Trade Fraud* (New York: St. Martin's Press, 1991), pp. 46–47.
39. Ibid., p. 48.
40. T. Grennes, "The Multifiber Arrangement and the Management of the International Textile Trade," *Cato Journal* Spring/Summer 1989, p. 127.
41. W. Cline, *The Future of World Trade in Textiles and Apparel* (Washington, DC: Institute for International Economics, 1987), pp. 194–196.
42. K.A. Elliott and G.C. Hufbauer, *Measuring the Costs of Protection in the United States* (Washington, DC: Institute for International Economics, 1994).
43. J.W. Merline, "Trade Protection: The Consumer Pays," *Consumers' Research*, August 1989, p. 16.
44. Ibid., p. 17.
45. Ibid.
46. L.C. Hunter, "U.S. Trade Protection: Effects on the Industrial and Regional Composition of Employment," *Federal Reserve Bank of Dallas Economic Review*, January 1990, p. 4.
47. Bovard (1991), p. 94.
48. Ibid., pp. 75–76; R. Klav, "Free Trade a Sweeter Deal for Everyone," February 27, 2002, <http://www.mackinac.org/article.asp?ID=4096>, accessed June 14, 2002.
49. J.A. Frankel and D. Romer, "Does Trade Cause Growth?" *The American Economic Review* 89: 379–399, 1999; D. Dollar and A. Kraay, "Trade, Growth, and Poverty," *Working Paper No. 2615* (Washington, DC: World Bank, 2001), <http://econ.worldbank.org/files/2207_wps2615.pdf>, accessed June 15, 2002; J.D. Sachs and A. Warner, "Economic Reform and the Process of Global Integration," *Brookings Papers on Economic Activity* 1: 1–118,

1995; J. Gwartney, C. Skipton, and R. Lawson, "Trade Openness, Income Levels, and Economic Growth, 1980–1998," in Gwartney and Lawson, pp. 71–87.
50. L.W. Reed, *Great Myths of the Great Depression* (Midland, MI: Mackinac Center for Public Policy, 1998), <http://www.mackinac.org/archives/1998/sp199801.pdf>, accessed June 15, 2002.
51. Lappe et al., pp. 25, 35.
52. P. Mauro, "The Effects of Corruption on Growth, Investment, and Government Expenditure: A Cross-Country Analysis," in K.A. Elliot, ed., *Corruption and the Global Economy* (Washington, DC: Institute for International Economics, 1997), pp. 83–107.
53. For details, see <http://www.libertario.org/en/>, accessed June 15, 2002.
54. Gwartney, Skipton, and Lawson, pp. 82–84.
55. Dollar and Kraay, op. cit.
56. Ibid., p. 76.
57. de Soto, p. 175.
58. Bethell, p. 199.
59. K. Deninger and L. Squire, "Economic Growth and Income Inequality: Reexamining the Links," *Finance & Development* 34: 38–41, 1997, <http://www.worldbank.org/fandd/english/pdfs/0397/0140397.pdf>, accessed April 23, 2002.
60. Ibid.
61. J. Gwartney and R. Lawson, *Economic Freedom of the World 1997* (Vancouver, BC: Fraser Institute, 1997), p. 75.
62. E. Contoski, *Makers and Takers: How Wealth and Progress Are Made and How They Are Taken Away or Prevented* (Minneapolis: American Liberty, 1997), p. 8.
63. P. Fallon and Z. Tzannatos, *Child Labor: Issues and Directions for the World Bank* (Washington, DC: World Bank, 1998), <http://www.wds.worldbank.org/servlet/WDSContentServer/WDSP/IB/1998/02/01/000009265_3980319100151/Rendered/PDF/multi_page.pdf>, accessed June 24, 2002.
64. F. Siddiqi and H.A. Patrinos, "Child Labor: Issues, Causes, and Interventions," *Working Paper HCOWP 56* (Washington, DC: World Bank, (no date given)), <http://www.worldbank.org/html/extdr/hnp/hddflash/workp/wp_00056.html>.
65. P. Krugman, "Hearts and Heads," *New York Times*, April 22, 2001, <http://www.stanford.edu/~armin/hb145/krugman.html>, accessed October 29, 2002.
66. R. Ray, "Child Labor, Child Schooling, and Their Interaction with Adult Labor: Empirical Evidence for Peru and Pakistan," *World Bank Economic Review* 14: 347–367, 2000.
67. "A Back Door into the Amazon," *Economist*, February 11, 1989, p. 39.
68. S. Hecht, "Local Heroes," *New Internationalist*, April 1990, pp. 19–20.
69. R. Stavenhagen, "Report of the United Nations Special Rapporteur on the Situation of Human Rights and Fundamental

Freedoms of Indigenous People," *E/CN.4/2002/97* (Washington, DC: United Nations Commission on Human Rights, 2002), <http://www.tebtebba.org/tebtebba_files/ipr/97AV.pdf>, accessed June 15, 2002.

70. C. Burnside and D. Dollar, "Aid, the Incentive Regime, and Poverty Reduction," *Working Paper No. 1937* (Washington, DC: World Bank, 1998); J. Isham, D. Kaufmann, and L. Pritchett, "Civil Liberties, Democracy, and the Performance of Government Projects," *World Bank Economic Review* 11: 219–242, 1997.

71. Dollar and Pritchett, op. cit.

72. L.M. Litvan, "Do We Still Need a World Bank? Private Funds Dwarf Official Aid to Poor Nations," *Investors Business Daily*, October 3, 1996, pp. A-1–A-2.

Chapter 19: Is Communism Really Dead?

1. R.J. Rummel, *Death by Government* (New Brunswick, NJ: Transaction Publishers, 1994), pp. 4–5.

2. S. Dentzer, J. Trimble, and B.B. Auster, "The Soviet Economy in Shambles," *U.S. News & World Report,* November 20, 1989, p. 36.

3. Because 25% of the agricultural output was produced on 2% of cultivated land in private hands, 12.5% of Soviet food came from every 1% of the land that was privately farmed. Furthermore 75% of the food came from the remaining 98% of available farmland; hence state-sponsored farming produced 0.77% of the Soviet food supply for every 1% of land cultivated. Thus, private farming is more than 16 times as productive as collective farming (i.e., 12.5/0.77 = 16.23).

4. M.B. Zuckerman, "Russian Roulette," *U.S. News & World Report*, November 20, 1989, p. 100.

5. Dentzer et al., pp. 25–26.

6. Zuckerman, op. cit.

7. Y.N. Maltsev, "The Soviet Medical Nightmare," *The Free Market*, August 1990, p. 4.

8. D.K. Willis, *Klass: How Russians Really Live* (New York: St. Martin's Press, 1985), p. 183.

9. N. Eberstadt, *The Poverty of Communism* (New Brunswick, NJ: Transaction Books, 1988), pp. 12–14.

10. H.S. Katz, "How the Commies Stole Thanksgiving," *The Gold Bug*, December 1984, pp. 6–8; R.W. Grant, *The Incredible Bread Machine*: *A Study of Capitalism, Freedom, and the State* (San Francisco: Fox & Wilkes, 1999), pp. 93–95.

11. Willis, pp. 2–3, 28–32.

12. Ibid., pp. 188–193.

13. M.S. Bernstam, *The Wealth of Nations and the Environment* (London: Institute of Economic Affairs, 1991), as cited in *Progressive Environmentalism: A Pro-Human, Pro-Science, Pro-Free-Enterprise Agenda for Change* (Dallas: National Center for Policy Analysis, 1991), pp. 11–14.

14. J. Thompson, "East Europe's Dark Dawn," *National Geographic*, June 1991, pp. 64–69.

15. J. Cherfas, "East Germany Struggles to Clean Its Air and Water," *Science* 248: 295, 1990.

16. H.F. French, "Eastern Europe's Clean Break with the Past," *World Watch*, March/April 1991, p. 23.

17. Ibid.

18. R. Waters, "A New Dawn in Bohemia?" *Sierra*, May/June 1990, p. 35.

19. K. Marx and F. Engels, *Basic Writings on Politics and Philosophy* (Garden City, NY: Doubleday, 1959), pp. 28–29.

20. M. Parenti, *Inventing Reality: The Politics of the Mass Media* (New York: St. Martin's Press, 1986), p. 27.

21. J. Baden, "Destroying the Environment: Government Mismanagement of Our Natural Resources," *NCPA Policy Report No. 124* (Dallas: National Center for Policy Analysis, 1986), pp. 20–21.

22. Institute for Justice, "Public Power, Private Gain: The Abuse of Eminent Domain," *Litigation Backgrounder* (no date given), <http://www.ij.org/cases/property/cokingbk.shtml>, accessed July 9, 2002.

Chapter 20: Making Our Nation Safe and Secure

1. A.C. Sutton, *Wall Street and the Bolshevik Revolution* (New Rochelle, NY: Arlington House Publishers, 1974), pp. 170–172; A.R. Epperson, *The Unseen Hand* (Tucson, AZ: Publius Press, 1985), p. 111.

2. Voline (V.M. Eikhenbanum), *The Unknown Revolution* (Detroit, MI: Black & Red, 1974), pp. 173–179.

3. A.C. Sutton, *Western Technology and Soviet Economic Development, 1917–1930,* Vol. I (Stanford, CA.: Hoover Institution Press, 1968), pp. 21–23, 42–44.

4. Sutton (1968), pp. 90, 207–209, 226, 262, 277–278, 289–291; A.C. Sutton, *Western Technology and Soviet Economic Development 1930–1945, Vol. II* (Stanford, CA: Hoover Institution Press, 1971), pp. 17, 71–72.

5. Sutton (1974), p. 59–161.

6. B.M. Weissman, *Herbert Hoover and Famine Relief to Soviet Russia, 1921–1923* (Stanford, CA: Hoover Institution Press, 1968), pp. 141–144.

7. A.C. Sutton, *Western Technology and Soviet Economic Development, 1945–1965, Vol. III* (Stanford, CA: Hoover Institution Press, 1973), pp. 3–14.

8. Sutton (1974), pp. 15–38; L. Abrahams, *Call It Conspiracy* (Seattle: Double A Publications, 1971), p. 112.

9. Epperson, pp. 330–332.

10. A. Wolynski, *Western Economic Aid to the USSR* (London: Institute for the Study of Conflict, 1976), pp. 8–9.

11. Ibid., p. 6.

12. A. Sutton, *Wall Street and the Rise of Hitler* (Seal Beach, CA: '76 Press, 1976).

13. M. Scranton, *The Noriega Years* (Boulder, CO: Westview, 1991), pp. 13–14; K. Buckley, *Panama: The Whole Story* (New York: Simon and Schuster, 1991), p. 14.

14. R. Flick, "How We Appeased a Tyrant," *Reader's Digest*, January 1991, pp. 39–44; C. Dickey and E. Thomas, "How Saddam Happened," *Newsweek*, September 23, 2002.

15. N.M. Ahmed, *The War on Freedom: How and Why America Was Attacked* (Joshua Tree, CA: Tree of Life Publications, 2002), pp. 41–54.

16. Associated Press, "Powell Announces Afghan Aid Program," May 17, 2001.

17. R. Brody, *Contra Terror in Nicaragua. Report of a Fact-Finding Mission: September 1984–January 1985* (Boston: South End Press, 1985), p. 10.

18. W. Blum, *The CIA: A Forgotten History* (London, UK: Zed Books, 1986), pp. 64–65.

19. Brody, pp. 28–124.

20. E. Margolis, "Anthrax and Abdul Haq: What Goes Around, Comes Around," *Inside Track on World News*, November 4, 2001, <http://www.bigeye.com/110401.htm>, accessed November 9, 2001.

21. Newsight, "Has Someone Been Sitting on the FBI?" *BBC News*, November 6, 2001, <http://news.bbc.co.uk/1/hi/events/newsnight/1645527.stm>, accessed December 31, 2001.

22. Brody, p. 16.

23. J. Marshall, P.D. Scott, and J. Hunter, *The Iran Contra Connection: Secret Teams and Covert Operations in the Reagan Era* (Boston: South End Press, 1987), pp. 10–11.

24. L. Cockburn, *Out of Control: The Story of the Reagan Administration's Secret War in Nicaragua, the Illegal Arms Pipeline, and the Contra Drug Connection* (New York: Atlantic Monthly Press, 1987), pp. 152–188; A. Cockburn and J. St. Clair *Whiteout: The CIA, Drugs and the Press* (New York: Verso, 1998), pp.1–28.

25. M. Levine, "I Volunteer to Kidnap Oliver North," <http://ciadrugs.homestead.com/files/ml-kiki-north.html>, accessed September 30, 2002.

26. "A Spreading Drug Epidemic," *Washington Spectator*, August 1, 1988, pp. 1–3; J. Marshall, "Drugs and United States Foreign Policy," in *Dealing with Drugs*, R. Hamowy, ed. (San Francisco: Pacific Research Institute for Public Policy, 1987), pp. 164–174.

27. J. Stockwell, *The Praetorian Guard: The U.S. Role in the New World Order* (Boston: South End Press, 1991), p. 118.

28. Scranton, pp. 13–14; Buckley, p. 14.

29. E. Giboa, "The Panama Invasion Revisited: Lessons for the Use of Force in the Post Cold War Era," *Political Science Quarterly* 110: 539–559, 1995.

30. M. Levine, "Mainstream Media: The Drug War's Shills," in K. Borjesson, ed., *Into the Buzzsaw: Leading Journalists Expose the Myth of a Free Press* (Amherst, NY: Prometheus Books, 2002), pp. 267–271.

31. Ibid., pp. 287–290.

32. Cockburn and St. Clair, p. 272.

33. For more details, see the Academy Award, winning film, "The Panama Deception," from the Empowerment Project, PO Box 2155, Chapel Hill, NC 27515, <http://www.empowermentproject.org>, accessed August 15, 2002,

34. K. Borjesson, "Editor's Introduction," in Borjesson, ed., p. 12.

35. These numbers may be inflated. See M. Murad, "Shouting at the Crocodile," in Borjesson, ed., pp. 77–102.

36. "Punishing Saddam," *60 Minutes*, May 12, 1996.

37. M.W. Herold, "U.S. Bombing and Afghan Civilian Deaths: The Official Neglect of 'Unworthy' Bodies," *International Journal of Urban and Regional Research* 26: 626–634, 2002.

38. M.W. Herold, "Recent 'Success' Tally of U.S. Bombs: Over 200 Civilians Are Killed to Get 1.5* Taliban Leaders," January 6, 2002, <http://www.cursor.org/stories/paktia.htm>, accessed August 26, 2002,

39. J. Steele, "Forgotten Victims," *Guardian*, May 20, 2002, <http://www.guardian.co.uk/analysis/story/0,3604,718635,00.html>, accessed September 1, 2002.

40. Herold, "U.S. Bombing and Afghan Civilian Deaths."

41. E. A. Neuffer, "Afghan Food Drops Found to Do Little Good," *Boston Globe*, March 26, 2002; Associated Press, "Doctors Without Borders Calls U.S. Food Drops 'Propaganda,'" October 8, 2001; A. Buncombe, "Don't Confuse Food Parcels with Cluster Bombs, Warns U.S.," Independent UK, October 30, 2001, <http://www.independent.co.uk/story.jsp?story=102228>, accessed October 30, 2001.

42. M.W. Herold, "Rubble Rousers: U.S. Bombing and the Afghan Refugee Crisis," March 16, 2002, <http://www.cursor.org/stories/rubble.htm>, accessed August 26, 2002; S. Peterson and S. Baldauf, "Setbacks in War Against Taliban: Week 4 of US Strikes Arrives Amid Mounting Civilian Toll and Death of a Rebel Commander," *Christian Science Monitor*, October 29, 2001; N. Koppel, "Red Cross Stunned by Bombing," *Washington Post*, October 27, 2001; Steele, op. cit.

43. "When the Body Count Doesn't Count," *New Zealand Herald*, January 17, 2002, <http://www.nzherald.co.nz/storydisplay.cfm?thesection=news&thesubsection=&storyID= 686660&reportID =61564>, accessed August 25, 2002.

44. CNN, "Robertson: Al Qaeda Renews Threats," *CNN.com*, October 15, 2001, <http://www.cnn.com/2001/WORLD/asiapcf/central/10/15/ret.robertson.otsc/>, accessed August 8, 2002.

45. N.K. Gvosdev and A.A. Cipriano, "Patriotism and Profit," *Honolulu Advertiser*, July 21, 2002.

46. "Military Assistance to the Afghan Opposition," *Human Rights Watch Backgrounder*, October 2001, <http://www.hrw.org/backgrounder/asia/afghan-bck1005.htm>, accessed September 1, 2002; for updates, summaries, and reports on this topic, see Human Rights Watch documents at <http://www.hrw.org/campaigns/afghanistan/women.htm#Alliance>, accessed September 1, 2002.

47. B. Dehghanpisheh, J. Barry, and R. Gutman, "The Death Convoy of Afghanistan," *Newsweek*, August 26, 2002, pp. 20–30.

48. U.S. Senate, 94th Congress, 1st Session, "Hearings Before the Select Committee to Study Government Operations with Respect to Intelligence Activities," Vols. I–VII, 1975.

49. Blum, pp. 44–55, 133–161, 284–291.

50. R. Paul, "U.S. Taxpayers Send Billions to Our Enemies in Afghanistan," *Texas Straight Talk*, November 5, 2001, <www.house.gov/paul/tst/tst2001/tst10501.htm>, accessed November 11, 2001.

51. D. Kiefer, "S.F. Attorney: Bush Allowed 9/11," *San Francisco Examiner,* June 11, 2002, < http://propagandamatrix.com/sf_attorney_bush_allowed_911.htm>, accessed September 7, 2002.

52. J.-C. Brisard and G. Dasquié, *Forbidden Truth: U.S.-Taliban Secret Oil Diplomacy and the Failed Hunt for bin Laden* (New York: Thunder's Mouth Press/Nation Books, 2002).

53. Associated Press, "Official: 15 of 19 Hijackers Were Saudi," *USA Today*, February 6, 2002, <http://www.usatoday.com/news/world/2002/02/06/saudi.htm>, accessed September 5, 2002.

54. Ibid.; G. Papast and D. Pallister, "FBI Claims bin Laden Inquiry Was Frustrated: Officials Told to 'Back Off' on Saudis Before September 11," *Guardian*, November 7, 2001.

55. Brisard and Dasquié, pp. 34, 41.

56. G. Langer, "Poll: Bush Approval Rating 92 Percent," *ABCNews.com,* <http://more.abcnews.go.com/sections/politics/dailynews/strikes_poll011010.html>, accessed September 7, 2002.

57. R.B. Stinnett, *Day of Deceit: The Truth about FDR and Pearl Harbor* (New York: Simon & Schuster, 2000), p. 33.

58. For a copy of this memorandum, see Stinnett, pp. 271–277.

59. Stinnett, p. 120.

60. Al-Quds al-Arabi, "Text of Fatwah Urging Jihad Against Americans," February 23, 1998, <http://www.ict.org.il/articles/fatwah.htm>, accessed August 25, 2002; L. Beyer, "Roots of Rage: Osama's Endgame," *Time*, October 15, 2001.

61. For a comparison of the two tyrants, see R.J. Rummel, Death by Government (New Brunswick, NJ: Transaction Publications, 1997) pp. 8, 10, 79–90, 111–121.

62. T. Fleming, *The New Dealers' War: Franklin D. Roosevelt and the War Within World War II* (New York: Basic Books, 2001), pp. 134, 204–205, 465.

63. A. Armstrong, *Unconditional Surrender: The Impact of the Casablanca Policy upon World War II* (New Brunswick, NJ: Rutgers University Press, 1961), p. 211.

64. Fleming, pp. 434–435.

65. Ibid., pp. 503–504.

66. Ibid., pp. 540–543.

67. Ibid., p. 526.

68. Ibid., p. 530.

69. Ibid., p. 188.

70. Armstrong, p. 262.

71. Fleming, pp. 530, 532.

72. Ibid., pp. 538–539.

73. Ibid., p. 544.

74. C. Johnson, *Blowback: The Costs and Consequences of American Empire* (New York: Henry Holt, 2000), p. 11.

75. M. Ijaz, "Clinton Let bin Laden Get Away," *Honolulu Advertiser,* December 7, 2001.

76. "Gallup International Poll on Terrorism in the U.S.," Gallup International, September 2001, <http://www.gallup-international.com/terrorism.htm>, accessed November 14, 2001.

77. N. Wooner, "Millions of Afghan Lives or One Life in Terre Haute?" *Michigan Daily Online*, October 17, 2001, <http://www.michigandaily.com/vnews/display.v/ART/2001/10/17/3cb2fe9cb8611?in_archive=1>, accessed October 6, 2002.

78. M. Colby, "School Girl Gets the Boot for Anti-War Opinions," *Counterpunch,* November 7, 2001,<http://www.counterpunch.org/colby3.html>, accessed November 11, 2001; L. Messina, "Jury: Anarchy Club OK: Katie Sierra Gets Mixed Response in Suspension Case," *Charleston Gazette Online*, July 13, 2002, <http://www.wvgazette.com/news/News/2002071222/>, accessed August 25, 2002.

79. K.P. O'Meara, "Police State," *Insight*, November 9, 2001, <http://www.insight-mag.com main.cfm?include=detail&storyid=143236>, accessed September 9, 2002.

80. J. Turley, "Camps for Citizens: Ashcroft's Hellish Vision. Attorney General Shows Himself as a Menace to Liberty," *Los Angeles Times*, August 14, 2002.

81. D. Campbell, "Rights Groups Move to End Secrecy over 1,000 Arrests," *Guardian*, November 2, 2001.

82. R. Paul, "Military Tribunals Put Our Justice System on Trial," December 6, 2001, <http://www.antiwar.com/paul/paul15.html>, accessed September 9, 2002.

83. D. Campbell, "U.S. Sends Suspects to Face Torture," *Guardian*, March 12, 2002.

84. M. Isikoff and D. Klaidman, "The Hijackers We Let Escape," *Newsweek*, June 10, 2002, pp. 20–28.

85. C. Rowley, "Memo to FBI Director Robert Mueller," *Time.com*, May 21, 2002, <http://www.time.com/time/nation/article/0,8599,249997,00.html>, accessed September 1, 2002.

86. R. Axelrod, *The Evolution of Cooperation* (New York: Basic Books, 1981), p. 131.
87. "Persian Gulf Policy," in *Cato Handbook for Congress: 105th Congress* (Washington, DC: Cato Institute, 1999), <http://www.cato.org/pubs/handbook/hb105-46.html>, accessed February 25, 2002.
88. K. Follett, *On the Wings of Eagles* (New York: Signet, 1984).
89. R. Marcinko, *Rogue Warrior* (New York: Pocket Books, 1992), pp. 229–234.
90. D. Alden, "Soldiers R US: The Corporate Military," August 30, 1999, <http://www.enterstageright.com/archive/articles/0999soldrus.htm>, accessed September 5, 2002.
91. Marcinko, p. 235.
92. F.M. Stern, *The Citizen Army: Key to Defense in the Atomic Age* (New York: St. Martin's Press, 1957), pp. 156–158.
93. I. Piazza, "Front Sight Vows to Press FAA to Restore Pilot's Ability to Defend the Cockpits," *Front Sight Press Release*, September 14, 2001, <http://www.front-sight.comgun_school_for_pilots_complete.htm>, accessed October 14, 2001.
94. Rummel, pp. 15, 27.
95. R.A. Waters, "When Order Breaks Down," *Keep and Bear Arms.com*, October 22, 2001, <http://www.keepandbeararms.com/information XcIBViewItem.asp?ID=2725>, accessed October 22, 2001; Libertarian Party,"Repeal Gun Control Laws That Leave Us Defenseless Against Evil Terrorists," *Press Release,* October 31, 2001.
96. C. Donaldson-Evans, "WTC Survivors Wonder: Where Is That $1 Billion in Donations?" *Fox News*, October 12, 2001.
97. J. Bamford, *Body of Secrets: Anatomy of the Ultra-Secret National Security Agency from the Cold War Through the Dawn of a New Century* (New York: Doubleday, 2001), pp. 82–94. For excerpts, see <http://www.whatreally happened.com/northwoods.html>, accessed September 12, 2002.
98. C. Cerf and H. Beard, *The Pentagon Catalog: Ordinary Products at Extraordinary Prices* (New York: Workman, 1986).
99. Marcinko, pp. 330–363.
100. H. Bachmann, "Bomb Shelters: A Cold War Refuge Is Hot Again," (no date) <http://www.time.com/time/europe/specials/changes/shelters.html>, accessed September 9, 2002; M. Shields, "Ever Cautious Swiss Drill for Nuclear Accident, Reuters News Service, November 12, 2001, <http://www.planetark.org/dailynewsstory.cfm/newsid/13263/story.htm>, accessed September 9, 2002.
101. P. Richter, "U.S. Works Up Plan for Using Nuclear Arms," *Los Angeles Times*, March 9, 2002.
102. A.D. Morse, *While 6 Million Died: A Chronicle of American Apathy* (New York: Ace Publishing, 1968), p. 205.
103. Ibid., pp. 212–213; 218–219.

104. M. Henry, "Voyage of the Damned," *Jerusalem Post*, July 1998, <http://www.cdn-friends-icej.ca/antiholo/voyage.html>, accessed on August 1, 2002.
105. S. Abrahamsen, "The Rescue of Denmark's Jews," in L. Goldberger, ed., *The Rescue of the Danish Jews: Moral Courage Under Stress* (New York: New York University Press, 1987), p. 10.
106. H. Pundik, "Herbert Pundik," in Goldberger, ed., p. 95.
107. Ibid., pp. 77–94.
108. L. Goldberger, "Leo Goldberger," in Goldberger, ed., p. 164.
109. Abrahamsen, p. 11.
110. J. Hæstrup, "The Danish Jews and the German Occupation," in Goldberger, ed., pp. 51–52; Pundik, pp. 95–97.
111. Hæstrup, pp. 22, 28.
112. Morse, pp. 253, 308.
113. Ibid., pp. 253–281.
114. Ibid., pp. 293–297.
115. C. Hiaasen, "A Piracy Done with Fines," *Knight-Ridder Service*, November 6, 1993.
116. J.L. Simon, *Immigration: The Demographic and Economic Facts* (Washington, DC: Cato Institute, 1995), pp. 31–32.
117. For a review of these studies, see Simon, pp. 19–30.
118. D. Card, "The Impact of the Mariel Boatlift on the Miami Labor Market," *Industrial Relations Section Working Paper #253*, May 1989, <http://www.irs.princeton.edu/pubs/pdfs/253.pdf>, accessed August 26, 2002.
119. G. Garvin, "No Fruits, No Shirts, No Service: The Real-World Consequences of Closed Borders," *ReasonOnLine*, April 1995, <http://reason.com/9504/garvin.apr.shtml>, accessed August 20, 2002.
120. Simon, p. 30.
121. Garvin, op. cit.
122. A. Rabushka, *From Adam Smith to the Wealth of America* (New Brunswick, NJ: Transaction Books, 1985), p. 127.
123. Simon, pp. 47–48.
124. H. Smith, "Should We Have Spotted the Conspiracy?" *Frontline*, <http://www.pbs.org/wgbh/pages/frontline/shows/network/should/>, accessed October 5, 2002.
125. B. Netanyahu, ed., *Terrorism: How the West Can Win* (New York: Avon Books, 1986), p. 9.
126. Rewards for Justice Program, <http://www.rewardsforjustice.org>, accessed October 7, 2001.
127. L.J. Sechrest, "Let Privateers Troll for bin Laden," *Independent Institute Opinion Article*, September 30, 2001, <http://www.independent.org/tii/news/010930Sechrest.html>, accessed November 11, 2001.

Chapter 21: A New Age or a New World Order?

1. J.L. Simon, *The Ultimate Resource 2* (Princeton, NJ: Princeton University Press, 1996), pp. 97–108.

2. T.P. Soubbotina, *Beyond Economic Growth: Meeting the Challenges of Global Development* (World Bank: Washington, DC, 2000), pp. 1–6, <http://www.worldbank.org/depweb/beyond/beyondco/beg_03.pdf>.

3. United Nations Population Division, Press Briefing, March 21, 2000, <http://www.un.org/News/briefings/docs/2000/20000321.populationbrf.doc.html>, accessed September 21, 2002.

4. J.L. Bast, "Ending the Myth of Overpopulation," July 8, 1999, <http://www.heartland.org/perspectives/worldpopday.htm>, accessed September 21, 2002.

5. R.T. Simmons and U.P. Kreuter, "Herd Mentality: Banning Ivory Sales Is No Way to Save the Elephant," *Policy Review,* Fall 1989, 46-49.

6. Ibid.

7. Convention on International Trade in Endangered Species of Wild Fauna and Flora, "Proposal 11.23,"<http://www.cites.org/eng/cop/11/prop/23.pdf>, accessed October 1, 2002.

8. M. DeAlessi, *Private Conservation and Black Rhinos in Zimbabwe: The Savé Valley and Bubiana Conservancies,* (Washington, DC: Competitive Enterprise Institute, 2000).

9. R.H. Nelson, *Private Property Rights to Wildlife: The Southern Africa Experiment* (Washington, DC: Competitive Enterprise Institute, 2000).

10. E. Contoski, *Makers and Takers: How Wealth and Progress Are Made and How They Are Taken Away or Prevented* (Minneapolis: American Liberty Publishers, 1997), pp. 288–291.

11. "Siefgried and Roy," <http://www.siegfriedandroy.com/conservation/index.php>, accessed September 11, 2002.

12. T.L. Anderson and D.R. Leal, Enviro-Capitalists: Doing Good While Doing Well (New York: Rowman & Littlefield, 1997), pp.46-47.

13. Ibid., pp. 52-54.

14. (no author specified) "Partnerships Protect Snow Leopards," *Square One: Back to Grassroots Environmentalism* 2: 1–2, 2000.

15. J.A. Baden and D.S. Noonan, "Taking the Folly Out of the Act," <http://www.freeeco.org/pub/DD.ESA.html>, accessed October 8, 2002.

16. J.H. Adler, "Private Conservation Produces Public Benefits," *Intellectual Ammunition,* September/October 1996, p. 6.

17. R.J. Agnello and L.P. Donnelley, "Prices and Property Rights in the Fisheries," *Southern Economic Journal* 42: 253–262, 1979.

18. D.R. Leal, *Homesteading the Oceans: The Case for Property Rights in U.S. Fisheries* (Bozeman, MT: Political Economy Research Center, 2000), pp. 7–22.

19. B. Runolfsson, " Fencing the Oceans: A Rights-Based Approach to Privatizing Fisheries,"*Regulation* 20: 57–62, 1997.

20. M. De Alessi, *Private Reef Building in Alabama and Florida* (Washington, DC: Competitive Enterprise Institute, 1996).

21. Leal, pp. 22–23.

22. For the raw NASA satellite data, see <http://vortex.nsstc.uah.edu/data/msu/t2lt/tltglhmam_5.0>; for a graphical presentation of the same data, see <http://www.heartland.org/environment/oct00/track.htm>, accessed October 1, 2002; for surface temperature data (graphs and links to raw data), see <http://www.giss.nasa.gov/data/update/gistemp/>, accessed October 1, 2002.

23. W. Soon, S.L. Balinus, A.B. Robinson, and Z.W. Robinson, *Global Warming: A Guide to the Science* (Vancouver, BC: Fraser Institute, 2001), p. 19.

24. Ibid., p. 20.

25. T.R. Karl and P.D. Jones, "Urban Bias in Area-Averaged Surface Air Temperature Trends," *Bulletin of the American Meteorological Society* 70: 265–270, 1989.

26. Soon et al., pp. 19–21.

27. B. Lomborg, *The Skeptical Environmentalist: Measuring the Real State of the World* (New York: Cambridge University Press, 2001), pp. 260–263.

28. P.J. Michaels, "Long Hot Year," *Policy Analysis No. 329* (Dallas: National Center for Policy Analysis, 1998), p. 8.

29. See satellite data in reference 19 above, especially for June 1991 and August 1992 (0.8EC. difference); also El Niño effect (1.0EC. difference) April 1998 and June 1999.

30. Lomborg, p. 310.

31. Ibid., p. 307.

32. J. Hansen, M. Sato, R. Ruedy, A. Lacis, and V. Oinas, "Global Warming in the Twenty-first Century: An Alternative Scenario," *Proceedings of the National Academy of Sciences* 97: 9875–9880, 2000.

33. S.F. Singer, "The Science Behind Global Environmental Scares," *Consumers' Research,* October 1991, p. 17; see also surface temperature citations from reference 19.

34. Hansen et al. For an abbreviated version of reference 29, see <http://www.giss.nasa.gov/research/forcings/altscenario/>, accessed October 15, 2002.

35. Soon et al., pp. 34–40.

36. M. Markels Jr., "Fishing for Markets: Regulation and Ocean Fishing," *Regulation* 18: 73–79, 1995.

37. For information on the euro, see <http://www.euro.ecb.int/en.html>, accessed October 15, 2002.

38. P. Shishkin, "European Regulators Spark Controversy with 'Dawn Raids,'" *Wall Street Journal,* March 1, 2002.

39. " 'Metric Martyr' Loses Appeal," BBC News, July 15, 2002, <http://news.bbc.co.uk/1/hi/uk/england/2129528.stm>, accessed October 1, 2002.

40. British Weights and Measures Association,"The Legal Campaign," <http://www.bwmaonline.com/Legal%20Campaign.htm>, accessed October 1, 2002.

41. W.F. Jasper, "European Superstate in the Making," *New American*, May 6, 2002, pp. 23–27.
42. S. Bonta, "New Push for Global Taxes," *New American*, April 22, 2002, pp. 15–21.
43. D. New, *Michael New: Mercenary or American Soldier* (No publisher listed, 1998). For updates, see <http://www.mikenew.com/index.shtml>, accessed October 1, 2002.

Chapter 22: How to Get There from Here

1. S. Golberman, *Waiting Your Turn: Hospital Waiting Lists in Canada* (Vancouver, BC: Fraser Institute, 1990); J.C. Goodman and G.L. Musgrave, *Twenty Myths About National Health Care* (Dallas: National Center for Policy Analysis, 1991), p. 17; E. McCaughey, "No Exit: What the Clinton Plan Will Do for You," *New Republic*, February 7, 1994, pp. 21–25.
2. J.S. Morris, "How Do Canadians Cope?" *Heartland Perspective*, September 8, 1992.
3. *Why Do Prescription Drugs Cost So Much?* (Washington, DC: Pharmaceutical Research and Manufacturers of America, 2000), p. 18.
4. R.K. Bennet, "Your Risk Under Clinton's Health Plan," *Readers Digest*, March 1994.
5. Y. Maltsev and L. Omdahl, "A Socialized Health-Care Nightmare," *Freeman: Ideas on Liberty*, November 1994, pp. 590–594.
6. Goodman and Musgrave, pp. 12, 40.
7. R.E. Bauman, "70 Years of Federal Government Health Care: A Timely Look at the U.S. Department of Veterans Affairs," *Policy Analysis No. 207* (Washington, DC: Cato Institute, 1994).
8. *Rhetoric vs. Reality: Comparing Public and Private Health Care Administrative Costs* (Alexandria, VA: Council for Affordable Health Insurance, 1994), pp. 1–2.
9. R. Pear, "Medicare Paying Doctors 59% of Insurers' Rate, Panel Finds," *New York Times*, April 5, 1994, p. A-10.
10. Freedom Network Partners, <http://www.free-market.net/partners>; Libertarian Oriented Organizations, <http://www.self-gov.org/liborgs/html>.
11. Cato Institute, 224 Second St., SE, Washington, DC 20003, (202) 546-0200; fax (202) 546-0728; <http://www.cato.org>.
12. Competitive Enterprise Institute, 1001 Connecticut Ave, NW, Ste. 1250, Washington, DC 20036, (202) 331-1010; fax (202) 331-0640; <http://www.cei.org>.
13. Fraser Institute, 4th Floor, 1770 Burrard Street, Vancouver, BC Canada V6J 3G7, (604) 688-0221; fax (604) 688-8539; <http://www.fraserinstitute.ca>.
14. Future of Freedom Foundation, 11350 Random Hills Rd. Suite 800, Fairfax, VA 22030, (703) 934-6101; fax (703) 352-8678; <http://www.fff.org>.
15. Heartland Institute, 19 South LaSalle #903, Chicago, IL 60603, (312) 377-4000; fax (312) 377-5000; <http:www.heartland. org>.
16. Independent Institute, 100 Swan Way, Oakland, CA 94621-1428, (510) 632-1366; fax (510) 568-6040; <http://www.independent.org>.
17. Manhattan Institute for Policy Research, 52 Vanderbilt Ave., New York, NY 10017, (212) 599-7000; fax (212) 599-3494; <http://www.manhattan-institute.org>.
18. National Center for Policy Analysis, 12655 N. Central Expy., Ste. 720, Dallas, TX 75243, (214) 386-NCPA; fax (214) 386-0924; <http://www.ncpa.org>.
19. Pacific Research Institute for Public Policy, 755 Sansome Street, Ste. 450, San Francisco, CA 94111, (415) 989-0833; fax (415) 989-2411; <http://www.pacificresearch.org>.
20. Reason Foundation, 3415 S. Sepulveda Blvd., Ste. 400, Los Angeles, CA 90034, (310) 391-2245; fax (310) 391-4395; <http://www.reason.org>.
21. Political Economy Research Center, 502 S. 19th Ave., # 211, Bozeman, MT 59715, (406) 587-9591; fax (406) 586-7555; <http://www.perc.org>.
22. Alliance for the Separation of School and State, 4546 E. Ashlan, #3282, Fresno, CA 93726, (559) 292-1776; fax (559) 292-7582; < http://www.sepschool.org>.
23. Forfeiture Endangers American Rights, 265 Miller Ave., Mill Valley, CA 94941, <http://www.fear.org>, (415) 389-8551
24. Fully Informed Jury Association, P.O. Box 5570, Helena, Montana 59604-5570.
25. *Journal of Libertarian Studies*, Ludwig von Mises Institute, 518 West Magnolia Ave. Auburn, AL 36832-4528, (334) 321-2100; fax (334) 321-2119; <http://www.mises.org>.
26. Liberty Fund, 8335 Allison Pointe Trail, Suite 300, Indianapolis, IN 46250-1684, (317) 842-0880; fax (317) 577-9067; <http://www.libertyfund.org>.
27. Institute for Humane Studies, 4210 Roberts Rd., Fairfax, VA 22032, (703)323-1055; fax (703) 425-1536;<http://www.theihs.org>.
28. Cato Institute, op. cit.
29. Laissez Faire Books, 942 Howard, San Francisco, CA 94103, (800) 326-0996; fax (415) 541-0597; <http://laissezfairebooks.com>; Libertarian Press, P.O. Box 309 Grove City, PA 16127, (724) 458-5861; fax (724) 458-5962; <http://www.libertarianpress.com>; Liberty Audio and Film Service, 824 W. Broad St., Richmond, VA 23220, (804) 788-7008; Liberty Tree Network, 100 Swan Way, Suite 200, Oakland, CA, 94621-1428, (800) 927-8733; <http://www.libertytree.org>.
30. Mackinac Center, 140 West Main St., P.O. Box 568, Midland, MI 48640, (989) 631-0900; fax (989) 631-0964; <http://www.mackinac.org>.
31. Hillsdale College, 33 E. College St., Hillsdale, MI 49242, (517) 437-7341.
32. Advocates for Self-Government, 3955

Pleasantdale Rd., #106-A, Atlanta, GA 30340, (404) 417-1304; fax (404) 417-1305; <http://www.self-gov.org>.

33. "Libertarian Litmus Test: Are You Libertarian?" <http://www.self-gov.org/poll1208_libertarian_litmus_test2_b.htm>, accessed November 1, 2002.

34. Libertarian Party (USA), 2600 Virginia Ave., NW, Ste. 100, Washington, DC 20037, (800) 682-1776; <http://www.lp.org>.

35. "The Libertarian Party: Our History," <http://www.lp.org/organization/history;> accessed October 27, 2002.

36. For a current listing, see Libertarians in Public Office, <http://www.lp.org/organization/officials.php>.

37. "LP Officeholders in Two States Dramatically Cut Property Taxes," *LP News Online*, August 2002, <http://www.lp.org/lpnews/0208/propertytax.html>.

38. "San Diego LP Stops Tax Boost," *LP News*, April 1999, http://www.lp.org/lpn/9904-San-Diego.html; "Alachua County LP Defeats $200 Million Tax Increase," *LP News*, November 1998, <http://www.lp.org/lpn/9811-tax-FL.html>; "Colorado: LP Helps to Derail $16 Billion RTD Tax Increase," *LP News,* January 1998, <http://www.lp.org/lpn/9801-RTD.html>; "Toledo Libertarians Defeat Stadium Tax," *LP News,* July 1998, <http://www.lp.org/lpn/9807-stadium. html>; "Illinois Libertarians Help Defeat New Tax," *LP News,* May 1998, <http://www.lp.org/lpn/9805-IL-tax.html>; "Alabama Libertarians Beat $697 Million Tax Proposal," *LP News,* October 1998, <http://www.lp.org/lpn/9810-tax-AL.html>; "North Carolina LP Kills Stadium Tax," *LP News,* July 1998, <http://www.lp.org/lpn/9807-NC-stadium.html>, all accessed October 20, 2002. Alaskan libertartians also helped establish the Permanent Dividend (Tax) Refund and helped end the state income tax there (Ed Hoch and Dick Randolph, personal communications). Libertarian efforts to repeal the Massachusettes state income tax failed 55% to 45% in November, 2002, <http://www.lp.org/lpnews/0212/masstax.html>, accessed November 12, 2002.

39. Republican Liberty Caucus, 44 Summerfield St., Thousand Oaks, CA 91360, <http://www.rlc.org>.

40. International Society for Individual Liberty, 836-B Southampton Rd., #299, Benicia, CA 94510-1960, (707) 746-8796; fax (707) 746-8797; <http://www.lp.org>.

41. L. Louw and F. Kendall, *South Africa: The Solution* (Bisho, Ciskei, South Africa: Amagi Publications, 1986).

42. L. Louw and F. Kendall, *After Apartheid* (San Francisco: Institute for Contemporary Studies, 1987).

43. Ibid., p. 73.

44. D. Pearson and S. Shaw, "Winning Our First Amendment Suit Against the FDA," *Life Extension*, July 1999, <http://www.lef.org/magazine/mag99/july99-cover.html>.

45. W. Fallon, "FDA Suffers Second Massive Legal Defeat in Pearson vs. Shalala II," *Life Extension* Magazine, May 2000, <http://www.lef.org/magazine/mag2001/may2001_cover_pearson2_1.html>.

46. Free State Project, <http://www.freestateproject.org>.

47. R. Stewart, *Limón REAL: A Free and Autonomous Region* (Alajuela, Costa Rica: Rigoberto Stewart, 1999), <http://www.limonreal.com>.